AF821939

Ultimate Cisco Collaboration Infrastructure for Enterprise Solutions

Unlock the True Potential of Cisco Collaboration Infrastructure for Deploying and Managing Solutions for Enterprises

Lalit Pamnani

www.orangeava.com

First Published: August 2024

Published By: Orange Education Pvt Ltd, AVA™

Address: 9, Daryaganj, Delhi, 110002, India

275 New North Road Islington Suite 1314 London,
N1 7AA, United Kingdom

ISBN (PBK): 978-81-97396-68-7

ISBN (E-BOOK): 978-81-97396-61-8

Scan the QR code to explore our entire catalogue

www.orangeava.com

Dedicated To

My Family

Your love and support mean the world to me

About the Author

Lalit Pamnani holds a Bachelor's degree in Commerce and numerous IT certifications, the most notable being the prestigious CCIE in Collaboration. He is currently employed at a large enterprise, managing all facets of its Collaboration Infrastructure.

His passion for sharing knowledge is evident through his active blog, where he provides detailed guides on various collaboration technologies. His expertise has earned him recognition as a Cisco Champion for three consecutive years, and in 2021, his blog was honored among the Top 25 in the IT Blog Awards by Cisco.

Outside the digital world, he is an avid reader and enjoys Anime series adapted from Manga. As an adventure enthusiast, he loves cycling and trekking.

About the Technical Reviewer

Redouane Meddane has over a decade of experience in designing and implementing Cisco Security and Collaboration solutions, specializing in large deployments of Cisco Meeting Server and Cisco Unified Communication Manager. With a strong background in Cisco training, he has delivered more than 100 official courses as a Cisco Certified System Instructor over five years, focusing on Routing/Switching, Collaboration, and Security, particularly video and voice solutions. Between 2019 and 2022, Redouane received six Cisco Instructors Awards, recognizing him among the top 5% of influential CCSIs for his high-quality training and exceptional performance across multiple Cisco technologies. He holds three CCNP certifications in Collaboration, Security, and Enterprise, as well as certifications from F5 (BIG-IP Administrator) and Palo Alto Networks (PCNSA).

In 2023 and 2024, Cisco honored him as a Cisco Designated VIP and Cisco Ambassador for his significant contributions and expertise in Cisco's online communities. Beyond his technical career, Redouane is a passionate author, having published five books with LULU Press, including titles such as OSPF *Demystified with RFC Request for Comments*, *Network Security All-in-one* ASA *Firepower* WSA *Umbrella* VPN ISE *Layer*, *Dial Plan Call Routing Demystified*: *Cisco Collaboration Technologies*, *Deploying Certificates on Cisco Meeting Server*, and *IP Routing Protocols All-in-one*: OSPF EIGRP IS-IS BGP *Hands-on Labs*.

Acknowledgements

I would like to express my heartfelt gratitude to my family and friends for their unwavering support and patience throughout this journey. Despite my limited availability in recent months, they have shown understanding and encouragement every step of the way.

A special thanks to my friend Mithun Padhya, whose expertise in audiovisual technology was invaluable in crafting one of the key chapters of this book.

I am also deeply grateful to our technical reviewer, Mr. Redouane MEDDANE, for his insightful feedback and suggestions, which have undoubtedly elevated the quality of this book.

Finally, I would like to extend my sincere appreciation to the AVA Orange team for their constant support and guidance throughout this process, ensuring a smooth experience.

Preface

Starting a career in the Collaboration (Unified Communications) domain can be overwhelming, with numerous technologies to learn and a confusing array of starting points. Even if your core responsibility is managing IP Telephony or Video Infrastructure, it's often expected that you have knowledge of adjacent technologies, as everything is interconnected.

This book covers all the relevant adjacent domains and technologies essential for most jobs in the Collaboration domain, while also providing in-depth coverage of crucial topics.

This book is designed to help IT professionals navigate the complex landscape of Cisco Collaboration solutions. From the fundamentals of collaboration technologies and deployment models to advanced concepts like dial plan configuration, media resources, and conferencing, this book offers a comprehensive overview. It also explores the Cisco Webex suite, hybrid solutions, and edge servers, giving readers a holistic understanding of Cisco's collaboration offerings.

This book is divided into 13 chapters, covering a wide range of topics essential for mastering Cisco Collaboration Infrastructure. The details are as follows:

Chapter 1. Introduction to Modern Collaboration Technologies: This chapter will introduce the basics of collaboration technologies, their evolution, and modern deployment models such as On-premises, HCS, Hybrid, and SaaS. It will explore the pros and cons of each model and provide real-world scenarios to help readers understand the collaboration tool landscape.

Chapter 2. Understanding Cisco Collaboration Solutions: This chapter will break down Cisco Collaboration solutions, explaining each component, such as CUCM, Voice Gateway, Edge servers, PSTN, IM/VM, SRST, and contact center features, in different topologies. It will also focus on understanding design criteria and redundancy at node, site, and data center levels.

Chapter 3. Managing Endpoints and Users: This chapter will discuss essential network services in Cisco Collaboration, including NTP, DHCP, DNS, TFTP, and PoE. It will show readers how to navigate the CUCM GUI, configure global settings, and understand endpoint registration in a cluster environment. The chapter will also cover COP files, software bundles, user authentication, authorization, and directory integration for endpoints in CUCM.

Chapter 4. Mastering CUCM Call Control and Telephony Features: This chapter will provide a deep understanding of CUCM call control and telephony features. It will cover call processing, routing, and Class of Control configuration, including partitions, calling search spaces, forced authorization codes, and client matter codes. The chapter will also explore CUCM telephony features such as call waiting, hold, transfer, forward, speed dial, call park, barge, privacy, shared lines, BLF, call pickup groups, hunt groups, extension mobility, and intercom.

Chapter 5. Dial Plans - Basics to Advance: This chapter will offer a comprehensive understanding of call control and dial planning. It will start with an introduction to dial plans, cover SIP trunk and voice gateway configuration, and explain dial plan configuration and transformation mechanisms in CUCM. The chapter will also cover advanced concepts such as globalized dial plans, time-of-day routing, automated alternate routing (AAR), and URI dialing.

Chapter 6. Media Resources, Conferencing, and AV Solutions: This chapter will cover media resources, conferencing, and audiovisual solutions for meeting rooms. It will start with an understanding of media resources and conferencing, including Media Resource Groups (MRGs), Media Resource Group Lists (MRGLs), codec technologies, Media Termination Points (MTPs), transcoders, annunciators, Music on Hold, and conferencing in CUCM. The chapter will then explore audiovisual solutions for meeting rooms, such as meeting room endpoints, scheduling systems, wayfinding, One Button to Push (OBTP), wireless sharing, RoomOS customization and integration, advanced AV technologies, environmental considerations in AV room design, hot desking, and digital signage systems.

Chapter 7. Exploring Cisco Collaboration Cloud, Hybrid and Edge: This chapter will explore Cisco's collaboration cloud offerings, including the Webex suite, hybrid solutions, and edge servers. It will provide an overview of Webex Meetings, Messaging, Calling (Webex Go and Webex Calling for Microsoft Teams), Webinars, and Vidcast, along with Webex real-time media models. The chapter will also cover Webex hybrid solutions, such as Webex Hybrid Calendar, Directory Service, Webex Edge (Video Mesh and Edge for Devices), and cloud-connected UC, as well as edge servers like Cisco Expressway and Cisco Unified Border Element.

Chapter 8. Understanding Signaling and Media Protocols: This chapter will discuss the significance of standards and protocols in VoIP and explore signaling and media concepts. It will cover SIP call setup and tear-down processes, SIP components in Cisco's collaboration infrastructure (SIP REGISTRAR, PROXY, B2BUA), SIP headers, and SDP. The chapter will also examine real-time media protocols like RTP and RTCP.

Chapter 9. Deep Dive - Signaling and Media Protocols: This chapter will cover advanced topics in signaling and media protocols for IP telephony. It will explain the SDP offer/answer, including delayed offer, early offer, and early media, and discuss advanced SIP session flows such as call transfer and forward. The chapter will explore essential protocols in IP telephony, including DTMF and fax over IP, and examine NAT in collaboration, focusing on STUN, TURN, and ICE. It will also address network performance considerations and Quality of Service (QoS).

Chapter 10. Security, Compliance and Recovery: This chapter will cover the security, recovery, and compliance aspects of Cisco Collaboration solutions. It will start with security topics, including Transport Layer Security (TLS), certificates, Public Key Infrastructure (PKI) in Cisco UC, certificate types in CUCM and their usage, secure communication protocols, security measures, system hardening, and preventing toll fraud. The chapter will then discuss recovery strategies, focusing on Disaster Recovery Planning (DRP) for Cisco UC, backup, and restore processes, and address compliance issues, including data privacy in Cisco UC, regulations affecting Cisco UC services, and emergency calling.

Chapter 11. Troubleshooting Techniques and Tools: This chapter will cover troubleshooting techniques and tools used in Cisco Collaboration Infrastructure. It will start with Cisco's troubleshooting framework and provide real-world insights beyond the framework. The chapter will then explore various Cisco Collaboration troubleshooting tools, including the Dialed Number Analyzer, Route Plan Report, CLI commands, logs, Real-Time Monitoring Tool (RTMT), Cisco Bug Search tool, and Collaboration Solutions Analyzer.

Chapter 12. Automation and APIs in Cisco Collaboration: The chapter will introduce the concept of automation and APIs in the context of Cisco Collaboration solutions. It will explore various APIs available in Cisco Collaboration products, including APIs for Webex devices (xAPI and CE-Deploy), SBC and voice gateways, Cisco Meeting Server, CUCM, Cisco Expressway, and Webex, and provide an overview of how these APIs can be used to automate tasks and enhance functionality in a Cisco Collaboration environment.

Chapter 13. Additional Resources and Emerging Trends: The chapter will focus on continuous learning resources and future trends in collaboration technologies. It will provide a list of resources to help readers deepen their knowledge and stay current with advancements in the field, including design guides, configuration guides, forums, and virtualization wikis. The chapter will conclude by discussing emerging trends shaping the future of collaboration.

Throughout the book, practical examples and real-world insights will be provided to reinforce the concepts covered. By the end of this book, readers will have a comprehensive toolkit to excel in managing Cisco Collaboration Infrastructure, whether they are novice IT admins, professionals preparing for Cisco Collaboration exams, or experienced administrators looking to enhance their skills.

Get a Free eBook

We hope you are enjoying your recently purchased book! Your feedback is incredibly valuable to us, and to all other readers looking for great books.

If you found this book helpful or enjoyable, we would truly appreciate it, if you could take a moment to leave a short review with a 5 star rating on Amazon. It helps us grow, and lets other readers discover our books.

As a thank you, we would love to send you a free digital copy of this book, and a **30%** discount code on your next cart value on our official websites:

www.orangeava.com

www.orangeava.in (For Indian Subcontinent)

☑ **Here's how:**

Leave a review for the book on Amazon.

Take a screenshot of your review, and send an email to **info@orangeava.com** (it can be just the confirmation screen).

Once, we receive your screenshot, we will send you the digital file, within 24 hours.

Thank you so much for your support – it means a lot to us!

Colored Images

Please follow the links or scan the QR codes to download the ***Images*** of the book:

You can find code bundles of our books on our official Github Repository. Go to the following link to and QR code to explore the further:

https://github.com/orgs/ava-orange-education/repositories

Please follow the link to download the Colored Images of the book:
https://rebrand.ly/9l65y9n

In case there's an update to the code, it will be updated on the existing GitHub repository.

Errata

We take immense pride in our work at **Orange Education Pvt Ltd,** and follow best practices to ensure the accuracy of our content to provide an indulging reading experience to our subscribers. Our readers are our mirrors, and we use their inputs to reflect and improve upon human errors, if any, that may have occurred during the publishing processes involved. To let us maintain the quality and help us reach out to any readers who might be having difficulties due to any unforeseen errors, please write to us at :

errata@orangeava.com

Your support, suggestions, and feedback are highly appreciated.

DID YOU KNOW

Did you know that Orange Education Pvt Ltd offers eBook versions of every book published, with PDF and ePub files available? You can upgrade to the eBook version at **www.orangeava.com** and as a print book customer, you are entitled to a discount on the eBook copy. Get in touch with us at: **info@orangeava.com** for more details.

At **www.orangeava.com**, you can also read a collection of free technical articles, sign up for a range of free newsletters, and receive exclusive discounts and offers on AVA™ Books and eBooks.

PIRACY

If you come across any illegal copies of our works in any form on the internet, we would be grateful if you would provide us with the location address or website name. Please contact us at **info@orangeava.com** with a link to the material.

ARE YOU INTERESTED IN AUTHORING WITH US?

If there is a topic that you have expertise in, and you are interested in either writing or contributing to a book, please write to us at **business@orangeava.com**. We are on a journey to help developers and tech professionals to gain insights on the present technological advancements and innovations happening across the globe and build a community that believes Knowledge is best acquired by sharing and learning with others. Please reach out to us to learn what our audience demands and how you can be part of this educational reform. We also welcome ideas from tech experts and help them build learning and development content for their domains.

REVIEWS

Please leave a review. Once you have read and used this book, why not leave a review on the site that you purchased it from? Potential readers can then see and use your unbiased opinion to make purchase decisions. We at Orange Education would love to know what you think about our products, and our authors can learn from your feedback. Thank you!

For more information about Orange Education, please visit **www.orangeava.com**.

Table of Contents

CHAPTER 1
Introduction to Modern Collaboration Technologies

Introduction

This chapter introduces the basics of collaboration technologies. We will highlight the benefits they bring to business, chart their evolution over the years, and look at modern iterations of these tools. By understanding various deployment models, their pros and cons, and through real-world scenarios, we aim to give you a comprehensive understanding of the collaboration tool landscape.

Structure

In this chapter, we will discuss the following topics:

- Introduction to Collaboration Tools
- Benefits of Using Collaboration Tools
- Evolution of Collaboration Technologies
- Modern Collaboration Tools
- Different Deployment Models
- Pros and Cons of Different Deployment Models
- Revisiting Deployment Models with Scenarios

Introduction to Collaboration Tools

Collaboration technology comprises various tools and platforms designed to facilitate effective communication and collaboration in a professional setting. This umbrella term covers everything from straightforward messaging apps and email services to complex video conferencing tools and project management platforms - basically, any tool that enhances the ease and efficiency of joint work efforts.

Companies are now embracing flexible work practices, with remote work becoming common. In such a scenario, collaboration tools have shown their worth, filling the physical void between team members and facilitating a unified and consistent workflow.

The tools currently used have come a long way from their earlier versions. They have transitioned from basic messaging and email services to refined platforms offering various features, including video conferencing, real-time document collaboration, project tracking, and even customer support driven by artificial intelligence. This trend continues as we delve deeper into the domains of cloud computing and artificial intelligence.

Benefits of Using Collaboration Tools

Collaboration tools have become vital for business productivity in the post-COVID era, as many organizations have embraced flexible and remote working models. Here are some key benefits:

- **Improved Communication**: Collaboration tools such as Slack, Webex, Microsoft Teams, or Google Workspace enable instant communication among employees, irrespective of their geographical location. This helps to keep everyone in the loop and promotes a sense of unity within distributed teams.
- **Real-Time Collaboration**: Platforms such as Microsoft Office 365 or Google Docs enable multiple users to work on a document simultaneously. This enables real-time collaboration and feedback, reducing the time required to complete tasks.
- **Efficient Project Management**: Tools such as Trello or Asana allows clear task assignments, progress tracking, and deadline setting. This reduces the chances of tasks being overlooked or delayed, helping in maintaining productivity.
- **Centralized Information**: Collaboration tools provide a central place for all communications, files, tasks, and other project-related information. This makes it easier for team members to find the information required without filtering through countless emails.
- **Cost and Time Efficiency**: Travel costs and time can be significantly reduced as meetings, training sessions, or conferences occur online via video conferencing tools such as Zoom or Webex.

Let us take a closer look at how collaboration tools have evolved over time to meet the changing needs of businesses.

Evolution of Collaboration Technologies

Technology constantly evolves and improves; each advancement opens up new possibilities for other improvements. Looking back at the early to mid-2000s, there are some key factors to consider:

- Mobile phones were expensive
- Network availability was not as good
- The average internet speed was 1Mbps
- The global internet penetration rate was 10-15%

For Personal Use

In the early to mid-2000s, making phone calls and sending text messages (SMS) using the cellular network was common. AOL IM and MSN Messenger (later Windows Live Messenger) were the popular internet messaging tools that allowed real-time chat with friends and were widely used across the globe.

Skype, launched in 2003, made a huge impact and quickly became a go-to solution for making audio and video calls over the internet. Its peer-to-peer technology and high-quality calls were unique at the time. The combination of text chat, voice and video calls, and group conversations in all these formats contributed to Skype's popularity.

After 2010, as internet speed and penetration improved and smartphones became popular, numerous platforms and apps emerged, changing the way we communicate with friends and family. Tools such as Google Hangout, Facebook Messenger, WhatsApp, Facetime, and WeChat offered standard features such as text chat, voice/video calls, group conversations, and file sharing.

Our usage of and dependence on these tools changed post-COVID (2020 onwards). Previously, it was uncommon to see the same tools available for both business and personal use, and most business tools had more features and were not free. In and after 2020, tools such as Zoom, Webex, and Microsoft Teams became free for personal use and common for various purposes, such as online classes, brainstorming, and virtual gatherings.

For Business Use

Prior 2010, tools for meetings and webinars were specialized and expensive. Webex and GoToMeeting were popular choices for meetings and webinars, while other tools like IBM Lotus Sametime, Microsoft Office Communicator, and Jabber focused on instant messaging, audio, and video calls.

Between 2010 and 2015, these tools improved significantly as overall technology advanced, but they became highly scalable for large meetings and webinars only after 2015. In and after 2020, these tools underwent massive improvements in features and scalability.

To better understand the current state of collaboration technologies, it is essential to examine the key factors that have influenced their development and adoption.

Here are some factors that brought about fundamental shifts:

Launch of New Apps

Skype significantly impacted existing tools; it was easy to use, cheaper for voice/video calls over the internet, and affordable for international calls. Skype's popularity also influenced hardware, with many computers starting to include webcams as standard and accessories such as headsets, with microphones becoming popular. These factors influenced and improved existing tools available for business use for voice/video calls.

Another example is Slack. Before its launch in 2013, instant messaging focused on direct messages and group chats. One of Slack's defining features is its use of channels for team communication, allowing users to create channels around specific topics, projects, or teams. This makes conversations more organized, easier to follow, and simpler for new team members to catch up.

Slack also supports a wide range of integrations with other tools and services (Google Drive, Trello, Asana, GitHub, and many other productivity and business tools), making it a hub for work. Its powerful search feature allows searching the entire conversation history, and it provides extensive customization and bots that can automate tasks, send reminders, and integrate with complex systems, helping teams be more efficient.

Slack's success popularized the concept of a team chat platform as a core productivity tool, shifting businesses away from relying heavily on email for internal communication. Its popularity also led to the emergence of similar platforms, such as Microsoft Teams, which adopted many similar features. Other existing tools such as Webex Teams and Google Chat also evolved.

Impact of COVID

The COVID-19 pandemic and the resulting shift to remote work in 2020 brought significant changes, such as:

- Increased demand.
- New features and upgrades - for example, increased max participants in video calls, introduced breakout rooms, and security improvements.
- Webinars and Large Meetings: With in-person events being canceled, many

organizations have turned to online webinars and virtual conferences. This led to tools enhancing their features to support large-scale events.

- Integration and Interoperability: There was an increased focus on making sure various tools could work together seamlessly, as businesses were using a mix of different tools for communication, collaboration, and productivity.

When comparing collaboration tools for personal and business use, there are notable similarities and differences to consider.

Similarities:

- Features such as IM (direct or group), Audio, Video, and file sharing are standard and available in most apps.
- We use more than one app even if the same feature is available on both apps.
- Availability on mobile devices and good user experience are no longer optional.
- Security and data privacy are more important than ever.
- Should work from anywhere.

Differences:

- For personal use, we lean towards free service as there are many. For business use, a free service is rarely an option or preference.
- Integration of collaboration tools with other apps is advised for personal use but mostly optional; for business use, integration with other tools and services is a must.
- Different scale of usage.
- Businesses have higher security, data privacy, and regulatory compliance requirements. Enterprise-grade collaboration tools often offer advanced security features, data loss prevention, audit trails, and adherence to various compliance standards that are not typically required for personal use.
- In businesses, implementing new tools often involves structured training and change management processes to ensure all employees effectively adopt and use the tool. In contrast, individuals tend to adopt tools more informally, frequently basing their choices on factors such as ease of use and the preferences of their friends or family.

Modern Collaboration Tools: A Shift in Dynamics

The landscape of collaboration technologies has experienced a monumental shift in recent years. This evolution, driven by both technological progress and shifts in workplace practices, has reshaped our professional communication and collaboration methods. Before diving into these transformations, let us clarify what is meant by Unified Communications and Collaboration technologies.

Unified Communications (UC) and Collaboration technology are two different but closely related concepts that are crucial in modern business communications.

Unified Communications is an industry term used to describe the integration of enterprise communication services such as instant messaging (chat), voice (including IP telephony), mobility features (extension mobility, single number reach), audio, web and video conferencing, and desktop sharing.

Collaboration technology, however, refers to tools and platforms that allow teams to work together on projects or tasks, regardless of their location. This can include project management software, document sharing and editing platforms, social media tools, and other digital platforms that facilitate team collaboration.

For example, a UC solution might include voice and video calling capabilities, instant messaging, and file sharing. A Collaboration technology might then add the ability to simultaneously edit a shared document, assign tasks, manage projects, and more. Therefore, UC is more about facilitating communication, while Collaboration technology is about facilitating teamwork and shared productivity.

In the past, businesses used a collection of separate tools to cater to their communication needs. There would be one tool for emails, another for voice calls, and another for video conferencing. However, today's collaboration tools have evolved beyond this siloed approach, shifting towards an integrated platform-based model.

This shift towards platform-centric solutions serves several key advantages. Firstly, it enhances user experience by providing a unified interface for various communication channels. Secondly, these platforms can seamlessly integrate with other business tools and applications, improving workflow efficiency. For example, a modern collaboration platform might integrate with your CRM software, letting you pull up customer information during a support call or with your project management tool to discuss real-time task updates.

These modern platforms have several core components that set them apart from their predecessors:

- **Unified Communications**: Modern collaboration tools embody the principles of UC, integrating voice, video, messaging, and content sharing into a seamless user experience. For instance, Cisco's Webex platform blends all these elements, allowing users to switch between different communication modes effortlessly.
- **Integration and Interoperability**: Modern tools focus on interoperability, facilitating integration with many third-party applications and services. Your project management tool, CRM, or document management system can work

harmoniously with your communication platform. For example, Cisco's Webex app and devices let you join any meeting (Webex, Zoom, Google Meet, MS Teams) with additional configuration.

- **Cloud-driven**: Cloud-based platforms can rapidly scale to meet growing user demand, provide feature updates without needing physical installations, and reduce upfront infrastructure costs. Microsoft's Teams platform, Zoom, and Cisco with Webex exemplify this shift towards cloud-based, all-encompassing collaboration platforms. For example, the Sales team wants to host a webinar with 2000 participants, with an upgrade of license, most of these platforms will allow you to meet the need.
- **Platform-centric Approach**: Today, collaboration tool providers strive to create an ecosystem rather than standalone tools. The shift is towards platforms that offer a broad spectrum of services, keeping users engaged within their ecosystem. This strategy allows companies to ensure a uniform experience, integrate new features seamlessly, and offer comprehensive solutions to diverse organizational needs.
- **Artificial Intelligence and Machine Learning**: An integrated platform allows for incorporating advanced technologies like Artificial Intelligence (AI). AI can offer features like AI-generated summary of the meeting, real-time transcription and translation, sentiment analysis, and more. These advanced features significantly improve productivity and streamline communication in increasingly distributed teams.
- **Scalability and Flexibility**: Cloud-based collaboration platforms provide unparalleled scalability and flexibility, allowing organizations to scale up or down based on their requirements. This aspect becomes critical in rapidly changing scenarios, such as the global shift to remote work due to the COVID-19 pandemic.

The paradigm shift in collaboration technologies reflects our evolving workplace dynamics and the need for more integrated, efficient, and adaptive solutions. As we progress, these trends will likely solidify, further reshaping our conception of collaboration.

However, the shift to platform-based collaboration tools has its own challenges. Companies must consider data security, privacy, compliance with regional regulations, avoid vendor lock-in, and the seamless integration of new tools with existing workflows. With the rapid pace of innovation and increasing demand for efficient remote collaboration, the shift towards integrated platform-based collaboration tools is set to continue, revolutionizing how we work.

Let us explore the four main deployment models for collaboration tools: On-premises, Hosted Collaboration Solution (HCS), Hybrid, and Software as a Service (SaaS).

Dissecting Deployment Models: Unveiling the Pieces of the Puzzle

The four main deployment models are On-premises, Hosted Collaboration Solution (HCS), Hybrid, and Software as a Service (SaaS). The selection of a particular model depends mainly on the size of the business, available budget, existing IT infrastructure, and specific operational requirements.

- **On-premises**: The organization hosts all the infrastructure and software in-house in this model. The IT team manages, maintains, and updates the entire infrastructure. While this approach provides maximum control and customization, it requires significant upfront investment and ongoing management resources. This may be a viable choice for large businesses with complex collaboration needs and a robust IT infrastructure.
- **Hosted Collaboration Solution (HCS)**: In the HCS model, a service provider hosts the collaboration infrastructure in their data center, and the organization consumes it as a service. Maintenance and upgrade tasks fall under the service provider's scope, reducing the management burden on the organization's IT team. This model provides the benefits of an on-premises solution, such as customization, with a cloud solution's reduced complexity and cost benefits. The scope of this model varies from one service provider (or Customer) to another. Some service providers deploy/provide the option to have dedicated instances or shared infrastructure with different add-on services based on their capabilities and customer needs.
- **Hybrid**: The hybrid model combines on-premises and cloud-based solutions. Some elements of the collaboration suite are kept on-premises, while others are moved to the cloud. This model offers flexibility by allowing organizations to leverage the benefits of cloud services while maintaining on-site control over specific critical components.
- **Software as a Service (SaaS)**: This is the fastest-growing deployment model for collaboration tools. The entire collaboration suite is hosted in the cloud, and businesses consume it through a subscription model. The provider handles all updates and maintenance, relieving businesses of these responsibilities. Examples of popular SaaS solutions include Webex by Cisco, Microsoft Teams, and Zoom. SaaS models are beneficial for small to medium businesses without big IT teams or those seeking to reduce initial costs (reduced Capex).

Now that we have defined the deployment models, let us understand the factors that influence a company's choice of collaboration tools.

From a user's perspective, collaboration technologies appear as a single, unified platform. However, behind the scenes, these platforms often consist of multiple components stitched together. It is rare for a single vendor to provide all the tools in a collaboration suite, and even rarer for a company to adopt an entirely integrated solution from a single provider. Various factors, such as unique business needs, existing infrastructure, and budget constraints, influence a company's choice of collaboration tools.

Vendors typically bundle closely integrated services and features into distinct products that can be easily combined to create a comprehensive platform. If a vendor can not offer certain essential features, they often partner with specialized providers to offer tested integrations. These bundled services are tailored to market trends and customer needs. Some vendors prioritize open interoperability, allowing their products to work seamlessly with popular tools in the market.

For example - Microsoft Teams has limited call center (aka Contact center) features, so they provide tested integrations with third-party contact center solutions. See this for more details: https://learn.microsoft.com/en-us/microsoftteams/teams-contact-center?tabs=connect

Another example is Slack. Slack has limited web conferencing functionality but allows integration with popular video conferencing tools. See this for more details:

https://slack.com/intl/en-in/help/articles/208492868-Voice-video-and-screen-sharing-apps

The choice of deployment model also depends on a company's existing IT infrastructure and requirements. For startups with few employees and no prior investment in tools, choosing a bundled solution from a single vendor can be relatively straightforward. This is known as a greenfield deployment. In contrast, large global companies with established collaboration tools and extensive IT infrastructure may face a slower migration process when adopting new tools (Imagine a running Elephant taking a U-turn), as they need to consider their existing investments and workflows. This is referred to as a brownfield deployment.

Companies may choose not to use all services from a single vendor for several reasons:

- To protect the investment made in existing infrastructure
- To leverage the strengths of different vendors
- To address unique use cases that require specific solutions
- To support legacy infrastructure that is only compatible with certain vendors
- Migration is slow (Migration is a multi-year project, so only one feature is migrated to a new tool at a time)

For example, a large global company might use Microsoft Office 365 or Google Workspace for email, calendar, file storage, and productivity tools while using Slack for instant messaging due to its integration with other tools in their workflow. They may use Zoom for web conferencing and webinars but rely on Cisco's on-premises solution for voice calling. The company may have been using Avaya and Cisco contact center solutions and is now gradually migrating to a cloud-based Genesys contact center.

Additionally, large global companies may use different tools for specific departments or regions. For instance, the sales department might require different web conferencing tools to accommodate customers who can only join Webex or MS Teams meetings. In some countries or regions, the standard tool may not be available or may cause issues, necessitating the use of alternative tools.

Choosing a suitable deployment model is a critical decision for any organization. The choice should align with the organization's strategic goals, operational needs, and IT capabilities. As the business environment and collaboration technologies evolve, organizations may shift from one model to another to best meet their changing needs.

Pros and Cons of Different Deployment Models

As with any technology decision, each deployment model for collaboration tools has unique advantages and drawbacks. Understanding these pros and cons can guide you in selecting the most suitable model that aligns with your business objectives, budget, and IT capabilities.

We will delve into the pros and cons of each model to help guide your decision-making process (see *Table 1.1*) :

Deployment Model	Pros	Cons
On-Premises	High level of control and customization, data security and privacy, integration with existing infrastructure	High upfront costs, ongoing maintenance, management require skilled IT staff, and scalability can be challenging
Hosted Collaboration Solution (HCS)	Reduced maintenance and management, lower upfront costs than on-premises solutions	Dependence on the service provider, potential limitations on customization, can be more expensive over the long term compared to SaaS
Hybrid	Flexibility to choose where each component is hosted, balance of control, Scalability, can leverage existing infrastructure	Complexity of managing multiple deployment models, integration, Compatibility challenges, requires skilled IT staff to manage

Software as a Service (SaaS)	Low upfront costs, scalability and flexibility, automatic updates and maintenance, accessibility from anywhere	Potential limitations on customization and control, dependence on internet connectivity, possible concerns around data privacy and security

Table 1.1: *Pros and cons of deployment models*

Navigating the Deployment Maze: Factors and Scenarios

When deciding which deployment model to choose, organizations consider multiple factors. These factors include but are not limited to cost (including licensing), interoperability with existing tech infrastructure, feature needs, global support, security, and compliance requirements, the desire to avoid vendor lock-in, and in-house skill competency.

Let us consider three scenarios to understand these factors in a real-world context.

Scenario 1: A startup with 100 employees in one country

- **Cost and Licensing**: As a startup, minimizing initial costs is crucial. SaaS models, with their pay-as-you-go nature, can provide cost-effective collaboration solutions.
- **Interoperability**: As the technical infrastructure might still be under development, the startup may prioritize solutions that offer easy integration and flexibility.
- **Feature Needs**: With fewer employees, the startup may not require all the advanced features. Essential communication and collaboration tools may suffice.
- **Global Support**: Since the organization is localized in one country, global support may not be a crucial requirement.
- **Security/Compliance**: Basic security features would be sufficient, and if the startup does not have sensitive data to handle at the early stages, extensive compliance needs may not be a priority.
- **Avoid Vendor Lock-in**: The organization might want to avoid long-term commitments to a particular vendor at this early stage, so they prefer a solution that offers flexibility.

Scenario 2: A startup with 1,000 employees in five countries with PCI DSS compliance requirements

- **Cost including licensing**: With a larger size and presence in multiple countries, the organization might have a more substantial budget but still be conscious of costs.

- **Interoperability with other infrastructure**: The startup might have a more complex tech infrastructure at this stage, making interoperability an important factor.
- **Feature needs**: As the organization grows, it will need more sophisticated features such as advanced communication tools, file sharing, project management, and so on.
- **Global Support**: With its presence in multiple countries, global support becomes crucial.
- **Security/Compliance**: Compliance with PCI DSS would be a priority, making security a critical factor in decision-making.
- **Avoid Vendor Lock-in**: At this stage, the organization may want to maintain flexibility if it needs to switch vendors as it grows.

Scenario 3: A large company with 15,000 employees in 10 countries

- **Cost including licensing**: A large company would likely have a more substantial budget for IT investments. However, it would still look for cost-effective solutions that provide value for money.
- **Interoperability with other tech infrastructure**: Interoperability would be critical due to the extensive and complex existing tech infrastructure.
- **Feature needs**: A large company would have sophisticated needs, requiring a comprehensive set of features from collaboration tools.
- **Global Support**: With a presence in numerous countries, global support is a must.
- **Security/Compliance**: The organization would have stringent security and compliance requirements, considering the vast amount of sensitive data it handles.
- **Avoid Vendor Lock-in**: To maintain flexibility and avoid potential risks, the company might still want to avoid vendor lock-in, even at this size.
- **In-house skill competency**: A large company would likely have a competent in-house IT team to manage and maintain the chosen solution.

These were just a few factors in each scenario. There can be more, for example:

- **Scalability**: How easily the solution can accommodate growth or contraction in the organization.
- **Reliability**: The consistency and performance of the solution.
- **Vendor's Reputation and Stability**: The trustworthiness and financial stability of the vendor.
- **Disaster Recovery and Business Continuity Planning (BCP)**: Whether the

solution offers data backup, disaster recovery, and continuity planning features.

- **Mobility**: If the solution supports remote work or mobile access.
- **User Experience**: How user-friendly and intuitive the solution is for the end-users.
- **Training and Support**: The availability and quality of vendor's customer support and training resources for users.
- **Data Ownership and Portability**: Clarity about who owns the data and how easily the data can be moved or extracted from the solution.

These scenarios illustrate that selecting a deployment model is a strategic decision that depends on multiple factors unique to each organization. It is essential to understand these factors thoroughly to make an informed decision that best suits the organization's needs and circumstances.

Conclusion

This chapter helped us understand how important collaboration tools are in today's connected business world. These tools are not just for communicating; they also help teams work better together , improve workflows, and provide better customer service.

We looked at how these tools have changed over time, from early instant messaging and internet phone services to today's advanced platforms such as Microsoft Teams, Slack, Zoom, and Cisco Webex. Modern collaboration focuses on providing one integrated platform to meet all communication and collaboration needs.

We also learned about different ways to set up these tools: On-Premises, HCS, Hybrid, and SaaS. Each has its own advantages and disadvantages. On-premises solutions give you more control but need a lot of money and maintenance upfront. SaaS solutions are flexible and can grow with your business, but might limit customization and data control.

When choosing how to set up collaboration tools, we have to think about many things like cost, compatibility, features, global support, security, avoiding being stuck with one vendor, and having the right skills in-house. It is about finding a solution that fits your organization's needs, budget, and plans for the future, not just getting the most features or the lowest price.

This chapter gives us a big-picture view of collaboration tools. The next chapter will focus on understanding how Cisco's Collaboration Solution works.

Multiple Choice Questions

1. What key trend has driven the development of collaboration tools from simple messaging applications to all-inclusive platforms?
    a. Increase in remote working and need for virtual collaboration
    b. Rise in the cost of cloud storage
    c. Growing popularity of cryptocurrency
    d. Advances in virtual reality
2. Which deployment model for collaboration tools provides the most control but requires significant upfront costs and continuous maintenance?
    a. SaaS
    b. On-Premises
    c. Hybrid
    d. HCS
3. What is one factor that does not affect the decision-making process when selecting a deployment model for collaboration tools?
    a. The organization's size and geographical spread
    b. The existing technical infrastructure
    c. The company's marketing strategy
    d. The allocated budget for IT expenditures
4. When considering a collaboration solution, why is it essential to consider the long-term cost implications of different deployment models?
    a. It can affect the overall operational efficiency
    b. It influences the organization's ability to scale and adapt
    c. Both a and b
    d. None of the above

Answers

1. a
2. b
3. c
4. c

Further Reading

To improve your understanding and broaden your perspective, explore the following topics. Remember to tailor your research based on your organization's specific needs and always discern between genuine insights and industry trends.

- **Investigate the Evolution of Collaboration Tools**: Track the historical journey of collaboration tools from their inception to the present day and identify the key technological advancements that have driven this evolution. Example- what tools have you had in your organization in the last 10 years, and what led to the current state.
- **Analyze the Key Players in the Market**: Conduct an analysis of the leading players in the collaboration tool market, including Microsoft Teams, Slack, Zoom, and Cisco Webex. Understand their unique selling propositions, core features, and the industries they primarily cater to.
- **Perform a Cost-Benefit Analysis**: Conduct a cost-benefit analysis of buying, leasing, and subscription models for collaboration tools. Do not limit your exploration to financial implications; consider the impact on operations, adaptability, and future scalability.
- **Examine the Impact of COVID-19**: Investigate how the COVID-19 pandemic affected the use of collaboration tools in businesses and in your own organization. (Hint: Start with news articles and industry reports from 2020-2021).
- **Research the Role of Global Support**: Understand the importance of global support for organizations with international operations. Learn how vendors cater to this need and what it implies for choosing collaboration tools.
- **Assess the Implications of Vendor Lock-in**: Research the concept of vendor lock-in. Understand its potential risks and the strategies organizations can adopt to avoid when choosing collaboration tools.
- **Study Interoperability**: Understand the importance of interoperability in today's business environment. Learn how collaboration tools integrate with other business systems and why this is essential.
- **Delve into Licensing Models**: Look deeper into the licensing models of different collaboration tools. How do they impact scalability and cost-effectiveness? (Hint: Start with the official websites of the tools).
- **Understand the Future**: Research emerging collaboration technology trends. How might AI, Machine Learning, and other advancements change how we collaborate?
- **Security in collaboration tools**: Explore the security measures employed by popular collaboration tools to protect data. (Hint: Check out white papers and security reports from collaboration tool providers)

CHAPTER 2

Understanding Cisco Collaboration Solutions

Introduction

In this chapter, we will explore the Cisco Collaboration ecosystem. We will cover its architectural components and understand redundancy and licensing in detail. Whether you are new to Cisco or deepening your understanding, this chapter will equip you with the knowledge needed for a robust on-prem collaboration setup.

Structure

In this chapter, we will discuss the following topics:

- Deployment Models and Reference Architecture
- Core and Hybrid Components of Cisco Collaboration Solutions
- The Role of Virtualization in Unified Communications
- Key Design Criteria
- Understanding Redundancy in Cisco Collaboration
- Deployment Scenarios Example
- Navigating Licensing and Associated Costs

Deployment Models and Reference Architecture

Cisco is one of the key players with a significant market share in Unified Communications. Their solution is available as on-prem, hosted, hybrid, and Cloud/

SaaS offering (Webex). As learned in the last chapter, in the post-COVID era and with a platform-centric approach, the focus has shifted to cloud-based solutions, but it is not feasible/beneficial for all customers.

While some big providers/vendors (for example, Microsoft) have entirely shifted the focus to Cloud and stopped innovating for on-prem solutions, Cisco commits to continue innovating for on-premises solutions (and for Cloud). It helps those customers who gradually/partially want to move to Cloud or want to stay on-prem but still get the features/benefits of Cloud by having a hybrid model.

One of the key features of UC is IP Telephony, which is commonly used by all companies. It is the ability to make phone calls using an IP network instead of traditional phone lines. Cisco is the market leader in this space. Let us look at some stats from their Cisco Live 2020 presentation. (DGTL-PSOCOL-1101)

- They had a 45% market share in On-premise IP Telephony.
- 300,000 Companies use their Collaboration solution.
- 95% of these are large enterprises (Fortune 500)

One of the key differences between a Cloud (SaaS) offering and On-prem is that, in a cloud offering, the vendor/service providers have an entire service designed for you. They provide 2-3 options to choose from based on your need, and as a customer, you need to use them as it is with some minor modifications to meet your needs. This model also locks customers in and forces them to use most components from the same provider or their partner.

In on-prem, the vendor sells the license/software and hardware (optional- if Virtualized) to the customer and has some recommendations for architecture. These are pieces that need to be stitched together. The good thing about this model is that customers can modify/remove the parts they do not need. There is flexibility and fewer chances of lock-in, and it is easy to use/integrate components from other vendors if the customer wants to.

In both cases, customers do not need to have complete expertise around the whole architecture. Most vendors (or their partner or external consultant) offer services to help customers design, deploy, and troubleshoot the infrastructure.

Let us look at the preferred Collaboration design recommended by Cisco. Understanding what each component does and how they provide a particular feature is essential. We will also discuss which components are redundant and how design can be changed in various ways. This is based on the 12.5 version, but the foundation remains the same if you have a higher or lower version (maybe a minor difference).

Unified Communications Deployment Models

A deployment model specifies the location of core servers and components within an organization. This arrangement shapes network efficiency, cost, and system redundancy.

Depending on the organizational scale, geographic dispersion, and specific operational needs, there are different models to consider. Let us explore the three primary models:

- **Campus deployment model**: All servers/components are in the same location/ office. It can be in the same or a different building within the campus and connected through high-speed LAN or MAN.
- **Centralized deployment model:** Core Servers are located in the central/ headquarters site or data center, and some components such as Voice gateway and media resources are distributed across multiple remote sites (local to branch offices). Central and remote sites are connected by WAN. Example- large company with various offices in a Country/Continent.
- **Distributed deployment model**: Multiple Centralized deployment models are interconnected. Example- very large company with many offices WW (across multiple continents).

We will discuss this in detail with more context and examples later in this chapter. These deployment models can have many variations, but the concepts remain the same.

Reference Architecture

Here is a diagram that depicts the centralized deployment model for Unified Communications:

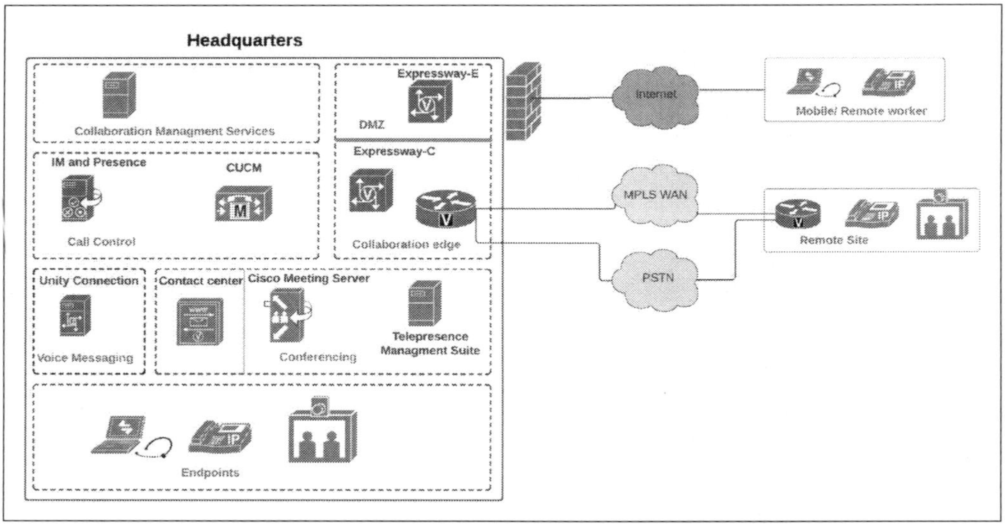

Figure 2.1: *Centralized deployment model*

This is a simplified On-prem design based on a centralized deployment model. Most of the infrastructure that provides core services is installed in the Company's Data center located in the headquarters, and the remote/branch site has a Voice gateway and endpoints. Most of these UC servers have complex integration with strict latency requirements within the cluster and with other servers, so it is better to have them installed in the same high-speed LAN.

In summary, all the endpoints register to the Call control server (CUCM), which integrates with Instant and Voice messaging, Conferencing, and edge components. Endpoints on remote/branch office also register to CUCM in the Central location, and in case network connectivity between the branch and central location is down, branch office endpoints fallback their registration to local Voice GW with SRST feature. All endpoints registered on the same call control servers can make calls to each other (assuming the dial plan is configured accordingly), and to make PSTN calls, CUCM sends calls through Voice Gateway, which can be local or centralized based on design. For SIP-to-SIP connectivity, CUBE is used. With integration to Webex cloud or to make business-to-business video calls, Expressway is used. Remote workers from home (Internet) have their endpoints registered through Expressway to CUCM using a VPN-less feature called MRA.

Components of Cisco Collaboration Solutions

Let us understand what each type of component does in this architecture.

Endpoints

In unified communications, endpoints refer to the devices or apps people use to access and interact with communication services and applications. With the recent addition of headsets to their lineup, Cisco offers a wide range of both hardware and software-based endpoints. Cisco also supports the usage of third-party endpoints in their deployment, but the features will be limited. You can find the extensive list of endpoints here: https://www.cisco.com/c/en_in/products/collaboration-endpoints/product-listing.html

Modern endpoints are designed to provide a seamless and intuitive user experience, enabling individuals to stay connected and collaborate effectively from different locations and devices.

Common types of endpoints are as follows:

- **IP Phones**: Desk phones connected to the network and use Internet Protocol (IP) to transmit voice calls. IP phones often provide advanced features beyond traditional analog phones, such as call transfer, conference calling, and directory access. Cisco has different models in their catalog- affordable full-featured VoIP (7800 series) phones, conference room phones with large speakers, phones with cameras, and colored displays to support video calls (8800 series). A wide range of phones allows customers to buy the right phone for specific needs. Knowledge workers may need an IP phone with more features, and if using it for long hours, they may need to connect their headset. But you can install a simple phone for the lobby and common area. If you need the phone in a conference/meeting room, you may prefer the phone with a good built-in speaker and mic. And for the receptionist or administrative assistants, they may need a phone that supports extra lines (or a key expansion module), so they can manage multiple calls.

- **Video Conferencing Endpoints**: Cisco is the market leader in this category. These devices are designed specifically for video conferencing. They include room-based video conferencing systems equipped with cameras, microphones, and displays to facilitate high-quality video meetings. Think of the quality difference, such as playing video games on PlayStation/Xbox compared to mobile gaming. Similarly, these video conferencing endpoints provide an immersive experience compared to joining the meeting from a computer/smartphone. Different models range from something you can have on your desk (Cisco desk pro) to an endpoint with a large display to use as a digital whiteboard to something you can install in a small (Webex room kit mini) or large conference room with multiple large displays connected (Webex room series). We will discuss this in detail in another chapter.
- **Softphones**: Softphones are software applications that run on computers, laptops, tablets, or smartphones. They emulate the functionality of physical phones, allowing users to make voice and video calls over the Internet using a headset or the built-in microphone and speakers. Example- Cisco IP Communicator, discontinued by Cisco in 2021.
- **Unified Communications Clients**: These software clients combine various communication channels (voice, video, messaging, and so on.) into a single interface. They often integrate with other applications, providing a unified experience. Cisco Jabber is an example of such a client. Even though Cisco recommends using the Webex app, which offers more features, they still support Jabber clients. One of the key reasons is that the Webex app needs connectivity to the Cloud, and not all customers want that, so some customers still prefer to use the Jabber client.
- **Collaboration Apps**: These software applications provide communication and collaboration features, such as instant messaging, Voice/Video calls or conferences, presence status, Persistent team/topic-focused chat, file sharing, and more. Example: Cisco Webex app that provides more features than Jabber, and it can now work in hybrid or cloud-only mode. It can utilize some features from On-prem infrastructure and other Cloud features.

Call Control

Call control refers to managing and directing voice and video communication sessions between different endpoints.

CUCM

Cisco Unified Communications Manager (CUCM) is the heart of Cisco collaboration services. As per the latest (CUCM 14) datasheet, over 300,000 customers worldwide use CUCM and over 120 million Cisco IP phones and soft clients are deployed.

https://www.cisco.com/c/en/us/products/collateral/unified-communications/unified-communications-manager-callmanager/data-sheet-c78-744937.html

All the endpoints register on CUCM. CUCM manages the routing of voice and video calls. It handles call setup, termination, and features like call hold, transfer, and conference.

Key functions of CUCM are:

- Call Routing and Control
- Unified Messaging
- Integration with other UC apps
- User Directory and Profiles
- Device provisioning and Management

We will cover these features in detail in upcoming chapters.

Unified CM Cluster Overview

CUCM cluster allows multiple servers, termed as nodes, to operate as a unified IP PBX system. This supports scalability, redundancy, and system resilience.

Server Node Roles:

- **Publisher**: Acts as the central database server. It is the only one with full read and write access to the configuration database. Usually, there is just one publisher per cluster. It is recommended to have a dedicated publisher in the cluster with over 1250 users for optimal telephony performance.
- **Subscriber**: They pull their database information from the publisher but use their local copy for faster initialization. They can function in various roles, such as:
  - **Call Processing**: Handles call functions when its specific service is enabled.
  - **TFTP**: Distributes files such as device configurations and firmware. It

might be best to dedicate a node to this function in larger clusters (over 1250 users).

  - **Media Resource**: Provides features such as conferencing, music on hold, and announcements. Depending on the scale, dedicated nodes might be advisable.

Additional Services:

- **CTI Manager**: Connects Cisco CallManager to TAPI or JTAPI apps. Maximum of eight nodes with this service in a cluster.
- **Unified CM Applications**: Include services such as Cisco Unified CM Assistant, extension mobility and Web Dialer.

Cluster Configuration:

It is possible to mix VM configurations in a cluster, but it is not recommended because capacity is limited by the smallest VM configuration.

Different hardware platforms can be combined, but this might impact capacity. Server specifications and platform rules must be taken into account.

Recommendation:

- Use the same VM configuration across all nodes if possible.
- It is ideal to keep all cluster nodes within the same LAN or MAN. Follow WAN clustering guidelines if spanning over IP WAN.
- A maximum of 20 server nodes in a cluster, but only eight of them can be call-processing subscribers.
- For two-node clusters, limit the user count to 1250. Beyond that, consider having separate server nodes.

Cisco IM&P

Cisco Instant Messaging and Presence (IM&P) extends call control capabilities to instant messaging and presence services within the UC environment. IM&P facilitates real-time text-based communication and provides information about the availability and status of users. Key aspects of call control in Cisco IM&P include:

- **Presence Management**: IM&P tracks users' availability, status, and location across different devices and platforms. It lets users see whether their contacts are online, busy, away, or offline.
- **Instant Messaging**: IM&P enables users to exchange text messages in real-time. It supports one-on-one chats, group chats, file sharing, and emoji reactions.

- **Integrated Communication**: IM&P seamlessly integrates with voice and video communication. Users can initiate calls directly from the instant messaging interface, promoting quick and efficient collaboration.
- **Unified Contacts**: IM&P often integrates with other applications to provide a unified contact list. This list combines email, phone, and IM contacts in a single interface.

Voice Messaging

Cisco Unity Connection is a unified messaging platform with many features.

At its core, CUC is designed to enhance voice messaging workflows. It provides voicemail, integrated messaging (voicemails sent to email), and automated attendant features, allowing users to manage their voice messages in versatile ways.

Some of the key features are:

- **Voicemail Storage**: Unity Connection stores voicemail messages in user mailboxes, making them accessible from various devices and locations.
- **Integrated Messaging**: Voicemails can be integrated with email inboxes, allowing users to receive voicemail notifications via email and access voicemails using the same client.
- **Personalized Greetings**: Users can set personalized greetings, including standard greetings, out-of-office messages, and more.
- **Message Synchronization**: Unity Connection synchronizes voicemail messages across devices, ensuring users can access their messages on their preferred endpoints.
- **Message-Waiting Indicator**: Users are notified of new voicemails through message waiting indicators on their devices.

In addition to these advanced voice messaging functionalities, Cisco Unity Connection extends its capabilities to streamline call-handling processes.

Some of these features resemble call center components similar to those found in Cisco Unified Contact Center Express (UCCX). However, Cisco Unity Connection primarily focuses on essential features for call management.

- **Call Handlers**: Act as automated attendants, greeting callers and providing routing options.

  Example: Imagine calling a company and being greeted by a message that asks you to press "1" for sales, "2" for tech support, or "3" for general inquiries. This ensures your call reaches the appropriate department without delays.
- **Directory Handlers**: Enable callers to search and connect with users or departments.

Example: When you call a company and want to speak with a specific person, the directory handler lets you search for them by entering their name or extension.

- **Interview Handlers**: Collect caller information via predefined questions.

  Example: Imagine calling a customer feedback line where you are prompted to rate your experience on a scale of 1 to 5. Your responses are recorded, helping the company understand and improve its service based on customer feedback.

- **Greetings Management**: User-managed voicemail and call greetings.

  Example: You can record a personalized voicemail greeting for your colleagues or customers.

- **Routing Rules and Schedule**: Calls after business hours can be routed to a voicemail box with a "We're closed now, but we will get back to you" message.

Conferencing

Let us delve into two core conferencing components in the Cisco Collaboration suite: CMS and TMS.

Cisco Meeting Server (CMS)

CMS is Cisco's On-prem conferencing solution, allowing for adaptable and scalable video, audio, and web meetings with various devices and platforms.

Cisco acquired Acano in 2016, a firm known for its video infrastructure and collaboration software. The technology from Acano was then integrated and rebranded as the Cisco Meeting Server (CMS).

CMS allows participants from various devices, including video endpoints, phones, and web applications, to join meetings. It can also integrate seamlessly with Cisco Unified Communications Manager (CUCM) and other third-party systems.

The primary operating system for CMS is Linux-based. It utilizes WebRTC for its web clients and employs Session Initiation Protocol(SIP) for call signaling.

Main Features:

- **Multi-Platform Collaboration**: CMS is designed to bridge the gap between various conferencing solutions. Whether participants use Skype for business, traditional video conferencing endpoints, or join via a browser using WebRTC, CMS brings them together in one meeting.
- **Adaptive Call Quality**: CMS adjusts call quality based on the network conditions. So, if bandwidth drops, CMS will adjust to ensure the call continues, even if at a reduced quality.

- **Advanced Scalability**: CMS can scale from small to large multi-site deployments, offering an optimal experience for SMBs and large enterprises. Its clustering ability ensures that thousands of users can be accommodated simultaneously.
- **Space-based Conferencing**: CMS uses a concept of "spaces" for meetings. Every user can have a dedicated space or virtual meeting room to host ad-hoc or scheduled meetings.
- **Enhanced Security**: CMS secures interactions between specific services such as the call bridge, web bridge, and database services using TLS and digital certificates, ensuring robust encryption and authentication of data exchanges. In addition to standard encryption, CMS offers features such as "lobby lock" allowing meeting hosts to approve participants before joining a space and lock a meeting once all participants have joined.
- **Recording and Streaming**: CMS has built-in recording and streaming capabilities, enabling meetings to be broadcast to larger audiences or stored for future reference. The Recorder provides the ability to record meetings and save the recordings on a Network File System (NFS) document storage. CMS streamer integrates with any streaming platform that supports RTMP(S) (YouTube, Facebook, and so on). The recommended platform for integrating with the CMS Streamer is the Vbrick DME external streaming server, which Cisco has successfully tested.
- **API Customization**: CMS offers a comprehensive set of APIs, allowing businesses to customize and integrate it with their specific business processes or applications.

TelePresence Management Suite (TMS)

TMS is a central hub for managing and monitoring Cisco TelePresence endpoints and infrastructure. It centralizes and simplifies many tasks associated with managing a large-scale video infrastructure.

TMS offers a unified dashboard for overseeing Cisco TelePresence systems. It also integrates with enterprise calendaring systems, providing video conference scheduling and resource reservation functionalities.

TMS is designed for on-premises deployment and operates seamlessly alongside other Cisco collaboration tools.

The platform for TMS is the Windows Server. It connects with Active Directory for user management and employs LDAP for directory services.

Cisco has announced the end of the sale and end of life for TMS and has recommended customers consider the migration. Details here: https://www.cisco.com/c/en/us/products/collateral/conferencing/telepresence-management-suite-tms/tele-manage-suite-eol.html

VQ Conference Manager DMA is the Cisco recommended on-premise replacement for Cisco TMS. You can find more details about it here: https://www.vqcomms.com/tms-replacement/

Main Features of TMS:

- Centralized Management
- Smart Scheduling
- Real-time Monitoring & Alerts
- Phonebook Services
- Usage and Performance Analytics
- Bandwidth Management
- Upgrade Management

PSTN and Voice Gateway Integration

With organizations increasingly relying on IP networks, there remains a need to interface with the traditional PSTN. This is where voice gateways come into play.

Voice gateways are intermediaries, ensuring seamless communication between IP-based systems and the PSTN.

This section will delve into the intricacies of the PSTN, its integration with IP networks, and the role of voice gateways in bridging these two worlds.

Public Switched Telephone Network (PSTN)

The PSTN is the traditional telephone network that uses circuit-switched telephony between telephones for voice communication. It consists of a global collection of interconnected public telephone networks, both commercial and government-owned.

In our context, when referring to the PSTN, we are discussing the network used to make traditional telephone calls instead of calls made over the Internet.

It is important to understand the key difference between the Internet and PSTN as both are interconnected public networks.

Attributes	**Internet**	**PSTN**
Network type	Packet-switched: Data is broken into packets, sent independently, and reassembled at the destination.	Circuit-switched: A dedicated path is reserved for the duration of a call, ensuring a constant, uninterrupted connection.
Origins and Design	Designed for a variety of traffic types. Can handle web browsing, file transfers, voice calls, and more.	Originally optimized for voice communication over long distances with clarity and reliability.

Flexibility and Services	Supports a variety of applications, from multimedia to integrations with other software.	Primarily limited to voice calls but offers high reliability and quality for these communications.
Reason for Existence	Adaptability and support for diverse applications including voice services.	Reliability in regions without high-speed internet, consistent voice call quality, regulatory requirements, legacy infrastructures.

***Table 2.1**: Key differences between the Internet and PSTN*

Organizations require PSTN connectivity to make or receive calls to/from the traditional phone network. This is typically achieved by leasing Direct Inward Dialing (DID) numbers and connections from a service provider.

Cisco Voice Gateway Options

Cisco offers a variety of voice gateways to cater to different organizational needs.

Cisco ISR 4000 Series are multifunction devices offering routing, security, and voice gateway capabilities. You can find more details here: https://www.cisco.com/c/en/us/products/collateral/routers/4000-series-integrated-services-routers-isr/data_sheet-c78-732542.html

Gateway Protocols:

The term "gateway" is used because it serves as an entry and exit point between two different networks. It essentially facilitates a transition between circuit-switched (traditional telephony) and packet-switched (modern IP-based) networks.

- **SIP**: Chosen for its flexibility, scalability, and adherence to open standards. Given that many modern unified communications solutions and providers support SIP, it is a natural choice for businesses that want a future-proof setup or work with various vendors.
- **MGCP**: Preferred in setups where centralized control is essential. Dial plan can be managed from CUCM. With MGCP, when using ISDN, the Q.931 signaling is backhauled to the CUCM. This means that the CUCM gets a clearer picture of the call setup and teardown process and can control it more granularly. In contrast, with protocols like H.323, the Q.931 signaling remains at the gateway, meaning that the CUCM has to rely on interworking and does not get the same visibility into the ISDN signaling process.
- **H.323**: This might be the choice for legacy systems or when working with specific older hardware or setups. It is less prevalent due to SIP's rise but still found in many enterprises that adopted VoIP in its early days.

It is important to know the difference among these protocols.

Feature/Protocol	**SIP**	**MGCP**	**H.323**
Dial Plan Control	Distributed	Centralized on CUCM	Distributed
Port Number	5060 (default)	2427 (call control), 2727 (media)	1720
Codec Negotiation	Yes	Limited	Yes
Signaling	Direct or Proxy	Centralized (Call Agent)	Direct or Gatekeeper

***Table 2.2**: Difference between Gateway protocols*

Collaboration Edge Solutions

Collaboration Edge Solutions helps different networks, protocols, and devices work together. In this section, we will look at two main components: CUBE, which manages voice and video sessions for SIP connections, and Expressway, which provides safe access to collaboration tools, connecting outside devices to company networks without needing VPNs.

CUBE

Cisco Unified Border Element (CUBE) is a network border element that facilitates SIP-based voice and video connectivity between different networks.

It acts as a voice and video gateway, offering interconnectivity between SIP trunks, service providers, and enterprise networks.

While voice gateways primarily deal with transitioning voice communications from digital and analog systems to VoIP, CUBE handles the more intricate responsibilities of session management for SIP trunking. It offers transcoding, security, and quality of service (QoS) and supports rich media sessions, including voice, video, and instant messaging.

CUBE is primarily used in SIP Trunking scenarios for connecting enterprise networks with Service Providers or interconnecting different VoIP solutions within a large enterprise.

Common features are:

- **Interoperability**: Provides seamless interoperability between different vendor solutions and protocols.
- **Security**: Offers features such as toll fraud prevention, encrypted voice and video, and denial-of-service protection.

- **Session Management**: Manages signaling and media streams while ensuring the quality and reliability of sessions.
- **Transcoding**: Facilitates conversion between different codecs to ensure compatibility.
- **QoS**: Ensures high-quality voice and video communication even in challenging network conditions.
- **Protocol Interworking**: Offers seamless conversion between different voice and video protocols.

Cisco provides CUBE in various formats:

- **Integrated Service Routers (ISR)**- Suitable for branch and smaller office locations.
- **Aggregation Services Routers (ASR)**- Ideal for larger enterprise or service provider settings.
- **Virtual CUBE (vCUBE)**- A software solution that can be hosted on virtual platforms.

The terms SBC and CUBE are often used interchangeably. While CUBE predominantly aligns with Cisco's ecosystem, integration with SBCs from other vendors such as Ribbon and AudioCodes is feasible via SIP trunks. However, it is essential to verify Cisco's support and testing for specific scenarios. Even though untested configurations might work, they could present troubleshooting challenges.

Expressway

Cisco Expressway is a versatile component that offers secure firewall traversal, remote access, and video interoperability for collaboration services.

While Voice Gateways and CUBE focus on voice and video session management, Expressway is tailored to enable secure remote and mobile access to collaboration tools without VPNs. Its core functionality revolves around providing edge services – facilitating access for external devices into the enterprise network.

- **Expressway-C (Core)**: Resides inside the enterprise network and is responsible for registration, call control, and service discovery.
- **Expressway-E (Edge)**: Sits at the edge of the enterprise network (usually in a DMZ) and serves as the traversal server, allowing secure communication between devices inside and outside the enterprise without exposing the internal network.

Main Features:

- **Mobile and Remote Access**: Securely connects mobile and remote workers to the enterprise collaboration tools without a VPN.

- **Firewall Traversal**: Navigate through firewalls without compromising security or requiring complex configurations.
- **B2B Communication**: Facilitate business-to-business video and voice calls.
- **End-to-End Encryption**: Ensures secure communication from device to device, even across public Internet.
- **Unified Communications Proxy**: Provides registration, call control, and provisioning for remote devices.
- **Interoperability**: Integrate non-Cisco endpoints and infrastructure into the collaboration environment.
- **Cloud Integration**: Connect on-premises infrastructure with Cisco cloud services.

We will understand these features in detail in another chapter.

Survivable Remote Site Telephony (SRST)

Survivable Remote Site Telephony (SRST) is a Cisco feature that provides high availability for branch office voice networks. It is deployed on Cisco Integrated Services Routers (ISRs) in branch sites. When the WAN link is up, the branch office uses the central UC server for call processing. If the WAN link goes down, SRST on the ISR takes over the call processing duties locally.

While centralized UC solutions are efficient, they rely heavily on WAN connectivity. If a branch office loses connection to the central UC server, it could be left without telephony services. SRST provides a fallback mechanism in such situations, enabling local call-processing capabilities so that the branch can continue its operations despite WAN failures. Though SRST is distinctively Cisco, it is essential to understand that this idea of localized fallback is a standard feature aligning well with any centralized deployment type across the industry. In the Cisco ecosystem, with their IP phones, its SRST. Similarly, other industry players such as Avaya, Ribbon (SBA in Skype for Business), and Poly have features that fulfil similar roles, providing resilience and continuity tailored to their specific deployments.

SRST capabilities are built into Cisco's ISR routers. Depending on the ISR model and its resources, a specific number of phones can be supported in SRST mode. Cisco offers a range of ISRs suitable for different sizes of branch offices, from small to large.

Main Features:

- **Fallback Call Processing**: SRST automatically detects a WAN failure and switches to local call processing mode.
- **MGCP Fallback**: If the branch uses MGCP with the central UC, SRST can seamlessly transition the phones to SIP or SCCP for local call processing.

- **Basic Call Services**: Supports essential call services such as call hold, transfer, conference, and voicemail.
- **E911 Support**: Ensures emergency calls are routed correctly, even in fallback mode.

Contact Center

UCCX is a part of Cisco's Unified Communications suite, specifically designed for small to medium-sized businesses (SMBs) to offer a feature-rich contact center solution without the complexity and overhead of larger systems.

While UCCX caters mostly to SMBs, it is essential to note that Cisco also offers the UCCE- a full enterprise version to cater to larger organizations with more extensive and intricate requirements.

Other on-prem contact center solutions can be considered as alternatives depending on the organization's unique requirements. However, the focus in this section will remain primarily on the capabilities of UCCX.

Main Features:

- **Automatic Call Distribution (ACD)**: Efficiently routes incoming calls to the most suitable agent or department.
- **Interactive Voice Response (IVR)**: Provides automated interaction with callers, gathering information and routing calls accordingly.
- **Skills-Based Routing**: Assigns calls to agents based on their specific skill sets, ensuring callers get the best assistance.
- **Real-Time and Historical Reporting**: A comprehensive view of contact center metrics enables informed decision-making.
- **Computer Telephony Integration (CTI)**: Allows integration with third-party applications, enhancing agent productivity.
- **Workforce Management**: Assists in agent scheduling, forecasting call volumes, and managing agent adherence.
- **Multichannel Capabilities**: Besides voice, UCCX supports email, web chat, and social media interactions.
- **Finesse Desktop**: A web-based agent and supervisor desktop that provides a collaborative experience.
- **CRM Integration**: Can be seamlessly integrated with popular CRM systems to offer agents a unified view of customer data.

Other Components (Good to Know)

This section briefly highlights additional Cisco components not depicted in the reference diagram but play specific roles in unique scenarios.

Cisco Emergency Responder (CER)

The Cisco Emergency Responder (CER) is an advanced solution engineered to enhance the emergency calling functionality offered by Unified Communications platforms. Its main objective is to provide accurate and rapid location-based information of the caller to emergency services, ensuring the quickest possible response in critical situations.

With the adoption of IP-based telephony, traditional location-based methods to identify the source of a 911 call became less reliable. Given that IP phones can be moved easily within and between office locations, there needs to be a way to accurately pinpoint the exact location of an emergency caller.

CER is deployed within an organization's network, often alongside other Cisco UC applications. It interfaces with CUCM for call control and phone tracking, and its database stores detailed location information for each device. The system continually monitors the network for any changes in the location of devices.

CER operates with Cisco's Unified Communications Manager (CUCM) to deliver:

- **Dynamic Tracking**: CER can track the location of IP phones, even if they are moved, ensuring accurate location information.
- **On-Site Security Notifications**: When an emergency call is made, CER can notify on-site security personnel with details about the caller's location, allowing for an internal response while waiting for emergency services.
- **Automatic Public Safety Answering Point (PSAP) Routing**: CER ensures that emergency calls are routed to the correct PSAP based on the caller's location.

Cisco VG Series Gateways

Cisco VG Series Gateways bridges an organization's analog devices and digital VoIP network. They enable legacy analog devices like fax machines, phones, and modems to interact seamlessly with modern IP telephony systems.

Cisco VG Series Gateways perform the following functions:

- **Signal Conversion**: They convert analog voice signals to digital signals suitable for VoIP and vice versa.
- **Integration with IP PBX**: These gateways can be seamlessly integrated with Cisco's Unified Communications Manager (CUCM), enabling centralized call control and Management.

- **Fax and Modem Support**: They ensure reliable fax and modem traffic transmission over VoIP systems.

Cisco Unified Communications Manager Ecpress (CME) and Session Management Edition (SME)

Cisco Unified Communications Manager Express (CME), the compact version of CUCM with limited features, is often used for small to medium-sized deployments **or** as a fallback mechanism on remote sites.

Session Management Edition (SME) is similar to CUCM, which provides centralized call routing and dial plan aggregation between different Cisco Unified CM Clusters in multisite distributed call processing deployments.

Core and Hybrid Components of Cisco Collaboration Solutions

There is a growing need for collaboration tools that offer both on-premises and cloud functionality. Cisco provides solutions that span both environments. These are often called Hybrid solutions, integrating on-premises Cisco components with cloud-based services, primarily through the Cisco Webex platform.

Webex Media Node

Webex Media Node is a bridge between on-premises infrastructure and the Webex cloud, providing better quality user experiences, especially when large traffic volumes are involved. It locally processes audio, video, and data-sharing streams for Webex Meetings, optimizing the media path to reduce latency and improve quality.

- Deployed on-premises.
- Connects directly to Cisco Webex in the Cloud.
- By processing media locally, it reduces the bandwidth requirements on external connections, saving costs and enhancing quality.

Expressway Connectors for Hybrid

Expressway connectors offer integration options that connect on-premises environment to Cisco cloud services. These are software applications that run on the Cisco Expressway platform.

Main Features:

- **Hybrid Call Service**: This connector allows Webex Teams clients to register to CUCM and place/receive calls like any other endpoint in the organization.

- **Calendar Integration**: Synchronizes on-premises calendars with Webex Teams, enabling one-click-to-join functionality for meetings.
- **Directory Integration**: Synchronizes on-premises directory services with the Cloud.

The Role of Virtualization in Unified Communications

With virtualization, a single physical server can run multiple Cisco Collaboration "servers" or "virtual machines." This approach has several advantages over traditional deployments, where applications run directly on the hardware platform. It can significantly reduce server, electricity, cooling, and rack space costs. To enable virtualization, a hypervisor is installed directly on the physical server to manage the virtual machines. In the case of Cisco Collaboration, the VMware ESXi Hypervisor is the required hypervisor.

Each virtual machine has associated virtual hardware resources such as virtual CPU, virtual memory, and virtual disk. Those resources are defined for each Collaboration application in predefined templates distributed through an Open Virtualization Archive (OVA), an open standards-based method for packaging and distributing virtual machine templates. For many of the Cisco Collaboration applications, several VM configuration options are available when deploying an OVA to provide different capacity options. OVAs must be used when installing a Cisco Collaboration application, not only to define the correct virtual hardware resources but also to ensure that the virtual disks are not misaligned with the host physical disks, which would impact the storage performance.

For more information on the considerations for designing and deploying virtualization of Cisco Unified Communications applications, refer to the information available at https://www.cisco.com/go/virtualized-collaboration

Call Processing Hardware

Selecting the right hardware is a critical step when setting up Cisco Collaboration solutions. While the choice largely depends on specific business needs and existing infrastructure, understanding the nuances of each option can significantly impact performance, scalability, and total cost of ownership. In this section, we'll explore three primary hardware options that Cisco recommends for different scenarios and requirements. More details here: https://www.cisco.com/c/dam/en/us/td/docs/voice_ip_comm/uc_system/virtualization/cisco-collaboration-infrastructure.html

Tested Reference Configuration (TRC)

- Built on Cisco Unified Computing System (UCS) servers.
- Defined limited hardware configurations, validated with Cisco Collaboration apps for performance, capacity, and application co-residency.
- Intended for those needing validated infrastructure or unfamiliar with virtualization.

Cisco Business Edition 6000 and 7000

- Packaged solutions including hardware, virtualization software, and Cisco apps.
- Pre-configured hardware tested with Cisco Collaboration apps.
- BE6000 has two versions: BE6000M and BE6000H. BE7000 also has BE7000M and BE7000H.

Specifications-based Hardware

- Offers flexible configurations and can adjust CPU, number of cores, storage type, and more.
- Hardware can be from Cisco or other vendors listed in the https://www.vmware.com/resources/compatibility
- Not explicitly validated by Cisco for collaboration apps, so performance isn't guaranteed.

Key Design Criteria for Cisco On-Prem Centralized Deployment Model

The following criteria offer a comprehensive view, addressing the nuances of sizing, network demands, and overall system optimization.

This overview is a simplified explanation meant to provide a fundamental grasp of the design criteria. For an in-depth understanding and intricate details, it is recommended to refer Cisco's System Reference Network Design (SRND) document or directly engage with a Cisco representative.

Sizing Your System

In this section, we will explore the key factors to consider when determining the right size and scale for your system.

- **Assessing Needs:** Understand both current and future requirements, such as concurrent calls, endpoints, and additional features.

- **Tools Available**: Leverage tools such as the Sizing Tool and Capacity Calculator to inform your decisions.
- **Key Considerations**:
  - **Growth**: Plan for expansion and scalability.
  - **Feature Set**: Estimate bandwidth requirements for voice, video, and other applications.
  - **Reliability**: Ensure redundancy and failover mechanisms.
  - **Integrations**: Recognize that integrating third-party systems might demand extra resources.
  - **Traffic**: Plan for peak usage periods.
  - **Network**: Ensure infrastructure can handle the requirements, considering aspects such as latency, jitter, and QoS.
  - **Bandwidth**: Strategize around endpoint and video demands; always maintain a bandwidth buffer.
  - **Embracing Virtualization**: Reference Cisco Collaboration Virtualization guidelines for determining VM specifications.

Network Requirements in Data Centers and Branch Sites

Let us understand essential network criteria for maintaining efficient operations in data centers and branch sites.

- **Within the Data Center:**
  - **CUCM**: Maintain an RTT ≤ 80ms for conversations within the cluster.
  - **CUC & UCCX**: Prioritize a latency ≤ 40ms when collaborating with CUCM.
- **Server Communication:**
  - **Achieve low latency:** < 150ms for effective server-to-server interactions.
- **Branch Infrastructure:**
  - **Local Voice Gateways**: Implementing local gateways can enhance call quality, reduce latency, and ensure continuous service.
- **WAN Considerations:**
  - Even with local processing, some traffic might traverse the WAN. Prioritize exceptional QoS. If RTT exceeds 150-200ms, consider dedicated connections.
  - **Quality Over Quantity**: High latency can degrade voice and video quality and disrupt app synchronization.

Ensuring an optimal setup for Cisco collaboration not only necessitates careful planning but also consistent monitoring to adapt and evolve with your organization's needs.

Understanding Redundancy in Cisco Collaboration

When we talk about redundancy in Unified Communications and IT infrastructure at large, we are referring to the practice of ensuring system availability and mitigating service interruptions. This is accomplished by creating backups or failover systems. These backups can be organized at various levels: node, site, and data center.

Node-Level Redundancy:

- **Importance**: If a single server or node fails, others can take over its duties. This ensures smooth operations with minimal interruptions.
- **Standard Practice**: In a Unified CM cluster, you have the publisher and multiple subscribers. While the publisher manages the primary database, subscribers can handle calls even if they lose connectivity with the publisher. Similar planning required for other components.
- **Recommendations**:
  - Deploy a balanced number of call processing nodes to distribute load and prevent one from being overwhelmed.
  - Ensure there is a failover strategy in place. If one node encounters issues, traffic should automatically divert to another.

Site-Level Redundancy:

- **Importance**: This level of redundancy ensures that even if an entire site (such as an office or a building) faces an outage due to reasons being natural disasters, power cuts, or major network issues, the functions can be taken over by another site.
- **Standard Practice**: In many large enterprises, there might be primary and secondary sites, both equipped to handle the company's full operations. If the primary site goes down, the secondary can become the primary until the original is restored.

Data Center-Level Redundancy:

- **Importance**: Redundancy at this level ensures business continuity even if an entire data center faces an issue.
- **Standard Practice**: Companies might have multiple data centers in different geographic locations. If one fails, the other can take over.

- **Recommendations**:
  - Like site redundancy, choosing geographically diverse locations for data centers can mitigate risks from regional events like natural disasters.
  - Regularly test failover procedures to ensure a smooth transition in case of emergencies.
  - Ensure adequate network connectivity between data centers to handle load during transition periods.

In conclusion, redundancy at all levels—node, site, and data center—is crucial for ensuring business continuity and high availability. Depending on the organization's scale, budget, and operational criticality, businesses can decide how deep they want to go into each redundancy level. As systems and networks grow more complex, the integration of multi-level redundancy becomes a necessity rather than a luxury.

Let us understand this with more context. This is a simplified explanation.

Node-Level Redundancy

In this section, we will delve into the specifics of ensuring redundancy at the node level, exploring various components and their respective strategies to maintain continuous service.

- **Call Control (CUCM and IM&P):**
  - **Unified CM Cluster Services**: A standard CUCM cluster inherently supports redundancy with a maximum of 20 nodes (up to 8 nodes for call processing). In case a node fails, devices seamlessly transition to another subscriber.
  - **IM&P Strategy**: Embraces a redundancy model similar to that of CUCM.
- **Voice Messaging (CUC)**: Implements an active/standby server redundancy model.
- **Contact Center (UCCX):** Adopts an active/standby redundancy model.
- **Conferencing (CMS and TMS)**:
  - **CMS**: Utilizes a clustering approach, where tasks are redistributed to other nodes if one fails.
  - **TMS**: Incorporates a secondary mirrored server to maintain high availability.
- **Gateways and PSTN Integration**: Redundancy is achieved by establishing paired setups; a secondary gateway is engaged if the primary one fails.
- **Collaboration Edge Solutions (Expressway and CUBE)**:
  - **Expressway**: Clustering is employed across both its forms, promoting load distribution.
  - **CUBE**: Employs a box-to-box redundancy approach.

- **Survivable Remote Site Telephony (SRST)**: In the event of WAN link failures, SRST serves as a safety net, allowing local routers to assume call processing responsibilities.

In larger infrastructures, the distinction between site and data center redundancy can blur. Nodes might be spread across various sites or data centers, demanding:

- **Network Considerations**: Ensure latency remains within solution limits and that bandwidth can accommodate peak loads, especially during failover scenarios.
- **Strategic Node Distribution**: Distribute nodes with potential risks in mind. For instance, do not cluster all nodes in regions vulnerable to similar natural disasters.
- **Interconnected Failover**: Sometimes, an entire site might act as a node in a broader data center strategy, with multiple sites offering failover options for each other.

In conclusion, understanding and implementing redundancy concepts will improve the resilience and reliability of Cisco On-prem Centralized Deployment Model, ensuring smooth business communication.

Deployment Scenarios Example

Deploying Cisco Collaboration systems goes beyond technical terminology; it is about tailoring them to real-world business needs. Different enterprises, regardless of size, require unique collaboration solutions. The following scenarios demonstrate how to craft these tailored solutions for varying scales of operations.

Scenario 1: MNC with HQ in Singapore and Branches in APAC

Let us start by examining a scenario of a multi-national company, headquartered in Singapore, with numerous branch offices spread across the APAC region.

Headquarters (Singapore):

- **Endpoints**: Based on requirements.
- **Call Control**: Centralized CUCM and IM&P.
- **Messaging**: Centralized CUC.
- **Contact Center**: UCCX (if required).
- **Conferencing**: Centralized CMS and TMS.
- **Gateways/PSTN**: As per local norms, centralized or local options.
- **Edge**: Expressway (remote access) & CUBE (SIP trunking).
- **SRST**: Not needed.

Branch Offices (APAC):

- **Endpoints**: Various IP, video, and software endpoints.
- **Call Control**: Register to HQ's CUCM.
- **Messaging**: Access HQ's CUC.
- **Conferencing**: Utilize HQ's CMS & TMS.
- **Gateways/PSTN:** Local or through HQ.
- **Edge**: Rely on HQ's Expressway & CUBE.
- **SRST**: Vital for call functions.

Key Points:

- **PSTN**: Evaluate latency, rules, and DID adherence.
- **Redundancy**: Mandatory at key junctions.
- **Bandwidth**: Need sufficient from HQ to branches.
- **Security**: Ensure secure inter-site communication.

Scenario 2: Small to Medium Enterprise (SME) in Tokyo with Multiple Branch Offices within Country

Transitioning to a smaller scale, this scenario centers around an SME located in Tokyo, exploring how it ensures connectivity and collaboration across its national branches.

Headquarters (Tokyo):

- **Endpoints**: Cisco 7800 series IP phones & Jabber.
- **Call Control**: CME via Cisco ISR routers—ideal for smaller user counts.
- **Voice Messaging**: CUE with voicemail & auto-attendant, paired with CME.
- **Integrated Solution**: BE4K provides unified call control, voicemail, and conferencing.

Branch Offices:

- **Endpoints**: Cisco 7800 series & Jabber.
- **Call Control**: Access Tokyo's CME using MPLS.
- **Voice Messaging**: Access Tokyo's CUE.
- **Local Continuity**: SRST for resilience during WAN disruptions.

Scaling Strategy:

- **Call Control**: If surpassing CME's 300-user limit, transition to CUCM.

- **Messaging**: Upgrade from CUE to CUC for enriched messaging.
- **Conferencing**: Integrate Cisco Meeting Server for heightened demands.
- **WAN**: Optimize links or integrate SD-WAN for superior voice/video.
- **Edge & Security**: Add Expressway & CUBE as Business grows.

Regulations & Telephony:

- Adhere to Japan's strict telecom rules.
- PSTN setups should respect local mandates.
- For HQ-centric PSTN, ensure impeccable voice quality.
- As you scale, refine dial plans and localization accordingly.

SMEs benefit from initial adaptability with compact solutions. But as the company expands, embracing more scalable systems becomes crucial. Proactive planning facilitates smoother growth and sustained efficiency.

Scenario 3: Multinational Enterprise Spanning 20 Countries

In this scenario, we will delve into the complexities and demands of a large multinational enterprise that operates across 20 different countries. Scenario 3 can be viewed as an expanded version of Scenario 1, where instead of a single headquarters serving multiple branch offices in one region, we now have multiple regional clusters, each serving its geographical area similar to how the Singapore HQ served its branches in Scenario 1.

Let us start by looking at high-level simple diagram which shows how different regions have separate clusters connected through SME.

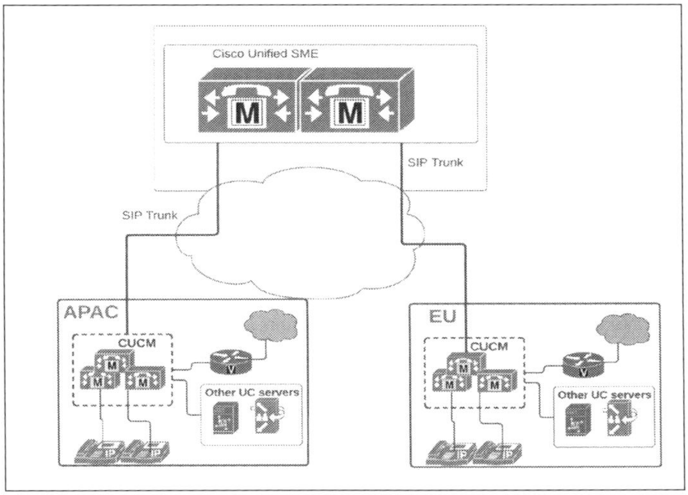

Figure 2.2: *Simple illustration of Distributed deployment model*

Operating across 20 nations requires a large enterprise to adopt a unified yet distributed centralized UC deployment model. This optimizes performance, ensures adherence to local telecom regulations, and guarantees robust disaster recovery.

Motivations for Distributed Clusters:

- **Latency**: VoIP sensitivity demands minimized latency via local clusters.
- **Scale**: Distribute endpoint demands to avoid overburdening a solitary cluster.
- **Design**: Regional clusters aid easier Management and localized configurations.
- **Regulation**: Adherence to country-specific telecom regulations.
- **Localization**: Simplified Management of time zones, local preferences, and routing.
- **Disaster Recovery**: Geographical spread guarantees uptime amidst local disruptions.

Cluster-to-Cluster Coordination:

- **SIP Trunks**: Facilitate inter-cluster calls.
- **Session Management Edition (SME)**: Acts as a central routing hub, streamlining the routing logic and facilitating smoother integration between clusters. SME is not mandatory. Each CUCM cluster can have SIP trunks to other cluster as well.

Key Elements:

- **Dial Plan**: Maintain a consistent, non-clashing dialing structure.
- **Bandwidth**: Plan for extensive video call bandwidth demands.
- **Codecs**: Deploy G.729 for inter-cluster communications and G.711 for intra-cluster.
- **Fallback**: Set alternate call paths during WAN disruptions.
- **Security**: Prioritize mutual TLS for SIP trunk.
- **QoS**: Ensure voice and video packets take precedence.
- **Localization**: Stay aligned with regional telecom norms and user preferences.

Navigating Licensing and Associated Costs

It is important to understand all cost factors associated to deployment. This is a general overview; the specifics can differ based on individual organizational requirements and deployment details.

Note: The Flex Plan model attempts to simplify Cisco's licensing, but intricacies persist. Always consider consulting with a Cisco representative for exact details.

Licensing Breakdown:

- **Endpoints**: Licenses correspond to device registrations, including IP phones and video systems on the Call Control server.
- **Call Control (CUCM) and IM&P**: Flex Plan's user-centric licenses replace the older UCL and CUWL models, with IM&P integrated under the Flex Plan model.
- **Voice Messaging (CUC)**: Voicemail boxes are encompassed in the Flex Plan without separate charges.
- **Contact Center (UCCX):** Licenses differ based on agent functionalities.
- **Conferencing (CMS and TMS)**: CMS uses participant licenses, while TMS requires licenses for specific features.
- **Gateways, PSTN Integration and Collaboration Edge Solutions**: Most are primarily free of licensing, though some modules, such as DSP and the likes of Expressway (RMS licenses) and CUBE (session-based), might have distinct licenses.
- **SRST**: Licenses depend on either user or phone counts.
- **Additional Features**: Tools like Unified Attendant Console, Cisco Emergency Responder (CER), and VG Series Gateways have their own licensing needs.

Costing Breakdown:

- **Endpoints**: Covers hardware, maintenance, and accessories.
- **Call Control (CUCM), IM & P, Voice Messaging (CUC), Contact Center (UCCX), and Conferencing (CMS and TMS)**: These typically involve costs for hardware (example, BE6000 for CUCM), virtualization, maintenance, and in some cases, potential network bandwidth upgrade charges.
- **Gateways, PSTN Integration and Collaboration Edge Solutions**: Costs can be related to hardware, the IOS License, specific collaboration features, and regular maintenance. For instance, Expressway and CUBE also factor in virtualization costs.
- **SRST**: Primarily linked to the IOS license and specific router hardware.
- **Additional Features**: Each, be it Unified Attendant Console, Cisco Emergency Responder (CER), or VG Series Gateways, carries its set of associated costs.

Comparing Cloud-based Solutions (SaaS) vs On-premises Deployment

From a cost perspective, cloud-based (SaaS) and traditional on-premises deployments differ significantly in how businesses incur and manage expenses:

Cloud-based Solutions (SaaS):

- **Subscription Model**: Costs are primarily operational (OPEX), involving monthly or annual subscription fees.
- **Minimal Upfront Hardware Costs**: Since infrastructure is hosted by the provider, there's little to no CAPEX involved.
- **Inclusive Maintenance**: Updates, maintenance, and some levels of support are usually included in the subscription.
- **Scalability**: Costs can flexibly scale up or down based on usage, aiding in budget predictability.

On-premises Deployment:

- **Upfront Hardware and Licensing**: Significant capital expenditure (CAPEX) on hardware, data centers, and initial software licenses.
- **Ongoing Maintenance**: Costs associated with regular software updates, security, and infrastructure maintenance.
- **Depreciation and Renewal**: Over time, hardware needs replacement, and licenses may require renewal.
- **Fixed Infrastructure**: Scalability often requires additional investments and can be less agile compared to cloud solutions.

Conclusion

In this chapter, we took a closer look at the Cisco Collaboration ecosystem. We explored different deployment models, the key components of Cisco's solutions, and the importance of virtualization in unified communications. Redundancy was highlighted as a crucial aspect to ensure continuous communication. We also navigated the practical elements of licensing and costs, emphasizing the distinctions and implications of on-prem versus SaaS models.

Grasping these foundational elements is crucial to effectively design, deploy, and maintain collaboration infrastructure. As we move on to the next chapter, we will dive deeper into the specifics of features and endpoints, providing a hands-on perspective on managing and registering within the Cisco Collaboration deployments.

Multiple Choice Questions

1. What is the primary function of Cisco Unified Communications Manager (CUCM)?

   a. Video Conferencing

   b. Voicemail Management

c. Call Control

d. PSTN Integration

2. Which component is primarily responsible for voice messaging?

a. CUCM

b. CUC

c. Expressway

d. CMS

3. What does SRST stand for?

a. Simple Remote Site Telephony

b. Secure Remote Site Telephony

c. Survivable Remote Site Telephony

d. Server Remote Site Telephony

4. In which deployment model is it essential to consider latency, scale, and better design across continents?

a. Localized deployment

b. Centralized deployment

c. Distributed centralized deployment

d. Hybrid deployment

5. For which component would you primarily consider SIP session licensing?

a. CUCM

b. Expressway

c. CUBE

d. CMS

6. Which component primarily handles conferencing?

a. CUC

b. CUBE

c. CMS

d. SRST

7. Which solution is generally recommended for small to medium enterprises as an all-in-one box?

    a. CUCM

    b. BE4k

    c. Expressway

    d. TMS

8. In a SaaS solution like Webex, licensing costs are typically based on which model?

    a. One-time purchase

    b. Subscription

    c. Free-for-all

    d. Lifetime

9. Which Cisco component is primarily responsible for emergency response?

    a. Expressway

    b. CUC

    c. CER

    d. CMS

10. Which of the following is NOT a deployment model for Unified Communications?

    a. Centralized

    b. Distributed

    c. Hybrid

    d. Singular

Answers

1. c
2. b
3. c
4. c

5. c
6. c
7. b
8. b
9. c
10. d

Further Reading

Same as the last chapter, to improve your understanding and broaden your perspective, explore the following topics on your own. Remember to tailor your research based on your organization's specific needs and always discern between genuine insights and industry trends.

- **Cisco vs. Competitors:** Analyze how Cisco's collaboration tools compare with competitors such as Avaya and Microsoft. Understand the strengths, weaknesses, and unique features each provider offers.
- **Total Cost of Ownership:** Conduct a deeper analysis of the costs of setting up, maintaining, and scaling Cisco's collaboration solutions. Incorporate costs such as hardware, licensing, training, and support into your evaluation.
- **Cisco's Planning and Design Tools**: Explore the tools Cisco provides for planning and design. How do they streamline the implementation process? Checkout some related Cisco's documents.

  https://www.cisco.com/c/dam/en/us/td/docs/voice_ip_comm/uc_system/virtualization/cisco-collaboration-infrastructure.html

  https://www.cisco.com/c/dam/en/us/td/docs/voice_ip_comm/uc_system/virtualization/cisco-collaboration-virtualization.html

  https://www.cisco.com/c/dam/en/us/td/docs/voice_ip_comm/uc_system/virtualization/collaboration-virtualization-sizing.html

  https://cucst.cloudapps.cisco.com/help/UC_Sizing_Tools_FAQ.pdf
- **Global Integration and Support:** Evaluate how Cisco's collaboration tools cater to globally distributed organizations. How does Cisco ensure consistent quality and support across different regions?
- **Interoperability with Third-Party Systems**: Explore how Cisco's solutions integrate with non-Cisco solutions. Is it straightforward, or are there challenges to be aware of?
- **Dive Deeper into Deployment Models**: Study the benefits and challenges

of different Cisco deployment models, such as distributed and hybrid deployments. How do they cater to varying organizational needs?

- **Exploring Cisco's Voice Gateway Options**: Look into Cisco's diverse voice gateway options. How do they differ in terms of functionality, scalability, and cost?
- **SRST**: Study the intricacies of Survivable Remote Site Telephony (SRST). Understand its critical importance in scenarios of network failures.
- **Network Requirements for Collaboration**: Delve into the network infrastructure requirements necessary for optimal functioning of Cisco Collaboration Solutions. What are the bandwidth and latency requirements? Check the bandwidth calculator tool from Cisco https://cway.cisco.com/vc-calculator/
- **Scenarios for Growth**: Research how organizations can scale their Cisco Collaboration Solutions as they grow. What are the changes required at different user thresholds?
- **All-in-One vs. Modular**: Investigate the pros and cons of opting for an all-in-one solution such as BE4k for SMEs vs. a modular approach using separate components.
- Check Cisco's Product Quick Reference Guides and Cisco Commerce Workspace(CCW) https://apps.cisco.com/Commerce/guest
- Explore feature navigator and SIP-profile test tool. These tools offer invaluable information that can be instrumental for daily operations.

  https://cfnng.cisco.com/
  https://cway.cisco.com/tools/SipProfileTest/

CHAPTER 3
Managing Endpoints and Users

Introduction

In this chapter, we will discuss essential network services crucial for collaboration. Then we will navigate through the CUCM GUI interface, along with CUCM global parameters. Our attention then shifts to the nuances of provisioning endpoints in CUCM, exploring the intricacies of the phone boot-up and registration processes. The chapter concludes by examining the relevance of COP files and software bundles, user authentication and authorization mechanisms, and the significance of directory integration within CUCM.

Structure

In the chapter, we will discuss the following topics:

- Getting Hands-On: Setting Up Your Lab Environment
- Essential Network Services in Cisco Collaboration – NTP, DHCP, DNS, TFTP and PoE
- Navigating Cisco Unified Communications Manager (CUCM) GUI
- Configuring Global Settings: Understanding Enterprise and Service Parameters
- Endpoint Registration in Cluster Environment
    - Device pool – Usage and Importance
    - Cisco Unified Communications Manager (CUCM) Group Overview
    - Phone/Endpoint Registration Process
    - Security and Trust Establishment (ITL/CTL)
- Cop Files and Software Bundles in CUCM
- User Authentication and Authorization in CUCM
    - User Account Types in CUCM

    - Access Control Group and Roles
- Directory Integration in CUCM for Endpoints
    - UDS Phonebook in Cisco

Getting Hands-On: Setting Up Your Lab Environment

From this chapter, we will delve into the practical aspects and hands-on procedures. The appropriate lab environment is essential if you are keen on trying these out. Here are your options:

DIY Lab Setup

You can build your own lab environment using these suggestions.

- Use simulation platforms such as GNS3 or EVE-NG.
  https://www.gns3.com/
  https://www.eve-ng.net/
- Install virtualization software for CUCM and related components.
- Obtain bootable images for CUCM and others. Note: You will need a Cisco contract linked to your Cisco login.
- Ensure you have a high-spec PC or consider cloud hosting (for example, GCP).

Cisco's Pre-Built Lab Environments

You can use Cisco's publicly available sandbox for practice.

- **Cisco dCloud Labs**: Exclusive access for those authorized by Cisco or its partners.

  https://dcloud.cisco.com/
- **Cisco DevNet Sandbox**: Open to all; it just requires a Cisco login. Great for practice.

  https://developer.cisco.com/docs/sandbox/#!collaboration

Essential Network Services in Cisco Collaboration

When configuring a Cisco Collaboration environment, several fundamental network services ensure efficient operations. Understanding these is very important before we get into CUCM-related configuration.

Network Time Protocol (NTP)

NTP is a service that synchronizes the clocks of computer systems over networks. NTP uses the UDP protocol and operates on port 123.

NTP is essential for Cisco Unified Communications Manager (CUCM) clusters. Many enterprises use dedicated NTP appliances, while others might rely on server solutions, including Linux servers running the `ntpd` service. Some even use routers or switches as their NTP sources.

For security and accuracy, large enterprises often use a mix of private NTP servers (inside their network) and authoritative, external NTP servers such as pool.ntp.org.

Note: While many Cisco solutions can use Windows Servers for NTP, Cisco Unified Communications (UC) Solutions, such as CallManager, Cisco Unity, and Instant Messaging and Presence, cannot. The primary reason is that Windows Time Services often utilize the Simple Network Time Protocol (SNTP), which Linux-based systems, namely CUCM, find challenging to synchronize with. Instead, UC solutions mandate using either a Linux-based or Cisco IOS-based NTP source. Acceptable sources include Linux NTP servers, Cisco IOS NTP sources, and Nexus OS NTP sources. Using a Windows NTP server with CUCM is not supported. It may work, but you will see a warning when running diagnose or pre-upgrade cop file.

- **Practical Tip**: Restrict NTP traffic to only known NTP servers and clients within your enterprise for security.
- **Configuration Tips**: For redundancy, set up at least three NTP servers; the publisher syncs with an external primary source, while subscribers derive their time from the publisher. Always use stratum 1 or 2 NTP servers for your CUCM. It is crucial for call logs, time-based access, and billing to have accurate time stamps.

Dynamic Host Configuration Protocol (DHCP)

DHCP assigns IP addresses and other network configurations to devices on a network automatically. DHCP servers such as Microsoft's DHCP service in Windows Server, ISC DHCP on Linux, or even appliances like Infoblox are common in large-scale deployments.

It provides hosts with essential configurations, such as IP address, subnet mask, and the TFTP IP address pointing to the TFTP service on a CUCM node.

DHCP can come from platforms such as CUCM, CUCM Express, or routers. However, CUCM's DHCP is primarily tailored for IP phones and might not suit vast networks exceeding 1000 phones.

- **Practical Tip**: Reserving IP addresses for critical devices, such as conference or front desk phones, ensures they always have the same IP, simplifying troubleshooting.

- **DHCP Operation**: The process includes:
  - **Discovery**: The device sends a DHCPDISCOVER message.
  - **Offer**: The DHCP server responds with a DHCPOFFER.
  - **Request**: The device requests the IP offered with DHCPREQUEST.
  - **Acknowledgment**: The server acknowledges with DHCPACK, completing the process.
- **IP Reservation**: This is when a specific IP address is reserved in the DHCP server for a particular MAC address. This ensures that the device is always assigned the same IP.
- **IP Helper**: Within local networks (LANs), DHCP protocol relies on broadcasts to request IP addresses. However, these broadcasts remain restricted to their originating broadcast domain, typically the same VLAN, and cannot cross Layer 3 boundaries, such as routers.

  Enterprises avoid placing a DHCP server in every broadcast domain or VLAN for efficiency in larger setups. Instead, they centralize it to serve multiple domains. But how can devices across various domains reach this server when broadcasts do not cross routers?

  This is where the *IP Helper* (or *DHCP relay agent*) functionality on routers or Layer 3 switches comes into play. When a DHCP request is broadcasted on a VLAN, the router interface of that VLAN captures the request. Using the IP Helper functionality, the router then changes the request from a broadcast to a unicast, directing it specifically to the DHCP server's IP address, even if that server is on a different VLAN or network.

  If a local voice gateway router is set up as the DHCP server for a particular VLAN or domain, there is no need for the IP Helper address since the DHCP requests are served locally.

Domain Name System (DNS)

DNS translates domain names to IP addresses. Many large enterprises use Microsoft's DNS services on Windows Server. It often gets its records from top-level domain servers or other authoritative DNS servers.

DNS typically uses UDP for its queries but can also use TCP, especially for longer responses. Both use port 53.

CUCM can use either DNS names (default) or IP addresses.

- **Configuring CUCM to Use DNS for Resolving Other Servers Addresses**: When setting up external integrations or services, CUCM may need to communicate with other servers, and you can specify either their DNS names or IP addresses.

- **Specifying CUCM's Identification (FQDN or IP Address)**: When referencing or identifying the CUCM itself, you can use its Fully Qualified Domain Name (FQDN) or IP address.
- **Practical Tip**: If using DNS, ensure redundancy with at least two DNS servers. This prevents a single point of failure, which could disrupt services.

Trivial File Transfer Protocol (TFTP)

TFTP is a simple file transfer protocol that moves files to and from remote machines. TFTP uses the UDP protocol and operates on port 69. In DHCP, "option 150" is essential. It provides IP phones with the address of the TFTP server. Without it, phones would not know where to fetch their configuration and other essential files.

Here is how CUCM leverages TFTP:

- **Stored Data**: The TFTP service in CUCM acts as a repository and delivery mechanism for various configuration and firmware files necessary to operate IP phones and other UC endpoints. TFTP houses various crucial files, from phone configurations and firmware updates to security and localization files.
    - **Phone Configuration Files**: These contain essential details such as the prioritized list of CUCM servers the phone should register with.
    - **Phone Firmware Files**: When phones boot up, they check their firmware version against the load parameter in their configuration file downloaded from the TFTP server. If an update is necessary, the phone will then download the correct firmware version from the TFTP server.
    - **Certificate and Security Files** include Certificate Trust List (CTL) and Identity Trust List (ITL) files. When present, they ensure the phone can verify the authenticity of its configuration files, confirming they come from a trusted source.
    - **Localization Files**: Network locales for country-specific tones and user locales for display languages.
    - **Ringer and Softkey Files**: Custom ring tones and softkey configurations.
- **Practical Tip**: Always monitor and backup the TFTP directory in CUCM. It contains critical files essential for phone functionalities.

If the TFTP service fails or is misconfigured, phones might not retrieve their configuration or firmware updates. This could result in phones failing to register, display incorrect information, or operate with outdated firmware, compromising functionality or security.

Newer Cisco phones sometimes prefer the HTTP protocol (port 6970) for its enhanced speed and efficiency.

Power over Ethernet (PoE)

While Power over Ethernet (PoE) is not technically a network service in the traditional sense, its relevance and importance in Cisco Collaboration cannot be overstated. Given its critical role in powering collaboration endpoints, discussing PoE in this context is vital.

Power over Ethernet (PoE) is a key feature for Cisco Collaboration endpoints, enabling power delivery to networked devices via standard Ethernet cables. Originating from Cisco's innovation in 2000, this technology has substantially evolved, adjusting to the demands of various networked devices, from IP phones to security cameras. Originally, Cisco termed PoE as inline power. Now universally termed as PoE.

When considering Cisco Collaboration endpoints, particularly IP phones and video conferencing units, the ability to power devices through the Ethernet connection simplifies deployments. This is both a cost-saving and an operational efficiency benefit:

- **Simpler Cabling**: Reduces the need for separate power and network cables
- **Cost-Efficient**: Consolidates backup power into centralized locations, reducing installation costs.
- **Energy Efficient**: When combined with Cisco's EnergyWise and Energy-Efficient Ethernet, PoE aids in sustainable energy management and lower energy costs.
- **High Availability**: Ensures uninterrupted services crucial for critical applications.

Understanding power classes and types is essential for maximizing PoE efficiency in Cisco Collaboration. Devices such as the Cisco IP Phone 8845 and 8851 belong to distinct power classes, which determine their power consumption. Familiarity with power budgets is crucial for device provisioning. For instance, the Cisco IP Phone 8851, as a class 4 device, might use up to 25.5W, but its consumption can vary depending on real-time demands.

Note: Verifying specific power consumption and class details with the latest Cisco documentation or product datasheets is always a good idea.

Understanding Standards:

Cisco's early PoE products differ from the IEEE 802.3af standard, especially in power availability, detecting devices, and disconnecting power. To determine if IP phones follow Cisco's PoE or IEEE 802.3af, look into Cisco's Power over Ethernet indications.

- **Functionality Highlights:**
  - Cisco switches, namely the Catalyst 9300, cater to both old and IEEE 802.3af devices.

- Be wary: third-party devices on the Catalyst 9300 may differ in power pin setups.
- Cisco PoE-friendly devices use the Cisco Discovery Protocol (CDP) to state power requirements.

- **Efficiency Insights:**
  - CDP is adept at redirecting unused power back to the PSE pool.
  - IEEE 802.3af might sometimes over-allocate. CDP keeps this in check.

It is crucial to know which pins give power. Earlier setups might have checked only data pins, leading to disruptions for some devices.

Navigating Cisco Unified Communications Manager (CUCM) GUI

The Cisco Unified Communications Manager(CUCM) Graphical User Interface (GUI) is the central point for configuring and managing all aspects of the Cisco Unified Communications system.

Apart from the web-based GUI, administrators can also access CUCM via SSH. This provides a command-line interface, handy for specific tasks, troubleshooting, or when the web interface is inaccessible. While the GUI is more visual and intuitive, the SSH interface is more direct and powerful for advanced users.

Use SSH only for direct database queries, system restarts, or specific issues requiring a command-line approach.

Accessing CUCM Web GUI

Enter the IP address or Fully Qualified Domain Name (FQDN) of the CUCM into a web browser. As you see in this picture, you can choose the administrative interface or the Self-Care Portal from the main page.

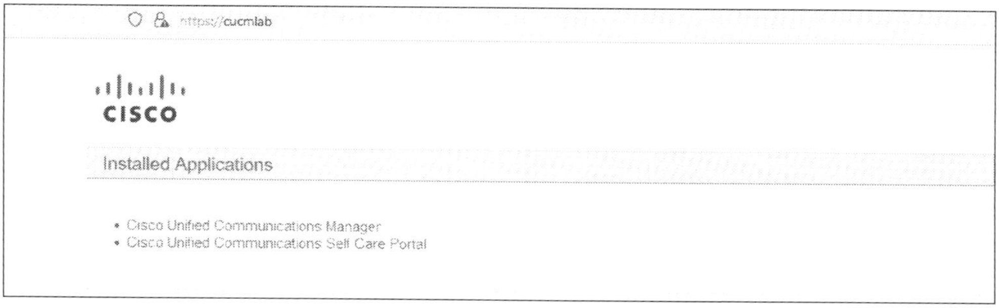

Figure 3.1: CUCM GUI

Self Care Portal

As you see in this picture, users can access the Self-Care Portal by navigating to **`https://<IP`** address or **`FQDN>/ucmuser/.`** It offers the flexibility to adjust phone settings such as speed dials and ring tones, set up voicemail preferences, modify IM & Presence status, and download plugins for phones and Jabber.

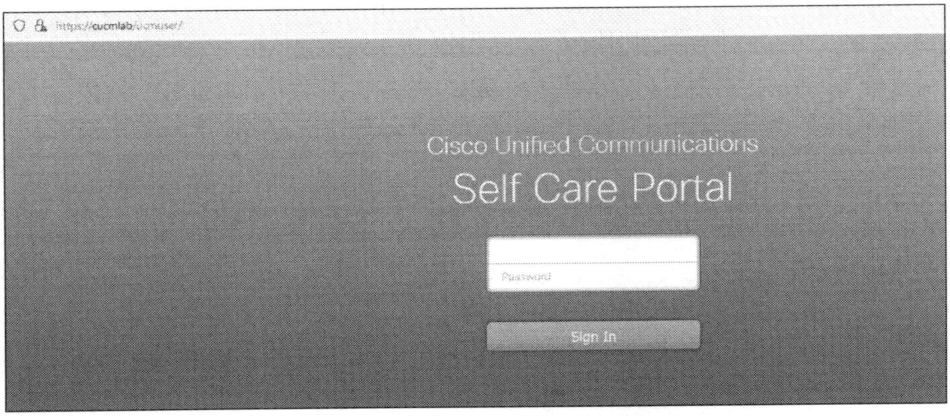

Figure 3.2: *CUCM Self-care portal*

CUCM Administration

Main dashboard for admins. As you see in this picture. the top right navigation bar houses several tools:

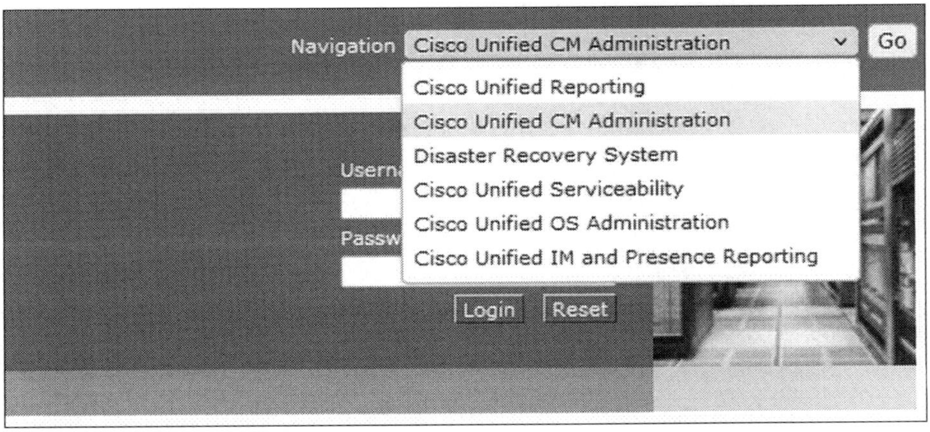

Figure 3.3: *CUCM Admin interfaces*

- **Cisco Unified Reporting**: Generates reports for troubleshooting by consolidating cluster data, helping to identify discrepancies or issues.

- **Cisco Unified CM Administration**: This is where most administrative tasks happen. Manage phones, users, define call routing logic, handle media resources, and more.
- **Disaster Recovery System**: Schedule backups, create restore points, and ensure the system can recover from unforeseen disasters.
- **Cisco Unified Serviceability**: Ensure the smooth operation of the cluster. Manage services on each node, restart them if needed, and monitor the health of services.
- **Cisco Unified OS Administration**: Manage the underlying operating system, oversee patches, and maintain the system's stability.
- **Cisco Unified IM and Presence Reporting**: Delve into IM & Presence analytics. This is essential for organizations that want insights into their messaging platforms.

Configuring Global Settings: Understanding Enterprise and Service Parameters

Managing a Unified Communication (UC) environment involves getting familiar with its core settings. In the Cisco Unified Communications Manager (CUCM), these foundational settings are located within the Enterprise and Service Parameters. They set the groundwork for all device configurations in the system.

Before we discuss endpoint configurations, we must grasp these global settings in CUCM.

System > Enterprise Parameters

Enterprise Parameters define the default system behavior. The Enterprise Parameters section in CUCM provides a unified platform to adjust settings that impact the entirety of the **CUCM cluster**. These parameters are generally set during the initial setup and fine-tuned as the system grows or when specific global changes are required.

Making changes to Enterprise Parameters can have widespread implications. Always review and test changes in a controlled environment before applying them system-wide.

To access these settings, head to `System > Enterprise Parameters`. Let us understand it with an example. As you see in this picture on the left side you have parameter name and on the right side it shows the default setting. You can choose to change the setting **cluster wide** from here.

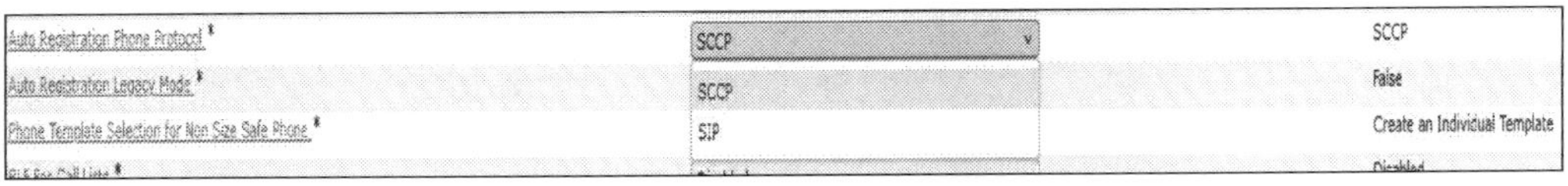

Figure 3.4: *Enterprise parameter – Auto Registration Phone Protocol*

Auto Registration Phone Protocol defines the default protocol for phones using auto-registration. It can be set to SIP or SCCP based on your organization's preference.

System > Service Parameters

Service Parameters, on the other hand, are more granular. They adjust the operational aspects of specific services running on the CUCM.

The Service Parameters section is crucial for tailoring service-specific configurations based on **individual nodes** in your CUCM cluster. Each node can have varying settings, allowing administrators to customize their network behavior according to each location's unique requirements.

They define behaviors for individual services on a server or cluster-wide basis. For instance, parameters related to the Call Manager service might define the maximum number of logged-in devices per user or set up timers for specific call-related functions.

Service Parameters allow for nuanced control. However, adjusting them without understanding can lead to unexpected system behaviors.

To access these settings, head to **`System > Service Parameters`**. Let us understand it with example. As you see in *Figure* 3.5, **`OffNet to OffNet Transfer`** are highlighted.

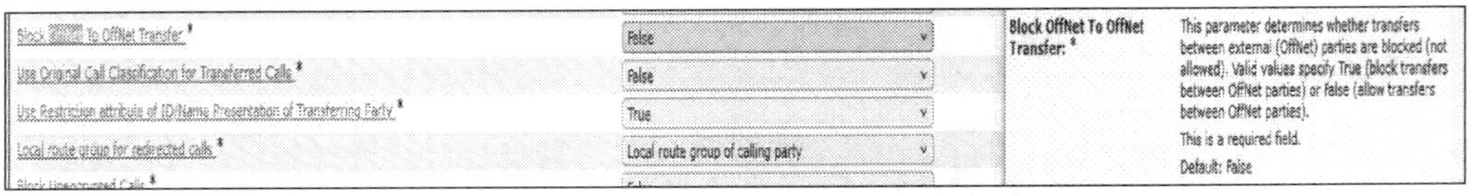

Figure 3.5: *Service parameter – OffNet to OffNet Transfer*

This is used to control whether calls that come in from the PSTN (**`OffNet`**) can be transferred back out to the PSTN (**`OffNet`**). If it is not managed correctly, it can lead to toll fraud or unexpected high call charges.

We can change it to **`'Restricted'`** to prevent potential abuse, though this can depend on your business needs.

Endpoint Registration in Cluster Environment

In a Cisco Unified Communications environment, endpoint registration is fundamental for devices such as IP phones or software-based communicators to be operational. We will delve into the specifics of the IP phone registration process with CUCM below. Furthermore, we will discuss how to provision, key settings in the device pool, and the phone boot-up/registration process.

Endpoint Provisioning Methods in CUCM

It is essential to understand the methods available in CUCM for provisioning devices. Whether it is for a single device or in bulk, CUCM provides various ways to ease the process:

- **Auto Provisioning**: CUCM automatically detects and configures new devices. Ideal for swift, large-scale deployments or short-term setups. However, it is less suitable when exact configurations or strict device controls are mandatory.

  Auto-provisioning can lead to unauthorized registrations, expose default settings, increase the risk of DoS, and may cause data leakage or eavesdropping threats. Only use auto-provisioning temporarily, monitor device registrations, segment networks, and customize default templates for better security.

  1. In CUCM, ensure the **`TFTP`** and **`CallManager`** services are active and running. You will find it in **`Serviceability > Control center`** – feature services.

Figure 3.6*: Control center- Feature services*

As you see the status in this figure.

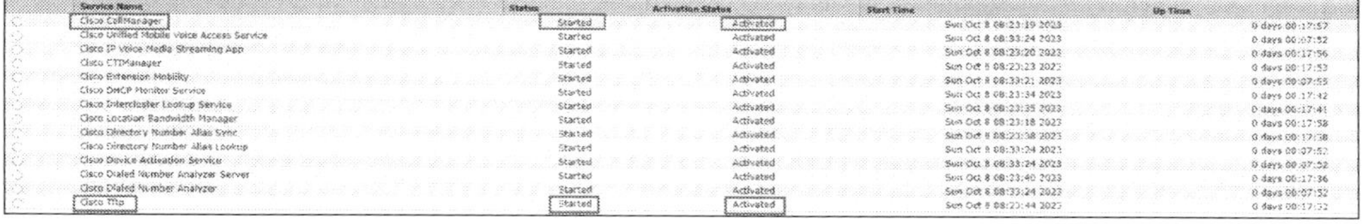

Figure 3.7*: Call Manager and TFTP service status*

2. Navigate to **System > Cisco Unified CM.**

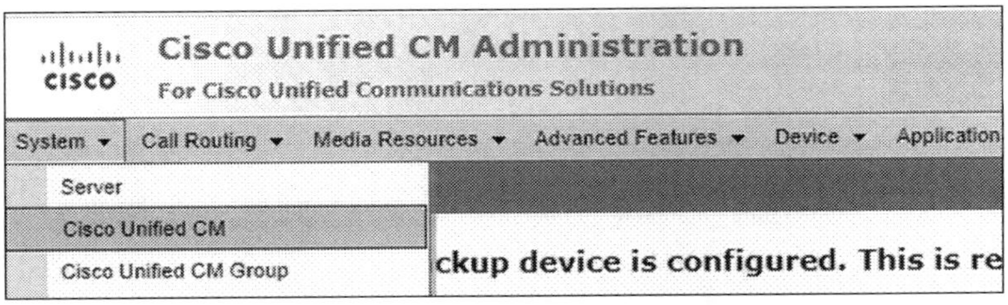

***Figure 3.8**: Navigate to System > Cisco Unified CM*

3. For each server listed, uncheck the option "**Auto-registration Disabled on this Cisco Unified Communications Manager**".

4. Configure the **Directory Number (DN)** range as necessary for auto registration.

   In this figure you can see, on CUCM Pub, **Auto registration disabled** is unchecked, **Directory Number** range is specified and templates are selected. You will need to do this for each node.

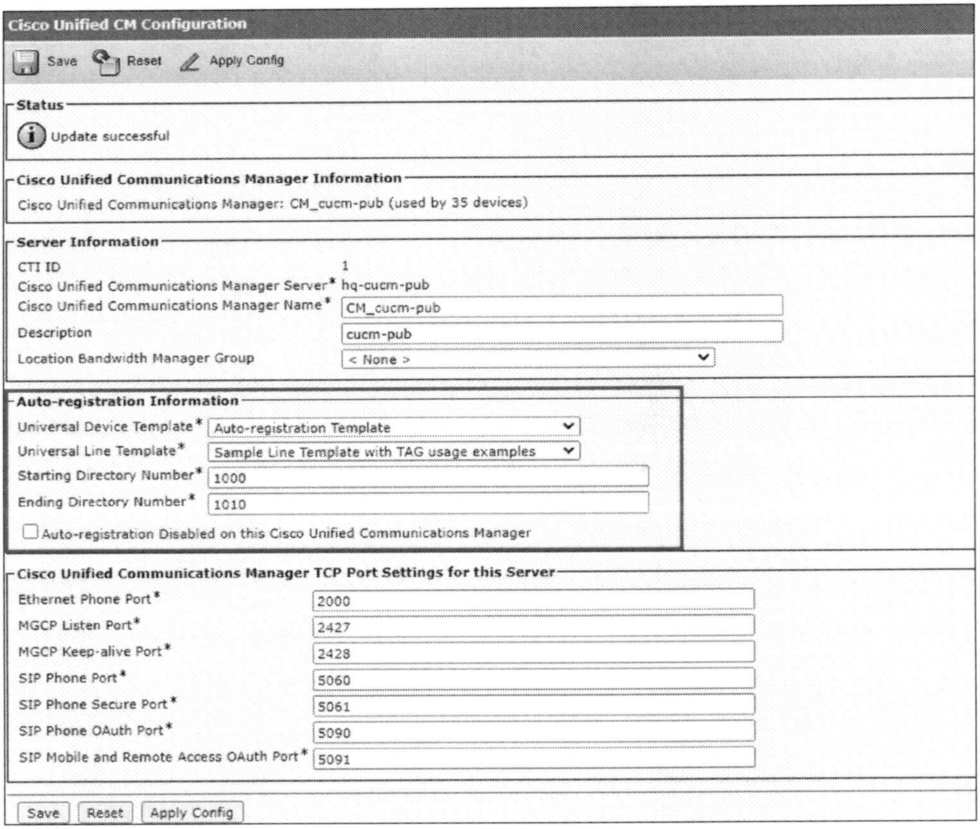

***Figure 3.9**: Auto-registration configuration*

- **Bulk Provisioning**: Use the Bulk Administration Tool (BAT) in CUCM to simultaneously add multiple devices/users via CSV files or templates. Perfect for mass deployments with known configurations.

  1. Navigate to **`Bulk Administration > Upload/Download Files`**. Prepare your CSV files with the necessary device information, upload them to CUCM.

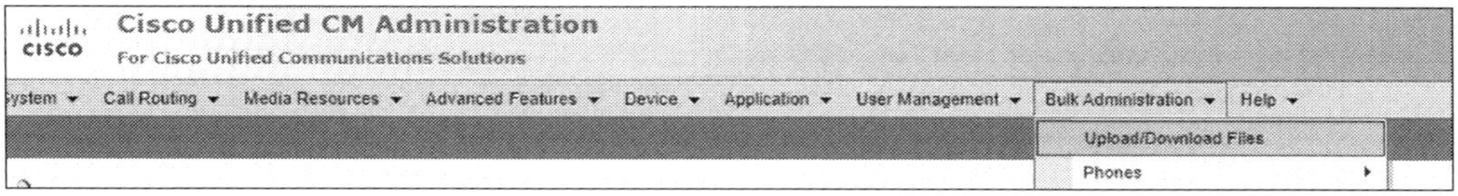

***Figure 3.10**: Bulk Admin > Upload files*

While uploading a file, you need to select target and transaction type as you see in this figure.

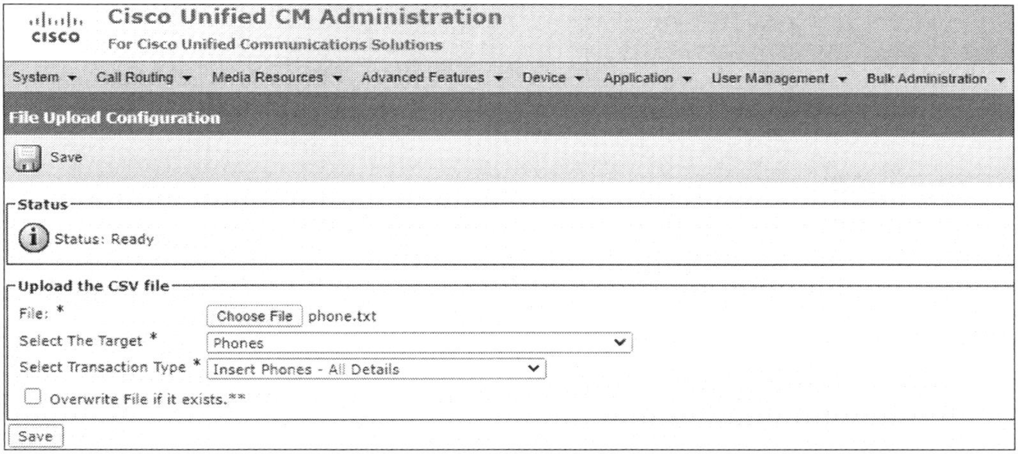

***Figure 3.11**: Upload file*

2. Then go to **`Bulk Administration`** > **`Phones`** > **`Insert Phones`** and select your uploaded file. After configuring any additional settings, execute the BAT process and monitor it through **`Bulk Administration`** > **`Job Scheduler`**.

   You can also find a sample file on this page.

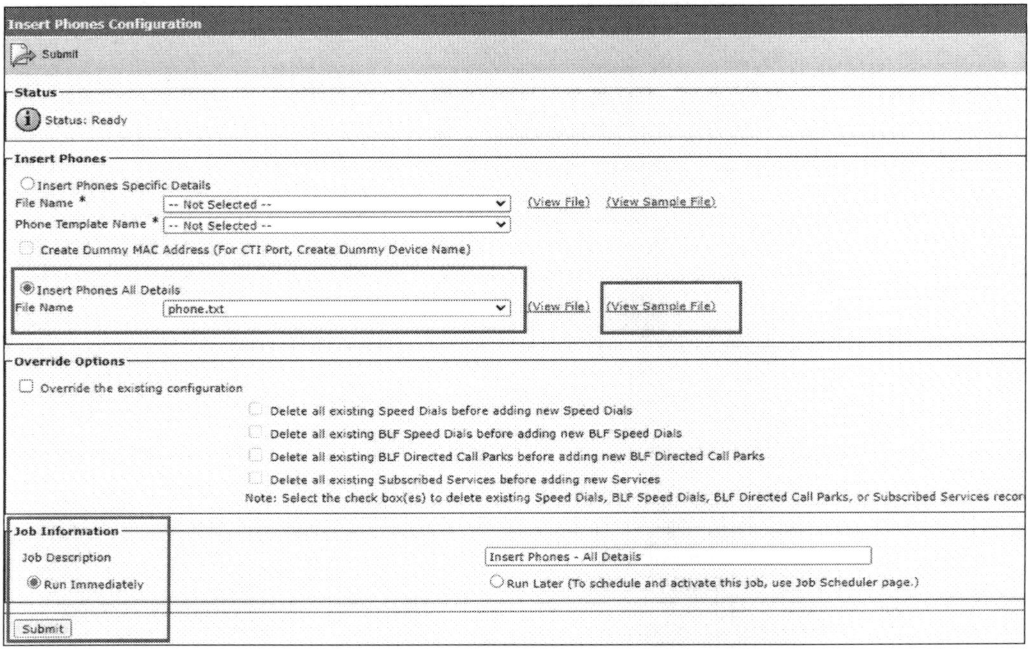

Figure 3.12: *Insert Phones*

- **Manual Provisioning**: Directly adding each device or user in CUCM. This method is most fitting for small setups or addressing unique configurations.

  Though End-of-Life, the Cisco IP Communicator (CIPC) offers a representative example of this process, mirroring the behaviour of hardware phones. Following are the steps to add a CIPC phone in CUCM:

1. **CUCM Services Check:** Certain services must be active and running:
   a. Cisco CallManager
   b. Cisco TFTP
2. CIPC should have connectivity to the CUCM, typically requiring VLAN setups, DHCP (or Static IP) configurations.
3. Log into **`CUCM CM Administration`**.
4. Navigate to **`Device > Phone`**.
5. Click **`Add New`**.
6. You will see options to choose **`Phone type`**, choose **`Cisco IP Communicator`**.
7. Choose the device protocol, **`SIP`** or **`SCCP`**. We will discuss this in detail later.
8. Input the MAC Address of the CIPC (For CIPC, this can be a generated value).

9. **Device Pool:** A collection of system-defined settings, such as regions and locations. We'll cover these in detail later.
10. **Phone Button Template:** Defines the layout of the lines, speed dials, and services.
11. Select the **`Device Security Profile`** and **`SIP Profile`** (or SCCP based on your protocol selection). These define the device's security and signaling behaviors.
12. **`Save.`**
13. Click **`Line [1].`**
14. **Assign a Directory Number**: This is the number assigned to the device. It can be a simple 4-digit extension or a more complex pattern.
15. Adjust the Route Partition if necessary.
16. Fill in other attributes like **`Display`**, **`Alerting Name`**, and more.
17. Launch CIPC on your PC.
18. Check under **`Settings`** that the TFTP points to the CUCM.
19. If it is not auto-detected, manually provide the CUCM TFTP server address.
20. Restart the CIPC for it to fetch its configuration.

Now you can check if CIPC is registered with CUCM.

1. On the CUCM, follow **`Device > Phone`**.
2. Find your device using either **`Directory Number`** or MAC address filters.
3. Confirm that the device status shows **`Registered`**.
4. If it is not showing as registered, check the following:
    a. Verify network connectivity.
    b. Double-check TFTP settings on the CIPC.
    c. Validate the MAC address and its configuration on CUCM.
    d. Review the CUCM services.

The nuances of the registration process might vary slightly depending on the device type, but the core understanding remains pivotal. Later in this chapter, we will understand the phone boot up and registration process in detail.

Specific phone models might mandate additional configurations or parameters. However, for the most part, the process we have outlined using CIPC closely mirrors the process for many other Cisco phone models. If there are specific requirements or parameters for certain models, they would usually be outlined in the device's respective documentation.

Session Initiation Protocol(SIP) and Skinny Client Control Protocol (SCCP)

In Cisco Unified Communications Manager (CUCM), the two primary signaling protocols for endpoint registration and call operations are Session Initiation Protocol (SIP) and Skinny Client Control Protocol (SCCP).

SIP is an industry-standard protocol developed by the IETF. It is versatile, handling not only voice but also video and messaging. When provisioning a SIP phone in CUCM, a SIP profile is typically defined, setting its behavior and features.

SCCP, often called "Skinny," was Cisco's answer for their early IP phones before SIP's widespread adoption. SCCP phones communicate their capabilities during registration and have unique settings within CUCM without the need for SIP profiles.

SIP is becoming the protocol of choice in modern unified communications due to its flexibility and standardization. However, SCCP still finds use in specific Cisco environments and legacy setups. Knowing the nuances of these protocols is essential, especially when provisioning endpoints in CUCM. We will discuss these in detail in another chapter.

Device Pool in CUCM

Understanding the Device Pool in CUCM is crucial. It determines the cluster-wide settings for devices, ensuring they operate within the desired parameters and simplifying the configuration and management of multiple devices.

A Device Pool in CUCM groups together a series of system attributes devices use. Instead of assigning each setting individually to every device, CUCM administrators can group common settings into a Device Pool and then apply the entire pool to new devices, thus streamlining configuration.

Architecture Decisions

In defining a Device Pool, several key considerations come into play:

- **Geographical Location**: Often, devices in the same geographic location share common attributes, so they can be grouped under the same Device Pool.
- **Purpose or Functionality:** For instance, a Device Pool for conference rooms might differ from one meant for executive offices.
- **Redundancy and Failover Needs**: Some areas might require higher availability

than others, influencing which Call Manager Group are listed in their Device Pool.

Key Parameters in a Device Pool

Here are the primary parameters in a Device Pool and a brief explanation of each:

- **Call Manager Group**: This determines the primary and backup CUCM servers the device will use.
- **Date/Time Group**: Defines the time zone for the devices in this pool.
- **Region**: This sets the codec (that is, G.711, G.729, and so on) for calls within and between different regions.
- **Media Resource Group List**: Determines which media resources (conference bridges, transcoders, and so on) the device can access.
- **SRST Reference**: Defines the fallback router the device should register with if it loses connectivity to all its CUCM servers.
- **Network Locale**: Dictates the device's language for displaying network and user messages.
- **Device Mobility Info**: This is used to adjust the calling search space (CSS) and other settings when a device roams to a different location.
- **AAR Group**: Used for automated alternate routing, allowing calls to be rerouted through the PSTN if WAN bandwidth is insufficient.

Cisco Unified Communications Manager (CUCM) Group

A CUCM group defines a prioritized list of up to three Unified CM servers. Endpoints primarily register with the first server in this list. If it becomes unavailable, the endpoint attempts to register with the next server on the list.

The decision to use one Unified CM Group Design over another is determined by factors such as redundancy requirements, load distribution, failover efficiency, and administrative preferences.

There are two primary design types to consider: the 1:1 Unified CM Group Design and the 2:1 Unified CM Group Design. Each offers a different approach to balancing redundancy and efficiency.

1:1 Unified CM Group Design

In a 1:1 design, each call-processing server is paired with its own dedicated backup server. If a primary server fails, the endpoints registered to it switch to its dedicated backup.

For example, let us consider Company ABC with 20,000 users. If they deploy three servers, one solely dedicated to CUCM TFTP and only two nodes with call-processing service, each primary server will handle 10,000 phones. However, if one call-processing server fails, the remaining one wouldn't handle the entire 20,000-user load. Hence, a 1:1 design for this scenario requires four servers: two actively supporting 10,000 users each and two servers on standby as backups.

Figure 3.13 shows two primary servers, each supporting 10,000 users, with each having its own dedicated backup server.

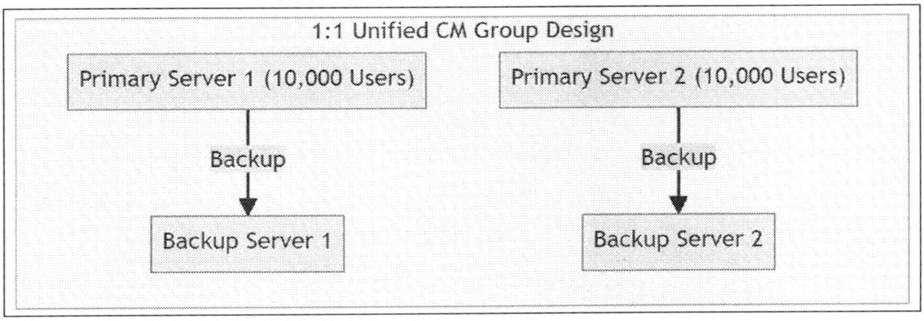

Figure 3.13: *1:1 Unified CM Group Design*

2:1 Unified CM Group Design

In a 2:1 design, two primary servers share a single backup. Only three servers are needed for 20,000 users: two active ones handling 10,000 users each and a third as a backup for both. This reduces infrastructure costs but comes with a risk: if both active servers fail simultaneously, the backup would be overloaded.

The decision between 1:1 and 2:1 design revolves around balancing costs and risks. While 2:1 saves on infrastructure, 1:1 offers more reliability. It is crucial to carefully consider each deployment's specific needs and tolerances.

Figure 3.14 illustrates two primary servers, each handling 10,000 users, sharing a single backup server.

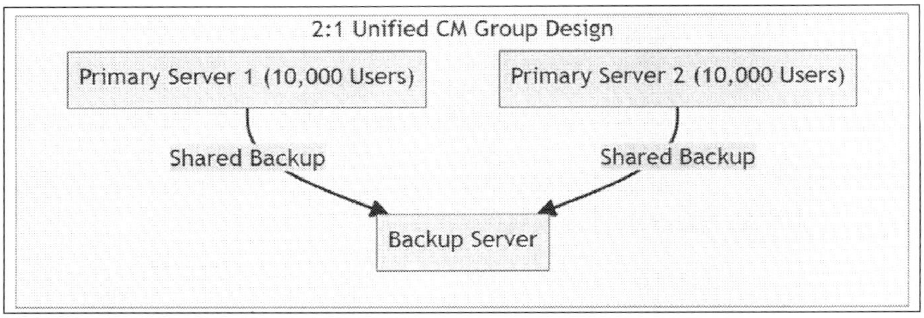

Figure 3.14: *2:1 Unified CM Group Design*

Phone/Endpoint Registration Process

Now that we have understood the provisioning process and essential parameters. Let us understand what goes behind the scene when endpoint bootups and try to register to CUCM.

- **Power Acquisition:**
  - **Power over Ethernet (PoE)**: Endpoints can obtain power through a PoE switch or a midspan injector.
  - **Power Cubes**: Traditional power adapters plugged directly into a wall socket, delivering power via the phone's rear power plug. These were popular before PoE became a commonplace solution for powering phones.
  - **Larger Telepresence Devices**: Devices needing more power than PoE offers must connect directly to mains power.
- **Loading Firmware**: After powering up, the phone loads its local copy of the firmware, known as the phone load, stored in the device's flash.
- **Voice VLAN Detection**: The endpoint determines if a Voice VLAN is configured. If not, it queries the switch for voice VLAN using the Cisco Discovery Protocol or Link Layer Discovery Protocol(LLDP).
- **Voice VLAN Assignment**: With voice traffic isolated in its own VLAN, QoS policies can be applied to prioritize this traffic over regular data traffic.
  - After getting the Voice VLAN ID, the IP phone will send voice packets with a tag corresponding to the Voice VLAN. This way, the switch knows to treat these packets with the appropriate priority.
  - If a user connects a computer to the PC port on the back of the IP phone, the data packets from that computer will remain untagged. This ensures they are treated as regular data traffic by the switch.
- **IP Configuration**: The endpoint retrieves its IP settings, which can either be statically configured or obtained via DHCP. Beyond the basic network settings, the phone also needs the TFTP server's IP address, typically provided by the DHCP server using scope option 150.
- **Fetching Configuration from TFTP**: The endpoint contacts the TFTP server using its IP to request its configuration. This configuration specifies the Call Manager nodes for phone registration.
- **Security and Trust Establishment (ITL/CTL)**: If a security profile is set up, the phone will also download the ITL or CTL file from the TFTP server. This step is crucial as it establishes the security trust for the phone's registration and further operations. The phone can trust the CUCM and other phones based on these files.

- **Firmware Version Check**: The configuration file downloaded from the TFTP server indicates the required firmware version in its 'load information' or 'load' parameter. The phone compares this version against its currently installed firmware. If there's a mismatch, the phone retrieves the specified firmware version from the TFTP server and typically restarts to apply the update.
- **Registration**: The endpoint registers with the designated CallManager node, receiving its full configuration (directory number, ringtones, button templates, and softkey templates) upon successful registration.

Take a look at this diagram; it provides a visual representation of the phone boot-up process, which might make it easier to grasp.

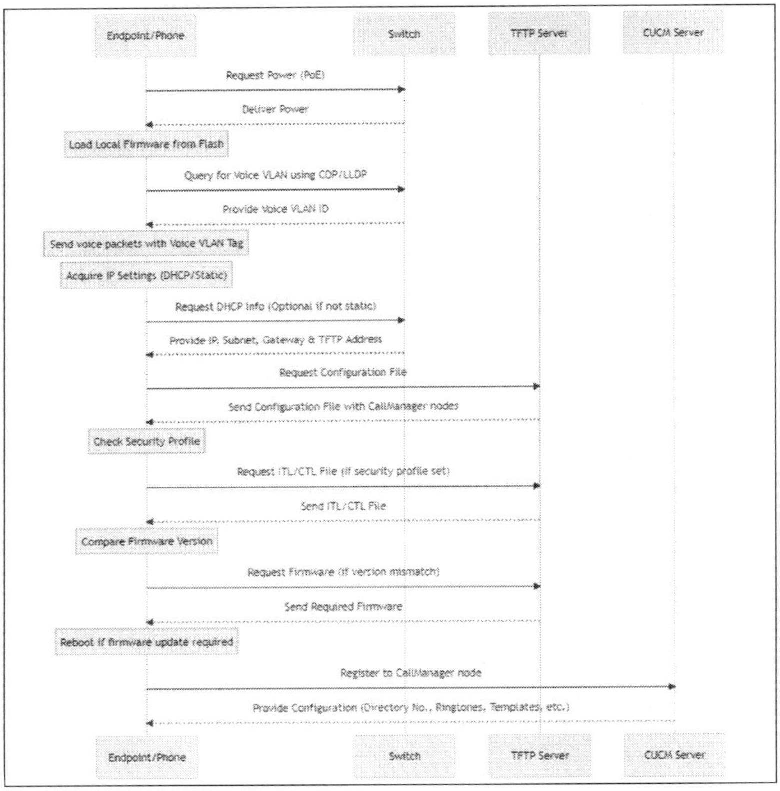

***Figure 3.15**: Phone bootup/ registration process*

Here are some pointers to help you troubleshoot if there is any issue in phone boot up or registering the phone to the CUCM.

- **Power Issues**: Verify switch PoE support. For non-PoE scenarios, confirm power cube or mains connectivity availability.
- **Firmware Issues**: The firmware might be the issue if the boot-up stalls or acts erratically. A manual firmware update may be necessary.

- **VLAN Misconfigurations**: If the phone does not get the Voice VLAN info, ensure the switch has it correctly configured and that CDP or LLDP is operational.
- **TFTP Server Inaccessibility**: Ensure the TFTP server is up and its address is correctly provided via the DHCP scope option.
- **Registration Errors**: In case of registration denial, validate that the phone's details align with server records

Security and Trust Establishment (ITL/CTL)

Among all the steps, often the most confusing point is how ITL/CTL work and what is the use of it.

ITL/CTL ensures that phones connect only to legitimate servers and does not become susceptible to man-in-the-middle attacks or other security threats.

To ensure secure communications and protect against potential threats, the Cisco Unified Communications Manager (CUCM) uses two primary files: the Initial Trust List(ITL) and the Certificate Trust List(CTL).

- **CTL (Certificate Trust List)**: This is used primarily for securing phone-to-CUCM communications. It is a file containing certificates, including the Certificate Authority Proxy Function (CAPF) certificate and the TFTP server certificate. When a phone is presented with a CTL, it establishes trust with the CUCM by validating against this list.
- **ITL (Initial Trust List)**: This file is more common in recent deployments. It essentially replaced the CTL in newer versions of CUCM. The ITL provides a simpler mechanism for establishing trust and is automatically generated by the CUCM. It contains the certificates of servers that the phone can trust. When the phone downloads this file from the TFTP server, it essentially "learns" which servers (like TFTP, CUCM, etc.) are trustworthy. Any server not on this list is treated as untrustworthy.

In technical terms, when a phone tries to connect to a server (such as the CUCM), the server presents its certificate to the phone. The phone then checks this certificate against the ones stored in its CTL/ITL. If there is a match, the phone trusts the server and continues the connection process. If not, the phone treats the server as potentially malicious and refuses to connect.

Cop Files and Software Bundles in CUCM

To ensure the smooth functioning of a Cisco Unified Communications environment, two essential components come into play: COP files and software bundles. Each has distinct roles in enhancing or maintaining system and endpoint functionalities.

COP Files

Cisco Options Package (COP) files are software packages used within Cisco Unified Communications Manager (CUCM) environments. Though not exclusively tied to CUCM, they can also be present in other Cisco products. Their primary role is to act as installer packages that add, modify, or remove features on the CUCM platform.

The file extension for these packages is ".cop.sgn". The '.sgn' suffix stands as an assurance that the file is signed, thereby confirming its authenticity as a genuine, unchanged file from Cisco.

Different Types of COP Files in CUCM are:

- **Feature COP Files**: Introduce new features or capabilities.
- **Update COP Files**: Deliver bug fixes or minor tweaks to existing functionalities.
- **Locale Updates**: Bring in new language packs or refine the current ones.
- **Device Support**: Occasionally, when introducing a brand-new Cisco device model, a COP file fills in the support gap until the device gains native support in a subsequent CUCM release.

These files are installed via the CUCM OS Administration page, and post-installation, certain COP files might require a system restart contingent on the nature of the modification.

Software Bundles

Software bundles, specifically crafted for endpoint firmware management in CUCM, house the requisite files to drive firmware transitions (either upgrade or downgrade) for Cisco endpoints, such as IP phones or video devices.

After installing the software bundle, you need to restart TFTP service, only then the firmware files become accessible to the endpoints.

Software bundles focus strictly on endpoint firmware, leaving the core functionalities or features of CUCM untouched.

The installation of a software bundle has the potential to modify the default load specified in CUCM. So, when a new device of a specific model is added and lacks a dedicated load name in its config, CUCM assigns the default load to it. This helps to maintain consistent firmware versions organization-wide.

For specific requirements, administrators can configure specific firmware versions to devices by setting the load name manually in the CUCM device configuration.

User Authentication and Authorization in Cisco Unified Communications Manager (CUCM)

Authentication verifies the user identity, ensuring they match their claims. In general, this involves cross-referencing credentials such as usernames and passwords against a database or directory.

Authorization determines the actions an authenticated user can or cannot perform, defining their system access level.

In the Context of CUCM:

- **Authentication in CUCM**: Ensures users, devices, and applications interfacing with CUCM are validated, safeguarding against unauthorized access.
- **Authorization in CUCM**: Upon authentication, users or applications receive varied permissions based on their CUCM roles or profiles. For instance, an administrator may have advanced control, whereas an end user only accesses personal settings.

There are multiple authentication mechanisms available in CUCM. These are:

- **Passwords**: CUCM end-user passwords can include alphanumeric ASCII characters and all ASCII special symbols. The system performs trivial credential checks, disallowing easily hackable credentials. There are specific non-trivial password criteria, such as containing three of the four allowable characteristics: uppercase, lowercase, number, and symbol.
- **PINs**: End users can access phone features from their PC via GUI using user/password credentials. However, when leveraging the telephony user interface, a PIN is used instead. PINs for CUCM end-users can only contain digits between 0 to 9.
- **LDAP Synchronization**: When CUCM is set up for LDAP synchronization, user accounts stored in the LDAP database get replicated to CUCM. Despite this, much of the user data remains modifiable solely through LDAP, barring some parameters like password and PIN. The synchronization process uses the directory synchronization (DirSync) service on CUCM.
  - **LDAP Authentication**: Instead of storing passwords in the CUCM database, LDAP authentication authenticates users against the LDAP directory. This process works in conjunction with LDAP synchronization.

Depending on whether LDAP integration, synchronization, or authentication is used, user data storage varies. As you see in this table:

Criteria	No LDAP Integration	LDAP Synchronization	LDAP Authentication
Personal/Organizational Settings	Local users only	LDAP (read-only in CUCM)	LDAP (read-only in CUCM)
Password	Local	Local	LDAP
CUCM settings (for example, PIN, Roles, Groups)	Local	Local	Local

Table 3.1: *User data storage* ***difference in non-LDAP, LDAP sync and LDAP authentication***

In cases of LDAP synchronization, personal and organizational settings originate and reside in LDAP. With LDAP authentication, user passwords are governed by the LDAP database, while other CUCM settings remain under CUCM Administration, only stored in the CUCM database.

User Account Types in CUCM

There are two types of users provisioned in CUCM - End users and Application users.

- **End Users:**
  - Linked to individual persons for personal use.
  - Interactive logins.
  - Can be integrated with LDAP.
  - Creation methods include manual input, importing, or replication from LDAP servers.
- **Application Users**:
  - Application users in CUCM are specialized accounts linked to particular CUCM features or applications, rather than individuals. These accounts are essential for non-interactive system processes that need to authenticate but aren't tied to a specific person. For instance, integrations between CUCM and other platforms, or features such as an auto attendant, may utilize application users.
  - Non-interactive logins.
  - Created locally on CUCM as LDAP is not supported.

Some users might need advanced access to handle certain aspects of CUCM administration, and this additional access comes with specific roles and permissions.

Access Control Group and Roles

Access Control Groups in CUCM function as sets of permissions or access rights. They dictate what actions a user can or cannot perform within the system.

When a user is associated with an Access Control Group, they inherit all the permissions assigned to that group. Multiple groups can be applied to a user, allowing a combination of permissions. This modular approach simplifies the management of access rights across many users.

Roles are bundled into groups. A group can have multiple roles, and when a user is added to a group, they inherit all the roles of that group.

End-users or application users are assigned to one or multiple groups, thereby determining their overall set of permissions.

Let us understand this by an example. Consider a corporation where there are IT administrators, phone operators, and general employees. Each of these categories will have different permissions in the CUCM environment.

This diagram visualizes the hierarchy of the user management system in CUCM. At the base level, we have specific roles that grant distinct permissions. These roles are grouped together in Access Control Groups to streamline user management. Finally, individual users are associated with one or more of these Access Control Groups, thereby inheriting the permissions of all the roles within those groups.

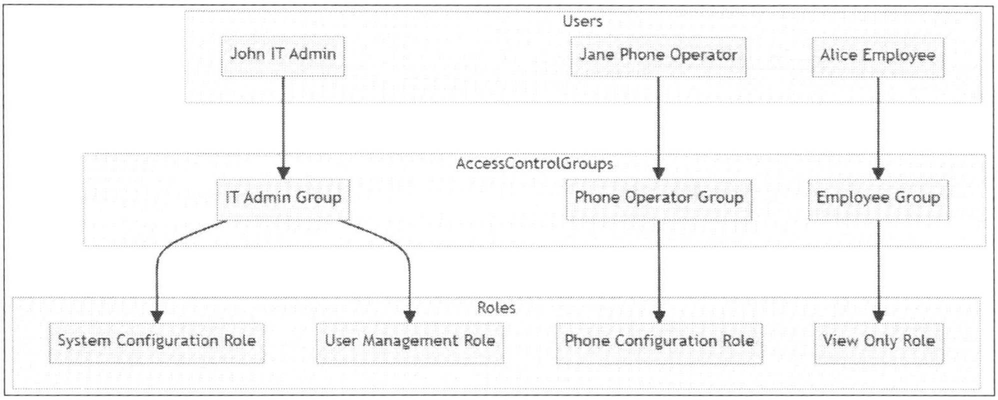

Figure 3.16: *Users, Access Control Groups and Roles*

Directory Integration in CUCM for Endpoints

Directory integration enables your endpoints, like IP phones and soft clients, to be in harmony with centralized directory services, thereby enhancing user experience and operational efficiency.

At its essence, directory integration is about synchronizing data between CUCM and external directory services, predominantly LDAP. This ensures automatic, error-free updates of user and device details.

Whether it is an IP phone displaying the caller's name or Cisco Jabber fetching contact information, endpoints are continuously tapping into directory services for essential data.

The operational aspect of directory integration with CUCM involves multiple stages, each crucial for ensuring that endpoints have the latest data:

- **Setting up Directory Services**: This involves configuring the CUCM with details of the LDAP server, search base parameters, and more.
- **Mapping LDAP Attributes**: To display data correctly, CUCM fields are mapped to specific LDAP attributes. This ensures accurate data representation in the CUCM.
- **Synchronization Routines**: Periodic syncs between CUCM and LDAP are essential to keep both databases updated. Though typically automated, manual syncs can also be triggered when needed.

Once set up, endpoints can access directory information from CUCM or, based on configurations, make direct queries to the directory service.

UDS Phonebook in Cisco

The User Data Services (UDS) phonebook acts as a central repository in the Cisco Collaboration suite:

- UDS is a protocol designed for Cisco Collaboration endpoints, such as Jabber, allowing them to retrieve contact details directly from the CUCM without the need for an external directory.
- While LDAP remains the primary directory service, UDS complements it, ensuring that even if LDAP is unreachable or specific data is not on LDAP, endpoints can still access essential contact details.
- UDS integrates smoothly alongside LDAP, ensuring endpoints always have access to the latest contact information, thus offering a holistic directory solution for all Cisco Collaboration tools.

In essence, directory integration in CUCM guarantees your endpoints are always in sync with user and device databases, leading to an enriched user experience and operational efficiency.

Conclusion

In this chapter, we discussed the process of provisioning endpoints, focusing on their integration with CUCM. The insights gained about essential network services, user authentication, and authorization, combined with the core elements of CUCM, will be indispensable as we delve into CUCM call control and telephony features in the subsequent chapter. Before progressing, it is advisable to familiarize yourself further with the CUCM GUI to solidify your understanding.

Multiple Choice Questions

1. Which of the following is NOT a core service in the Cisco Collaboration environment as covered in this chapter?
    a. Network Time Protocol (NTP)
    b. Hypertext Transfer Protocol (HTTP)
    c. Trivial File Transfer Protocol (TFTP)
    d. Dynamic Host Configuration Protocol (DHCP)
2. In the Cisco Unified Communications Manager (CUCM) GUI, where can you primarily configure global settings?
    a. System > Global Settings
    b. System > Enterprise Parameters
    c. Settings > Global Config
    d. CUCM > Global Parameters
3. What design provides each call-processing server with a single backup server in a CUCM environment?
    a. Unified CM Group Design 1:2
    b. Unified CM Group Design 2:2
    c. Unified CM Group Design 1:1
    d. Unified CM Group Design 2:1
4. Which of the following is NOT a method of endpoint provisioning in CUCM as discussed in the chapter?
    a. Manual Configuration
    b. Auto-Registration
    c. TFTP Provisioning
    d. Bulk Administration Tool

5. During the phone registration process in CUCM, which service is primarily responsible for providing the configuration file to endpoints?
   a. Network Time Protocol (NTP)
   b. Domain Name System (DNS)
   c. Trivial File Transfer Protocol (TFTP)
   d. Dynamic Host Configuration Protocol (DHCP)
6. The "IP helper" command is mainly used for which purpose in the Cisco environment?
   a. Resolving domain names.
   b. Forwarding broadcast requests for IP addresses.
   c. Assisting with IP routing.
   d. Providing IP security.
7. LDAP authentication in CUCM is primarily used to:
   a. Synchronize user directories.
   b. Authenticate users against a centralized directory.
   c. Facilitate IP phone registration.
   d. Manage device pools.
8. Which statement about Power over Ethernet (PoE) is true?
   a. PoE is used to deliver data only across Ethernet cables.
   b. PoE allows devices to receive power and data using a single Ethernet cable.
   c. PoE can only be used with wireless devices.
   d. PoE requires a dedicated power line separate from the data connection.

Answers

1. b
2. b
3. c
4. c

5. c
6. b
7. b
8. b

Further Reading

Like the previous chapter, to improve your understanding and broaden your perspective, it is suggested to explore the following topics on your own. Remember to tailor your research based on your organization's specific needs and always discern between genuine insights and industry trends.

- **DHCP Pool Diversification**: Research how enterprises segregate their DHCP pools based on distinct services. Understand the criteria and the advantages of such segmentation.
- **Power over Ethernet (PoE) In-depth**: Investigate more about PoE technology. Examine the network switches in your environment and consult their datasheets to determine how many devices they can concurrently power using PoE.
- **CUCM Parameters Exploration**: Familiarize yourself with the various enterprise and service parameters within CUCM. Identify which parameters are critical for day-to-day operations and which might be specific to certain deployments.
- **Device Pool Deep Dive**: Extend your research to fully understand all the attributes within a device pool in CUCM. Recognize the implications of each parameter and how they might affect endpoint functionality.
- **Account Management in CUCM**: Examine the default roles and access groups provided in CUCM. Determine their permissions and use cases, and consider how you might need to modify or create new roles for specific needs.
- **Phone Model Variation**: Register different models of phones to your CUCM. Observe the settings that are either unique or vary based on the phone model. This hands-on activity will help you appreciate the nuances and customization options available for different endpoint types.
- **COP Files and Bundles**: Research more about the application of COP files and how they enhance or modify CUCM functionalities.

  You can search for *Unified Communications Manager Utilities- COP-Files* and you will get to the Cisco downloads webpage. Look at their readme notes to understand what particular cop file do.

CHAPTER 4
Mastering CUCM Call Control and Telephony Features

Introduction

In this chapter, we will look closer at CUCM Call Control and several important telephony features commonly used in enterprises with IP telephony deployments. We will dig into the Class of Control (CoC) and see why it is crucial for managing call restrictions and permissions, followed by exploring setting up different CUCM Telephony Features. We will discuss the use of features such as Call waiting, hold, transfer, forward, Speed dial, Call Park, Barge and privacy, Shared line and BLF, Call pickup group, Hunt group and Extension Mobility along with their configuration steps.

This chapter will provide a brief overview of call routing in CUCM and also set the stage for the next chapter, where we will get into the details of Dial Plans and call routing in CUCM.

Structure

In this chapter, we will discuss the following topics:

- Call Processing and Routing Overview
- Class of Control Overview and Configuration
    - Partitions and Calling Search Spaces (CSS)
    - Forced Authorization Codes (FAC) and Client Matter Codes (CMC)
- CUCM Telephony Features, Overview and Configuration
    - Basic Call Control Features - Call Waiting, Hold, Transfer, Forward, Speed Dial, Call Park, Barge and Privacy

- Call Coverage Features - Shared Line and BLF, Call Pickup Group, Hunt Group
- Advanced Features - Extension Mobility, Intercom

Call Processing and Routing Overview

In IP telephony, especially with CUCM, the Directory Number (DN) is vital. Just think of DN as the phone number assigned to a device or user. So, when you make a call, you are calling a DN, and based on it, CUCM decides where that call should head and how it gets there.

It is essential to understand that, in CUCM, DNs are not just limited to individual phone lines. A variety of elements can have a DN. Example:

- **Phone Line**: This is the most basic application of DN. Just like your personal phone has a number, in CUCM, every registered phone will have a unique DN assigned to it.
- **Hunt Pilot**: A Hunt Pilot is the DN you dial to reach a hunt group. Dialing this number utilizes the associated hunt list to direct the call based on a specified distribution algorithm. We will discuss it in detail later in this chapter.

These are the most common usage, but there can be others such as Voicemail Pilot, Call park number range, and so on. To re-emphasize, `Directory Number (DN)` is pivotal in CUCM, acting as the primary means of addressing.

When dialing a number within a CUCM environment, multiple factors and configurations influence how the call is processed and routed.

When a user lifts the handset, it is termed as going "off-hook." In such scenarios, phones typically send dialed digits to CUCM one-by-one (digit-by-digit). However, based on specific configurations or user actions, phones might collect the entire dialed sequence and then send it all together (enbloc) to CUCM.

- **Digit-by-Digit Analysis**: As you dial a number, CUCM evaluates each digit in real-time against its database. This allows for flexible routing but can sometimes introduce delays, mainly when applying inter-digit timeouts. Inter-digit timeout is configured to pause that CUCM waits between digits, determining if the user has finished dialing or if more digits are coming.
- **Enbloc Analysis**: CUCM waits for the complete number to be entered before initiating its analysis. This method is particularly common with external incoming calls where the entire dialed sequence is received at once.

Let is understand this by the example of overlapping DNs 1234 and 12345.

When a user goes off-hook and starts dialing, if they dial 1234, CUCM could potentially route the call immediately, thinking it is a complete match. However, what if the user intended to dial 12345? Here lies the challenge. CUCM would typically rely on inter-digit timeout to determine if another digit is forthcoming. If the inter-digit timeout expires after 1234 and there is no further digit, CUCM routes the call to 1234. If the user continues with a "5" before inter-digit timeout, CUCM routes it to 12345.

This may rarely happen if the default inter-digit timeout (15 seconds) has been changed to very low, and the user is dialing each digit very slowly (taking a longer pause than the timer).

In enbloc, since the entire number is presented to CUCM at once, there is no ambiguity. If the dialed number is 12345, then CUCM will route it correctly. Overlapping DNs present fewer challenges in enbloc dialing.

Calls coming from outside networks generally arrive enbloc since the external System sends the full dialed number simultaneously, but calls initiated within the CUCM system can be processed using either digit-by-digit or enbloc methods based on configurations and dialing behaviors.

Before introducing partitions and CSS, it is worth noting that, in its basic form, CUCM matches dialed numbers against its internal database. Depending on the match found, it directs the call. We will discuss call routing multiple times in this and the next chapter.

Class of Control

In CUCM, controlling who can call which numbers is crucial. This is achieved using "Class of Control," primarily using Partitions and Calling Search Spaces (CSS).

Partitions and Calling Search Spaces (CSS)

During digit analysis, CUCM is not just looking at the dialed number. It is also considering the CSS of the device making the call. The System scans the partitions listed in the device's CSS to find a match. CSS works like a filter, allowing or denying access to different partitions.

Every time a device makes a call, CUCM goes through the partitions in the device's CSS. The System searches for the best match, considering both the dialed digits and the partitions the device can access. Partitions in the CSS list dictate which numbers or patterns the device can see and call. If the System finds an equally good match in two partitions, the order in the CSS list breaks the tie, selecting the pattern in the earlier listed partition.

- **Partitions**: Think of a partition as a labelled box where you can put specific directory numbers (DNs) and route patterns. This labelling allows for specialized reachability and routing. For example, you could have a partition named **"Executives"** that holds the DNs of the top management in a company.

- **Calling Search Spaces (CSS)**: A CSS is like a checklist. When a device wants to make a call, it checks off against its CSS list to see which partitions it is allowed to look into. So, if a device's CSS includes the **"Executives"** partition in its CSS, it can call the DNs in that room. Without access, the call would not go through.

To re-emphasize, partitions are just labels on DNs; it is the CSS that defines who you can call or not. Consider this example: DN 1234 and DN 2345 are both in a partition named **"A."** If DN 1234 is assigned to a phone with a CSS that can access partition **"A,"** it can dial DN 2345. However, if the phone with DN 2345 does not have a CSS that lists partition **"A,"** it would not be able to dial DN 1234, even though they are in the same partition.

There is a default partition named **<None>.** Initially, all DNs reside here until custom partitions are created. **<None>** partition is available to all CSS. For predictability and security, moving all critical DNs out of the **<None>** partition to custom partitions is recommended.

Figure 4.1 illustrates the process of assigning a CSS to various elements within the Cisco Unified Communications Manager (CUCM). On the left side of the diagram, we see the **"Source"** components, which include IP phones, gateways, trunks, translation patterns, and voicemail ports. It is the administrator's responsibility to assign the appropriate CSS to each of these elements based on their specific calling requirements and constraints.

The right side of *Figure* 4.1 depicts the **"Destination"** components, which encompass directory numbers, meet-me numbers, translation patterns, directory URIs, route patterns, SIP route patterns, and call park numbers. The administrator must assign each of these components to a suitable partition, effectively organizing them into logical groups based on their intended reachability and functionality within the CUCM ecosystem.

The central concept illustrated in *Figure* 4.1 is the mapping of the CSS (assigned to the source components) to the partition (assigned to the destination components). This mapping ultimately determines which devices can reach specific destinations based on the partitions included in their assigned CSS. By carefully defining these relationships, administrators can create a secure and customized calling environment that meets the unique needs of their organization.

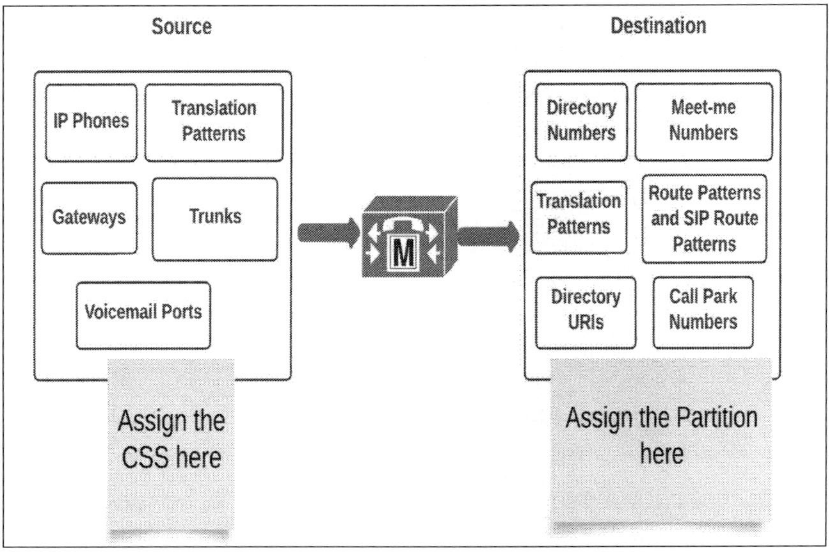

Figure 4.1: *Partition and CSS*

Creating Partition and CSS are very easy. As you can see in *Figure* 4.2, Go to **`Call Routing > Class of control > Partition`** or **`CSS`**, to create a new (or to view existing) Partition or CSS.

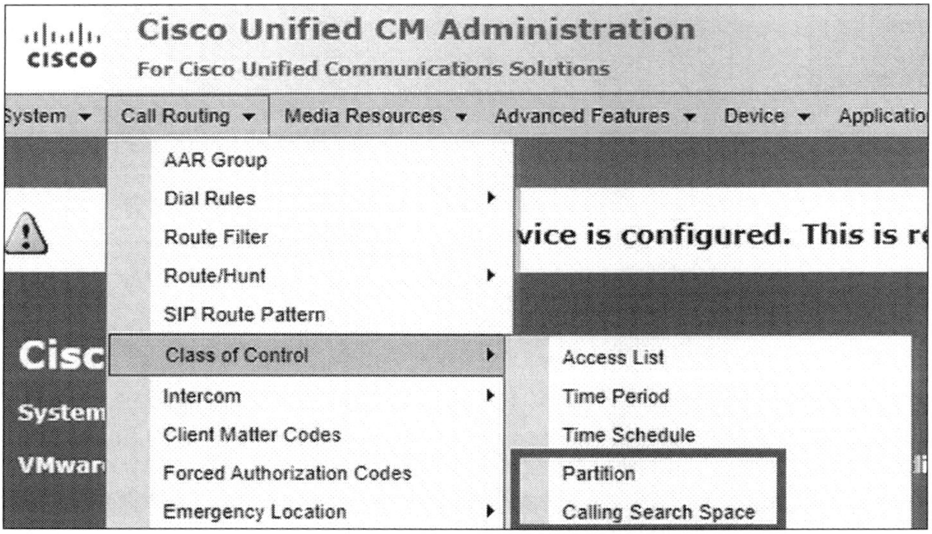

Figure 4.2: *Navigating to Partition and CSS*

As you see in *Figure* 4.3, You simply need to enter the name and click on **Save**.

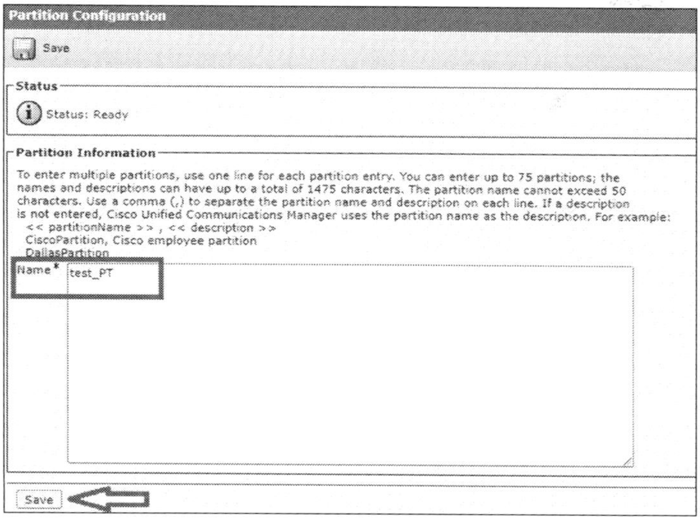

Figure 4.3: *Creating a new Partition*

When you create a CSS, as you can see in *Figure* 4.4, you need to add a partition to it. You can change the sequence of partitions as well.

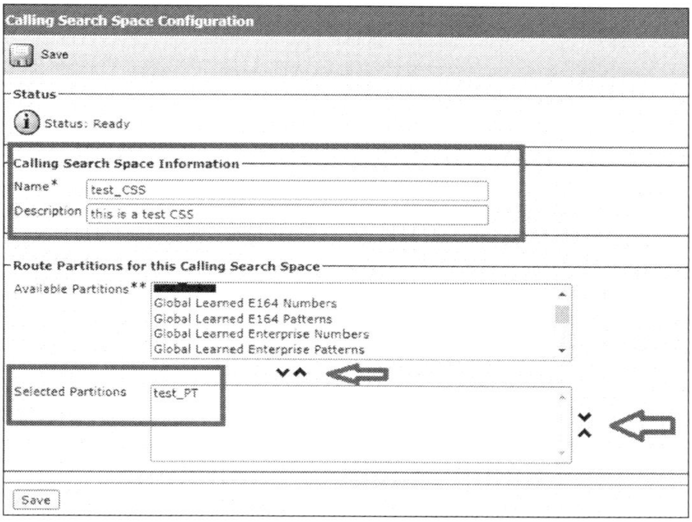

Figure 4.4: *Creating new CSS*

CSS Concatenation

There can be a scenario when both a phone's Directory Number (DN) line and the phone device itself (often referred to as the device profile) have Calling Search Spaces (CSS) assigned; there is a combination mechanism in place. This mechanism is often referred to as the "CSS concatenation."

Here is how it works:

- **Line Level CSS (DN CSS)**: This CSS is assigned directly to the line (or DN) on the phone. It is considered "closer" to the user or more specific.
- **Device Level CSS (Phone CSS)**: This CSS is assigned at the phone device profile level.

Here in *Figure* 4.5, you can see the CSS assigned on device level.

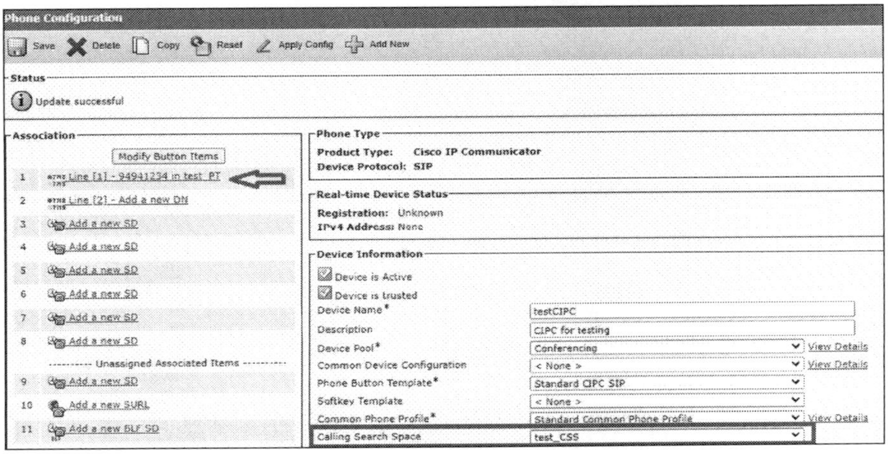

***Figure 4.5**: CSS assigned on device level*

As shown in *Figure* 4.6, If you click on line/DN, you can see the partition and CSS assigned to it.

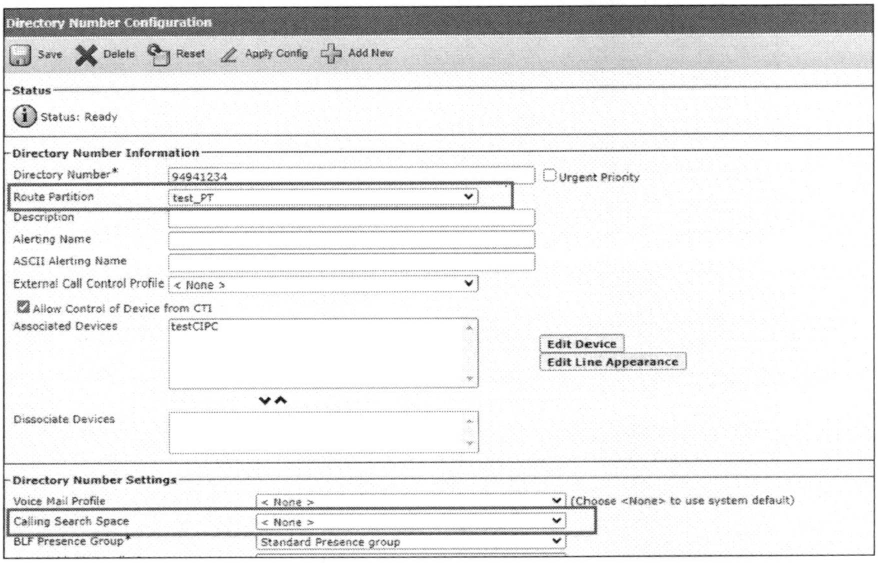

***Figure 4.6**: Partition and CSS assigned on DN*

When a user makes a call from a phone with both Line and Device CSS configured:

1. CUCM first looks at the Line Level CSS (DN CSS). It will use this CSS to match the dialed number against partitions listed within this CSS.
2. If a match is not found in the DN CSS, CUCM will then proceed to look at the Device Level CSS (Phone CSS).
3. The final resulting CSS that CUCM uses to route the call is a concatenation of the DN CSS followed by the Phone CSS. It essentially extends the search space by looking at the line's partitions first and then the device's partitions.

As you can see in *Figure 4.7*, the CSS is assigned at two distinct levels: the Line level (CSS - Line) and the Device level (CSS - Device). The Line CSS contains partitions that are specific to the phone line, such as those governing international and national calling privileges. This allows administrators to grant certain users the ability to place calls to these destinations based on their individual roles and requirements.

The Device CSS, in contrast, includes partitions related to the capabilities of the physical device itself, such as mobile and conference calling functionality. When a user initiates a call, CUCM first searches the Line CSS to determine if the dialed number is permitted. If no match is found, it then proceeds to search the Device CSS. This two-tiered approach provides administrators with a high degree of granular control over calling permissions, taking into account both the user's line and the device they are using.

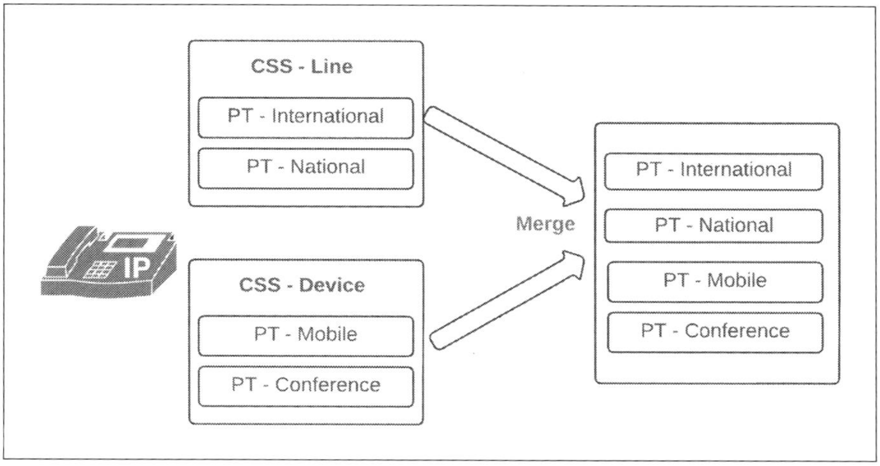

Figure 4.7: *CSS concatenation*

This concatenation mechanism allows administrators to provide more granular control and flexibility. Commonly, general access rights are given at the phone level, while more specific rights (such as access to executive DNs) might be given at the line level.

Key Considerations for Partition and CSS Configuration

For seamless call routing in CUCM, strategically design and assign your Partitions and CSS. Here are some key things to keep in mind.

- **Planning and Design**: Before deploying, you should have a clear map of which devices or users need access to which numbers. This helps in designing the partitions and CSS effectively. It is good practice to use clear, descriptive names for partitions.
- **Unique DN within a Partition**: A DN must be unique within a single partition. This means you cannot have two identical DNs in the same partition (CUCM will give an error). For instance, if DN **`"1000"`** exists in the partition **`"Sales_PTN"`**, you cannot create another DN **`"1000"`** within that same partition.

  However, the same DN can exist in different partitions. While you cannot have another DN **`"1000"`** in **`"Sales_PTN,"`** you can have a DN **`"1000"`** in, let's say, **`"HR_PTN."`** This means two different devices or functions can have the DN **`"1000",`** but they are differentiated by being in separate partitions.
- **DNs Across Partitions**: The ability to differentiate the same DN in various partitions allows for more precise control over who can call whom. A phone's Calling Search Space (CSS) can be configured to access one partition and not the other, effectively controlling its reachability to different **`"1000"`** extensions.
- **Assignment of Partitions and CSS**: Most elements that can be dialed (such as DNs, route patterns, and translation patterns) have a partition assigned. Anything that initiates a dialing process (such as phones, gateways, trunks) typically has a CSS. Some elements, such as translation patterns and phones, can have both, a partition (for its DN) and a CSS.

Forced Authorization Codes (FAC) and Client Matter Codes (CMC)

There is often a need to regulate who can make certain types of calls and track calls for billing or internal accounting. This is where FAC and CMC come into play.

- **Forced Authorization Codes (FAC)**: FAC is a feature that requires a user to enter a unique code before making specific types of calls, usually long-distance or international ones. It is like a PIN code for dialing. This ensures that only authorized individuals can make such calls. When a user tries to make a call that requires FAC, CUCM prompts for a code. If the entered code is valid, the call proceeds; if not, the call is denied.

- **Client Matter Codes (CMC)**: While FAC controls call access, CMC is more about tracking. It is used in businesses where call costs must be allocated to specific clients or projects. Before or after making a call, the user is prompted to enter a CMC. This code is then logged with the call details, helping with call accounting and billing processes.

Both FAC and CMC offer an additional layer of control and accountability over call activities. They integrate with the Class of Control, ensuring that while users have the required access, there is a mechanism to authorize and track their call activities.

Let us look at the steps on how to configure FAC and CMC:

1. Define the FAC or CMC.

   a. Go to **`Call Routing > Forced Authorization Codes`** or **`Client Matter Codes.`**

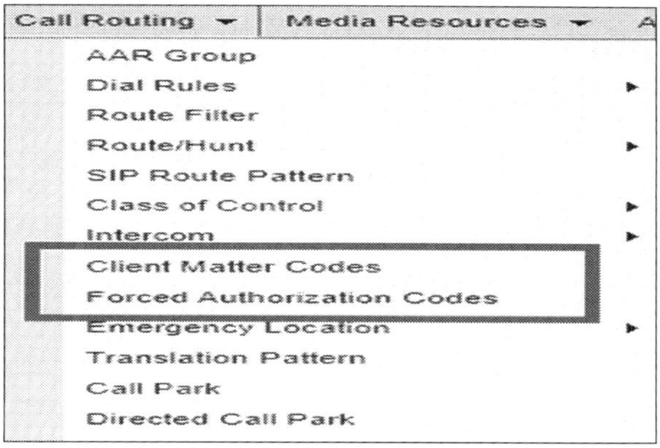

Figure 4.8: *Navigating to FAC or CMC*

   b. Click **`"Add New"`** and fill in the details, including the code itself and a description. In the case of FAC, you need to define the Authorization level.

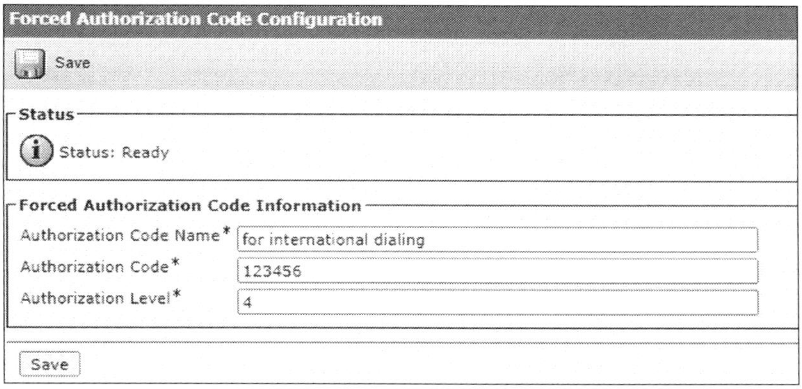

Figure 4.9: *Creating FAC*

2. Update Route Pattern or Route List.

   a. Navigate to the relevant Route Pattern.

   b. Under the **"Route Pattern Configuration",** check the box to require the Forced Authorization Code or Client Matter Code. In the case of FAC, you need to specify the required authorization level value.

   We will discuss the Route pattern in the next chapter. For now, keep in mind that the Route pattern is used in CUCM to match specific dialing patterns and send the calls out to other Infrastructure components (PSTN, SIP trunk/Gateway or other CUCM clusters).

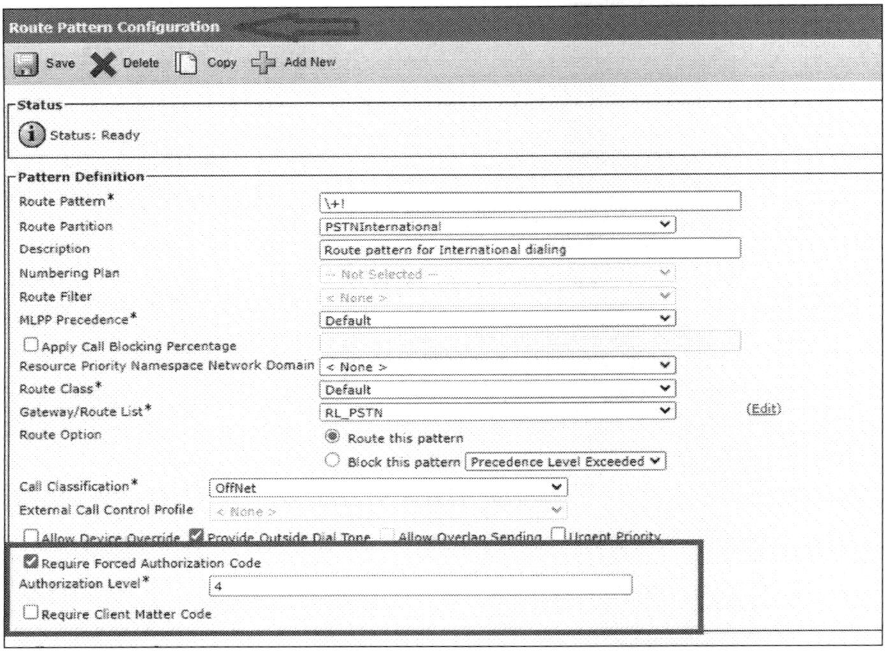

***Figure 4.10**: Applying FAC on the route pattern*

Now when user make a call, if their CSS allows that call then they will be asked this code. They need to be made aware to enter this code and then only their calls will work.

CUCM Telephony Features

The dynamics of today's communication landscape are enriched by intricate needs and scenarios where even a simple call can have multiple layers of functionalities. Cisco Unified Communications Manager (CUCM) stands out as a robust IP PBX solution precisely because it transcends basic telephony. It is not just about connecting two endpoints but catering to advanced requirements that actual business scenarios demand.

In this section, we will look into various telephony features which are commonly used.

Let's conceptualize a fictional company, **`"ABC Corp",`** a mid-sized tech company with several departments:

- **Research and Development (R&D) Department**: A bustling hub where developers and researchers work on the next big software product.
- **Sales and Marketing Department**: The face of the company. They liaise with clients, pitch products, and drive company sales.
- **Human Resources (HR) Department**: They manage employee welfare, hiring, benefits, and internal company events.
- **Support Department**: The troubleshooters, assisting customers with product issues.
- **Management**: The decision-makers, including the CEO, CFO, and other executive roles.

We will use the example of ABC Corp throughout this chapter when explaining various features.

Basic Call Controls

These controls allow users to manage and manipulate calls to suit their immediate communication needs. We will also discuss speed dial in this section.

Call Waiting

When a user is on a call and a second call comes in, Call Waiting provides a beep to inform the user of the incoming call.

Team Leaders in the Sales Department, who might be discussing with one client, can be alerted if another client is trying to reach them simultaneously. This ensures that vital calls are not missed, even during other engagements.

Let us look at the steps.

1. Navigate to **`Device > Phone`** in CUCM Administration.
2. Select the desired phone device.
3. Within the **`Directory Number Settings`**, Locate the section labelled **`"Multiple Call/Call Waiting Settings on Device [device name]."`**

4. Set the Maximum Number of Calls to a value that suits the needs. A common setup might be **`'2'`** to allow one active call and one call on hold (or waiting).

   Configure the Busy Trigger to a desired value. If set to **`'1'`**, it means the line will send a busy signal or forward the call (based on further configurations) when there is one active call, while allowing the user to be notified of another incoming call.

5. Save and apply the changes.

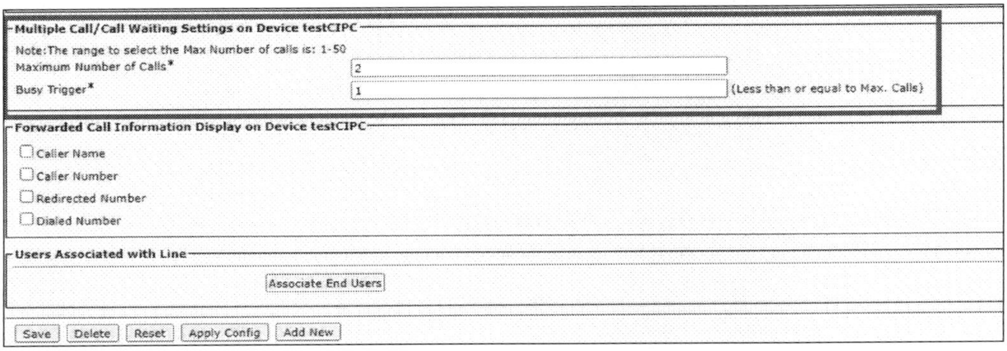

***Figure 4.11**: Setting call waiting on DN*

Call Hold

`"Hold"` is a feature that lets you temporarily pause an ongoing call, freeing up your line to make or receive another call.

In the R&D Department of ABC Corp, developers might be on calls with partners to discuss a software product's technicalities. Suppose they need to quickly refer to documentation, get clarification from a colleague in the same room, or receive/make another call. In that case, they can place the call on hold, get the information, and then return to the call without disconnecting.

Configuration Steps:

1. In CUCM Administration, navigate to **`Device > Phone`**.
2. Select the phone device you want to configure.
3. Ensure that the phone's softkey template includes the **`"Hold"`** softkey in the **`"Connected"`** call state.
4. Save and apply the configuration.

You can create a new Softkey template as well. Let us look at the steps for creating a softkey template and assigning it to the device. This will be useful for many features we will explore in this chapter.

1. Navigate to **`Device > Device settings > Softkey Template`** in CUCM Administration.

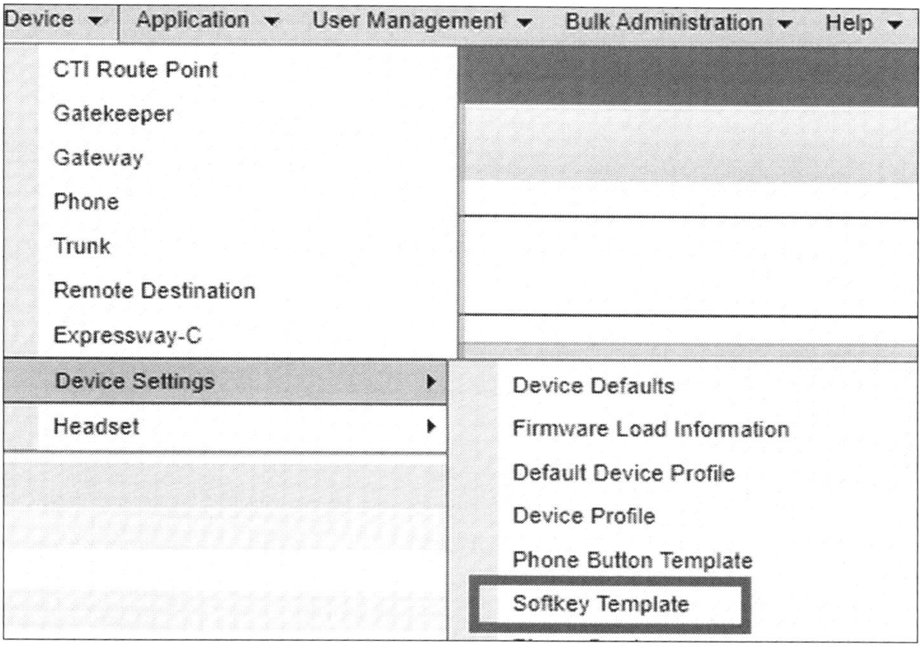

Figure 4.12: *Navigating to the Softkey template*

2. Add New.

3. Configure the name and description and click on **`Save`**.

4. From related links, go to **`Configure Softkey`** layout

Figure 4.13: *Configuring the new Softkey template*

5. Select a call state where you want to add a softkey.

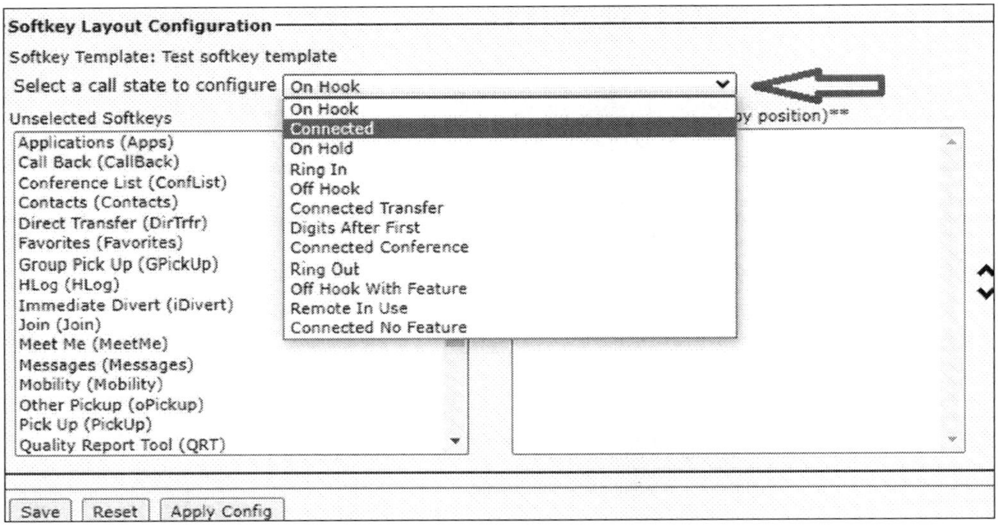

Figure 4.14: *Configuring the new Softkey template in a connected state*

6. As you see in *Figure* 4.15, you need to select the softkey from the left side and click on the arrows in mid to select them. Once you see them on the right side, it means those are selected. You can also change the order of keys.

7. Once changes are made, save it.

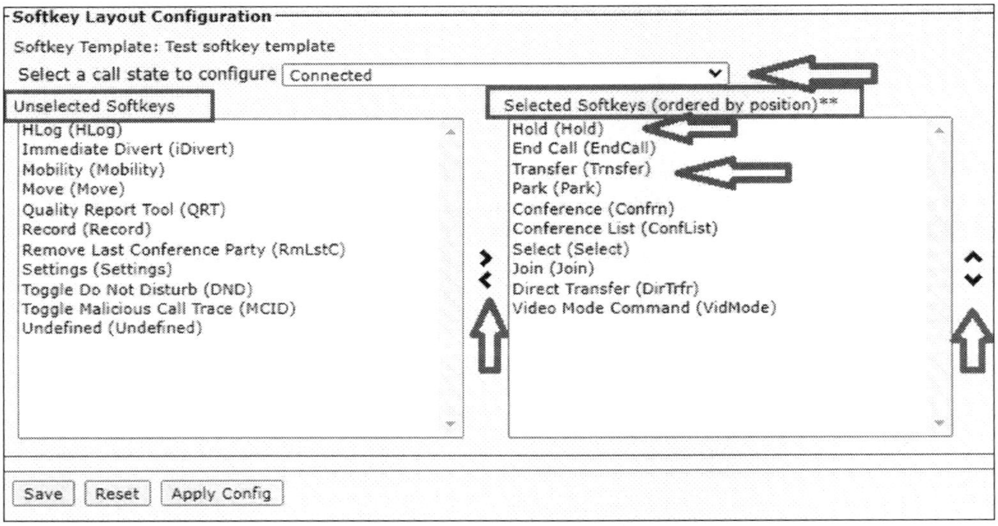

Figure 4.15: *Adding options in the new Softkey template in a connected state*

8. Apply this on your device/phone if not done already.

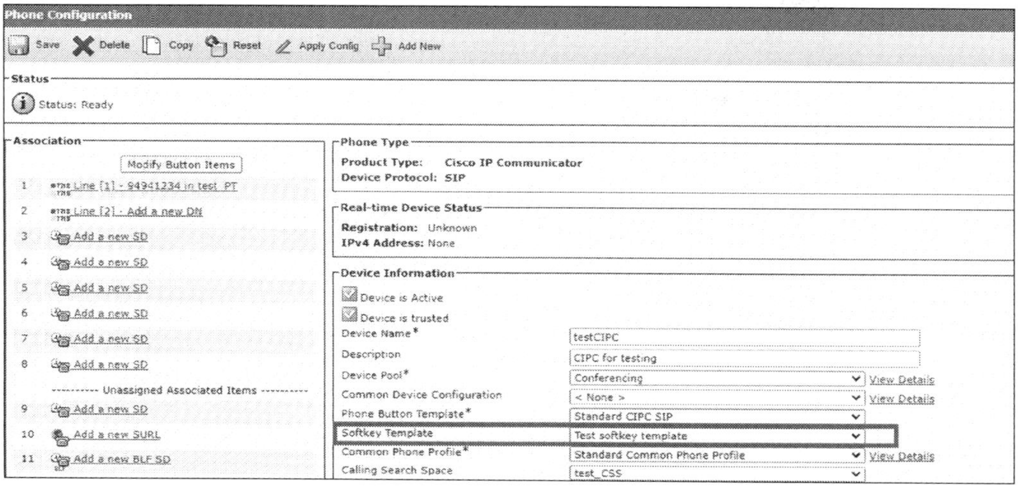

Figure 4.16: *Applying new Softkey template to phone*

Call Transfer

Transfer lets you send an active call to another extension or external number.

The Receptionist at ABC Corp frequently uses this feature. If a client calls the mainline asking to speak with someone from Sales, the Receptionist can quickly transfer the call to the required individual or department.

Configuration Steps are easy, we just need to add a softkey.

1. Navigate to **`Device > Phone`** in CUCM Administration.
2. Select the phone device for configuration.
3. Ensure that the softkey template for the phone has the **`"Transfer"`** softkey in the **`"Connected"`** call state. We already saw the in *Figure* 4.13.
4. Save and apply the changes.

Call Forwarding

Call forwarding automatically sends incoming calls to another predetermined extension or number based on conditions set (example, always forward, forward when busy).

The Management team at ABC Corp, especially during out-of-office hours or during meetings, can set their lines to forward calls to their assistants or voicemail to ensure no important calls are missed.

Let us look at the steps.

1. In the CUCM Administration, go to the Directory Number configuration page.
2. Find the directory number you want to configure for forwarding.

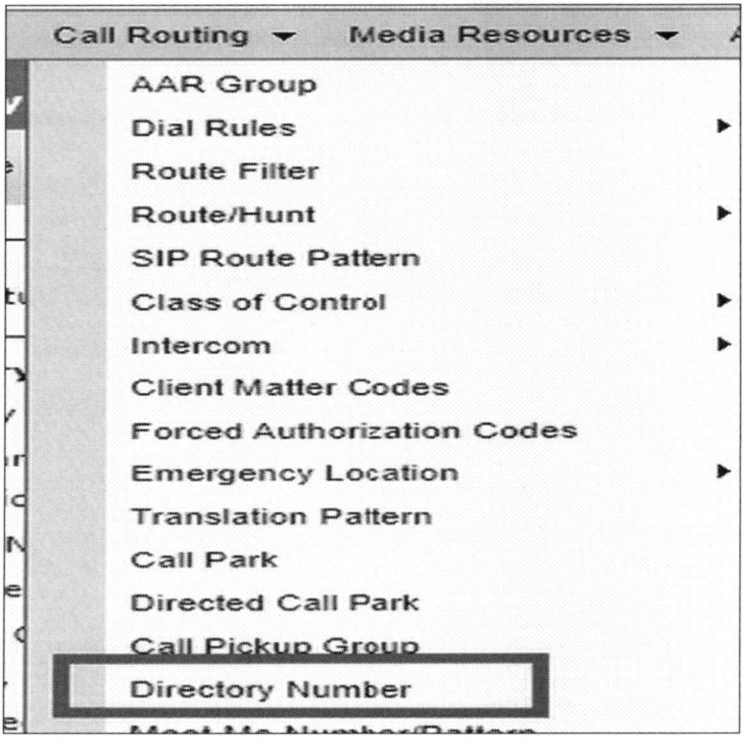

Figure 4.17: *Navigating to the directory number*

3. In the **`Call Forward`** and **`Call Pickup Settings`** section, set the desired forwarding behavior (e.g., **`"Forward All"`** to always forward calls).
4. Enter the destination number or extension for forwarded calls.
5. Save and apply the configuration.

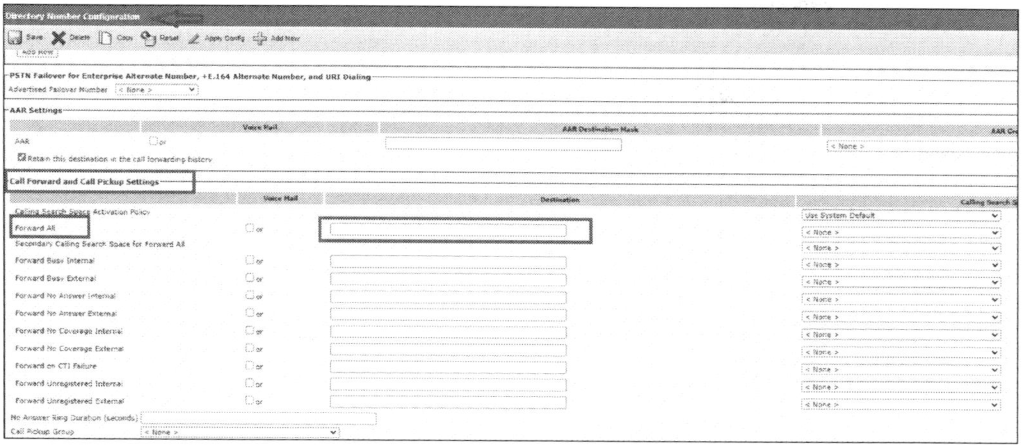

Figure 4.18: *Setting call forward*

Administrators can also enable users to control forwarding directly from their IP phones, which can streamline user experience. Administrators can add a softkey to facilitate this:

1. In the CUCM Administration interface, navigate to **`'Device'`** **`>`** **`'Device Settings'`** **`>`** **`'Softkey Template'`**.
2. Select the softkey template associated with the user's device.
3. Under **`'Configure Softkey Layout'`**, add the **`'CFwdAll'`** softkey to the **`'On Hook'`** state (or as applicable).
4. Save and apply the configuration.
5. Ensure that the modified softkey template is applied to the user's device.

Users can also manage all forwarding settings via Self-Care Portal by navigating to **`https://<IP address or FQDN>/ucmuser/.`** This allows users to manage their call routing preferences directly without administrator intervention.

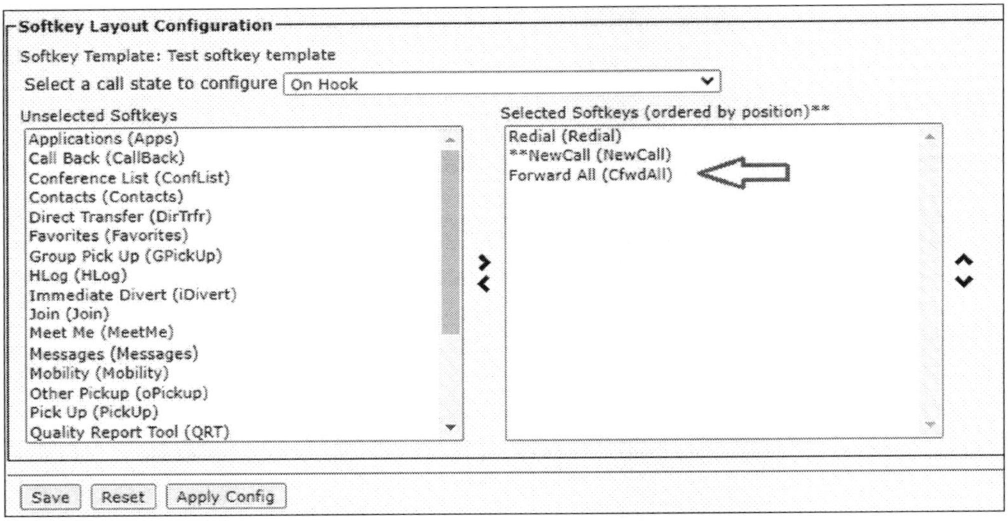

***Figure 4.19**: Call forward all in softkey template*

Speed Dial

Speed Dial allows users to associate frequently dialed phone numbers with specific buttons or indexes on their phone. Instead of dialing the full number, users can simply press a designated button or a short key sequence to place the call.

Imagine a manager at ABC Corp frequently liaising with key clients, suppliers, or other department heads. Instead of dialing their numbers every time, the manager can use Speed Dial buttons for instant communication.

- Users can set up Speed Dial through their user web pages in CUCM or directly on their IP phones, depending on the phone model and configuration.
- In the user interface, they can assign specific numbers to available speed dial buttons or indexes.
- To dial, users simply press the button associated with the desired Speed Dial entry. On some phones, they might select an index and then press a **`"Speed Dial"`** softkey or a similar function.

Admin can also configure a Speed dial from the CUCM phone configuration.

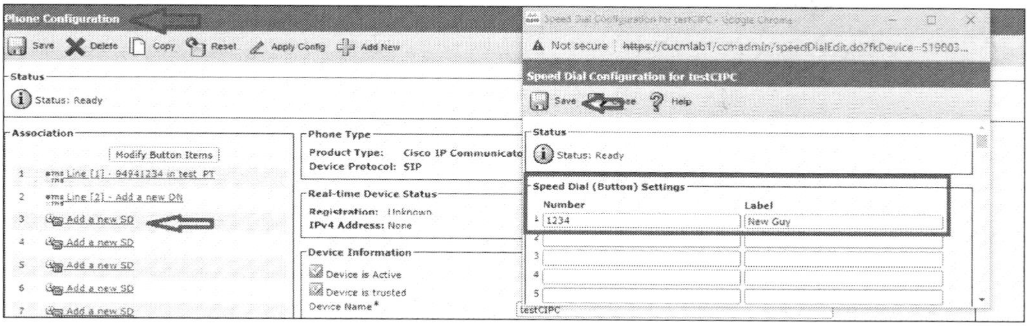

Figure 4.20: *Speed dial config on the device*

Call Park

Call Park is a telephony feature that allows a user to place a call on hold at one telephone set and continue the conversation from any other telephone set. The call is "parked" on a designated extension, freeing up the initial phone line. Someone else, even at a different location, can then retrieve the call by dialing the specific parked extension.

At ABC Corp's headquarters, the reception desk often receives calls intended for personnel who might be away from their desks. With Call Park, the Receptionist can park the call and announce over the office PA system or send an instant message that there is a call waiting for a specific individual on a particular extension.

Or, when a crucial client calls with specific concerns that only a particular sales rep can address or a technical issue that requires a certain support agent, the call can be parked until the appropriate person is located and can retrieve the call.

The exact configuration steps can vary, but here is a general approach:

1. Define Call Park Range:
    a. Navigate to **`Call Routing > Call Park`**.

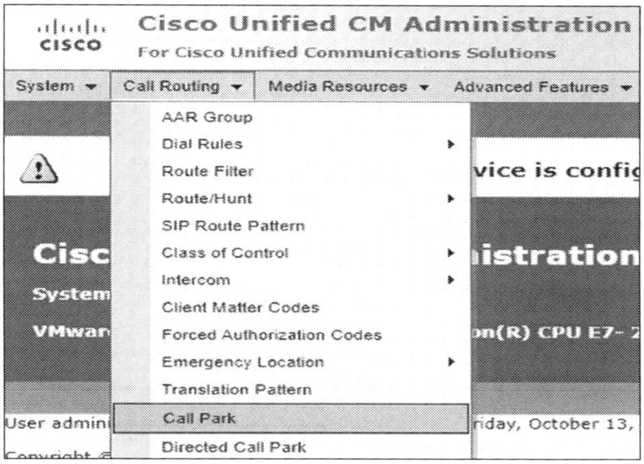

Figure 4.21: *Navigating to Call Park*

   b. Enter the call park extension number. You can enter literal digits or the wildcard character X (the system allows one or two X). For example, enter 8555 to define a single call park extension number of 8555 or enter 85XX to define a range of call park extension numbers from 8500 to 8599.

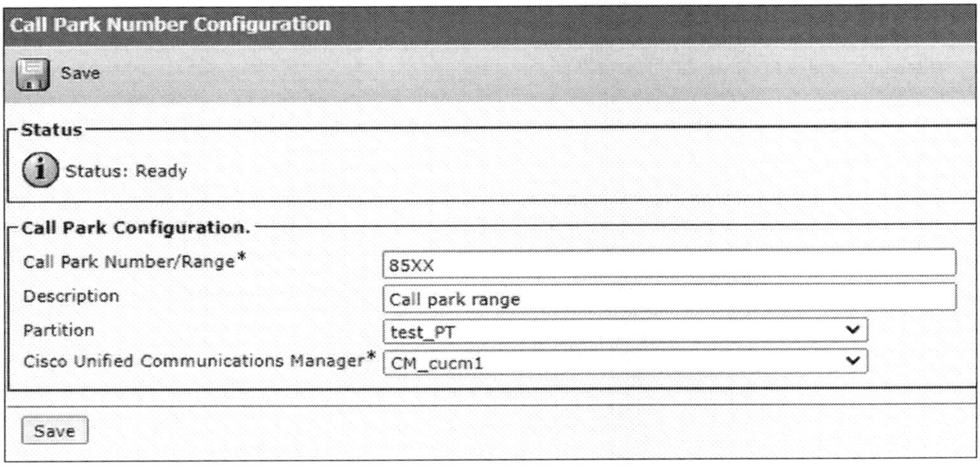

Figure 4.22: *Call Park number configuration*

2. **Assign Call Park to a Softkey:**

   a. Go to **`Device > Device Settings > Softkey Template`**.

   b. Choose the template you're using for your phones.

   c. Ensure the **`"Park"`** softkey is available in the **`"Connected"`** call state.

3. **Apply to Devices**:

   a. If you made changes to the softkey template, ensure that the updated template is assigned to your devices. You might need to reset or restart phones for the changes to take effect.

4. **Retrieve Parked Calls**:

   a. A user can park a call by pressing the **`"Park"`** softkey during a call. The system will then announce the extension where the call is parked.

   b. To retrieve the parked call, any user can dial that extension from another phone.

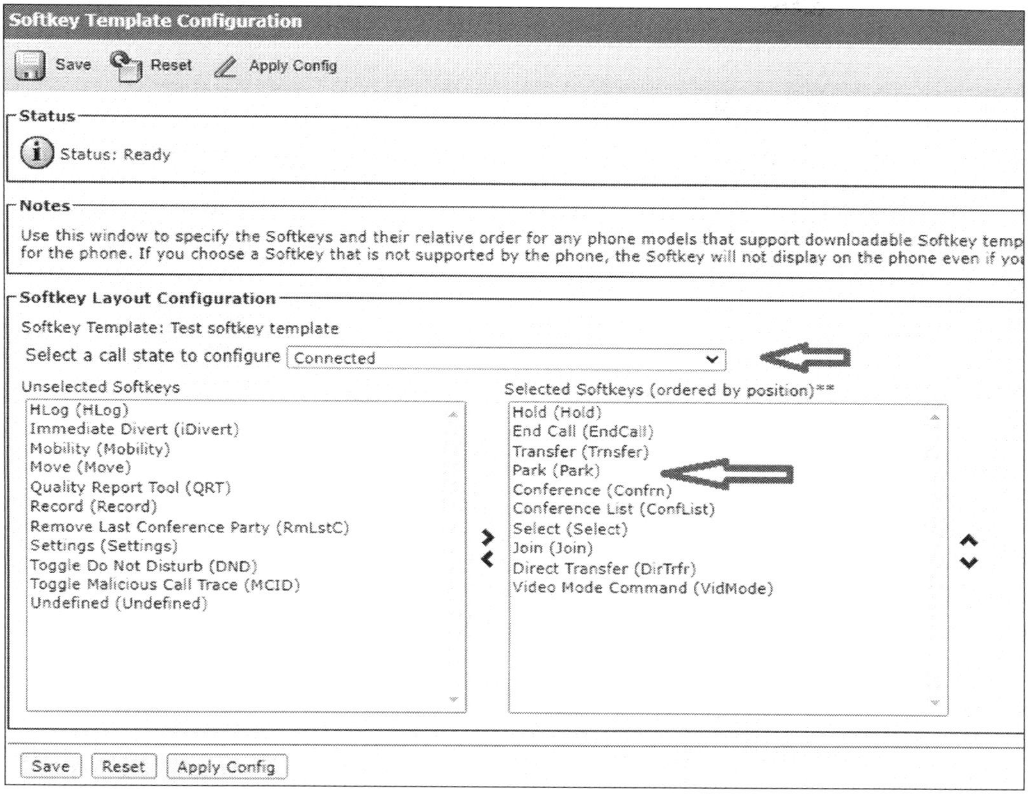

***Figure 4.23**: Call Park softkey configuration*

Note: Set up a **`Call Park Reversion`** timeout to avoid lost calls. If a parked call is not picked up within a specified time, it can revert to ringing at its original location or another designated number to ensure the call isn't missed.

1. **`System > Service Parameters`**. Select the desired node as **`Server`** and the service as **`Cisco CallManager (active)`**.
2. Set the **`Call Park Reversion Timer`** for each server in a cluster that has the Unified Communications Manager service and Call Park configured.
3. The default is 60 seconds. This parameter determines the time that a call remains parked. When this timer expires, the parked call returns to the device that parked the call.

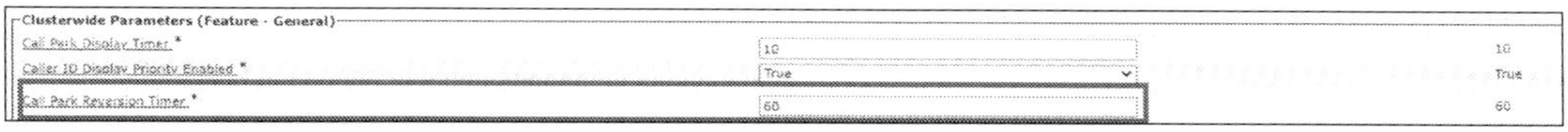

***Figure 4.24**: Call Park revision timeout from service parameters*

Barge and Privacy

Barge is a feature that allows a third person to join an ongoing call. Imagine two colleagues on a call, and a supervisor wants to jump in to provide immediate feedback or clarification; they can do just that with Barge. It is like walking into a room where two people are talking and joining their conversation.

The privacy feature ensures that a call remains private and cannot be interrupted or joined using the Barge feature. It is a safeguard to maintain the confidentiality of a call.

The Privacy feature is linked to the Barge functionality. It's designed to prevent unauthorized Barge actions on a call. If Barge isn't enabled or used in your environment, then the Privacy feature is unnecessary, as someone cannot intrude on the call. Understanding this dependency is essential to avoid unnecessary configuration and use these features effectively.

We will stick to the overview of this feature and not cover the config steps.

Call Coverage Features

These features ensure that incoming calls are attended to, even if the primary recipient is unavailable, optimizing responsiveness and collaboration.

Shared Lines and Busy Lamp Field (BLF)

Shared Lines allow a single **`Directory Number (DN)`** to appear and ring on multiple devices. BLF is a feature on IP phones that indicates the call status of another line or extension, it is a visual cue showing whether a specific line or extension is busy (on a call) or available.

Shared Lines provides:

- **Efficiency**: Ideal for teams or departments like the Support team at ABC Corp, where shared responsibilities ensure quicker response times.
- **Flexibility**: Allows multiple team members to handle calls for a specific DN, ensuring no call goes unanswered.

BLF provides:

- **At-a-Glance Availability**: Users can instantly determine if a colleague is on a call, aiding in decision-making for call transfers or initiations.
- **Enhanced Collaboration**: Team members can quickly see if a colleague is free before attempting to reach out, reducing unnecessary call attempts.

The reception desk at ABC Corp utilizes Shared Lines for the main company number, ensuring any of the available receptionists can answer. Team leads in various departments may use BLF to monitor the availability of their team members.

Let us look at the steps on how to configure these features.

Shared Lines Configuration:

- In the CUCM Administration interface, navigate to the desired DN.
- Assign this DN to multiple devices. Simple as that.

BLF Configuration:

- Navigate to its configuration page for the desired phone in the CUCM Administration interface.
- Configure a BLF / speed dial.
- Save and reset the phone for the changes to take effect.

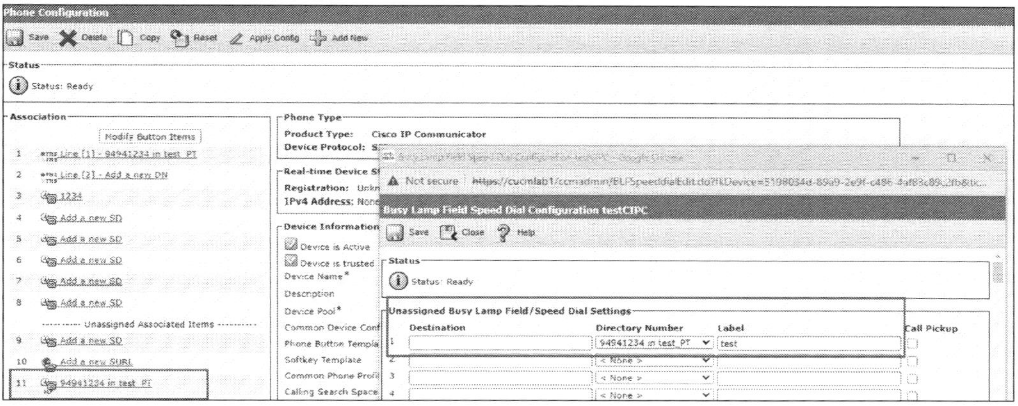

Figure 4.25: *BLF config on phone*

Call Pickup Group

Call pickup group is a feature that lets you answer a colleague's ringing phone from your own. Say you are at ABC Corp and a nearby phone rings, but the owner is not around. With Call Pickup, you can answer it from your own desk.

Let us understand the different types of Call Pickup in brief:

- **Group call Pickup**: Allows users to answer calls for another pickup group. Users must dial the specific call pickup group number and use the `"GPickUp"` softkey.
- **Other Group Pickup**: Enables users to pick up calls within an associated group to their own. When activated, the system searches for the incoming call in associated groups and makes the call connection. `"OPickUp"` is used for this feature.
- **Directed Call Pickup**: Allows users to pick up a specific ringing call by dialing its Directory Number (DN). Users press `"GPickUp"` or `"Group Pickup"` and

enter the DN of the ringing device. The privilege of picking up an incoming call using this feature is controlled through an associated group mechanism.

- **Busy Lamp Field (BLF) Call Pickup**: Notifies a user about a waiting call on a BLF DN and allows them to pick it up. A flashing BLF SD button indicates an incoming call, which can be picked up by pressing the button if Auto Call Pickup is configured. Otherwise, the phone must be off the hook, or the answer key should be pressed.

We will briefly cover the steps to configure Group Call Pickup in CUCM. Please check the Feature Configuration Guide of CUCM for detailed steps.

1. **Creating a Pickup Group**:
   a. Navigate to `Call Routing > Call Pickup Group`, then click `Add New`.

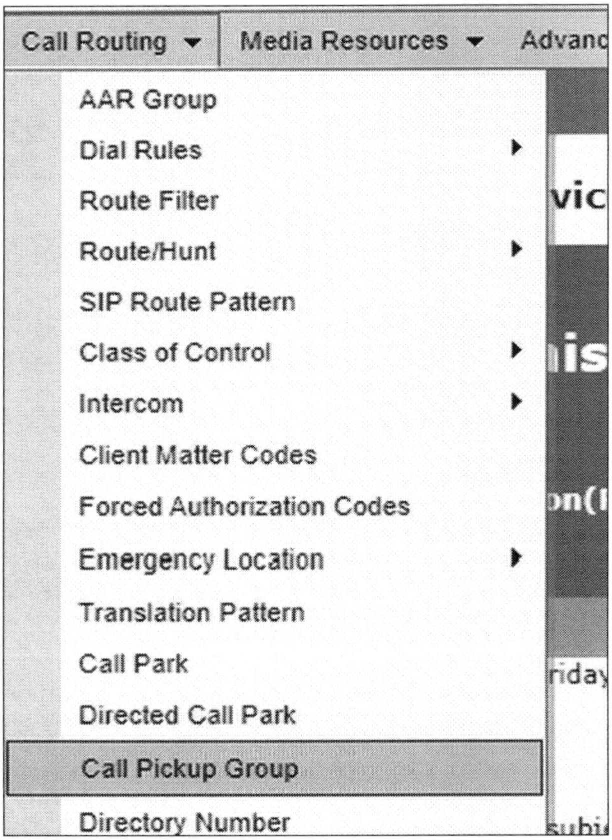

Figure 4.26: *Navigating to Call Pickup group*

   b. Assign a name and description for the pickup group, then click `Save`.
   c. Add respective `Directory Numbers (DNs)` or lines to define the group.

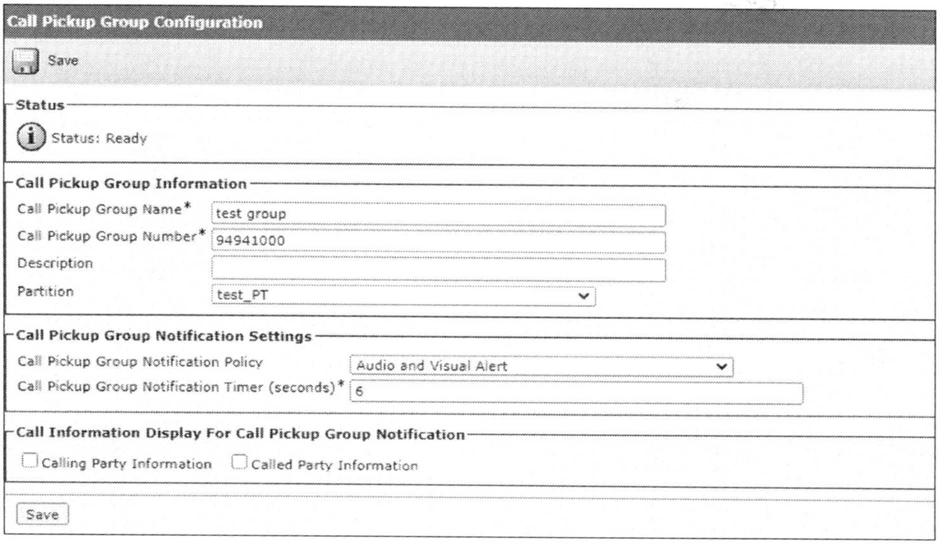

Figure 4.27: *Call pickup group config*

2. **Activating Softkeys**:

    a. Navigate to **`Device > Device Settings > Softkey Template`** in CUCM Admin.

    b. Choose the relevant softkey template, then click **`Configure Softkeys`**.

    c. Under both **`"On Hook"`** and **`"Off Hook"`** call states, ensure **`"Pickup"`** and **`"Group Pickup (GPickup)`** softkeys are added to the Selected Softkeys box.

    d. Choose the position/order for the softkeys and click **`Save`**.

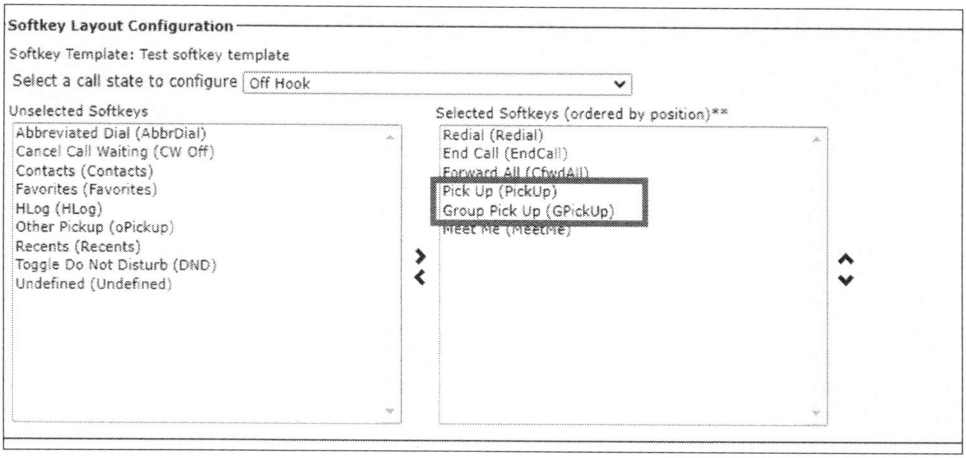

Figure 4.28: *Pickup and group pickup in softkey template*

3. **Assigning Phone to Pickup Group**:
   a. Navigate to **`Device > Phone`**.
   b. Search and select the phone device that you want to link to the pickup group.
   c. Under **`Associated Items`**, go to the line you want to associate and click on its line number.
   d. Under **`Call Pickup Group`**, select the created pickup group from the drop-down menu.
   e. Click **`Save`**, then **`Apply Config`**.

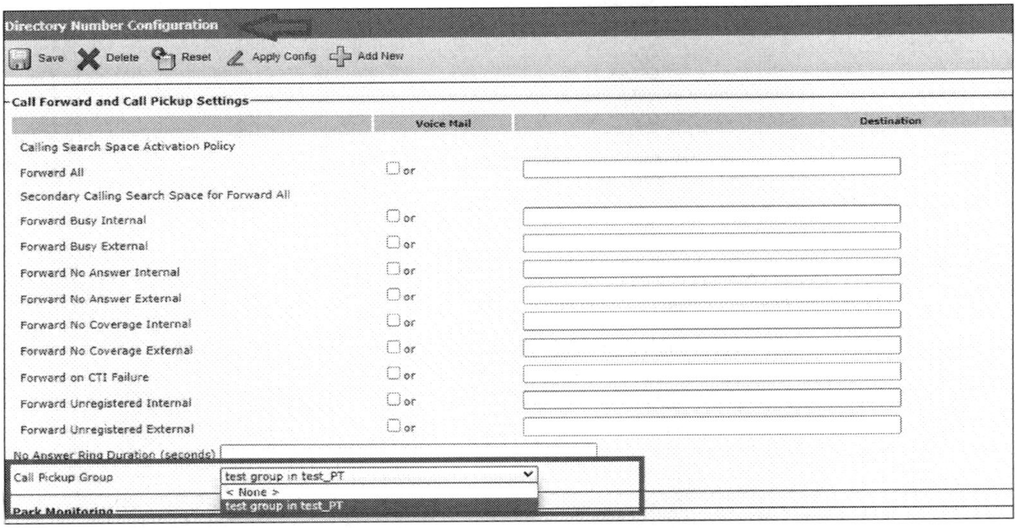

Figure 4.29: *Call pickup group configuration in DN*

It is essential that ABC Corp trains employees and sets clear guidelines on when and how to use the Call Pickup feature, ensuring both operational efficiency and respect for individual boundaries.

Hunt Group

A Hunt Group is a collection of directory numbers (DNs) that are grouped and processed in a specific order based on a predefined hunting mechanism. If the primary line in the group is busy or does not answer, the call "hunts" for the next available line in the group to ring.

In the ABC Corp context, if the main sales line is busy, potential clients are not left waiting. Their call can be immediately rerouted to another sales executive.

Different Types of Hunt Algorithms:

- **Top Down (Linear)**: Calls start with the first line and move down the list sequentially, trying to find an available line.
- **Circular**: After offering a call to a line, the system shifts to the next line for subsequent calls, cycling through the group.
- **Longest Idle**: Calls are routed to the line that's been free for the most extended period.
- **Broadcast**: Every phone in the group rings simultaneously, and the first to answer secure the call.

As you see in *Figure* 4.30, When a call comes in to the Hunt Pilot (91123456789), it is directed to the Hunt List. The Hunt List contains two Line Groups in this example, and the linear hunting process begins.

The system starts with Line Group 1, which is the first preference in the linear hunting order. It attempts to connect the call to the first available extension within Line Group 1, which is 1111. If extension 1111 is busy or unavailable, the system tries the next extension in the line group, which is 1112.

If all extensions in Line Group 1 are busy or unavailable, the linear hunting process moves to Line Group 2, which is the second preference. The system then attempts to connect the call to the first available extension within Line Group 2, starting with 2111 and then moving to 2112 if necessary.

If all extensions in both Line Groups are busy or unavailable, the call may be forwarded to voicemail or another designated destination, depending on the Hunt Group configuration.

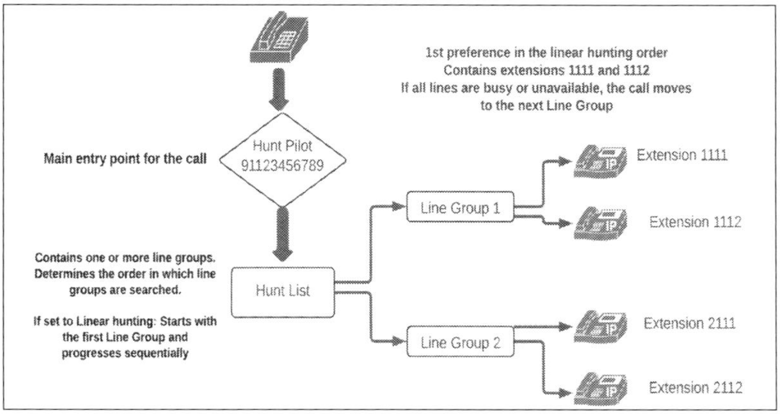

***Figure* 4.30**: *Hunt Group*

Let us look at the config steps for the hunt group in CUCM.

1. Create the Hunt Group (often referred to as **`Line Group`** in CUCM).

   a. Navigate to **`Call Routing > Hunt/Line Group`**.

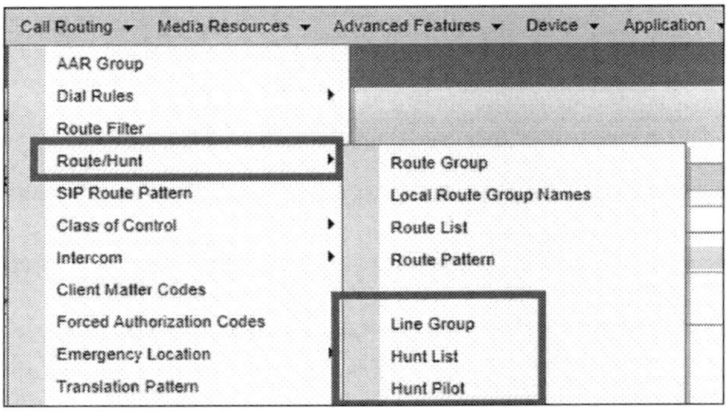

Figure 4.31: *Navigating to hunt group*

b. Click **"Add New"** to create a line group.

c. Here, you will specify the hunt algorithm and pick directory numbers or lines that are part of this group. The algorithm determines the order in which the lines in the group are rung.

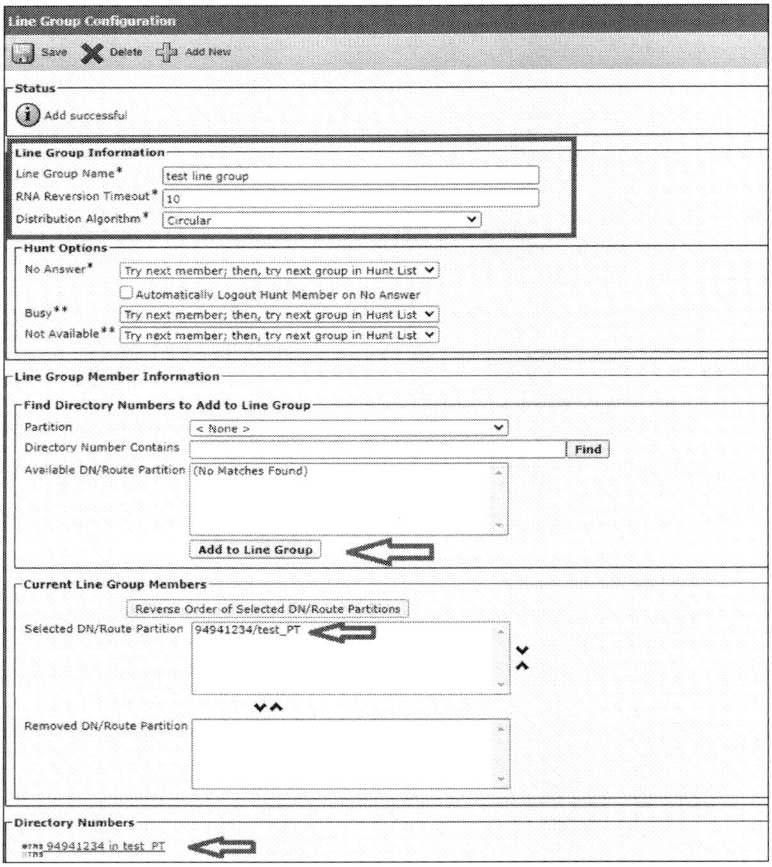

Figure 4.32: *Creating line group*

2. Define a Hunt List.

   a. Navigate to **`Call Routing`** in the CUCM administration interface.

   b. Go to **`Hunt/Hunt List`** and add a new list.

   c. Add a line group to it. This is essentially a container in which you can place one or more line groups. If the first group is unavailable, the system will go to the next group on the list.

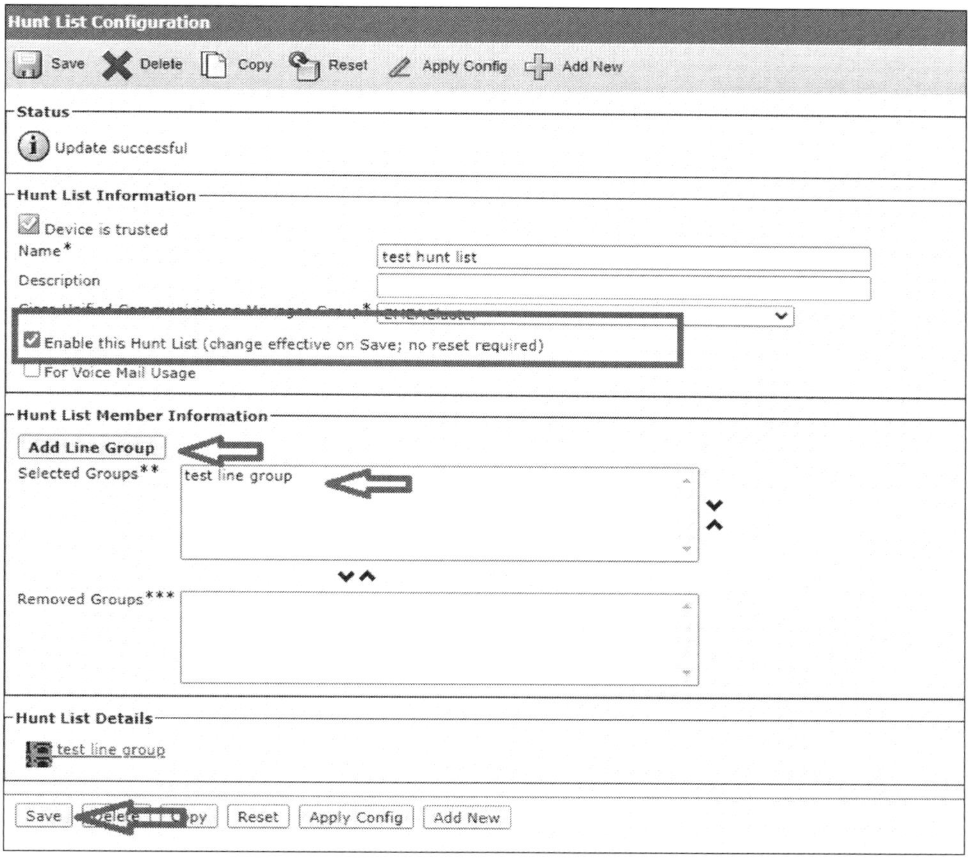

***Figure 4.33**: Creating hunt list*

3. Configure a Hunt Pilot.

   a. Under **`Call Routing`**, go to **`Hunt/Hunt Pilot`**.

   b. Assign a directory number that users will dial.

   c. Associate the Hunt Pilot with the Hunt List you created. When this number is dialed, CUCM uses the hunt list and line group to direct the call accordingly.

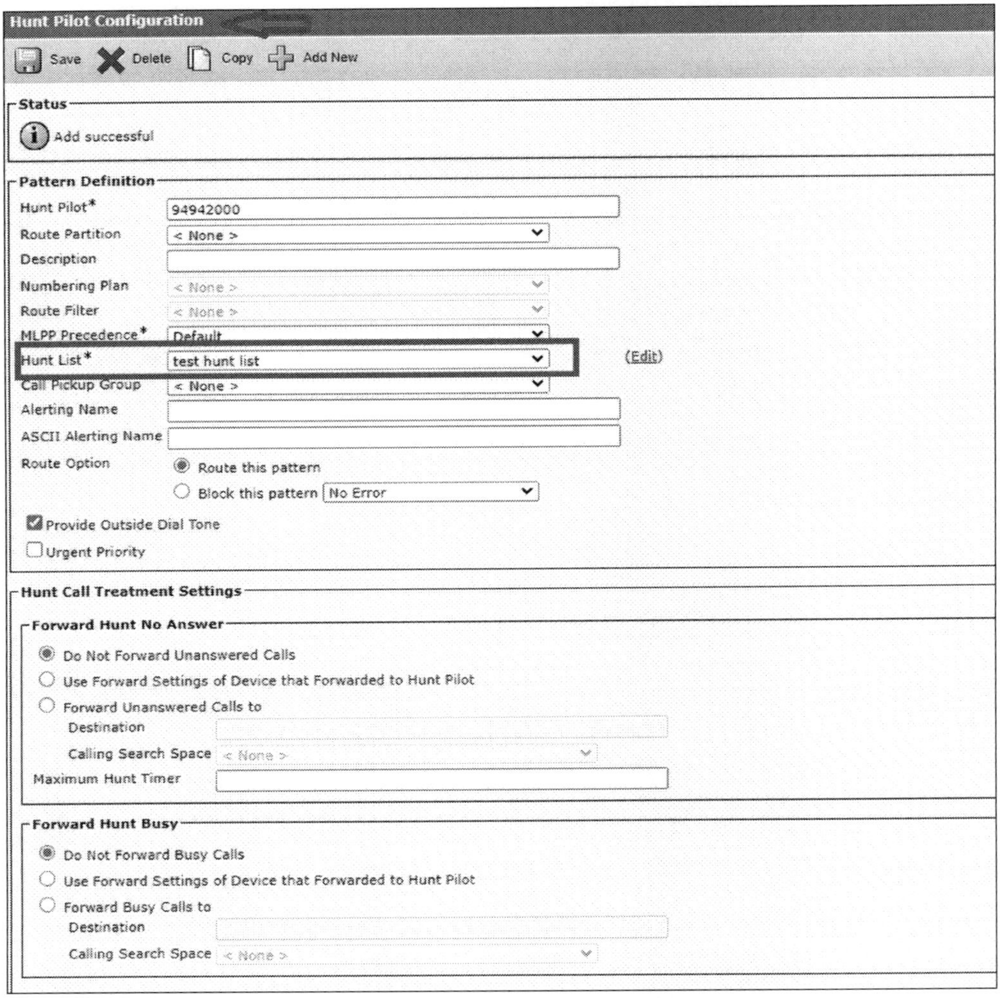

***Figure 4.34**: Creating hunt pilot*

4. Customize Forwarding Settings.

    a. Within the **`Hunt Pilot`** settings, specify what should happen if no one in the Line Group answers. This could be forwarding to another DN, voicemail, or perhaps playing a busy tone.

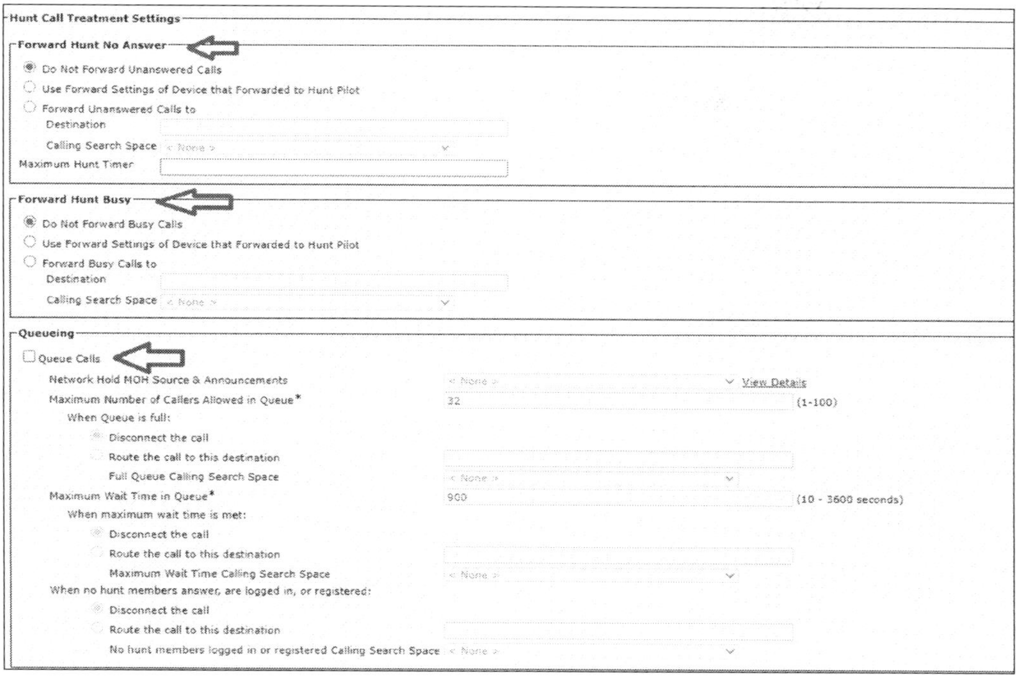

Figure 4.35: *Additional config in hunt pilot*

Advanced Features

These features in CUCM offer specialized solutions for unique communication needs, providing more flexibility and control in specific scenarios. Let us explore these in detail.

Extension Mobility

Extension Mobility is a Cisco Unified Communications Manager (CUCM) feature that allows users to associate their phone number and user profile with any Cisco Unified IP Phone. By logging into any phone, users can access their personal settings, such as line appearances, speed dials, and services, temporarily making that device "their" phone.

As the support team in ABC Corp works in shifts, the next person coming in can use the same desk and log into the phone, making it their own for the duration of their shift.

When executives visit the R&D Department or any other department in ABC Corp, they can log in to any phone, ensuring they remain reachable on their number.

Let us look at the configuration steps.

1. Ensure the Extension Mobility Service is Running:

   a. Navigate to **Cisco Unified Serviceability > Tools > Service Activation**.

   b. Ensure the **'Cisco Extension Mobility'** service is activated.

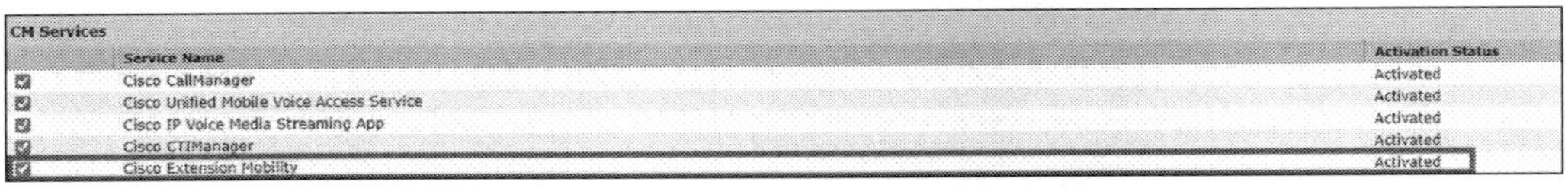

***Figure 4.36**: Extension mobility service*

2. Create Extension Mobility Service:

   a. Go to **Device > Device Settings > Phone Services** from the CUCM Administration interface.

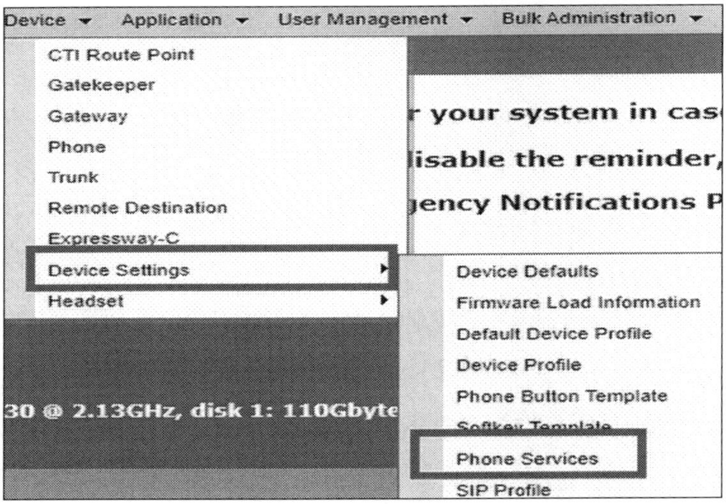

***Figure 4.37**: Navigating to phone services*

   b. Click **'Add New'**.

   c. Enter the Service Name, for instance, **"Extension Mobility"**, and the Service URL (which usually follows the format http://<CUCM IP Address>:8080/emapp/EMAppServlet?device=#DEVICENAME#).

   IP Address is the IP address of the CUCM, where Cisco Extension Mobility is activated and running.

   d. In the **Service Type field**, choose whether the service is provisioned to the Services, Directories, or Messages button.

e. Save the service settings.

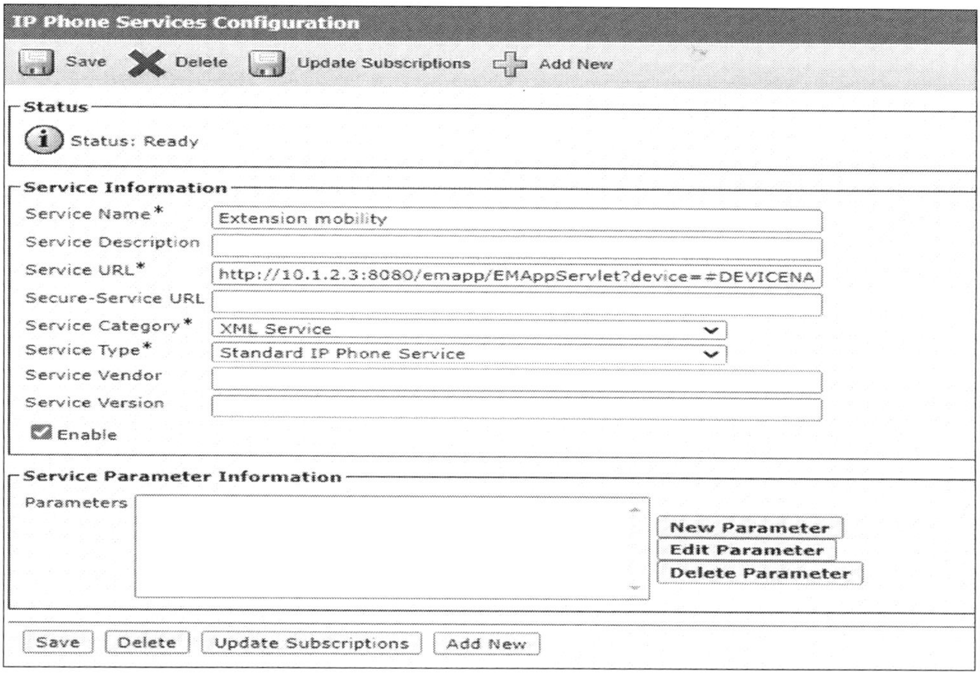

***Figure 4.38**: Creating Extension Mobility Service*

3. Create an Extension mobility Device Profile:

   a. Go to **`Device > Device Settings > Device Profile`**.

   b. This profile acts as a virtual device that maps onto a physical device when a user logs in to extension mobility.

   c. Click **`'Add New'`** and select the phone model and protocol.

   d. Configure the fields and save.

   e. From the Association Information section, click **`Add a new DN`**.

   f. In the **`Directory Number`** field, enter the directory number and click **`Save`**.

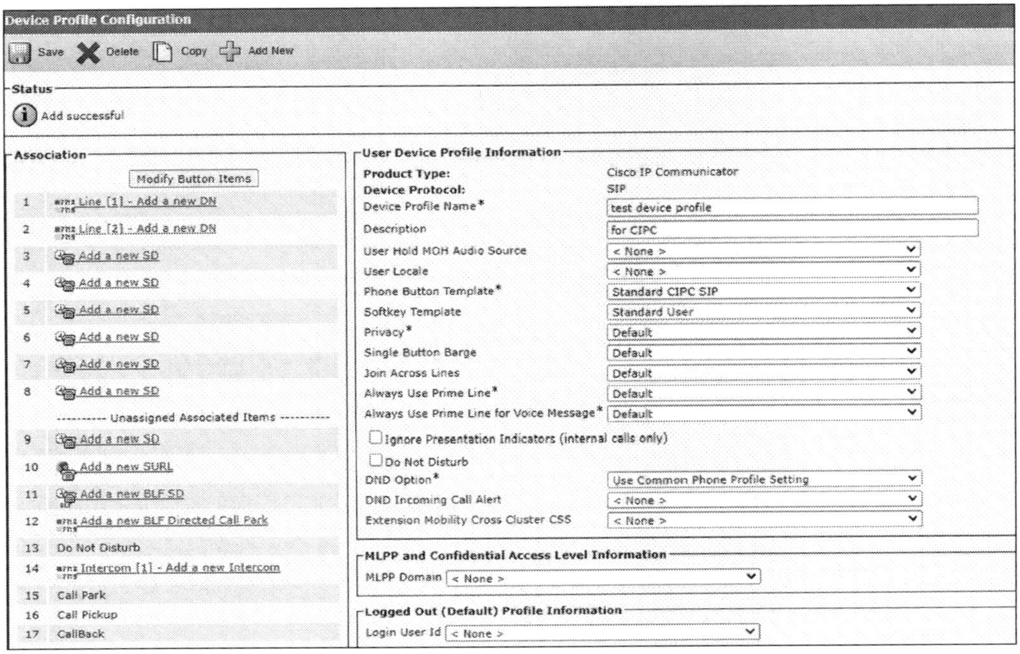

***Figure 4.39**: Creating device profile*

4. Subscribe the Physical Devices and device profile to the Extension Mobility Service for Users:

   a. Navigate to **`Device > Phone`**.

   b. Select the phone you want to enable.

   c. Under **`Related Links`**, choose **`'Subscribe/Unsubscribe Services'`**.

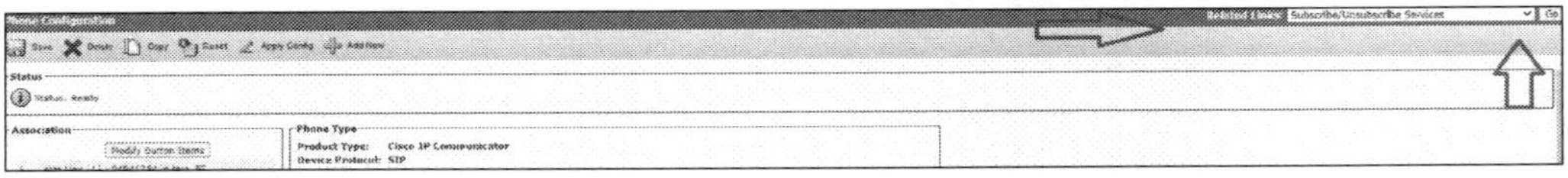

***Figure 4.40**: Navigating to Subscribe/ Unsubscribe services on the phone*

   d. Subscribe to the Extension Mobility service you created.
   Do the same steps for the device profile.

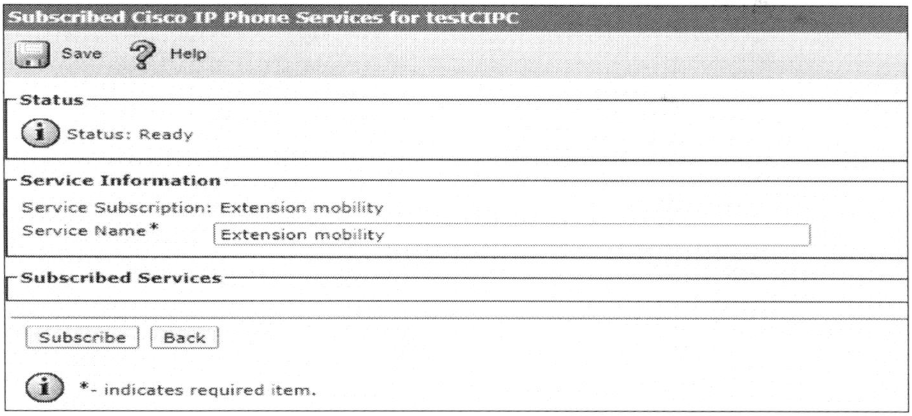

Figure 4.41: *Subscribing service to phone*

e. Return to the phone configuration, and in the Extension Information section, check **'Enable Extension Mobility'** and assign the device profile

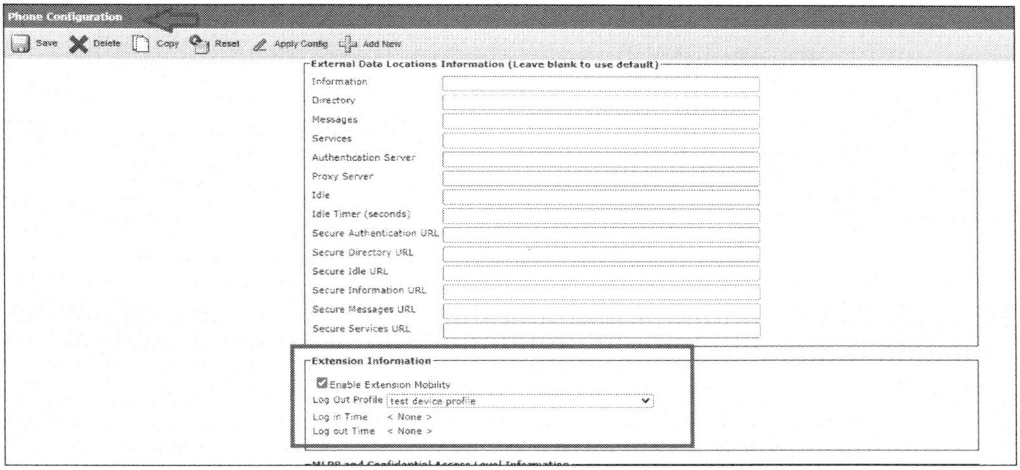

Figure 4.42: *Enable extension mobility on the phone*

5. Assign the Device Profile to the user:

   a. Navigate to **User Management > End User**.

   b. Locate and select the user.

   c. Under **Extension Mobility**, select the device profile.

   d. Assign a device profile to the user and set a PIN for them if not already set.

   This PIN should ideally be communicated to users securely, or they can be instructed to change it upon first login.

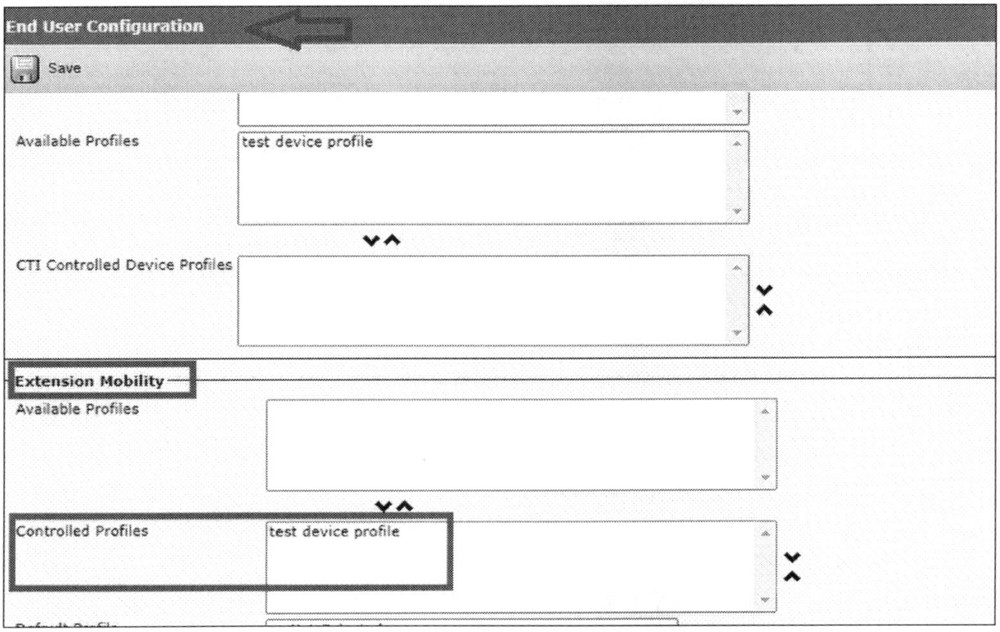

***Figure 4.43**: Assign device profile to end user*

6. Logging into a Phone Using Extension Mobility:
    a. On the phone, the user will press the **`'Services'`** or **`'Application'`** button.
    b. The user will choose **`'Extension Mobility'`** and input the credentials.
    c. The phone will restart and apply the user's profile.

Intercom

The intercom in the Cisco Unified Communications Manager (CUCM) system facilitates a direct line of communication between two designated phones. When initiated, the receiving phone auto-answers in speaker mode, paving the way for swift, hands-free exchanges.

The intercom is tailor made for speedy interactions or short messages, bypassing the traditional call-answer process.

Supervisors utilize the intercom in ABC Corp's manufacturing wing to issue rapid directives or safety alerts to control room operators.

Intercom is a niche feature and not very commonly used, so we will stick to the overview and not cover the config steps here.

Conclusion

In this chapter, we started with an overview of CUCM call processing and routing to establish foundational knowledge, which will aid in understanding numerous concepts in this and subsequent chapters. We then transitioned to the Class of Control, discussing partitions and Calling Search Spaces (CSS). Understanding Partition and CSS is imperative before delving into dial plan discussions and will be referenced several times in the next chapter.

Subsequently, we explored various CUCM features commonly utilized in telephony environments, such as Call Waiting, Hold, Transfer, Forward, Call Park, Call Pickup Group, and Hunt Group, advancing to topics like Extension Mobility and intercom.

It is important to take some time, do hands-on and test these features to see user experience and understand the configuration flow. Even if you forget most of the steps after a few months, understanding the logic of configuration will be useful to recall easily when required. Lots of these features are available on all telephony systems (even if it has a different name), be it on-prem or SaaS and are commonly used by companies.

In the next chapter, our focus will shift to Dial Plans.

Multiple Choice Questions

1. Which component in CUCM segregates the global dialable address space?
   a. Hunt Groups
   b. SIP Trunks
   c. Dial Peers
   d. Partitions
2. Which feature allows users to pick up a ringing call within their defined group?
   a. Call Transfer
   b. Call Parking
   c. Call Pickup
   d. Call Forwarding
3. In the context of CUCM, what does BLF represent?
   a. Best Line Forwarding
   b. Busy Lamp Field

c. Base Line Filtering

d. Business Line Facilitator

4. When a user wishes to temporarily store a call and retrieve it from another extension, which feature should they use?

    a. Call Forwarding

    b. Call Waiting

    c. Call Transfer

    d. Call Park

5. What feature allows an employee to log into any Cisco IP phone and acquire their user profile and settings?

    a. Forced Authorization Codes (FAC)

    b. Call Barge

    c. Extension Mobility

    d. Call Parking

Answers

1. d
2. c
3. b
4. d
5. c

Further Reading

Same as the last chapter, to improve your understanding and broaden your perspective, it is suggested to explore the following topics on your own. Remember to tailor your research based on your organization's specific needs and always discern between genuine insights and industry trends.

- **Class of Control in CUCM**: Consider a mid-sized tech firm, similar to ABC Corp, and ponder over designing partitions and CSS tailored to different departments.

  Explore best practices for designing partitions and CSS and evaluate how these configurations might differ or align with setups in other vendor ecosystems or infrastructure components.

- **Call Pickup Variations**: Explore scenarios where specific Call Pickup variations might be especially advantageous or potentially problematic.
- **Telephony Features**: Explore in depth the telephony features we covered in this chapter - call waiting, hold, transfer, forward, speed dial, call park, shared line and BLF, and hunt group.

Consider different organizational structures and sizes for each feature and investigate how configurations might be optimized for each scenario.

CHAPTER 5
Dial Plans - Basics to Advance

Introduction

Now that we've covered device registration, configuration, telephony features, class of control and other CUCM fundamentals in previous chapters, we'll dive into dial plans—the critical component that brings it all together. This chapter will equip you with the knowledge to design, configure, and optimize dial plans on CUCM.

We'll start with SIP trunks and gateways, the core connections that enable routing. Then, we'll explore dial plan components like route patterns, route lists, route groups and digit manipulation tools. You'll also learn advanced concepts like TEHO, globalized dial plans, URI dialing and time-of-day routing. By the end, you'll be able to analyze requirements, craft robust dial plans, and deliver excellent user experiences.

Structure

We will discuss the following topics:

- SIP Trunk : Overview and Configuration
- Voice Gateway Configuration in a CUCM
- Introduction to Dial plans
- Dial Plan Config and Transformation Mechanisms in CUCM
- Advanced Concepts - TEHO, Globalized Dial Plan, Time-of-day Routing, AAR Overview, URI Dialing
- Practical Dial Plan Scenarios

SIP Trunk: Overview and Configuration

SIP Trunking in CUCM enables a connection between the Cisco Unified Communications Manager (CUCM) and external entities such as SIP gateways, SIP

Proxy Servers, Unified Communications applications, conference bridges, and remote CUCM clusters. It uses the IP network to replace traditional telephone trunks, enabling direct communication between IP-based systems and the broader phone network.

SIP trunks can handle voice, video, and other multimedia communications through a single connection. You can assign up to 16 different destination addresses for a SIP trunk using IPv4 or IPv6 addresses, fully qualified domain names, or a single DNS SRV record.

Let's look at the configuration steps. Please note that these are just simple configuration steps, and based on specific requirements/scenarios or versions, you may have to do additional config to make it work. Check the System Configuration Guide for CUCM for the production environment config.

1. Creating a SIP Profile:

    a. Navigate to **`Device> Device Settings > SIP Profile`**.

    b. To edit an existing profile, find and select the required SIP profile; to create a new profile, click **`Add New`**.

    c. Choose the required SDP Transparency Profile and Normalization Script if necessary for interoperability.

    d. Look for the setting **`Enable OPTIONS Ping to monitor destination status for trunks`**. Set it to **`Enabled`**. This ensures that CUCM will send an OPTIONS request to the trunk's destination periodically.

    e. **OPTIONS Ping Interval**: This is the time interval (in seconds) at which CUCM sends the OPTIONS request. You can adjust this according to your needs.

    Utilizing the **`OPTIONS`** ping can help dynamic call routing decisions. CUCM can choose an alternate path or trunk for the call if a SIP trunk is detected as down.

    f. Save your changes.

    You can see these parameters In *Figure* 5.1.

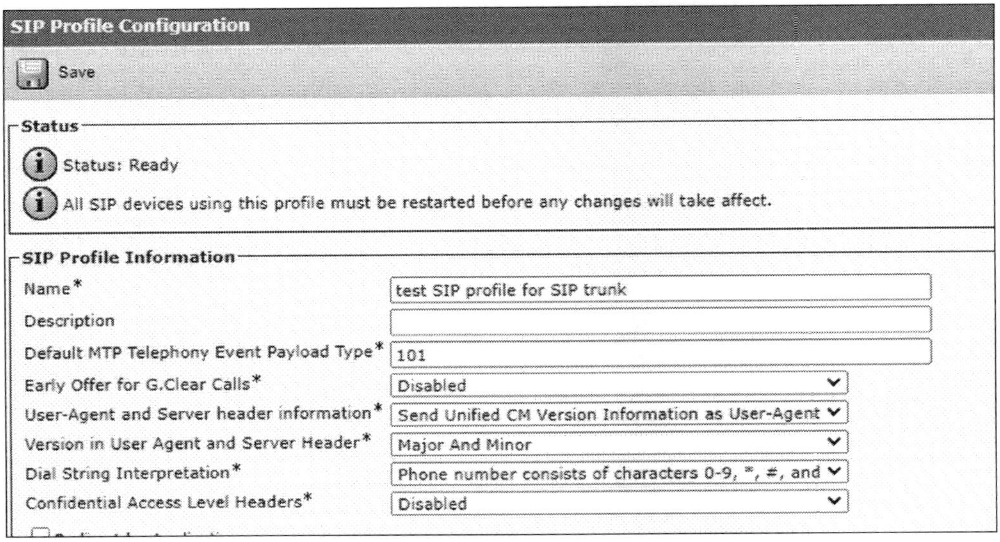

Figure 5.1: *Creating SIP Profile*

In SIP profile, you will see **`SIP OPTIONS Ping`** config as shown in *Figure 5.2*.

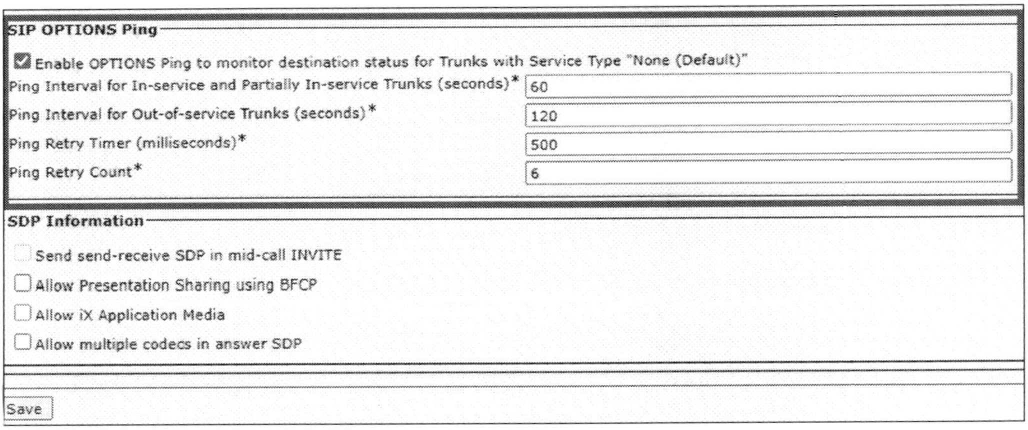

Figure 5.2: *OPTION ping in SIP profile*

2. Creating a SIP Trunk Security Profile:

    a. Go to **`System> Security > SIP Trunk Security Profile`**.

    b. Click **`Add New`**.

    c. If you're implementing SIP signaling encryption with TLS, ensure you select the **`Encrypted`** option under **`Device Security Mode`**, choose **`TLS`** for both incoming and outgoing transport types, and provide the X.509 certificate's subject name. We will discuss the secure SIP trunk in detail in a later chapter.

Or you can keep it as non-secure. Select the **`Transport type`**.

d. To enable digest authentication, check the respective box and set the **`Nonce Validity Timer`**.

e. Complete additional fields as per your requirements and click **`"Save."`**

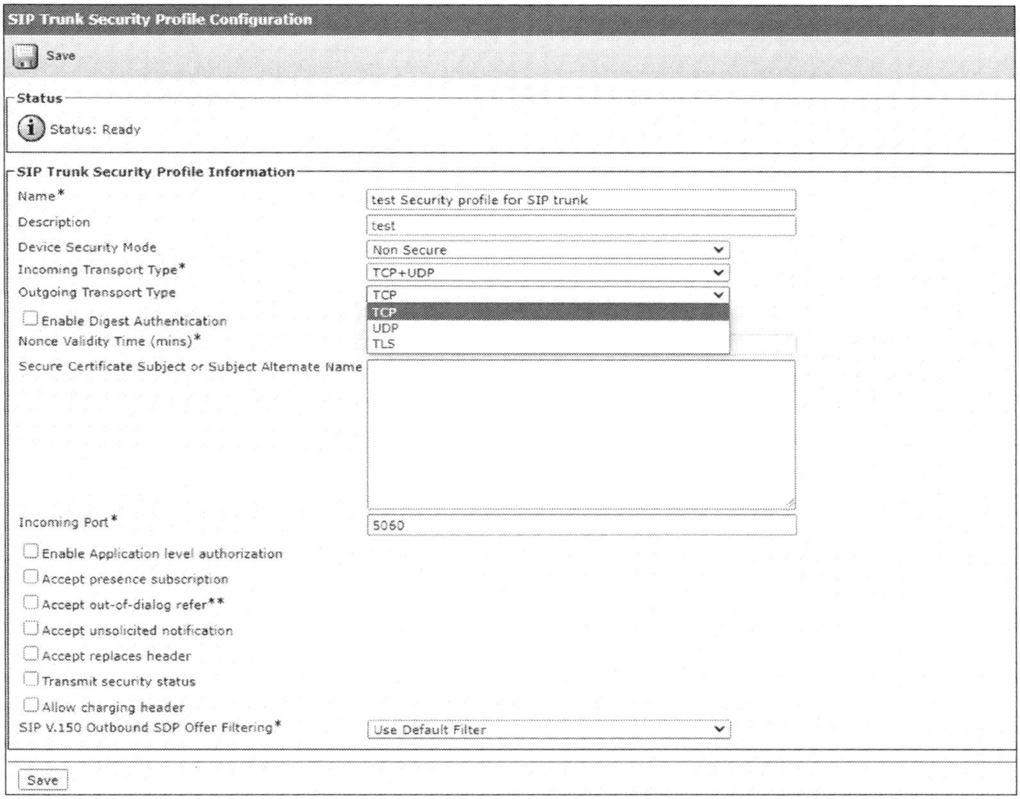

Figure 5.3: *Creating SIP trunk security Profile with different transport type*

3. Creating and configuring a SIP Trunk:

   a. Navigate to **`Device> Trunk`** and click **`Add New`**.

   b. Choose **`SIP Trunk`** from the drop-down menu. Configure the destination address for the SIP trunk, which could be an IPv4/IPv6 address, a fully qualified domain name, or a DNS SRV record.

   c. Assign a SIP Trunk Security Profile and SIP Profile from the drop-down menus.

   d. If necessary, attach a normalization script for the SIP trunk.

   e. Configure any additional settings as required and click **`"Save."`**

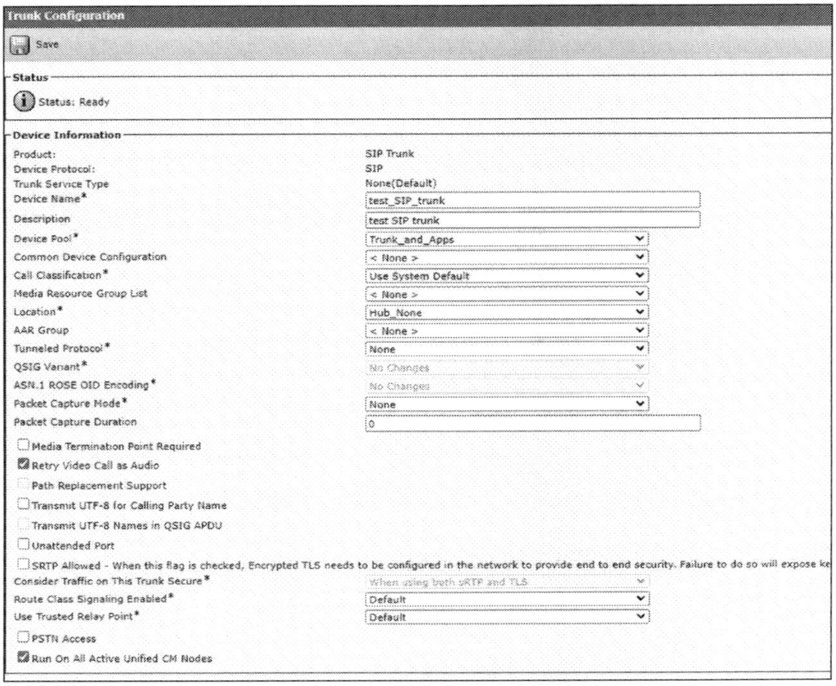

Figure 5.4: *Creating SIP trunk*

When you scroll down, you will see some important parameters as you can see in *Figure 5.5*

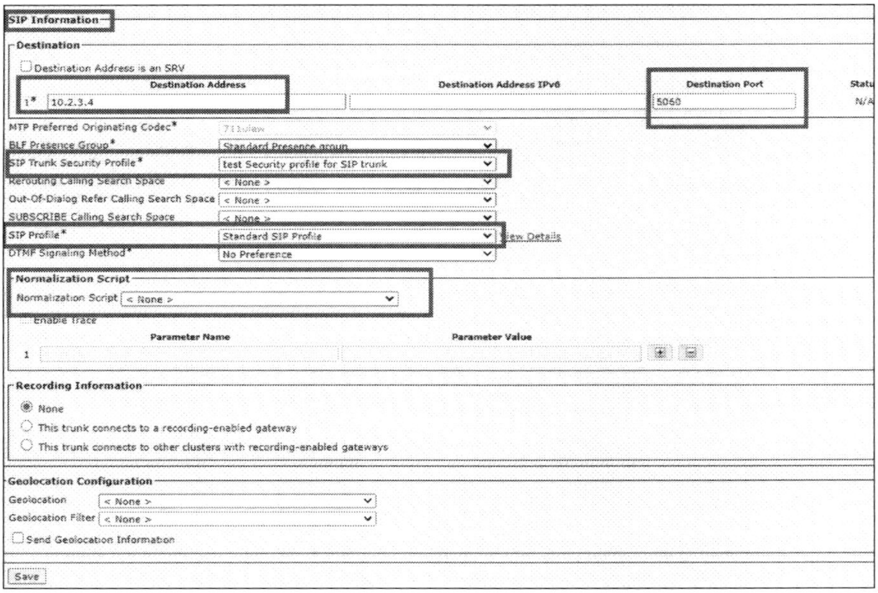

Figure 5.5: *Configuring parameters in SIP trunk*

The SIP trunk connection is a bidirectional communication pathway. If you configure a SIP trunk on one side (for example, in CUCM) but not on the other side (like on a third-party PBX or a SIP service provider), the trunk will not function. When a SIP trunk is established, there's a process of signaling negotiation that occurs between the two ends. They agree on certain parameters for communication, such as codecs, media types, and more. Without a properly configured trunk on the other end, this negotiation cannot happen.

For OPTIONS ping to function effectively, the other end of the SIP trunk (e.g., a gateway or another PBX) must be configured to respond to SIP OPTIONS messages. If the far end doesn't respond to the OPTIONS message or responds with anything other than a SIP 200 OK message, the CUCM might consider the trunk as **down** or **unavailable.**

At its core, a SIP trunk in CUCM doesn't provide functionality by itself. Instead, it serves as a pathway for SIP-based communications between CUCM and external entities, be it another PBX, a gateway, a service provider, or some other SIP-enabled device. When combined with other features like dial plans, conferencing capabilities, integration with edge devices, and other infrastructure components, the SIP trunk's actual value is realized. Think of it like a bridge; on its own, it connects two points, but the traffic (cars, people, etc.) that utilize the bridge and the destinations it connects give it real purpose.

The SIP trunk's role will become more apparent as we dive deeper into dial plans and conferencing topics. It acts as the foundational pathway over which many of these integrations operate.

Voice Gateway Configuration in a CUCM

A voice gateway bridges the digital world of VoIP and the analog or digital signaling of the Public Switched Telephone Network (PSTN) or legacy PBX systems. This integration allows calls to flow seamlessly between IP phones, traditional phones, and external phone lines. We discussed this in *Chapter 2, Understanding Cisco Collaboration Solutions*, along with different gateway protocols which can be used for integration with CUCM.

Let's look at the steps to configure an MGCP gateway in CUCM. We will revisit this topic in another chapter for SIP.

Before configuring the MGCP gateway:

1. Install and properly set up the gateway hardware
2. Vendor Interface Cards (VICs) should be correctly installed on the gateway
3. Use the CLI to configure the base IOS on the gateway

MGCP Gateway Configuration Steps:

1. Configure MGCP on IOS Gateway:
    a. Access your gateway's command line interface
    b. Enter global configuration mode using the configure terminal
    c. Enable MGCP with the command **`mgcp`**
    d. Specify your Unified Communications Manager server using **`mgcp call-agent <UCM_IP_Address> service-type mgcp version 0.1`**
    e. Apply relevant configurations for the interface using MGCP. For instance, for a T1 interface, you might use commands like **`controller T1 0/0/0`** followed by **`ds0-group 1 timeslots 1-24 type fxo-loop-start`**
2. Unified CM Administration Configuration:
    a. Navigate to **`Device> Gateway`** in Cisco Unified CM Administration
    b. Click **`Add New`**
    c. Choose your gateway model from the **`Gateway Type`** drop-down
    d. For protocol, choose **`MGCP`** and click **`Next`**
    e. Specify the domain name or IP address of the MGCP gateway
    f. Under **`Configured Slots, VICs, and Endpoints`**, select the slot and VIC type corresponding to your hardware setup
    g. Save your settings

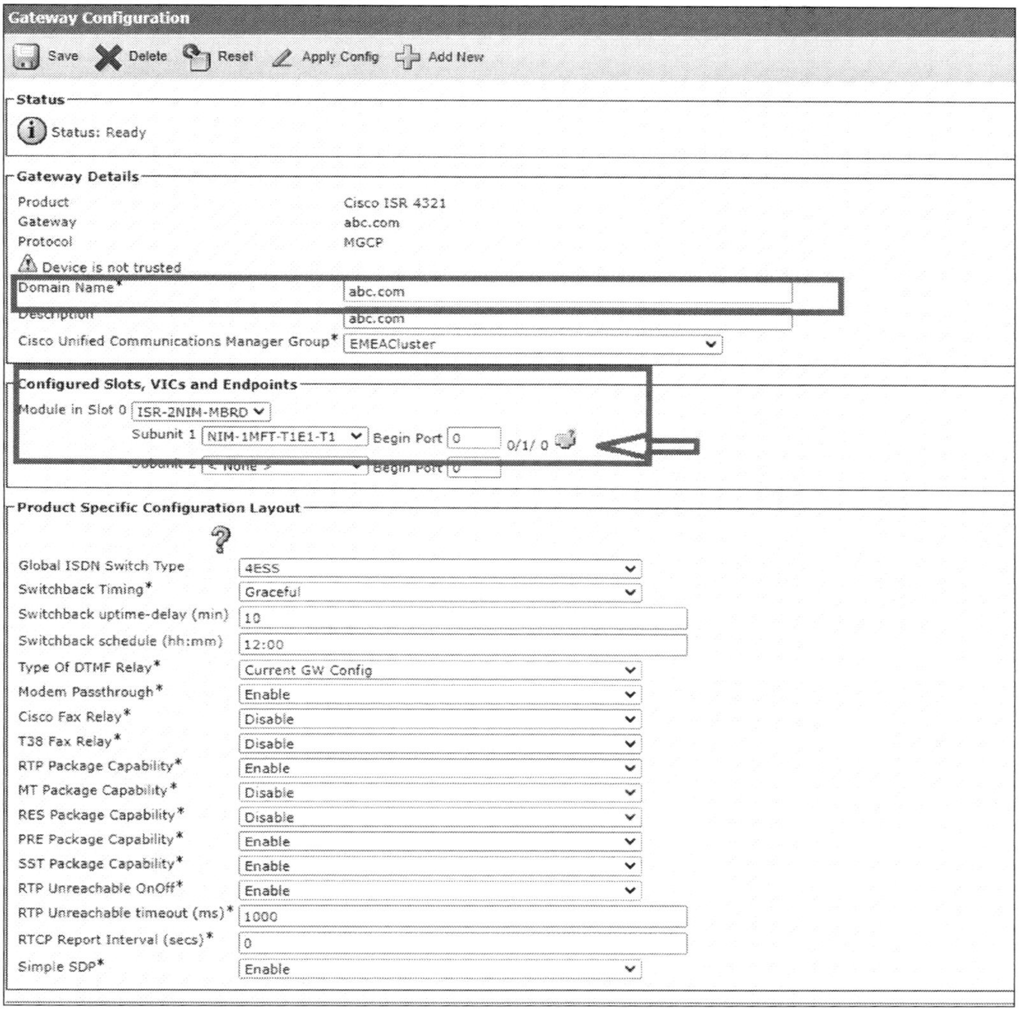

Figure 5.6: *Configuring gateway*

3. Port Configuration:

    a. You'll see available ports based on your chosen VICs within the same gateway configuration page

    b. Configure each port as required. This will often involve specifying port roles (for example, FXS, FXO, T1, E1) and other relevant settings

    c. Remember to save each port configuration

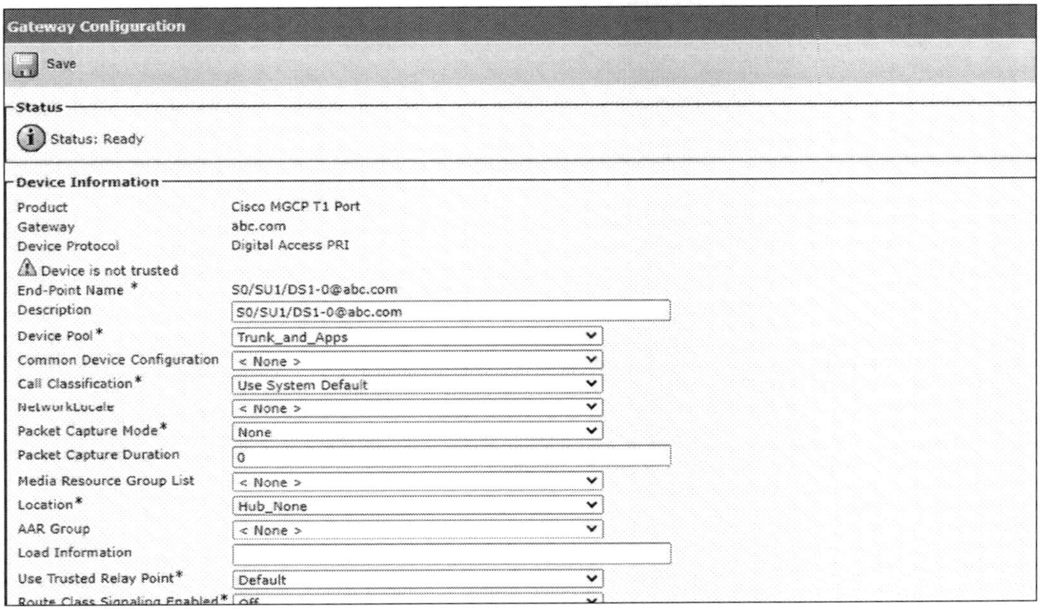

***Figure 5.7**: Configuring PRI in MGCP*

After completing the configuration, reset the gateway from the UCM administration interface to activate the changes.

Navigate to **`Device> Gateway`**, find your gateway, select it, and choose **`Reset`** to finalize your configuration.

Once the configuration is done, verify that MGCP is operational.

On the gateway, use the command **`show mgcp`** to verify the MGCP agent's state. You should see that the gateway is registered with the UCM.

These are just high-level steps, please check Cisco's official document for more detailed configuration steps.

Introduction to Dial Plans

When endpoints register with Cisco Unified Communications Manager (CUCM), their details, such as Directory Number (DN), are stored in the CUCM database. Additionally, there are other elements, not necessarily endpoints, that CUCM recognizes by their DN. A prime example is a Hunt Pilot, which facilitates hunting behavior across a group of directory numbers. With this information, CUCM can easily route calls between internal endpoints as determined by the Class of Control (Partition and CSS). However, for calls outside the CUCM environment, such as an external phone number or a different service, CUCM requires a Dial Plan to guide this external call routing.

Simply put, a dial plan in CUCM is a set of rules that guides how calls are routed. It's crucial for directing calls based on dialed number patterns. Think of it as a set of instructions: "If you see this number pattern, send the call this way."

Key Components:

- **Directory Numbers (DNs)**: Unique identifiers for endpoints in CUCM
- **Partitions and Calling Search Spaces (CSS)**: Define call permissions and visibility
- **Route Patterns**: Direct calls based on number patterns
- **Route Lists and Route Groups**: Organize routes and control path selection
- **Translation Patterns**: Modify dialed numbers for specific routing needs

We must understand few key points and context before planning and configuring dial plan elements. We will explore these before getting in to dial plan config and design.

Number-based vs. Domain-based Routing

In telephony, the routing of calls can primarily be done in two ways: based on numbers or domains.

Traditional Public Switched Telephone Network (PSTN) relies heavily on number-based routing. Specific number patterns are recognized here, and the call is routed accordingly. For instance, a call to **1-800-XXX-XXXX** might be routed to a business's toll-free line in the US.

PSTN operates under a more regulated and controlled environment. Service providers oversee the infrastructure and their operations are typically governed by national or international regulatory bodies. These entities ensure standardization and reliable service and even set pricing guidelines in many regions. This centralized control ensures the PSTN remains interoperable and consistent across vast geographical areas.

On the other hand, internet-based calls, especially those using technologies like SIP (Session Initiation Protocol), can leverage Domain Name System (DNS) for domain-based routing. Here, a call destined to sip:user@company.com would use DNS to resolve company.com to an IP address and then route the call to that address.

E.164 Standard and Direct Inward Dialing (DID) in PSTN

Within PSTN, the E.164 standard plays a pivotal role. E.164 is an ITU-T recommendation defining the international public telecommunication numbering plan used in the PSTN and other data networks. It ensures each Device on the PSTN has a globally unique number.

An E.164 number can have a maximum of 15 digits and is structured as follows:

- **Country Code (CC):** Up to 3 digits
- **National Destination Code (NDC):** Variable length
- **Subscriber Number (SN):** Variable length

This structured approach allows for calls to be efficiently routed within a country and internationally. Knowing the country code, for instance, can immediately determine the destination country of the call.

Opting for a connection from a PSTN provider or an ITSP (Internet Telephony Service Provider) is like purchasing an entry ticket into the telecommunication world. This connection provides you with the capability to make and receive calls. But to functionally make these calls, you need identifiers, essentially phone numbers, to act as your unique addresses.

This is where DID comes into the picture:

- **The Need for DIDs**: Consider a business scenario where you have an IP-based Private Branch Exchange (IP PBX) with 1000 users. Only some users in this vast pool need a direct line from the PSTN. Let's consider, 100 of these users, maybe senior executives or client-facing employees, must be reachable directly from the external world. To address this, you'd acquire 100 unique phone numbers or DIDs from the service provider.
- **How DIDs Work**: These acquired numbers are not tied to traditional analog lines but are instead mapped in your IP PBX system. When an external caller dials one of these DIDs, the service provider routes that call to your PBX. Your PBX then has instructions like, "For calls coming to DID number X, ring IP phone Y." This ensures that specific employees or departments can be reached directly.
- **Benefits of Using DIDs:**
  - **Direct Accessibility**: Allows external callers to bypass general company lines, auto-attendants, or receptionists, providing direct access to the intended recipient
  - **Cost Efficiency**: Businesses save costs with DIDs by only acquiring the number of direct lines they need instead of acquiring individual PSTN lines for every user
  - **Professional Image**: Offers direct lines to specific personnel or departments, projecting a more professional image and enhancing client relationships

- **Making Calls Using DIDs**: When a user associated with a DID makes an outbound call, the receiver sees that specific DID as the caller ID. This way, if the receiver needs to call back, they're directly connected to the original caller.

The remaining 900 users in our example who don't have DIDs can still make outbound calls. Their calls might display a general company number or any designated number as the caller ID. However, for inbound calls, they wouldn't have a direct line; callers would likely go through a main company number or directory.

In essence, DIDs offer a blend of direct accessibility and flexibility, enabling businesses to optimize their telecommunication strategy effectively.

Company-Specific Numbering Plan

Beyond the E.164 numbers, which are crucial for PSTN and global reachability, enterprises often deploy their own internal numbering plans for internal communication purposes. This is particularly useful for large organizations with multiple sites or departments, allowing for streamlined internal call routing and easier management.

For example: A company might define the range 2000-2999 for its headquarters, 3000-3999 for a remote manufacturing site, and 4000-4999 for a sales office in another city. When an employee dials an extension starting with 3XXX, the company's PBX knows to route it to the manufacturing site, regardless of the caller's location.

Difference Between PSTN E.164 Routing and Company-specific Routing

When a number adhering to the E.164 standard is dialed, the PSTN network using the country and area codes can deduce where the call should be directed. It's a standard followed worldwide, ensuring any E.164 compliant number can be reached from anywhere in the world. The entire telecommunication ecosystem abides by this to ensure interoperability.

Company-specific Routing is localized and confined to an organization's communication system. While the numbers might resemble regular phone numbers, they don't necessarily have to adhere to global standards. It's an internal convention that the company's telephony system recognizes and routes accordingly. It's a layer of abstraction on top of the underlying numbers. An internal number, say 2500, might map to a real-world E.164 number behind the scenes, but internal callers wouldn't need to know or dial that entire number.

The beauty of combining both systems is that a company can enjoy the benefits of global reachability with E.164 while maintaining a simplified, logical, and structured internal numbering plan for its employees. This internal structure allows for efficient call handling and management without overwhelming the users with lengthy or complicated number patterns.

Dial Plan Logic and Pattern Matching in CUCM

Before getting into config elements of dial plans, it's important to understand how they work. Dial plans need careful planning and testing before deploying/configuring in a production environment.

In a Cisco Unified Communications Manager (CUCM) environment, when a user dials a number, CUCM uses a set of established methods and principles to route the call correctly. Key among these are the Longest Match Principle (Most specific match) and Class of control considerations involving Partitions and CSS.

Longest Match Principle and Class of control Considerations

CUCM's routing logic begins with the Longest Match Principle, which selects the most specific route pattern that matches the dialed digits. However, before applying this principle, CUCM determines which patterns are accessible to the calling party based on their Calling Search Space (CSS).

We discussed the Class of control in the previous chapter, so we will not cover it in detail here. CSS is a collection of Partitions. Each partition can contain multiple route patterns (or multiple Route patterns can be in the same partition), and the CSS defines which of these Partitions the Device or user can access. When multiple route patterns match the dialed digits within the allowed Partitions, CUCM will prioritize the longest match.

Furthermore, if there are identical longest match patterns in different Partitions, CUCM will consider the order of Partitions within the CSS. It evaluates the Partitions in the order they are listed in the CSS, giving preference to the route pattern found in the first-listed partition that contains a match.

Example: Assume we have the following route patterns configured in two different Partitions that are included in the caller's CSS:

- `Partition A` contains `9[2-9]XXXXXX` for local off-net numbers (7 digits total after the prefix 9)
- `Partition B` contains `9[2-9]XXXXXXX` for long-distance off-net numbers (8 digits total after the prefix 9)

If a user with a CSS including both **Partition A** and **Partition B** dials **93251234**, CUCM will:

1. Assess which Partitions the user's CSS includes
2. From the accessible Partitions, select the longest pattern that matches the dialed number
3. Route the call using **9[2-9]XXXXXX** from **Partition A** because it's the longest specific match for the dialed string within the available Partitions

Pattern Urgency

In addition to the Longest Match Principle, CUCM can also be configured to recognize certain patterns as urgent, which instructs the System to route the call immediately upon recognition of the pattern without waiting for additional digits. This feature is often used for emergency numbers or service codes requiring immediate attention.

Example: 911 is configured as an urgent pattern. When a user dials 911, the call is immediately routed as per the emergency services route pattern without delay.

By aligning the Longest Match Principle with CSS and Partition logic, CUCM administrators can craft a dial plan that is precise in call routing and compliant with the organization's security and access policies.

Absolute vs. Wildcard Matches

An absolute match is when the dialed number corresponds exactly to a predefined route pattern. This one-to-one mapping is straightforward but can be impractical beyond a certain scale due to the sheer volume of patterns needed.

Example: A route pattern **914005551234** would be an absolute match for the dialed number **914005551234**, routing the call directly to that specific destination.

To accommodate a scalable and manageable dial plan, CUCM utilizes wildcards, which serve as placeholders for digit sequences, allowing for pattern generalization.

For example, the wildcards used in CUCM are:

- **X** matches any single digit from 0 through 9
- **!** signifies a variable-length string of digits and can be used to represent a block of numbers

We will revisit this in the config section.

Wildcards must be used judiciously. While they offer the flexibility to cover broad number ranges, they can also introduce ambiguity into the dial plan if not carefully planned. The goal is to find a balance where the number of route patterns is minimized while ensuring each pattern is as intentional and unambiguous as possible.

Example: A route pattern of **9X!** could match any number starting with a **9**, followed by any digit, and then any string of digits afterward. This pattern could route local, long-distance, and international calls if no more specific route patterns are defined. However, this could lead to unintended call routing unless more specific patterns are created for certain call types or destinations.

Creating individual route patterns for every possible dialed number in a large organization is virtually impossible. Instead, combining specific and wildcard patterns can streamline call routing. The design of these patterns must consider the various call types, lengths of numbers, and unique dialing requirements of the organization to avoid routing conflicts.

For instance, starting with broad wildcard patterns and refining more specific ones where necessary can effectively funnel the calls to the correct routes. This approach requires thorough testing and careful consideration of the dial plan's impact on call routing and digit manipulation.

Example:

- A general route pattern for local calls might be **9XXXXXXX**, where **9** is the access code for an outside line and the following **X's** represent the local 7-digit number.
- For long-distance, a pattern could be **91XXXXXXXXXX,** where **1** signifies long-distance within the country, followed by a 10-digit national number.

By using wildcard patterns in tandem with absolute matches, the CUCM dial plan becomes flexible and robust, supporting the needs of a growing and evolving organization without becoming unwieldy or overly complex.

Dial Plan Config and Transformation Mechanisms in CUCM

A robust dial plan is essential for any CUCM deployment. In this section, we will cover the key components and techniques used to design an effective call routing scheme. This includes dial plan elements like route patterns, route lists and route groups. We will also discuss important mechanisms like digit manipulation and transformations that adapt dialed numbers to meet business rules and technical requirements.

Route Pattern

The route pattern instructs the CUCM on how to route calls based on the dialed digits. It is a fundamental component of the CUCM dial plan. It analyzes the dialed digits and determines where to send the call - either directly to a gateway/trunk or to a route list.

When a user dials a number, CUCM checks if it matches any configured route patterns. If a match is found, the route pattern dictates the next hop.

Here's a simple relationship between Route Patterns (RP), Route Lists (RL), Route Groups (RG), and Voice Gateways/SIP Trunks.

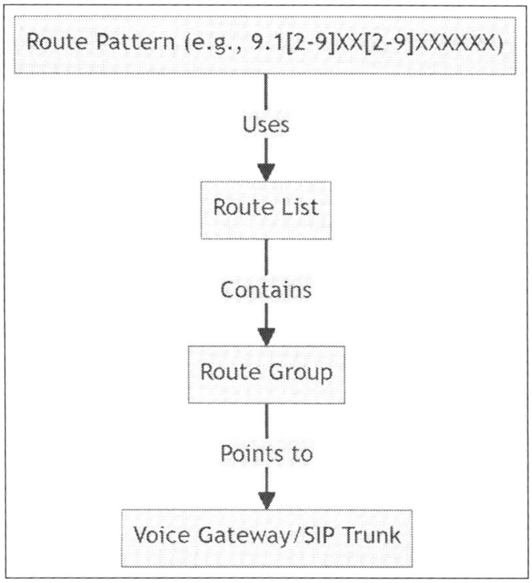

Figure 5.8: *RP-RL-RG-Trunk or Gateway*

The use of wildcards and special characters in route patterns makes the configuration more dynamic and allows a single pattern to match a variety of dialed numbers. This flexibility is beneficial in large organizations with complex dialing requirements.

It defines which route list or gateway a call should be sent to based on the dialed digits.

The table provides an overview of the key wildcards and special characters utilized in configuring route patterns in CUCM. A solid grasp of these special characters is crucial for designing route patterns that provide dynamic call-routing capabilities to match the organization's dialing requirements.

Character	**Description**	**Examples**
X	Matches any single digit from 0 through 9	9XXX matches 9000 to 9999
!	Matches one or more digits in the range 0 through 9	91! matches 910 to a string with twenty-two 9's after the initial 91
?	Matches zero or more occurrences of the preceding digit or wildcard	91X? matches 91 to 919 followed by twenty-one 9's

+	Matches one or more occurrences of the preceding digit or wildcard	91X+ is similar to the 91! example above
[]	Encloses a range of values	813510[012345] matches 8135100 to 8135105
-	Used inside square brackets to denote a range of values	813510[0-5] is the same as the previous example
^	Used inside square brackets to negate a range of values	813510[^0-5] matches 8135106 to 8135109
.	Serves as a delimiter. Separates internal digits from external ones	9.@ uses the initial 9 as an access code
+	Indicates the international escape character + is used as a dialable digit	Used to represent the international prefix
#	Signifies the end of a dialing sequence. It must be the last character	901181910555# denotes an end to the sequence
*	It can serve as an extra digit for special dialed numbers	*411 might connect to internal directory assistance
\+	A plus sign preceded by a backslash that is, \+, indicates that you want to configure the international escape character +	Using \+ means that the international escape character + is used as a dialable digit, not as a wildcard

Table 5.1: *Wildcards and Special Characters in Route Patterns*

Let's look at the steps to configure the Route pattern.

1. Navigate to **`Call Routing`**:
   a. Access the **`Call Manager Administration`** page
   b. Click on **`Call Routing`**, then **`Route/Hunt -> Route Pattern`**
2. Add New Route Pattern:
   a. Click on the **`Add New`** button
   b. Input your desired Route Pattern. For our scenario:

      Example: **`2X0X.XXXX`**
3. Important Parameters:
   a. **Partition**: Defines the logical partitioning of devices. Configure to restrict/allow calling between devices
   b. **Gateway/Route List**: Select the desired RL to process this pattern

c. **Urgent Priority**: Routes the pattern before the user finishes dialing

d. **Provide Outside Dial Tone**: Gives dial tone when users press an access code (like 9 for external calls)

e. **Discard Digits**: Choose from options such as `PreDot` to remove digits before the dot in the pattern. Useful to remove access codes

f. **Called Party Transformations**:

   i. **Prefix Digits**: Add specific digits before the called number

   ii. **Calling Party Transform Mask**: Alter the calling party number before routing

g. **OnNet/OffNet**: Designate the pattern as `OnNet` for internal calls or `OffNet` for external/PSTN calls

h. **Block Pattern**: Choose whether to allow or block this pattern

i. **Route Option**: Define how the call is routed

4. **Digit Manipulation**:

   a. **Calling Party Transformations**: Specify a calling Party Transform mask for calling party transformations

   b. **Called Party Transformations**: Specify a called Party Transform mask for called party transformations

   c. Transformation Examples:

      i. If you need a dialed number like `20020102` to be transformed to `020020102` before routing, you can utilize digit prefixing to add the 0 at the start

      ii. To change the caller ID presentation, use the calling party transformation mask

5. **Save and Apply**:

   a. After setting the desired configurations, click on the `Save` button. Ensure you also apply and reset affected devices/services for changes to take effect

Route Lists and Route Groups

A Route List determines the order of preference in which calls are routed to external destinations. These destinations can be the Public Switched Telephone Network (PSTN), a remote branch, or another organization.

The primary reason for using route lists is to provide a structured failover mechanism. If one route fails, the call can be sent via an alternate route.

- Attaches route list to multiple route patterns
- Serves as a prioritized list of route groups, offering alternatives if one route is unavailable
- Allows specific digit manipulation for each route group, useful for adapting to various gateway or trunk requirements
- Device-level transformations override route-pattern-level transformations

A Route Pattern (RP) can point directly to a trunk or gateway. However, this lacks flexibility. By using a RL, you can:

- **Prioritize Multiple Paths**: Define primary, secondary, tertiary paths, etc., for call routing based on availability and preference.
- **Digit Manipulation**: Customize how numbers are manipulated differently based on the chosen path.

Let's look at the steps to configure the Route list.

1. Navigate to Route Lists:
   a. Access the `Call Manager Administration` page
   b. Click on `Call Routing`, then `Route/Hunt -> Route List`
2. Add New Route List:
   a. Click on the `Add New` button
   b. Provide a descriptive name, for instance, `"EMEA_RL."`
   c. **CM Group**: If there's a specific CM group you want to associate the RL with, designate it here
3. Important Parameters:
   a. **Run On All Active Unified CM Nodes**: Offers redundancy by enabling the Route List to operate on multiple nodes
   b. **Route List Enabled**: Ensures the Route List is active
   c. **Route Groups**: Here's where you add RGs to the RL in your preferred sequence. The order is important as RGs will process calls based on this list
4. Associated Route Patterns:
   a. Link the RL to specific Route Patterns (RPs) to ensure calls matching those patterns are processed by this RL

5. Save and Apply:

   a. Click on **Save** after making configurations. Apply and reset any affected devices or services to ensure the changes are made

A Route Group directs calls to specific devices or groups of devices, providing the bridge between a logical call route and the physical Device(s) that handle the call.

It determines where a call can be sent, specifically to which Device or set of devices, like gateways or trunks.

- Points directly to physical or logical devices like gateways or trunks
- Offers different distribution algorithms like top-down or circular
- Supports various devices like MGCP gateways, SIP trunks, H.323 trunks, and more

In this diagram, we're expanding on the idea that a Route List can contain multiple Route Groups, and each Route Group can point to multiple Voice Gateways or SIP Trunks.

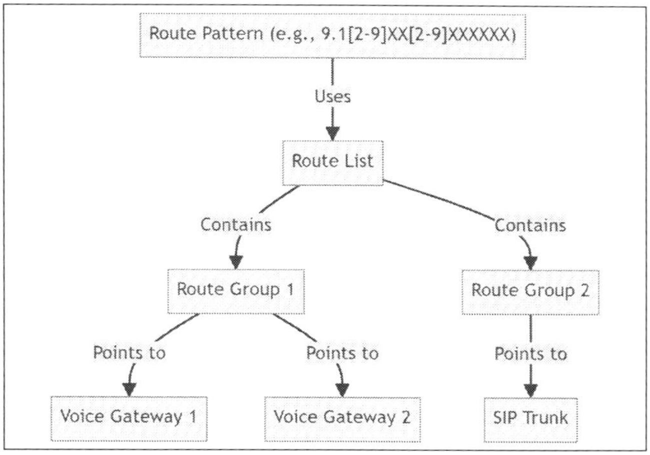

***Figure 5.9**: RP-RL-RG-Trunk or Gateway detailed diagram*

Let's look at the steps to configure the Route group.

1. Navigate to Route Groups:

   a. Access the **Call Manager Administration** page

   b. Click on **Call Routing**, then **Route/Hunt -> Route Group**

2. Add New Route Group:

   a. Click on the **Add New** button

   b. Provide a descriptive name, for example, **AP_RG**

3. Important Parameters:
    a. **Distribution Algorithm**: Defines how calls will be distributed among devices (trunks/ gateways) in the RG. Options typically include:
    b. **Top Down**: Calls are routed to the first available Device, moving to the next if the first is unavailable
    c. **Circular**: Calls are distributed evenly across all devices in the RG, with each new call going to the next Device in line
    d. **Selected Devices**: Add gateways, SIP trunks, or other routing devices to the RG. The order is essential as it determines call distribution based on the algorithm selected
4. Associated Route Lists:
    a. Assign this RG to one or multiple Route Lists, determining which RLs will process calls using this RG
5. Save and Apply:
    a. After setting configurations, click **`"Save."`** Also, ensure you apply and reset any affected devices/services for the changes to take effect

Local Route Group

The Local Route Group in Cisco Unified Communications Manager (CUCM) optimizes call routing in multi-site deployments by dynamically selecting the egress gateway based on the originating Device's location. Traditional setups require multiple route groups for each site's gateway, but with the Local Route Group, the call is directed through the gateway corresponding to the caller's location.

Here's how it works:

- Each Device Pool is associated with a specific Local Route Group, which points to the actual gateway for that location.
    - The Local Route Group is a setting within the Device Pool and not a separate entity
    - It leverages existing route groups by tying a Device Pool to a particular Local Route Group, enabling dynamic gateway selection based on the Device's location
- A single route pattern can point to a route list containing the Standard Local Route Group This group dynamically determines the right Local Route Group based on the calling device's Device Pool

Let's understand this with a diagram. In this representation:

1. The endpoint (phone) initiates a dial
2. The dialed pattern matches a Route Pattern (RP), which then uses a Route List (RL)
3. The RL first checks the Local Route Group (LRG)
4. The behavior of the LRG is determined by the Device Pool (DP) configuration of the calling device
5. The DP points to a specific Route Group via the LRG setting
6. If the LRG doesn't determine the route, or under other conditions, the RL can use a Standard Route Group
7. Both the Route Group defined by LRG and the Standard Route Group point to specific gateways or trunks

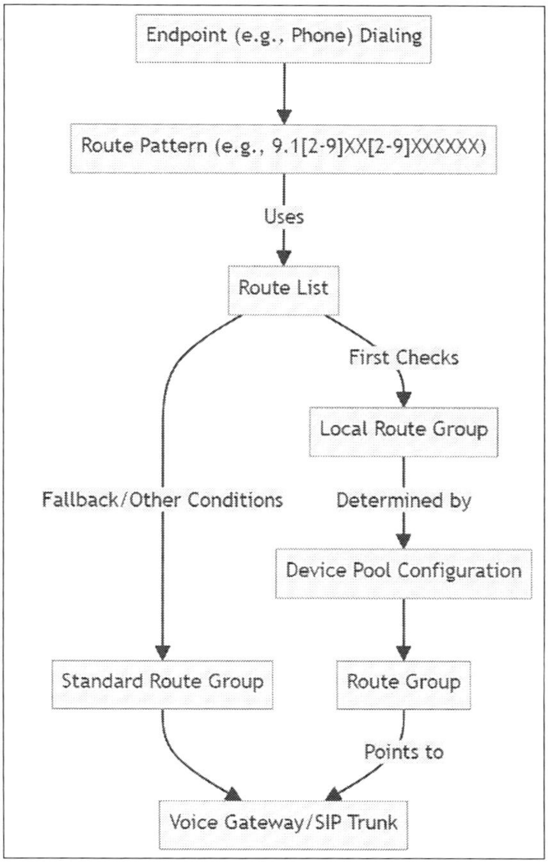

Figure 5.10: *Local Route group*

Number Transformation and Digit Manipulation in CUCM

CUCM provides tools for altering the calling and called numbers, which is critical for developing an efficient dial plan. These tools enable accurate call routing and number presentation, both internally and externally. Let's understand briefly about all the available options.

1. **External Phone Number Mask**: Set on the Directory Number configuration page, it dictates how an internal number appears to external callers. It is essential in Direct Inward Dial (DID) scenarios to present internal extensions in a specific format to the outside world.

2. **Transformation Patterns**: Transformation patterns in CUCM are designed to manipulate dialed digits in incoming or outgoing calls. These patterns are crucial when there is a need to alter the calling or called number before it reaches the phone or the Public Switched Telephone Network (PSTN).

    a. **Key Functions**:

        i. **Discarding Digits**: Remove unnecessary digits from a dialed number

        ii. **Prefixing Digits**: Add specific digits to a dialed number

        iii. **Calling Party Transformation Mask**: Modifies the appearance of the calling party's number

        iv. **Control Calling Party Number Presentation**: Manages how the calling number is displayed to the recipient

    b. **Types of Transformation Patterns**:

        i. **Calling Party Transformation Patterns**: Transform the calling number, such as replacing a caller's extension with the office's main number when calling the PSTN

        ii. **Called Party Transformation Patterns**: Transform the called number, like retaining only the last five digits of a dialed ten-digit number

    c. **Transformation CSS (Calling Search Space)**: It is crucial for associating specific calling or called party transformation patterns with various entities like devices, lines, SIP trunks, or gateways. It controls transformation patterns applicable in a given context, ensuring that the correct number manipulation is applied based on the originating or destination point of the call.

3. **Digit Manipulation at RP/RL/RG/GW Level**: Incorporated within route patterns, route lists, directory numbers, and at various system levels. Utilized for tasks like appending or stripping digits, prefixing numbers, and more.
   a. In Route Patterns (RP), it's used for broad, network-wide number changes
   b. Route Lists (RL) offer centralized digit manipulation across multiple Route Groups
   c. Route Groups (RG) provide location-specific digit adjustments
   d. Gateways (GW) enable final, gateway-specific number transformations
4. **Translation Pattern**: It modifies the calling or called number before making the call routing decision. Useful for adapting dialed numbers without altering the call's routing path, crucial for meeting diverse organizational dialing rules

   Applicable for incoming and outgoing calls, they adapt number formats to fit organizational standards

Let's understand in detail about Digit manipulation and translation patterns in CUCM.

Digit Manipulation at RP/RL/RG/GW Level

In CUCM, digit manipulation is integral to call routing, applied at different levels: Route Patterns (RP), Route Lists (RL), Route Groups (RG), and Gateways (GW). The order of preference in which digit manipulation occurs is crucial for creating an effective dial plan.

Order of Preference:

- **Route Pattern (RP)**: The starting point for digit manipulation, applied based on matched dialed number patterns
- **Route List (RL)**: Centralizing digit manipulation for all calls routed through the list
- **Route Group (RG)**: Customized for specific gateway or trunk requirements when a particular Route Group is selected
- **Gateway (GW):** The final stage of digit manipulation, specific to the physical or virtual gateway used for outbound calls

Let's understand these with examples:

1. **Route Pattern (RP) Level**:
   a. **Scenario**: Employees dial 9 to access an outside line, followed by the full 10-digit number (`9-212-555-1234`)

   b. **Context**: At the RP level, digit manipulation like predot removal can consistently strip unnecessary leading digits across the network
   c. **Impact**: Configuring the RP to discard the leading 9 before routing ensures only the 10-digit number is passed on. This avoids failed or misrouted calls due to extraneous leading digits

   In this case, the Route Pattern applies predot removal to strip access code 9 from all outbound calls. This simplifies the dial plan and eliminates dependence on users dialing external calls uniformly.
   Prepending area codes, stripping access codes, etc. are commonly utilized at the RP level for consistent network-wide digit manipulation needs. The broad scope of Route Patterns makes them ideal for organization-wide dialing rules.

2. **Route List (RL) Level**:
   a. **Scenario**: Inter-office calls using a 5-digit plan require conversion to full international numbers
   b. **Context**: RL level manipulation is vital for uniform digit manipulation across multiple Route Groups
   c. **Impact**: Configuring digit manipulation here ensures that all calls, regardless of the Route Group, are uniformly transformed, facilitating consistent internal-to-external number conversion
3. **Route Group (RG) Level**:
   a. **Scenario**: Different international call prefixes are needed for offices in different locations
   b. **Context**: RG level manipulation is tailored to the specific Route Group, ideal for location-specific dialing requirements
   c. **Impact**: This level enables precise manipulation, like adding "01144" for New York to London calls and "001" for London to New York, adhering to regional dialing practices
4. **Gateway (GW) Level**:
   a. **Scenario**: Stripping the local country code for outbound international calls through a specific gateway
   b. **Context**: GW level manipulation is the final adjustment stage, tailored to the gateway's requirements or external network standards
   c. **Impact**: This adjustment, such as removing the country code (+44) for outbound international calls, is crucial for correct routing in external networks

Digit manipulation often involves functions like prefixing, stripping, prepending, and appending digits to meet routing requirements.

Selective use of digit manipulation at different levels in CUCM provides granular control and flexibility in call routing. This structured approach ensures that calls are routed efficiently and accurately, aligning with the specific requirements of the network's call-routing strategy.

Translation Pattern in CUCM

A translation pattern in CUCM is a specific type of dial plan entity that allows the calling and called numbers to be modified as they pass through the CUCM. Unlike a standard route pattern that defines how calls are routed, a translation pattern is primarily concerned with number modification.

Key Points:

- Translation patterns do not route calls; instead, they change the dialed digits to a new pattern, which can then be routed by subsequent entities in the dial plan
- They can be used for various purposes, such as simplifying dial plans, accommodating legacy dialing habits, transforming numbers for site-specific requirements, and more
- These patterns can be set up with specific partitions and calling search spaces, ensuring they're applied only in specific scenarios or for particular devices

Let's understand the use of the translation pattern by example.

1. Employees at ABC's US offices frequently make local calls within their area but are often required to dial the area code as required for the 10-digit dialing plan. Create a translation pattern for 7-digit local numbers that automatically prepends the correct area code before the call hits the route pattern. For example, dialing **5551234** translates to **4155551234**, ensuring compliance with the 10-digit dialing plan without complicating the route pattern.
2. ABC is transitioning to a new dial plan with a different numbering scheme but wants to minimize disruption during the transition period.
   Translation patterns can temporarily support both the old and new dialing schemes, translating numbers from the old scheme to the equivalent numbers in the new scheme.

TEHO and LBR (Tail End Hop Off and Location-based Routing) Overview

TEHO is a form of Least Cost Routing (LCR) used to reduce call costs in multi-site Cisco environments. It routes calls through gateways near the destination number to minimize long-distance charges. TEHO is about routing phone calls wisely to save money.

The key steps are:

- Configuring dial patterns to identify calls intended for different regions
- Optimizing gateway and route selection based on call destination
- Choosing the gateway geographically nearest to the destination exchange to minimize distance

TEHO can save money on international calls, but it is only good if your network's bandwidth and QoS support it. If international calls are infrequent, the complexity of TEHO might not be worth it.

LBR focuses on routing calls based on the caller's geographic location, mainly to comply with local telecommunication laws and regulations.

In regions with strict telecom laws, LBR is essential to avoid legal issues, even if it means higher costs.

Configuration Steps for LBR in CUCM:

1. Define and assign geolocations in CUCM to represent physical areas
    a. Create a geolocation filter to specify which fields to use for policy decisions
2. Enable geolocation in the Enterprise Parameters and set the default policy action
3. Assign geolocations to device pools, which are assigned to devices and endpoints
4. Create logical partition policies using geolocation field values in CUCM. **`Call routing> Geolocation Policy > Logical Partition Policy`**
5. Configure the policy relationships between geolocations to allow or deny calls in CUCM.
    a. Go to **`Call Routing > Geolocation Policy > Logical Partition Policy Relationship`**
    b. Add source and destination policies and specify **`Allow`** or **`Deny`**
    E.g., allow **`"Local"`** to **`"Local"`** but deny **`"Local"`** to **`"National."`**
6. Enable location conveyance on SIP trunks and Intercluster Trunks (ICT) in CUCM.
    a. Go to **`Device> Trunk`**
    b. Edit trunk configurations

c. Check the Send Geolocation Information checkbox

d. This shares location in calls between clusters

Let's discuss when to use what (TEHO, LBR or other form of routing) and if we need to choose one for the entire deployment.

- Usually, calls can go through the user's local gateway, matched by Route Patterns and Local Route Groups in CUCM. This is straightforward and usually complies with most regional laws, but it may need to be more cost-effective for international calls.
- For international calls, consider routing them through a SIP trunk to exit from a local gateway in the destination country (TEHO). This can reduce costs significantly but is complex and requires good bandwidth management. Additionally, TEHO isn't legal in some countries.
- In regions where TEHO isn't viable, stick to local routing and implement Location-Based Routing (LBR) to adhere to local telecom regulations. LBR ensures compliance but might increase international call costs.

This is a general suggestion, please consider researching more for specific needs.

Globalized Dial Plan

Globalized call routing or a globalized dial plan is a paradigm shift from traditional dial plans in CUCM. It involves normalizing all numbers in the System to a single standard format, typically the +E.164 format, and then using transformations to adapt the numbers for presentation and routing based on the situation.

- **Uniformity and Consistency**: By using a standardized format, you avoid the complexities that arise from having various formats, which may differ by region, office, or function
- **Scalability**: As your organization grows or integrates with other systems or networks, having a standardized format ensures that new additions or integrations are smoother and less complex
- **Interoperability**: When using a globalized dial plan, it's easier to interoperate with other systems, such as SIP trunks or third-party PBXs

Let's understand the use case with a scenario.

ABC acquires a company, XYZ, in the EMEA region with its existing dial plan and infrastructure. ABC wants to integrate XYZ's infrastructure with minimal disruption but finds that XYZ's dial plan conflicts with ABC's existing EMEA dial plan.

Solution with Globalized Dial Plan:

1. **Normalization**: Implement translation patterns to normalize XYZ's dialed

numbers to the +E.164 format. ABC already has a globalized dial plan, so its numbers are already in this format

2. **Avoiding Conflicts**: Any potential conflicts (like overlapping extension ranges) between ABC and XYZ are resolved globally. Focusing on the global +E.164 numbers allows specific site or region-level conflicts to be more easily managed with localized transformations

3. **Unified Call Routing**: All call routing decisions, whether they are for ABC or XYZ numbers, are based on the +E.164 format. This ensures seamless call routing across both entities

4. **Egress Transformation**: Depending on the final destination, the +E.164 number will be transformed into the appropriate local format, ensuring that calls to the PSTN and between ABC and XYZ always use the correct local conventions

Outcome: The merger's integration process becomes smoother as the dial plans are managed globally. Both ABC and XYZ employees experience seamless calling, with the backend globalized dial plan handling all complexities.

Let's break down the configuration logic.

- **Ingress Digit Manipulation**: When a call enters the CUCM environment, the dialed number is immediately transformed into the globalized format (usually +E.164). This can be done using translation patterns, transformation patterns, or SIP normalization scripts.
- **Unified Call Routing**: All call routing decisions are based on this globalized format. This means that route patterns, dial plan logic, and configuration are done once and work globally.
- **Egress Digit Manipulation**: When the call is leaving the CUCM environment, the globalized number is then transformed into a format that the destination (whether it's an endpoint, gateway, trunk, or another system) understands and expects. This can be done using transformation patterns at the route list or route group level or using gateway or trunk settings.

This diagram may help you visualize the concept easily.

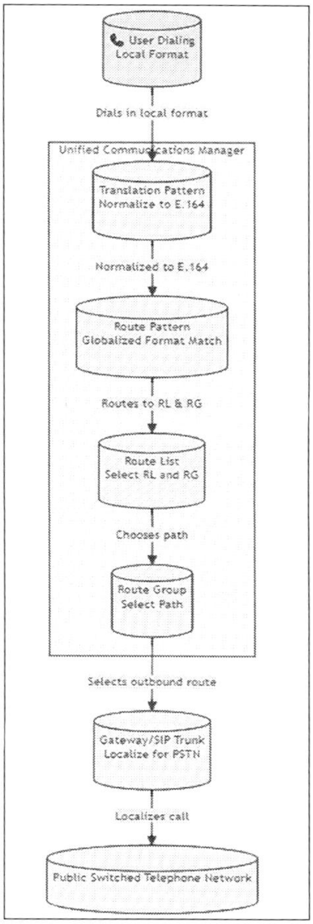

***Figure* 5.11**: *Globalized dial plan*

Remember, while a globalized dial plan simplifies and standardizes call routing in CUCM, the initial transition can be complex. Proper planning, testing, and documentation are essential for a successful implementation.

Let's understand this with another diagram using example and explanation.

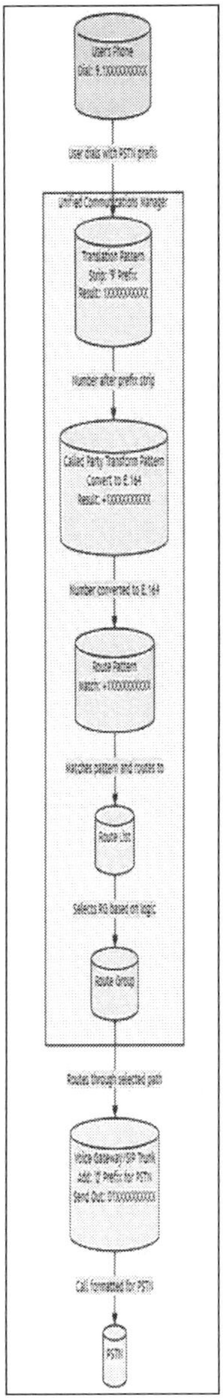

***Figure* 5.12**: *Globalized dial plan with example*

1. **User's Phone Dialing**: The user starts a call by dialing a number with a specific pattern, here represented as **`9.1XXXXXXXXXX`**. The 9 is a commonly used dial-out prefix in enterprise environments, signaling an external call.
2. **Translation Pattern Processing**: The Translation Pattern is hit first as per the Calling Search Space (CSS) configuration on the user's phone. The CSS dictates

which pattern the dialed string can match, and the Translation Pattern is configured to recognize the initial 9 and strip it, leaving `1XXXXXXXXXX.`

3. **E.164 Number Normalization**: The Called Party Transform Pattern is applied next. It's often placed on the Device or line level and set to execute after the Translation Pattern to normalize numbers to a standard format before hitting the routing logic. Here, it adds the `+1` to conform to the E.164 international standard, resulting in `+1XXXXXXXXXX.`
4. **Route Pattern Matching**: The globalized number in E.164 format is then matched against a Route Pattern that identifies the correct Route List (RL) for the call. The Route Pattern essentially links the dialed E.164 number to a defined path within the UCM.
5. **Route List and Route Group Selection**: The Route List contains a list of Route Groups (RG) and provides a prioritized list of routes. Based on the configured logic within the RL, a Route Group is selected to route the call.
6. **Outbound Routing via Voice Gateway/SIP Trunk**: The call is routed through the selected Route Group to a Voice Gateway or SIP Trunk. Before leaving the UCM, the number is formatted to meet the PSTN requirements. In this scenario, a 0 prefix is added to the call, converting the number to `01XXXXXXXXXX,` which is a format often required by PSTN providers in certain countries.
7. **Call Sent Out to PSTN**: The call, now in the correct format for the PSTN provider, is sent out via the Voice Gateway or SIP Trunk into the public switched telephone network (PSTN), where it will be routed to its final destination.

Throughout this process, the UCM handles the complex transformations of the dialed number, ensuring the user can dial in a familiar format. At the same time, the System adapts the number for proper routing and completion on the PSTN. This example demonstrates how a globalized dial plan can effectively manage call routing and number transformation within an enterprise telephony environment.

Time-of-Day Routing Overview

Time-of-Day Routing in CUCM lets you route calls differently based on the time or day. It adjusts call handling dynamically, ensuring callers get directed to the right place, whether it's during business hours, off-hours, or holidays.

- **After-Hours Support**: If a client calls the Support Department of ABC Corp after regular business hours, the call can be routed to an off-hours support team.
- **Holiday Routing**: During public holidays when ABC Corp is closed, incoming calls can be directed to a special holiday greeting and then to voicemail.

- **Lunch Hour Handling**: Between 12 PM and 1 PM, when many employees might be on lunch break, calls could be routed differently to ensure they're still answered.

Let's look at the config steps.

1. **Define Time Periods:**
   a. In CUCM, go to `Call Routing > Class of Control > Time Period`.
   b. Define specific blocks of time, like Business Hours, which might be set from 9:00 AM to 5:00 PM.
2. **Create Time Schedules:**
   a. Navigate to `Call routing> Class of Control > Time Schedule.`
   b. Combine one or more Time Periods into a Time Schedule. For example, you can create a Weekday Schedule using the Business Hours period from Monday to Friday.
3. **Assign Time Schedules to Partitions:**
   a. Go to `Call Routing > Class of Control > Partition`.
   b. When you create or modify a partition, there will be an option to associate a Time Schedule with it. This makes the partition active only during the specified times.
4. **Create Route Patterns:**
   a. Navigate to `Call Routing > Route/Hunt > Route Pattern.`
   b. Set up your primary route patterns and associate them with the partition on which you set the time schedule. This will be the route for the main active times.
5. **Handle Off-Hours Calls:**
   a. Create additional route patterns to manage calls outside the main active times. This can be in a partition without time restrictions or another partition with a different time schedule.
   b. The routing for these patterns can direct calls to voicemail, a different destination, or an after-hours service.
6. **Ensure Proper Ordering in Calling Search Spaces (CSS):**
   a. `Go to System> Class of Control > Calling Search Space`.
   b. The order of partitions in a CSS matters. Calls will be processed based on the order of partitions listed in the CSS. Ensure your main "active time"

partition is listed before the off-hours or unrestricted partitions, so during active times, the call will match the intended pattern first.

In essence, during active times, the System will first use route patterns in the time-restricted partition because of its position in the CSS. Suppose the time schedule for that partition is not currently active. In that case, it becomes invisible, and the call processing will move on to the next available partition and its associated route patterns.

Automated Alternate Routing (AAR) Overview

Automated Alternate Routing (AAR) is a feature in Unified CM designed to provide an alternate call path when the primary path between two devices within the same cluster lacks sufficient bandwidth. This determination is based on the location mechanism for call admission control.

Key Aspects of AAR:

1. **Usage Scenario**: AAR is primarily designed for deployments with multiple sites interconnected via WAN. For example, if a phone at Branch A tries to call a phone at Branch B, and the WAN link between them doesn't have enough bandwidth, AAR can re-route the call via the PSTN. Thus, the call starts as IP-based, shifts to TDM-based over the PSTN, and returns to IP-based at the destination.
2. **User Experience**: AAR can be set up to be transparent, allowing users to dial the on-net directory number without requiring any extra input, even if the call is re-routed through another network like the PSTN.
3. **Determining the PSTN Number**: AAR determines the alternate number using the dialed digits and the AAR Destination Mask of the called party. If the AAR Destination Mask isn't set, the External Phone Number Mask is used. This combination should produce a fully qualified number for routing through the alternate network. For instance, if a San Francisco phone (DN = 2345) dials an on-net DN in New York (1234), and the call is denied due to bandwidth, AAR uses the New York phone's AAR Destination Mask to produce a number routable via the PSTN.
4. **E.164 Numbering**: It's ideal for the AAR destination mask to be a fully qualified E.164 number. This makes the overall configuration of AAR simpler. In essence, the number contains all the necessary details to derive a PSTN-routable number regardless of the calling phone's location.
5. **Prefixing Access Codes**: Certain prefixes might be required for proper routing depending on the AAR destination. DNs in AAR are grouped, and prefix digits can be configured for each AAR group pair, even for calls within the same AAR group.

6. **Dial Plan and Routing**: AAR calls should go through a gateway at the same location as the calling phone, sending the completed dial string through the originating site's dial plan. Choose the correct AAR calling search space in the Unified CM Administration to achieve this. This configuration can be simplified by using a local route group in conjunction with a fully qualified E.164 address as the AAR destination.

URI Dialing in Cisco Unified Communications Manager (CUCM)

URI dialing and traditional numeric dialing have distinct characteristics and use cases within a telephony environment like Cisco Unified Communications Manager (CUCM). Let's discuss how they differ and how CUCM decides which routing method to use.

Differences Between Number and URI Dialing

Number Dialing:

- **Format**: Typically numeric, follows a structured pattern (e.g., E.164).
- **Routing**: Based on dialed digits that match route patterns, translation patterns, and possibly partition and calling search space (CSS) configurations.
- **Use Case**: Predominantly used for PSTN and internal telephony where a structured numbering plan is in place.
- **Integration**: Number dialing is well-integrated with traditional telephony systems and endpoints.

URI Dialing:

- **Format**: Alphanumeric, similar to an email address (e.g., alice@abc.com).
- **Routing**: Based on the domain part of the URI, which can be routed via SIP route patterns or domain-based routing rules.
- **Use Case**: Suited for IP-based communications, often used for calls over the internet, such as B2B calls, where the domain can be an internet domain.
- **Integration**: URI dialing is natively supported on IP-based systems and essential for integrating various internet communication services.

CUCM Routing Decisions: Number vs. Domain

CUCM decides whether to route a call based on the dialed digits or the domain part of a URI by analyzing the format of the dial string. If a user dials a numeric string, CUCM treats it as a traditional phone number and follows the number-based route patterns. If a user dials a string that contains non-numeric characters, particularly with an @

symbol, CUCM interprets it as a URI and will attempt to route it based on the domain portion of the URI.

However, it's essential to note that when a call is set up in a SIP environment, even if the routing decision is made using the numeric part (because the user dialed digits), the SIP INVITE that CUCM sends out will still contain a domain portion in the Request-URI. This is because SIP inherently works with URIs, so even when numeric routing is used, the SIP messages must still comply with SIP standards, including specifying a domain. The domain added by CUCM is typically the domain of the next SIP proxy or the destination domain.

This approach allows for a hybrid system where calls within an enterprise or to the PSTN can be handled using traditional numeric routing, while calls to other entities over the internet, like B2B calls, can utilize URI-based routing. The latter can provide more direct routing in IP-based networks, often resulting in better call quality and lower costs, as the calls can bypass the PSTN.

To manage this effectively in CUCM:

- **SIP Trunk Configuration**: Ensure SIP trunks are configured to handle the appropriate dialing format—number or URI—and that the domain is correctly appended to outgoing SIP messages when necessary.
- **Pattern Configuration**: Set up dialing patterns that accommodate both numeric and URI formats. For example, you might have a catch-all SIP route pattern for URIs (.*@abc.com) to route any call destined for abc.com domain.
- **Transformations**: Use transformation patterns to manipulate the calling or called party numbers for presentation purposes or compliance with the destination system's expected format.

By understanding these differences and how CUCM makes routing decisions, administrators can configure the System to handle both traditional and modern forms of communication efficiently, ensuring that users can make calls in whatever format they find most convenient.

Similar to Route pattern, you can create a SIP route pattern and associate it to a SIP trunk or RL. Here are the steps.

- Creating SIP Route Patterns for URI Dialing:
    1. Open **`Call Routing > SIP Route Pattern`**
    2. Click **`Add New`** to create a new pattern
    3. Enter the SIP route pattern that matches the format of the URIs you're using
    4. Assign a Partition and a SIP Trunk/Route List for call routing

Scenario: Designing a Global Dial Plan for Company ABC with Multiple CUCM Clusters

As your company expands globally, a structured dial plan is crucial for seamless communication. Let's walk through how to design a flexible plan that grows with you.

Imagine you work for ABC, a global company with offices worldwide. Thousands of employees are spread across different sites, but everyone needs to collaborate.

- **Company**: ABC
- **Offices**: 20 offices across Asia-Pacific (AP), Europe, Middle East, and Africa (EMEA), and the United States (US)
- **Employee Distribution**: Each branch accommodates up to 1000 employees, whereas major regional hubs can host up to 5000 employees.
- **Devices**: Generally, each employee is assigned one DN across all devices. Furthermore, each office is equipped with up to 100 common area devices.

Dial Plan Framework

A well-structured dial plan is essential for seamless internal and external communication. We propose an 8-digit numbering pattern, which facilitates future growth while maintaining the integrity of the current System.

Format: `RROODDDD`

- `RR`: Region Code
- `OO`: Office Code
- `DDDD`: Device DN

Region Codes:

- AP: `20`
- EMEA: `30`
- US: `40`

Office Codes:

- Major Hubs: `XX00`
- Other Offices: `XX01 - XX99` (enabling expansion of up to 99 offices)

Device DNs:

- **Common Area Devices**: `0001-0100`

- **Employee DNs**:
  - Major Hubs: **0101-5100**
  - Other Offices: **0101-1100**

  A 4-digit DN can range from 0001 to 9999. The first 100 DNs are reserved for common area devices, so these offices can accommodate up to 9,900 users.

Examples:

- A common area device in AP's main office: **20000050**
- An employee DN at AP's second office: **20020102** (representing the 102nd employee)
- A common area device in the EMEA main hub: **30000025**
- An employee DN at EMEA's third office: **30030101** (representing the 101st employee)

Benefits of This Approach:

- Up to 100 offices per region, preparing ABC for extensive growth.
- Consistent 8-digit format across all branches.
- Adequate numbering for all employees and common area devices.

Planning for Application DNs

Cisco Unified Communications Manager (CUCM) and other components in the Cisco Collaboration architecture often use several other Directory Numbers (DNs) and patterns for applications, services, and features beyond just endpoints. Here's how you can integrate these additional requirements into the dial plan based on Cisco's best practices:

1. **Service Prefixes**: Using specific prefixes for services can help segregate application-specific DNs from user endpoints. This helps in clear distinction and troubleshooting.

   Examples:

   a. Voice Mail Prefix: **9XXX**

   b. CTI Route Points: **8XXX**

   c. Hunt Pilots: **7XXX**

   d. Conference Bridges: **6XXX**

   e. Call Park: **5XXX**

   f. Meet-Me Conferencing: **4XXX**

... and so forth.

2. **Block Allocation**: Allocate specific, contiguous DN blocks for each application. This is particularly useful if you predict growth in a particular application, such as more CTI route points or additional hunt pilots.

   Examples:

   Voice Mail: **`9100-9199`**
   CTI Route Points for IVR: **`8300-8399`**

3. **Geographical Considerations**: If you have multiple sites, consider designating a site-specific prefix or suffix for services. This provides clarity when troubleshooting and ensures there's no overlap between different geographical locations.

4. **Flexibility for Growth**: Always leave a buffer. If you need a range of 100 DNs for a service in the near future, allocate a block of 200. This ensures you have numbers readily available without restructuring if there's unpredicted growth.

5. **Clarity and Simplicity**: Choose patterns that are easy to remember. For instance, having all voice mail DNs start with a '9' makes it simpler for IT teams and users.

6. **Pattern Consistency**: Maintain consistency in the number of digits for all service DNs. If you're using 4-digit DNs for endpoints, keep application DNs to 4 digits as well. This can help with pattern matching and partition configuration in CUCM.

7. **Partitioning and CSS (Calling Search Space):** It's recommended to use partitions and CSS effectively to segregate application DNs from user DNs. This ensures no overlap and provides an added layer of security and control. For instance, you might want only certain users or phones to access a specific hunt pilot or voice mail system.

High-Level Dial Plan Design

For Company ABC, each regional CUCM cluster will handle its internal call routing and also have specific configurations to route calls to other regions through inter-cluster trunks. Here's a high-level outline focused on the AP CUCM cluster:

1. **Internal Dialing within Clusters**:

   a. Utilize unique Directory Numbers (DNs) for devices, eliminating the need for Route Patterns (RPs) within the same cluster

   b. Apply Partitions and CSS to DNs to control intra-cluster calling capabilities based on Class of control requirements

2. **Inter-Cluster Routing**:

    a. **AP Cluster Configuration**:

        i. **Route Pattern for EMEA**: `30XXXXXX` within a partition accessible by CSS that includes inter-cluster routing privileges

        ii. **Route Pattern for the US**: `40XXXXXX` within a similar partition tailored for AP to US routing

    b. **EMEA Cluster Configuration:**

        i. **Route Pattern for AP**: `20XXXXXX` with a corresponding Partition and CSS setup for EMEA to AP routing

        ii. **Route Pattern for the US**: `40XXXXXX` for EMEA to US routing with appropriate Class of control settings

    c. **US Cluster Configuration**:

        i. **Route Pattern for AP**: `20XXXXXX` with Class of control considerations for US to AP routing

        ii. **Route Pattern for EMEA**: `30XXXXXX` tailored for US to EMEA connectivity

    These inter-cluster Route Patterns must be associated with the right CSS to ensure only authorized users can initiate calls to other clusters.

3. Local PSTN Breakout Configuration:

    a. Configure Local Route Groups in each cluster to match the local gateways for PSTN access

    b. Associate these Local Route Groups with Route Lists and set up the Route Lists with appropriate Route Patterns to match local, long-distance, and international dialing requirements

    c. In the AP CUCM cluster, for instance, create a Route Pattern like 9.@ with a Route List that points to the Local Route Group for PSTN access. This 9.@ pattern assumes 9 is the dial-out prefix used in your organization

    d. Ensure that each Device Pool has the correct Local Route Group configured so calls route via the nearest PSTN gateway

    e. Use Partitions to create a logical separation of these Route Patterns and CSS to assign them to users and devices based on their geographic location and calling privileges

4. Class of control Implementation with Partitions and CSS:

    a. Define Partitions representing different Class of control levels (e.g., `Internal_Calls, Local_PSTN, LD_PSTN, Intl_PSTN`)

    b. Within the CUCM, create Route Patterns for different call types and assign them to the corresponding Partitions. For instance, `91[2-9]XX[2-9]XXXXXX` could be a long-distance pattern in the `LD_PSTN` Partition

    c. Develop CSS that includes the necessary Partitions for each user group. For example, the CSS for regular employees may consist of `Internal_Calls` and `Local_PSTN` but not `Intl_PSTN`

    d. Apply these CSS to user Device Profiles or Line Appearances to control call permissions according to the Class of control policy

5. Emergency Dialing Strategy:

    a. Create a specific Route Pattern for emergency services, such as 911, and place it in an emergency services Partition (For example, `Emergency_Services`)

    b. Ensure that the `Emergency_Services` Partition is included in every CSS so that all users and devices can dial emergency numbers without restrictions

    c. Consider implementing Enhanced Location CAC to ensure that emergency calls are given priority and routed efficiently in the network

6. Service and Application Dialing Planning:

    a. Allocate specific Dial Plan Ranges and Partitions for services. For example, assign 7000-7999 for Meet-Me conferencing and place it in the `MeetMe_Conference` Partition

    b. Link these service Partitions to the respective CSS based on the level of access required by different user groups

    c. When creating CTI Route Points or Hunt Pilots, ensure they reside in their specific service Partitions and are accessible via the CSS assigned to the users who need to interact with these services

7. Dial Plan Redundancy and High Availability:

    a. Design alternative Route Patterns and Route Lists for redundancy, ensuring they point to secondary call paths (like a backup SIP trunk or gateway)

    b. Assign these backup Route Patterns to a Redundancy Partition and include this partition in the CSS for critical devices and users

   c. Test failover scenarios to confirm that calls re-route as expected during primary path failures

8. Scalability Provisions in the Dial Plan:

   a. Reserve number blocks within existing Partitions for future expansion. For example, if the current dial plan uses 2001-2500 for AP users, reserve 2501-3000 for future users

   b. When designing the CSS, consider future growth by leaving room to add new Partitions without needing major overhauls to the existing CSS structure
   Review the dial plan regularly and make incremental adjustments to accommodate new sites or services before reaching capacity limits

By following these technical guidelines, Company ABC can create a comprehensive dial plan that is prepared for current needs and future growth.

Conclusion

In this chapter, we have covered all the important aspects of SIP trunks, gateways, advanced features, and real-world scenarios. With this knowledge, you will be well-prepared to design and set up dial plans on CUCM that fit your organization's needs. You'll know how to plan, configure, optimize, and troubleshoot dial plans like a pro. We will revisit the dial-plan topic briefly in Chapter 7, Exploring Cisco Collaboration Cloud, Edge and Unified Communication Integrations, but we will look at it from the perspective of Expressway.

In the next chapter, we will explore media resources, conferencing, and audio-visual technologies that work hand-in-hand with Cisco video endpoints. This will give you an even better understanding of how everything fits together in the Cisco collaboration world.

Multiple Choice Questions

1. Which of the following is NOT a key component of a CUCM dial plan?

   a. Route Patterns

   b. Translation Patterns

   c. Calling Search Spaces

   d. Endpoint Firmware

2. What is the primary purpose of digit manipulation in a Cisco dial plan?
    a. To block certain call types
    b. To alter numbers for proper routing and presentation
    c. To allow only internal calls
    d. To convert analog signals to digital
3. What is the recommended approach for structuring directory numbers in an organization with multiple sites?
    a. random 4-digit extensions
    b. location-based contiguous ranges
    c. employee ID numbers
    d. letters and numbers
4. Which technique allows adapting call routing based on time and day?
    a. Local route groups
    b. Logical partitioning
    c. URI dialing
    d. Time-of-day routing
5. Which redundancy technique re-routes calls over PSTN when IP bandwidth is insufficient?
    a. Translation patterns
    b. Tail-end hop off
    c. Automated alternate routing
    d. Meet-me conferencing

Answers

1. d
2. b
3. b
4. d
5. c

Further Reading

Similar to the last chapter, it is suggested to explore the following topics on your own to improve your understanding and broaden your perspective. Remember to tailor your research based on your organization's specific needs and always differentiate genuine insights and industry trends.

In-depth SIP Trunk Configuration

- **Voice Gateway Protocols**:
  - Investigate the differences and use cases for MGCP, H.323, and SIP protocols in voice gateways
  - Examine fallback and redundancy options between these protocols
- **Route Pattern Optimization:**
  - Dive deeper into the nuances of wildcard usage in route patterns
  - Research the requirements and best practices for setting up route patterns for emergency services in different countries
  - Explore best practices for managing overlapping dial patterns
- **Creating Specific Route Patterns for Office Locations:**
  - Develop a detailed route pattern for a hypothetical office, considering local dialing practices and international access
  - Outline the necessary CSS and partitions for this route pattern, explaining how they segregate and grant call access
- **Advanced Route List and Route Group Design:**
  - Explore load balancing and call distribution methods within Route Groups
  - Study the use of Route Lists for complex call routing scenarios involving multiple gateways
- **Practical Applications of Digit Manipulation Techniques:**
  - Research scenarios where pre-dot, post-dot, and mid-string digit manipulation techniques are most effective
  - Explore case studies demonstrating the use of prefixing and stripping in complex dialing environments
- **Globalization and Localization in Dial Plans:**
  - Study E.164 Numbering and its impact on global dial plan designs
  - Explore how localization techniques vary in different regions
- **URI Dialing and Its Integration:**
  - Understand the integration of URI dialing with existing legacy systems

    - Explore the integration of URI dialing with LDAP and corporate directories
    - Investigate the role of URI dialing in unified communications and collaboration platforms

- **Advanced AAR (Automated Alternate Routing) Configurations:**
    - Delve into AAR setups for handling call overflows in multi-site environments
    - Investigate how AAR interacts with other CUCM features like Call Forwarding and Call Admission Control

- **Complex Time-of-Day Routing Scenarios:**
    - Research into dynamic time-of-day routing based on business hours, holidays, and special events
    - Explore scripting and automation to enhance time-of-day routing logic

Chapter 6
Media Resources, Conferencing, and AV Solutions

Introduction

This chapter explores media resources, conferencing, and audio-visual solutions in unified communications.

We first discuss different types of media resources and how they are assigned to Media Resource Groups Lists (MRGLs) to be consumed by endpoints. We also discuss various voice and video codecs, their differences, and how codec preferences can be configured in CUCM.

The chapter then delves into audio-visual technologies and how they transform the modern meeting room experience. We explore both Cisco's solutions and other products in the market to provide examples and context.

The explanations here are kept simple for easy understanding. In real-world deployments, extensive planning and testing would be required to implement these solutions. The products mentioned only provide examples and an overview of the technology capabilities.

Structure

We will discuss the following topics:

- Understanding Media Resources and Conferencing
    - Media Resource Groups (MRGs) and Media Resource Group Lists (MRGLs) in CUCM
    - Understanding Codec Technologies in CUCM
    - Media Termination Point (MTP)

  - Transcoders
  - Annunciator
  - Music on Hold
  - Conferencing
- Audio-visual Solutions for Meeting Rooms
  - Overview of Meeting Room Endpoints
  - Meeting Room Scheduling System
  - Wayfinding System
  - One Button to Push (OBTP) Overview
  - Wireless Sharing in meeting rooms
  - RoomOS Customization and Integration
  - Advanced AV Technologies
  - Environmental Considerations in AV Room Design
  - Hot desking and Digital Signage System

Understanding Media Resources and Conferencing

In Cisco Collaboration, media resources are pivotal for optimizing and integrating audio and video streams across various communication protocols and devices. These resources are categorized into two types: software-based and hardware-based. Hardware-based resources employ Digital Signal Processors (DSPs) for intensive processing, especially in voice and video applications. Software-based resources (Cisco IP Voice Media Streaming Application service in CUCM) manage operations like music on hold, announcement playing, and media termination point operations, thereby optimizing media streams in Cisco Unified Communications.

It's important to note that each type of media resource, whether hardware or software-based, must be added or registered in Cisco Unified Communications Manager (CUCM). After you configure media resources, these resources are organized into Media Resource Groups (MRGs) and Media Resource Group Lists (MRGLs), which can be assigned to individual devices or, more commonly, to device pools.

Media Resource Groups (MRGs) and Media Resource Group Lists (MRGLs) in CUCM

MRGs in CUCM are used to organize and manage media resources, like conference bridges, transcoders, and Music on Hold servers. An MRG:

- Allows you to group similar types of media resources. For example, you can create an MRG that contains all your conference bridge resources, including the CMS conference bridge.
- It can be configured based on geographical location, network bandwidth, or other organizational requirements, ensuring that media resources are efficiently utilized and available where needed.

MRGLs are collections of MRGs. An MRGL:

- Defines the order of preference in which media resources are allocated. They allow CUCM to prioritize which MRGs should be accessed when a media resource is required.
- Offers the flexibility to assign different combinations of resources to various devices or groups within the organization.

MRGLs can be assigned directly to devices (like IP phones or video conferencing units) or, more commonly, to device pools. This assignment determines which media resources are available to devices when needed.

As you see in *Figure 6.1*, Media Resources (such as Conference Bridges, Transcoders, etc.) are assigned to a Media Resource Group (MRG). This group is then included in a Media Resource Group List (MRGL), which can be assigned to a Device Pool. The Device Pool, in turn, allocates the media resources to individual Devices. Additionally, the MRGL can be directly assigned to Devices if needed, allowing for more direct resource allocation.

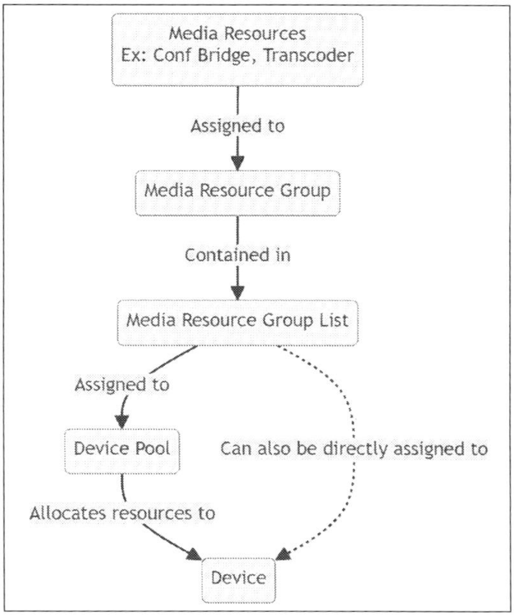

***Figure 6.1**: Media Resource Allocation*

As we delve deeper, we will explore the nuances of media resources in Cisco Unified Communications Manager. Before that, let's explore various codec technologies used in CUCM.

Understanding Codec Technologies in CUCM

Codecs, short for coder-decoders, are algorithms used to compress and decompress media streams, balancing the trade-off between quality, bandwidth usage, and computational requirements. Let's explore these in detail.

Voice Codecs Overview

The choice of a particular codec can significantly impact factors like bandwidth consumption, audio quality, and the overall user experience. Selecting the appropriate voice codec becomes crucial in a UCM environment, where network resources and communication needs vary. Let's examine some essential voice codecs in CUCM and their specific attributes and applications.

- **G.711 (µ-law and A-law)**: G.711, often referred to as the standard for voice telephony, operates in two variants: µ-law and A-law. µ-law is predominantly used in North America and Japan, while A-law is common in Europe and other parts of the world. Known for its wideband audio capabilities, G.711 provides high-quality voice transmission, making it ideal for environments where call clarity is paramount.

  This codec is the default choice for local telephony within regions with ample bandwidth availability.

- **G.729**: G.729 is renowned for delivering acceptable voice quality while consuming significantly less bandwidth than G.711. This codec is particularly advantageous in bandwidth-constrained environments, compressing audio data to a lower bit rate. It's ideal for scenarios such as remote office connectivity or WAN links where bandwidth efficiency is crucial. Despite its lower fidelity than G.711, G.729 balances audio quality and bandwidth utilization, making it a practical choice for many applications.
- **G.722**: G.722 stands out for its high-fidelity voice capabilities, surpassing G.711 in audio quality. It achieves this by utilizing a wider audio frequency range, translating to clearer and more natural voice communication. Although it offers enhanced audio quality, G.722 requires more bandwidth than G.729 but is on par with G.711. It is best suited for network environments where the available bandwidth can support its higher bit rate without adversely affecting other network services.

In addition to the standard voice codecs, CUCM supports advanced audio codecs that provide enhanced audio quality and adaptability under varying network conditions.

These advanced codecs are especially useful in scenarios where superior audio fidelity or specific network requirements are a priority. Let's delve into two such codecs: Opus and AAC-LD.

- **Opus**: The Opus codec stands out for its exceptional versatility and performance across many bitrates. It is unique in its ability to provide high-quality audio transmission both in low and high-bandwidth environments. Depending on the network conditions, Opus can dynamically adjust its bitrate, audio bandwidth, and complexity. This flexibility ensures optimal audio quality even in fluctuating network scenarios, making it highly effective for mobile communications and video conferencing in Cisco's UCM environment. Opus's capability to handle both narrowband and wideband audio frequencies further enhances its suitability for various use cases, ranging from simple voice transmission to high-fidelity music streaming.
- **AAC-LD (Advanced Audio Coding - Low Delay)**: AAC-LD is an advanced audio codec known for its high-quality audio transmission capabilities. It is designed to deliver near-studio audio quality, making it ideal for applications where audio clarity and fidelity are paramount. This codec is particularly favoured in high-definition telepresence and video conferencing solutions within Cisco UCM, where synchronization between audio and video is crucial. AAC-LD provides low-latency, high-quality audio transmission, ensuring a natural and immersive communication experience.

Now, let's explore Video Codecs.

Video Codecs Overview

Video codecs in CUCM play a crucial role in facilitating high-quality video conferencing and collaboration. Let's explore some of the prominent video codecs used in CUCM.

- **H.264 (Advanced Video Coding, AVC)**: H.264 is renowned for providing high-quality video at lower bit rates. Its optimal balance between video quality and bandwidth usage makes it the default choice in Cisco UCM for video calls, adaptable to various devices and network scenarios.
- **H.265 (High-Efficiency Video Coding, HEVC)**: HEVC offers a significant advancement in compression efficiency over H.264. It delivers superior video quality at about half the bit rate, making it ideal for high-definition video streaming in bandwidth-constrained environments. This codec is well-suited for next-generation video applications in Cisco UCM.
- **AV1 (Alliance for Open Media Video 1)**: AV1 significantly reduces bandwidth requirements while supporting next-generation content, addressing patent issues prevalent in previous codecs like HEVC. AV1 is an open, royalty-free video coding format created by the Alliance for Open Media beginning in 2015.

Its extensive toolset supports scalability, screen content coding, and AR/VR applications within a unified profile structure, enhancing interoperability.

In CUCM, you can define audio and video codecs system-wide through Service Parameters or at a more granular level using region settings associated with device pools. This flexibility allows for optimized codec usage based on network conditions and device capabilities.

Regions in CUCM are used to manage the audio codec preferences for calls between different areas of the network, especially when dealing with endpoints that support specific codecs. The configuration process involves defining a prioritized list of audio codecs, which CUCM uses to filter and select the best codec based on the maximum audio bit rate settings and codec support on both ends of a call. CUCM supports up to 2000 regions, offering extensive customization options.

In Cisco Unified Communications Manager, codec selection for intra-region and inter-region calls is governed by the 'Audio Codec Region Preference List.' This list prioritizes codecs in a specified order. Any unsupported codecs are initially filtered out during the codec negotiation process for a call setup. Additionally, codecs exceeding the maximum configured bitrate are excluded from consideration. Following their prioritized order in the list, the remaining codecs are then used to negotiate and finalize the codec selection for the call.

Here are the steps to Customize Audio Codec Preferences:

1. **Access Codec Preference List**: In CUCM Administration, go to **`System> Region Information > Audio Codec Preference List`**
2. **Add New Codec List**: Click **`'Add New'`** to create a new audio codec preference list
3. **Select Existing List**: Choose an existing list from the drop-down menu to use as a template
4. **Copy and Customize**: Click **`'Copy'`** and then modify the name and description of the new list. For example, name it **`'customizedCodecList'`**
5. **Prioritize Codecs**: Adjust the order of codecs in the list to reflect your preferences.
6. **Save Settings**: Once the list is customized, click **`'Save'`**

   As you can see in *Figure 6.2*, we are creating a new Audio Codec Preference List and have option to adjust order of codecs.

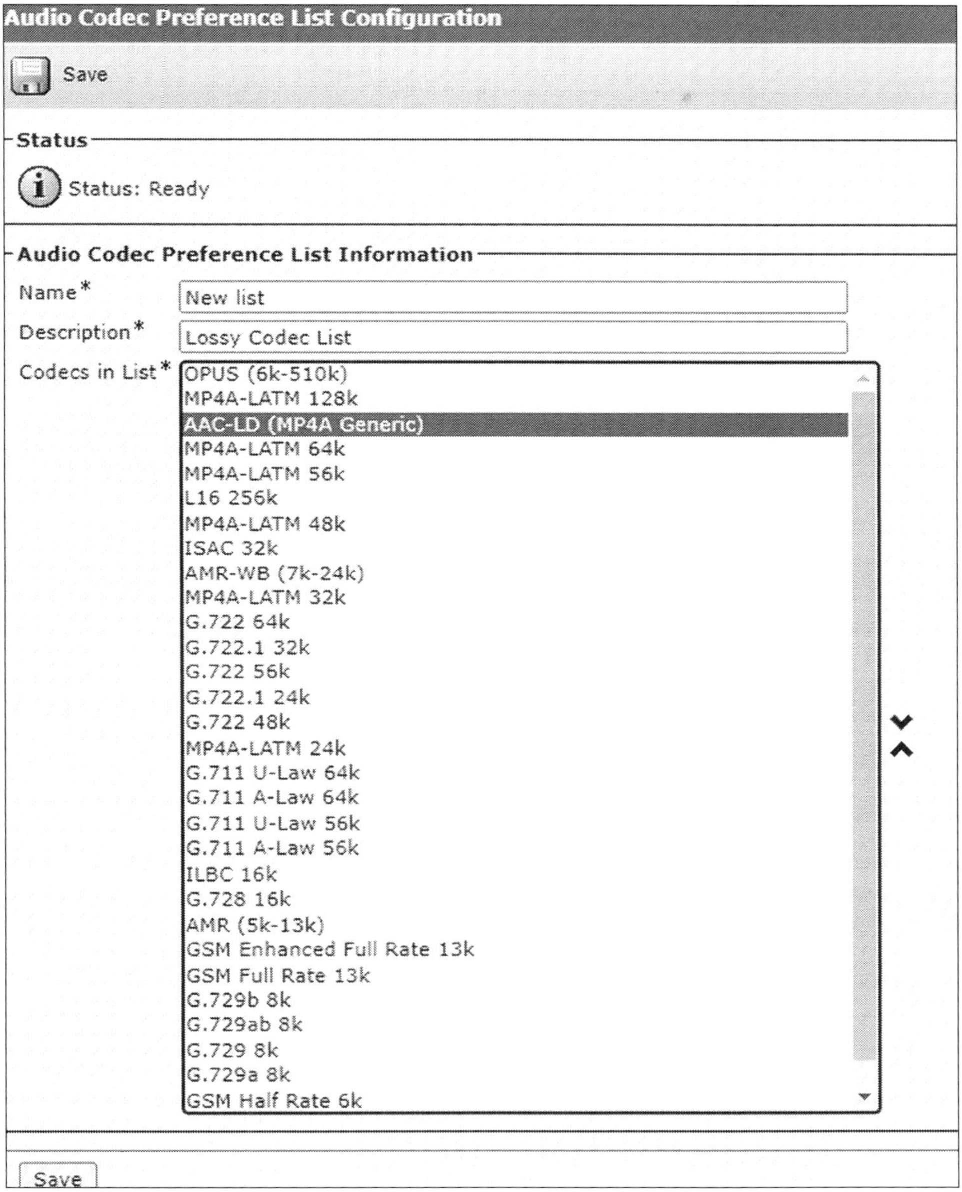

Figure 6.2: *Audio Codec Preference list config in CUCM*

7. **Apply to Regions**: As you can see in *Figure* 6.3, we are assigning the new codec preference list to specific region. This region can be assigned to device pools. All devices within these device pools will use the selected audio codec preferences.

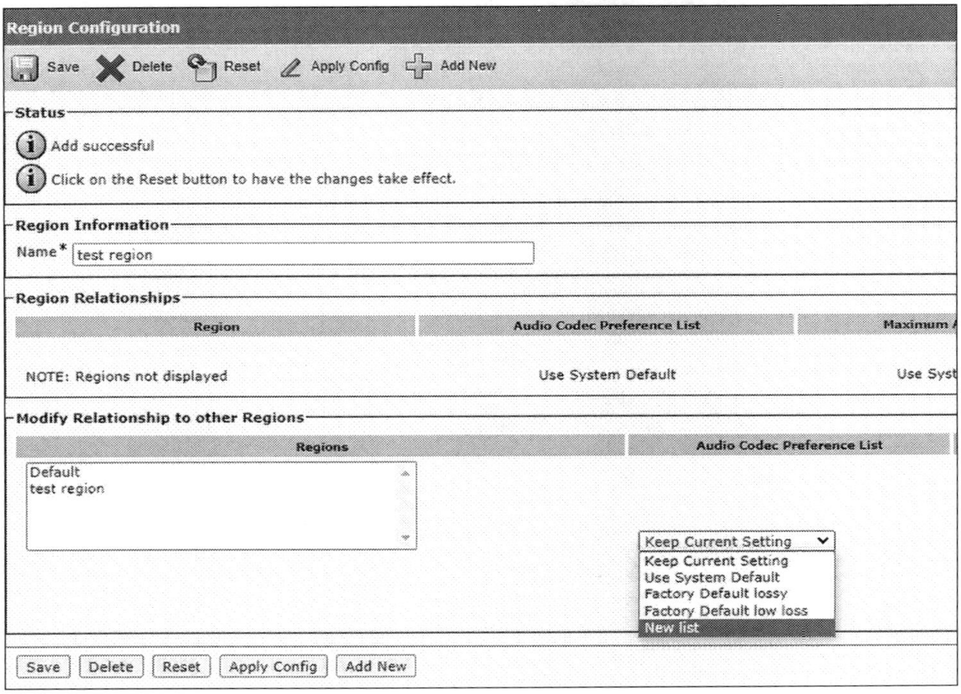

***Figure 6.3**: Assigning Audio Codec Preference list to Region in CUCM*

By following these steps and understanding the codec selection process, administrators can effectively manage and optimize audio and video codecs in CUCM, enhancing call quality and network efficiency.

Media Termination Point (MTP)

Media Termination Points (MTPs) are essential in the Cisco CallManager environment, primarily facilitating the bridging of media streams. They accept two full-duplex G.711 Coder-Decoder (CODEC) stream connections, passing streaming data between them while transcoding a-law to mu-law and adjusting packet sizes as necessary.

MTPs can also do the following:

- **DTMF Signal Conversion**: MTPs facilitate the conversion of Dual-Tone Multi-Frequency (DTMF) signalling methods, such as transitioning from in-band to out-of-band signalling (RFC 2833), ensuring compatibility between different transmission methods used by endpoints.
- **RTP Stream Conversion**: They convert IPv4 and IPv6 for RTP (Real-Time Protocol) streams.
- **SIP Early Offer Support**: MTPs are instrumental in delivering SIP Early Offer for SIP trunks.

MTP devices are automatically added upon activating the Cisco IP Voice Media Streaming Application service in CUCM. This service enables various functionalities, including MTP, Conference Bridge, Annunciator, and Music on Hold.

CUCM supports software MTPs in IOS gateways, hardware MTPs in IOS gateways, and software MTPs provided by the Cisco IP Voice Media Streaming service.

You can distribute MTPs across networked systems. However, Cisco advises against activating the Cisco IP Voice Streaming Media Application on a CUCM with high call-processing loads to prevent performance degradation.

Transcoders

Transcoders in CUCM are essential for seamless communication between endpoints using different voice codecs. They perform real-time conversions from G.711 to G.729, enabling compatibility during calls with differing codecs. CUCM automatically invokes transcoders as needed, making the process transparent to users and endpoints.

Transcoders in CUCM also offer Media Termination Point (MTP) functionality and come in various types, including hardware-based in IOS gateways and software-based via the Cisco IP Voice Media Streaming service.

The high-level steps are:

- Enabling DSP resources on supported Cisco IOS devices using the dspfarm command.
- Configuring the DSP farm profile with resources and control method (LTI or SCCP).
- Registering the DSP farm with CUCM for allocation.

Annunciator

An annunciator plays a crucial role in enhancing the user experience during calls. Its primary function is to play specific tones and announcements, useful in transferring a call over the Public Switched Telephone Network (PSTN) through an IOS gateway. These announcements might include notifications like call waiting tones, number unavailability messages, or pre-recorded informational messages, providing clear communication to callers during various call states.

When planning for an annunciator configuration, it's essential to consider its capacity. By default, a single annunciator supports 48 simultaneous streams. However, this capacity can be adjusted depending on the network infrastructure and server capabilities. On standalone servers, the annunciator can support a higher capacity—up to 255 simultaneous announcement streams, and with a high-performance setup, this number can even reach 400 streams.

Cisco CallManager provides a set of pre-recorded annunciator announcements, which organizations can customize according to their specific needs. Additionally, these announcements support localization, meaning they can be configured to play entirely in the System's locale settings. This feature is essential in multi-lingual environments or global organizations, where announcements need to be understood by a diverse user base.

Music on Hold

Music on Hold (MoH) in CUCM is a crucial feature enhancing the user experience during call holds. It is primarily a facility that allows organizations to play music or pre-recorded messages to callers on hold. The functionality of MoH relies heavily on the Cisco IP Voice Media Streaming service. When a caller is put on hold, the MoH feature is activated, streaming the chosen audio to the caller. This feature is crucial in providing callers with a more engaging and less monotonous experience, especially during extended wait times.

MoH can impact CPU performance, especially with a large number of active held calls or multicast MoH streams. So, activate the Cisco IP Voice Media Streaming application on servers without call processing to avoid performance impacts.

Conferencing

Conferencing is a core aspect of collaboration, enabling real-time communication among three or more people using voice and video technologies.

There are three types of conferences:

- **Instant or Ad Hoc Conferences**: These spontaneous conferences are not pre-scheduled. They typically evolve from a two-party call where additional participants are added on the fly.
- **Permanent or Rendezvous Conferences**: Participants dial into a predetermined number or URI to access these always-available conference resources. These are ideal for recurring meetings or open-room discussions.
- **Scheduled Conferences**: Pre-planned meetings with a specific start time and often reserved resources. They are optimal for formal gatherings and larger meetings.

For audio and video conferencing, in the Cisco Collaboration on-premises Preferred Architecture, Cisco recommends implementing the Cisco Meeting Server across the board for all types of conferencing. The Cisco Meeting Server should be set up in a clustered formation for enhanced reliability and scalability.

In today's fast-paced business environment, organizations increasingly rely on SaaS-based web conferencing tools that offer comprehensive functionalities, including audio, video, and screen sharing. This shift has led to a decline in the exclusive use of audio-only conferencing. Given this trend, our focus will be more aligned with current practices, highlighting the integration of CUCM and Cisco Meeting Server (CMS) for the conference bridge. In the next chapter, we will briefly discuss Webex Video Mesh used in hybrid setups with Webex.

Cisco Meeting Server (CMS)

Cisco Meeting Server (CMS) is a critical component in Cisco's suite of conferencing solutions, offering a versatile and comprehensive audio and video conferencing platform.

CMS has several components, including a call bridge that integrates with CUCM for call control. All conference calls - permanent, instant, and scheduled - are routed through a single SIP trunk from CUCM to the call bridge on the Cisco Meeting Server. Each call bridge in the CMS cluster requires a separate SIP trunk for optimal operation. Call bridge supports diverse conference types:

- **Instant or Ad Hoc Conferences**: These spontaneous meetings evolve from two-party calls. When a user escalates a call to a three-party conference, Unified CM sends an API request to CMS, creating a temporary virtual meeting space for the conference.

  When we add CMS as a conference bridge resource in CUCM, an HTTPS connection is configured and carries XML-RPC requests to the CMS nodes. This process is crucial for creating temporary spaces for hosting instant conferences. Once the conference is initiated, CUCM routes all participants to the designated space via the SIP trunk. Once the conference concludes, CUCM sends another API request to the CMS to remove that temporary space, ensuring efficient resource management.

  As we see in *Figure 6.4*, in the instant conference scenario, devices utilize a Media Resource Group List (MRGL) to access available media resources, including a Conference Bridge. This Conference Bridge is the Cisco Meeting Server (CMS), designated to handle multi-party calls. When a device initiates a conference, it connects to CMS via a SIP trunk.

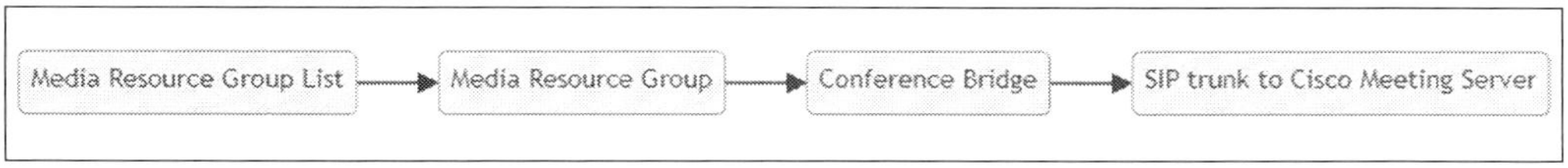

Figure 6.4: *Flow for Instant Conferences*

- **Permanent Conferences**: Utilizing Cisco Meeting Server Spaces, these conferences offer a permanent virtual meeting environment. Spaces are created as part of the user import process from LDAP and can be accessed anytime using a unique Space URI.

- **Scheduled Conferences**: Managed through Cisco TMS, these conferences are pre-planned with specific start times. Cisco TMS configures a range of numeric IDs for these conferences, creating an inactive Space on CMS for each ID. When a meeting is scheduled, Cisco TMS selects a dial-in number from this range and activates the corresponding space at the scheduled time, enabling participants to join the conference seamlessly.

  As we see in *Figure* 6.5, for permanent or scheduled conferences, the call flow starts when a device dials a number or URI matching a Route Pattern in CUCM. This pattern uses Route List, which organizes route groups in a specific order. Finally, like in the instant conference, the call reaches CMS via a SIP trunk.

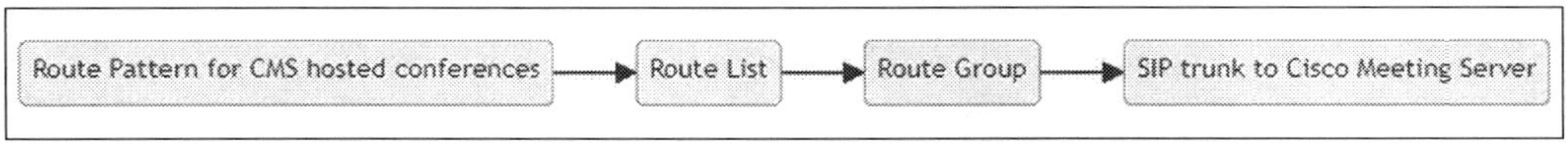

***Figure* 6.5**: *Flow for Permanent and Scheduled Conferences*

As we discussed the configuration of Route Patterns and SIP trunks in a previous chapter, we will not delve into these details here.

These are the steps to configure CMS as conference bridge in CUCM.

1. Navigate to **`Media Resources > Conference Bridge`**
2. Select **`Add New`**
3. Select **`Cisco Meeting Server`** from the **`Conference Bridge`** drop-down menu
4. Enter the conference bridge name
5. Select the SIP trunk towards CMS
6. Enter username and password of the account created in CMS with API privileges. CUCM will need this to send API requests for creating and removing temporary spaces in CMS
7. HTTP port is **`443`** by default
8. Save

You can see these configuration parameters in *Figure* 6.6.

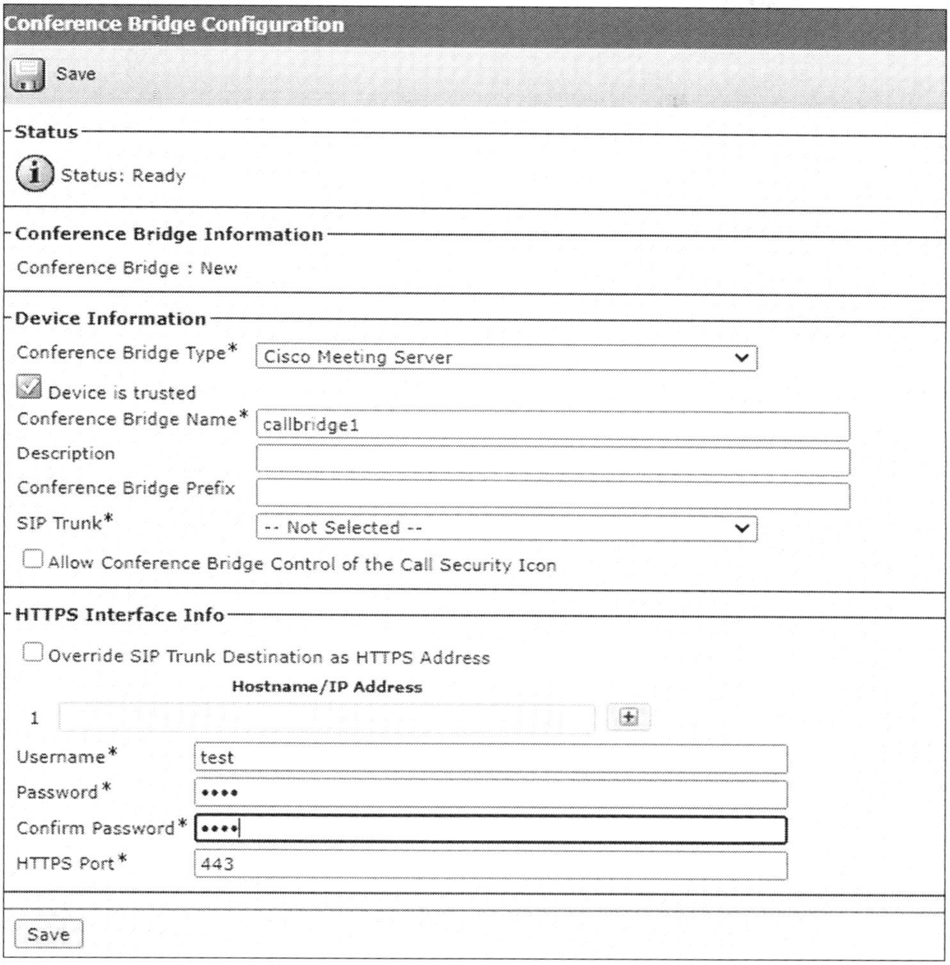

Figure 6.6: *CMS as Conference bridge in CUCM*

There are some pre-requisites related to certificates:

- Add the **`CMS Webadmin`**, **`Call Bridge`**, and **`Root`** certificates to the Call Manager trust store in CUCM. This is crucial for establishing a trusted connection between CMS and CUCM.
    - If you opt for a Non-Secure SIP trunk, uploading the Call Bridge certificate to the **`CallManager`**-trust store isn't required. However, you must upload the Root certificate which is signed by the Call Bridge certificate.
- The Hostname (FQDN of CMS) or IP address must be specified in the **`Webadmin`** certificate, either in the Common Name or the Subject Alternative Name field.

This concludes our Media resource and conferencing topic, let's move to Audio-visual solutions now.

Audio-visual Solutions for Meeting Rooms

Audiovisual solutions in meeting rooms have transformed from traditional projectors and conference phones to sophisticated environments encompassing a blend of technology and user experience. Over the years, these solutions have become central to a company's collaboration strategy, reflecting a shift towards more interactive, connected, and efficient workspaces. Today's AV solutions are about creating spaces that facilitate communication and enhance it through intuitive interfaces and seamless integration. Let's start with a user story to see how these technologies work together in a real-life scenario.

User Story: The Modern Collaborative Workspace Experience

Imagine Sarah, a project manager in a tech firm. Her day is filled with meetings, brainstorming sessions, and collaborative work. She begins by booking a meeting room directly from her calendar app which is seamlessly integrated with the company's room scheduling system. The System suggests the "Vista Room," which is perfect for her team of six and available at her preferred time.

Arriving at the office, Sarah uses the Wayfinding solution displayed on digital signage throughout the building to navigate to the Vista Room.

As she approaches, the room's sensor technology detects her presence and automatically checks her in. The environment is welcoming, with the room's lighting and temperature adjusted for comfort - a subtle but essential aspect of environmental considerations in AV room design.

Sarah initiates the meeting with a simple tap on the In-Room touch panel. The One Button to Push (OBTP) feature effortlessly connects her to the scheduled video conference, bringing in remote participants with crystal-clear audio and video quality. During the meeting, the team decides to share a presentation. Sarah uses the room's wireless sharing technology to project her screen onto the large display. This effortless sharing encourages more dynamic and interactive discussions.

After the meeting, real-time analytics and monitoring systems collect data on room usage and system performance. This data helps the IT department optimize resources and improve the user experience for future meetings.

Now, let's take a closer look at each technology, exploring how they function and their impact on collaboration.

Overview of Meeting Room Endpoints

In today's technologically advanced workspaces, meeting room endpoints facilitate seamless communication and collaboration. These endpoints can be peripherals (BYOD solution where you bring your laptop/device and use a camera, speaker, and mic from these Systems) or standalone systems with built-in operating systems and specialized features like Zoom rooms or Cisco endpoints.

- **Cisco Meeting Room Endpoints**: Cisco offers a comprehensive range of meeting room endpoints designed to cater to various room sizes and collaboration needs. These endpoints typically include features like high-quality video and audio capabilities, easy-to-use touch interfaces, and seamless integration with Cisco's collaboration platforms. Cisco endpoints are known for their reliability and advanced technology, though they can be higher in cost.

  You can find more details about Cisco endpoints here:
  https://www.cisco.com/c/en_in/products/collaboration-endpoints/index.html

  Cisco keeps innovating in the endpoint space. One of their recent endpoint features is People Focus. Like Zoom's Smart Gallery, Cisco offers a People Focus capability that provides an enhanced view of meeting participants. People Focus uses AI to automatically crop and optimize each participant's video feed, ensuring individuals are clearly visible even when sharing a meeting room, creating a more personalized view that feels more connected by using screen space better. You can learn more about People Focus here: https://help.webex.com/en-us/article/n997hz9/People-focus-on-Board,-Desk,-and-Room-Series

- **Microsoft Teams Rooms:** Microsoft Teams Rooms are designed to integrate seamlessly with the Microsoft Teams platform. Microsoft has its own hardware lineup and a robust partner ecosystem, offering a variety of endpoints from different manufacturers. These devices are optimized for Teams meetings, providing features like one-touch join, proximity join, and content sharing.

  Cisco has also made it possible to convert some of its endpoint models into Microsoft Teams Rooms, illustrating the versatility and adaptability of these systems. Microsoft Teams Rooms are known for their ease of use and deep integration with Office 365, although they are somewhat limited to the Microsoft ecosystem.

  You can find more details about Microsoft Teams Rooms here:
  https://www.microsoft.com/en-in/microsoft-teams/microsoft-teams-rooms

  https://www.webex.com/solutions/microsoft-teams-rooms-cisco-devices.html

- **Zoom Rooms**: Zoom Rooms provides a flexible and user-friendly solution for video conferencing, catering to different room sizes and configurations. These endpoints are designed to work seamlessly with the Zoom platform, offering features like wireless content sharing, interactive whiteboarding, and easy calendar integration. Zoom Rooms can be set up with various hardware from different manufacturers, providing cost and room setup flexibility.

  Key innovations like Smart Gallery and Intelligent Director make Zoom Rooms highly engaging. Smart Gallery shows each participant individually, ensuring remote users feel seen. Intelligent Director leverages AI and multiple cameras to frame active speakers or group conversations dynamically.

  You can find more details about Zoom rooms here :

  https://www.zoom.com/en/products/meeting-rooms/

- **Other popular endpoints**: Let's briefly explore what other popular endpoints are common choices.
  - **Logitech Rally Systems**: Logitech offers the Rally lineup of conference room cameras and audio devices that work with most major video conferencing platforms. They provide advanced features like stereo audio, PTZ cameras, and AI-based speaker tracking.
  - **Poly Studio and Studio X Family**: Poly offers the Studio and Studio X series of video bars and all-in-one systems with high-quality audio/video. They work with platforms like Webex, Zoom, Teams, etc.
  - **Jabra Panacast Cameras**: Jabra Panacast video cameras feature intelligent zoom and tracking capabilities. They function as USB peripherals that are compatible with all major video conferencing apps.
  - **Interactive Digital Whiteboards**: Interactive Digital Whiteboards are trending in modern workplaces for their ability to facilitate dynamic, visual collaboration, transforming traditional meetings into interactive sessions where participants can annotate, share, and edit content in real-time, fostering more engaging and productive discussions. Popular choices in the market are DTEN, Neat Board, Logitech Scribe, Microsoft Surface Hub, and Cisco Board Pro.

Meeting Room Scheduling System

Historically, meeting room management was manual, often involving physical sign-up sheets or basic digital calendars. As organizations grew and became more complex, this method proved inefficient, leading to conflicts, underutilization of spaces, and confusion. The evolution of Meeting Room Scheduling solutions began with digitizing room bookings, initially through standalone systems and later through integrated enterprise calendaring tools.

Meeting Room scheduling in modern organizations involves several interconnected components, each vital in ensuring seamless meeting experiences. Let's break down these components for a clearer understanding:

- **User Interface for Booking the Room**: This interface could be integrated within your company's internal portal, a web conference app like Webex, or a calendar application that is part of your email service, like Microsoft Outlook, if using Office 365 or Gmail interface for Google Workspace. Users typically book meeting rooms through these familiar interfaces.
- **Calendar Service**: This service manages the bookings for each meeting room and is usually a component of your enterprise email or messaging solution. Examples include Microsoft Exchange Server 2019, Office 365, and Google Workspace. Like individual users, each meeting room has a mailbox in the company's messaging/email service. When you reserve a room, it blocks the time slot in the room's calendar, preventing double bookings.
- **Room Scheduling Solution**: This solution syncs all the bookings from the calendar service to the touch panels outside the meeting rooms. It also facilitates room booking directly from these touch panels and ensures that any booking made is reflected in the central calendar service, maintaining consistent scheduling information. These touch panels also display the room's availability status (e.g., in use, available), often indicated with different colors.

  To optimize room usage, some scheduling systems incorporate check-in and check-out functionalities. If a user does not check in within a specified period from the start time of their booking, the System may automatically cancel the booking and free up the room. Similarly, a check-out feature allows users to end their reservation early if their meeting concludes before the scheduled time.
- **Video Endpoint / Codec with Touch Panel**: Meeting rooms might be equipped with video endpoints or codecs and hardware devices, designed for conferencing. With One Button to Push (OBTP) integration, the user's scheduled meeting appears on the touch panel, allowing them to join the meeting with a single tap. We will explore OBTP in more detail later in this chapter.
- **Conferencing Solution**: Conferencing solution provides a virtual meeting space where participants connect. It is a centralized media resource, facilitating audio and video transmission among all connected users.

It's important to note that a Meeting Room Scheduling Solution and touch panels outside meeting rooms, while beneficial, are optional. Organizations have the flexibility to set up their meeting rooms in a way that best suits their needs and infrastructure. One alternative is to have video endpoints in meeting rooms directly synchronize with the organization's calendar service.

In this setup, meeting details are reflected on the touch panel inside the meeting room, allowing users to view their scheduled meetings and join easily. This direct syncing with the calendar service simplifies the process and still provides a level of convenience for users.

Detailed guidance can be found in the 'Deployment Guide for Hybrid Calendar' and 'Hybrid Calendar Service with Microsoft 365 Integration' reference documents for those using Cisco Webex endpoints with Control Hub integration.

Similarly, for Zoom Rooms setup with Office 365, the 'Setting up Zoom Rooms with Office 365' document offers comprehensive instructions. These resources provide valuable insights.

While this approach streamlines the technology used in meeting rooms, it's worth mentioning that incorporating a Meeting Room Scheduling Solution can significantly enhance the user experience. It provides broader visibility of room availability, facilitates on-the-spot booking, and offers features like check-in/check-out to optimize room utilization. However, the choice ultimately depends on the organization's specific requirements, budget, and existing IT infrastructure.

The term 'Meeting Room Scheduling System varies across different vendors. For instance, Gartner refers to similar systems as 'Resource Scheduling Applications,' which encompass a broader range of functionalities but essentially serve the same purpose. To explore various solutions, you can refer to Gartner's reviews on Resource Scheduling Applications here: https://www.gartner.com/reviews/market/resource-scheduling-applications

In this discussion, we'll focus on two systems widely compatible with popular video endpoints and web conferencing solutions: the Zoom Room Scheduler system and the Cisco Webex Room Navigator. Let's dive into the details of each system.

Zoom Rooms Scheduler

The Zoom Room Scheduler is part of Zoom's Workspace solutions, including kiosks, digital signage, and room booking displays. These tools enhance office efficiency by managing meeting spaces and displaying information.

If you have a Zoom Room or phone license, the scheduler is usually included, but it's best to check with your Zoom Account Manager. Unlike producing its hardware, Zoom works with various hardware partners, offering a wide choice of compatible devices.

Key features of Zoom Room Scheduler:

- **Room Management Tool**: It uses a secondary touch panel as a room management tool, showing room availability and allowing reservations. This touch panel operates in scheduling display mode and is placed outside the meeting room.

- **Calendar Integration**: The System integrates with popular calendar services like Google Calendar, Office 365, or Microsoft Exchange, ensuring synchronized meetings and real-time updates on room status.
- **Scheduling Process**: Meetings can be booked through email clients like Outlook or directly from the scheduling display touch panel by tapping 'Reserve,' setting the meeting time and title, and inviting participants. The meeting is then added to the scheduling display, room controller, and the associated online calendar.

Administrators can manage the scheduling displays through the Zoom web portal, configuring the displays as devices associated with Zoom Rooms for efficient management. You can find more details in KB0061511 on Zoom support and also check their product detail here:

https://www.zoom.com/en/products/meeting-rooms/features/workspace/

Webex Room Navigator

The Webex Room Navigator can be used both inside and outside meeting rooms. Inside, it is used as an interface for the video endpoint. When mounted outside, it is a sophisticated room booking panel, displaying room availability and facilitating ad-hoc bookings.

It displays meeting room availability status and allows for ad-hoc meeting bookings or calendar checks. It features a coloured light strip indicating the room status: green for available, red for occupied, and yellow for an impending meeting or booked but unoccupied room.

The Cisco Webex Room Navigator can also be used effectively as a standalone device in rooms without a video conferencing endpoint. This adaptability ensures a consistent room management experience across various meeting spaces. The Room Navigator can be directly registered and managed through the Webex Control Hub when operating independently. This mode empowers it with comprehensive functionalities, including support for third-party web apps, room booking features, and extended integrations through xAPIs.

The Room Navigator retains its core room booking capabilities in its standalone form. It displays the room's availability status and enables the scheduling of instant meetings.

You can find more details here:

https://help.webex.com/en-us/article/iq6aw6/Room-Navigator-as-a-standalone-device#sx10_r_standalone_management

Now let's find that meeting room we just booked.

Wayfinding System

Wayfinding systems have become essential in enhancing the efficiency of navigating and booking meeting rooms in office environments, but their utility isn't limited to just corporate settings. Beyond corporate offices, wayfinding solutions are instrumental in educational campuses, healthcare facilities, retail spaces, and transport hubs, aiding users in navigating complex layouts and finding specific locations or amenities.

These systems provide several key functionalities:

- **Locating Scheduled Rooms**: Interactive maps enable users to locate their pre-booked meeting rooms easily.
- **Identifying Available Rooms**: Real-time availability of meeting rooms is displayed, assisting users in quickly locating an unoccupied room.
- **On-the-Spot Booking**: The wayfinding interface allows users to book available rooms directly, ensuring efficient utilization of meeting spaces.

Wayfinding systems integrate seamlessly with a facility's IT infrastructure, utilizing digital signage, interactive kiosks, and mobile applications. These components are connected to a central database, holding detailed maps and room information, ensuring the System reflects real-time room availability and facility layout changes. Advanced systems may include indoor positioning technologies, such as Wi-Fi triangulation or beacon technology, for more precise navigation.

Additionally, these systems are increasingly integrated with room booking systems, allowing users to view room availability and make bookings directly from the wayfinding interface. This integration is particularly beneficial in dynamic work environments where meeting spaces are frequently used.

Let's look at two solutions in the market to understand wayfinding solutions better. Appspace and 22 Miles are prominent examples that provide insights into the capabilities and features of modern wayfinding technologies.

- **Appspace Wayfinding Solution**: Appspace's solution is known for its efficient self-service kiosks and interactive directories, which are beneficial in simplifying navigation within office spaces. Its major strengths lie in device compatibility, enhancing flexibility for users across desktop and mobile platforms. Appspace's integration with office calendars and real-time availability updates are its strengths. However, it may not be as suitable for environments that require more advanced navigational tools.
- **22 Miles Wayfinding Solution**: 22 Miles distinguishes itself with its innovative interactive 3D mapping and AR technology, offering an immersive navigation experience. The solution is especially advantageous for its ADA-accessible routing and smart pathway automation. While these advanced technologies

provide detailed navigational assistance, they may also introduce higher costs or a more complex implementation process.

- **Customized Solutions:** For organizations with expertise in Crestron programming and a preference for custom solutions, developing a wayfinding system using Crestron hardware offers a highly tailored approach. This setup typically involves the use of Crestron's DGE100 (Digital Graphics Engine) and a Crestron controller, such as the CP4 or RMC4. Let's discuss in detail about different components and their functionality.
    - **Crestron DGE100**: The DGE100 is central to this setup, acting as the graphic engine. It's responsible for rendering the custom user interface, which in this scenario includes wayfinding maps and interfaces. This UI is developed using Crestron software.
    - **Crestron Controller**: The Crestron controller, such as the CP4 or RMC4, serves as the system's brain. It can be centralized to serve multiple DGE100 units across the network or configured to pair with individual DGE100s for dedicated control.
    - **Interactive Display Connection**: The DGE100 connects to large third-party touch displays, overcoming the size limitations of native Crestron touch panels.
    - **HDMI Input for Signage Content**: The DGE100 also has an HDMI input port, which feeds the output from any signage player like Brightsign. This will help embed and show signage content and the floor map (wayfinding) in a customizable layout as you design in Crestron software.

The key advantage of this setup is the ability to fully customize the layout and content of the wayfinding system. From the arrangement of floor maps to the integration of additional signage elements, the system can be tailored to meet the specific needs and preferences of your organization.

Crestron does not market these for wayfinding purposes. But, we can utilize the capabilities of this hardware combined with Crestron programming knowledge to make it a custom wayfinding solution.

Similar functionality can be achieved using the Extron ecosystem - Extron TLI Pro 201 (in place of DGE) paired with any Extron controller (e.g., IPCP Pro 250).

Refer to the schematic diagram in *Figure* 6.7, to understand the connectivity and interaction between the DGE100, the Crestron controller, and the interactive displays.

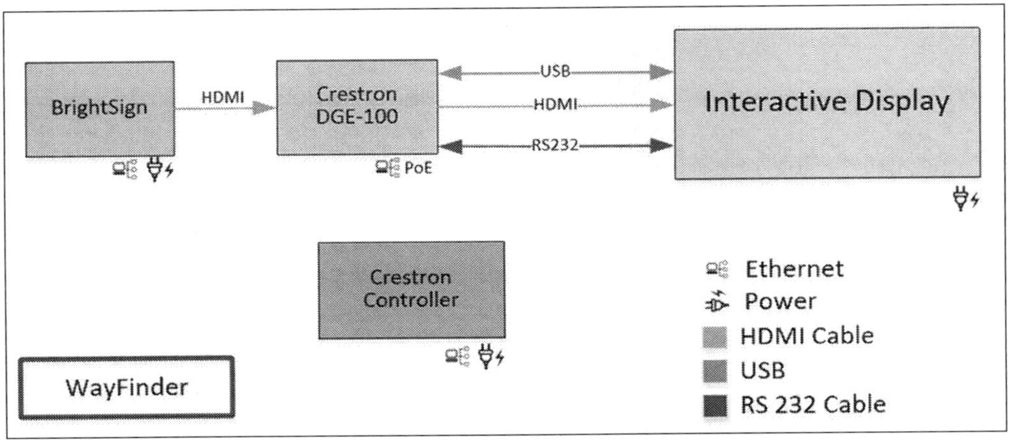

Figure 6.7: *Custom wayfinding System using Crestron*

Now that we have found the meeting room, let's connect to our meeting.

One Button to Push (OBTP) Overview

Attending meetings in a modern conference room can sometimes be a hassle, especially when it involves locating meeting IDs, understanding the correct dialing method, and navigating various meeting systems. OBTP streamlines this process significantly. When users enter a meeting room equipped with OBTP, they are presented with a straightforward option on the room's touch panel. A simple tap on 'Start Meeting' automatically connects them to the scheduled conference.

The workflow will be something like this:

- **Schedule Meeting**: A user schedules a meeting using a calendar service integrated with the Meeting Room system and conferencing service.
- **Sync to Device**: The meeting information is synchronized with the Meeting Room system.
- **Join with One Click**: A "Join" or "Start Meeting" button appears on the room's touch panel at the scheduled time. The user presses this button to start the meeting.

Let's understand how meeting information is synchronized to video endpoints or Meeting Room devices. We'll explore two different scenarios at a high level to provide a comprehensive understanding:

- Implementing Webex Hybrid Calendar with on-premises registered Cisco endpoints
- Zoom Rooms OBTP

In both scenarios, we are considering On-Premises Exchange. It's important to note that the integration process may differ slightly with cloud-based services like Office 365 or Gmail. Please refer to the respective service documentation for specific details on these variations.

Webex Hybrid Calendar with On-premises Registered Cisco Endpoint

As Cisco's TelePresence Management Suite (TMS) reaches its discontinuation, organizations are transitioning to more modern solutions like the Webex Hybrid Calendar Service for OBTP.

The primary distinction from the TMS-XE setup is the role of the Webex Control Hub in synchronizing calendar data to endpoints. In this configuration, there's no requirement for an on-premises TMS and TMS-XE server. The Control Hub effectively takes over the calendar syncing process, offering a more cloud-centric approach.

- **Meeting Booking in Outlook**: A user schedules a meeting in Outlook, choosing a meeting room. This room is linked to a service account in Exchange with a delegate's access to its mailbox. This service account is used by the Webex Hybrid Calendar service.
- **Calendar Sync with Webex calendar Connector**: The meeting details from the room calendar are synchronized to the Webex Control Hub through the Webex calendar connector on Exp-C.
- **Meeting Detail Sync to Endpoint**: The Control Hub then pushes these meeting details to the on-premises endpoint associated with the meeting room. This synchronization to the endpoint is facilitated via the Expressway-C connector, a component deployed within the on-premises infrastructure.
- **Meeting Start Option on Endpoint**: The endpoint displays the meeting details and provides a "Join" option at the scheduled meeting time. Users can initiate the meeting with a single click, connecting them directly to the Webex cloud meeting.
- **Conference Bridging by Webex Cloud**: The Webex Cloud platform handles the conferencing bridge, seamlessly connecting all participants in the meeting.

This is just a high-level overview. For more details, please check the Deployment guide for the Hybrid Calendar. Webex Hybrid Calendar also provides OBTP for third party meetings with specific configurations and pre-req, please check Cisco's documentation for details.

These high-level steps are almost identical to other services, like Zoom Room.

Zoom Rooms OBTP

Now, let's look at how OBTP works in Zoom Room.

- **Meeting Booking in Outlook**: A user schedules a meeting using Outlook, selecting a Zoom Room as the meeting location. This room is linked to a service account in Exchange with a delegate's access to its mailbox.
- **Calendar Sync with Zoom**: The Exchange service account, configured in Zoom, periodically checks the Outlook calendar for the Zoom Room. It fetches new meeting details using Microsoft Exchange Web Services (EWS).
- **Meeting Details Sync to Zoom Room**: Zoom Rooms automatically polls the calendar based on a predefined time interval set in the settings. Subsequently, the Zoom Rooms appliance relays this information to the room controller (the touch panel in the meeting room) and the scheduler, effectively updating them with the latest meeting schedule and details.
- **Endpoint Displays Meeting Information**: The Zoom Room controller updates its display to show the upcoming meetings, complete with all the relevant details and a "Join" button that becomes active at the scheduled meeting time.
- **Joining the Meeting via Zoom Room**: When it's time for the meeting, users in the Zoom Room can start the meeting by pressing the "Join" button on the controller. This action connects the room to the scheduled meeting on the Zoom Cloud.
- **Conference Bridging by Zoom Cloud**: The Zoom Cloud platform manages the conferencing bridge, ensuring all participants are connected and can interact effectively during the meeting.

For detailed steps, please check Zoom Calendar Integration documentation. Now, let's move on to Wireless Sharing in Meeting Rooms.

Wireless Sharing in Meeting Rooms

Wireless sharing technologies facilitate seamless sharing of content and presentations in meeting rooms and collaborative spaces without requiring physical cables or extensive setup.

It enables users to share content from their devices (laptops, tablets, smartphones) to a shared display (like a TV or projector). One of the most appreciated benefits is the reduced clutter, as wireless sharing eliminates the need for cables, tidies up the workspace and reduces potential connectivity issues. Additionally, they offer greater flexibility in room layout and seating arrangements, as users do not need to be tethered to a specific spot by physical connections.

Popular Wireless Sharing Solutions

Let's delve into the details of these technologies using examples like Barco Clickshare and Crestron.

- **Barco Clickshare**: Barco Clickshare is a wireless presentation system that allows multiple users to share content from their devices simultaneously. It typically involves a base unit connected to the display and a set of USB-powered devices called "Clickshare Buttons." Users connect these buttons to their devices to share content wirelessly.

  Their C-5 and C-10 models are focused on wireless presentation and collaboration, which are suitable for ad hoc screen sharing and basic collaboration features. They connect to room displays via HDMI for local content sharing from laptops.

  - **Challenges and Considerations**: Users need to plug in a USB device (Clickshare Button), which may only be convenient for some users, especially in a bring-your-own-device (BYOD) setting. They also have an app where you don't need the Clickshare Button. It may require the installation of drivers or applications, which can be a hurdle in environments with strict IT policies.

- **Crestron AirMedia**: Crestron offers a range of wireless presentation solutions, including the AirMedia series. These solutions allow users to present wirelessly using a simple app or, in some cases, native casting features of their devices. This solution enables wireless screen sharing from laptops and mobile devices to room displays over Wi-Fi. It connects to displays via HDMI and is mainly designed for local screen sharing.

In addition to third-party hardware solutions like Barco Clickshare and Crestron, organizations can leverage the apps of their web conferencing services for wireless sharing. This option can be particularly advantageous in environments where the organization already uses a specific web conferencing platform, as it can simplify the setup and provide a more integrated experience.

Zoom and Webex Apps for Wireless Content Sharing

In Zoom Rooms, sharing content using Wi-Fi is straightforward. The equipment in the room sends out special ultrasound signals. When you walk into the room with the Zoom app on your phone or laptop, the app hears these signals through your computer's microphone. This lets the app know it's near a Zoom Room and gets ready to share your screen. Your device needs to have a network reachability with Zoom Room, and you can start sharing your content with just a tap.

Webex works similarly when you're in a room with Cisco's video conferencing gear, like their Webex series endpoints. These devices also use ultrasound signals to talk to the Webex app on your device. When your app picks up these signals, it knows a Cisco device is nearby and gets ready to share your screen. Again, network reachability is required from your device to the Cisco endpoint.

Zoom and Webex use ultrasound signals to make the initial connection, but your network does the heavy lifting of sending your content from your device to the screen in the room. This setup is great because it means you don't need cables to share your content, but it also means that a good Wi-Fi connection is really important to avoid any lag or interruptions during your presentation.

Choosing the Appropriate Wireless Sharing Solution for Diverse Meeting Environments

Selecting an appropriate wireless sharing solution requires balancing technical capabilities with the specific needs of your meeting environments.

- **Integrated vs. Third-Party Solutions**: Products like Barco Clickshare and Crestron provide versatility, catering to diverse device ecosystems and room setups. These solutions often require additional connectivity hardware but are not restricted to specific software environments. They're suitable for varied meeting spaces, especially where technology integration is diverse.
- **Native wireless sharing features from Zoom and Webex** are best for organizations that predominantly use these platforms. These solutions provide smooth integration within their ecosystems but may offer limited flexibility in mixed-technology environments.

For organizations with a mix of advanced and basic meeting rooms, a universal third-party solution can ensure consistent user experiences across all spaces. For those heavily reliant on specific platforms like Zoom or Cisco, native wireless sharing solutions can maximize the utility of existing systems.

By carefully considering these factors, you can choose a wireless sharing solution that meets your technical needs and also aligns with your organization's user experience and operational efficiency goals.

Now let's delve into the customization possibilities with the Cisco Video endpoints, especially the new version of RoomOS.

RoomOS Customization and Integration Capabilities

RoomOS, the underlying operating system for Webex Devices, is an open platform with a versatile API, the xAPI, enabling profound customization and third-party extensions. These extensions can be developed by customers, partners, and third-party software developers, greatly enhancing the functionality of Cisco devices.

RoomOS supports various integration types, each with its specific connection method, network requirements, deployment strategies, and security models. The integrations all utilize the xAPI, differing mainly in their connection approach.

- **Macros**: JavaScript snippets running on the device, utilizing the xAPI library to interact with the device and receive feedback. Common use cases include custom UI actions, room control, and automated workflows. Macros run with either admin or integrator access, allowing broad API access but lacking fine-grained control over API permissions.
- **Cloud xAPI / Workspace Integrations**: These integrations run outside the collaboration device network and communicate with devices via the Webex cloud using REST APIs.
- **JSXAPI / Web Sockets**: A Node.js-based SDK that enables communication with devices on the same network using web sockets. This approach is versatile and allows for the use of external libraries but requires maintenance of device IP addresses, usernames, and passwords.
- **HTTP(S) API**: A stateless HTTP API using XML data for communication. It includes a webhook-like mechanism for device feedback. This approach is recommended for situations similar to JSXAPI but only where web sockets are not feasible, or feedback is not required.
- **RS-232 / SSH Connection**: These are cable-based connections for external room controllers like Crestron and Extron. They are typically used in the same room as the collaboration device and support various formats like command line, XML, or JSON.

These integrations can be helpful with other AV equipment, to extend Cisco endpoints functionality.

Now, let's explore customization in Room OS, including widgets, panels, and action buttons, which provide a versatile and user-friendly approach to tailor the functionality and interface of Cisco Webex devices.

Exploring Widgets and Panels for Room Navigator

RoomOS's UI panels and widgets are essential for creating custom user interfaces on Cisco devices. These interfaces can range from controlling room equipment like lights and temperature to automating tasks and providing user instructions.

UI Extensions on RoomOS devices enable developers to design panels and action buttons for custom functionalities. These extensions can appear as buttons on the home screen, call controls, or in the control panel, offering a variety of interactive possibilities.

Action buttons in RoomOS are designed to perform a single action when pressed. Developers can program these actions using the API command and the Macro Editor. For instance, creating an action button to display a message involves defining the button's ID, programming the action in the Macro Editor, and exporting the configuration to the device.

The event model of UI Extensions involves user interactions with general UI elements like buttons and sliders, triggering events. These events can be managed internally with macros or external integrations, such as virtual servers or Raspberry Pis. The bi-directional API allows real-time widget updates in response to changes, such as a light switch being toggled.

Widgets in RoomOS are programmed through the API or XML, and their behavior includes:

- Commands to change widget values
- Events triggered by user actions, such as pressing or releasing a button
- Interaction with the RoomOS through various modes, including terminal output and XML

Each widget on a panel must have a unique identifier or Widget ID, which links the UI to the device and the control system. This ID is included in all events associated with a widget and is used when sending commands to that widget.

To illustrate the practical application of widgets and panels in RoomOS, let's consider a scenario in a meeting room equipped with Cisco Webex devices. Let's understand how to create an intuitive and automated control system for various room elements like lights, blinds, and room temperature, enhancing the meeting experience.

1. **Develop a Custom Panel**: Utilizing the UI Extensions Editor, we create a custom panel named **`"Room Control Panel."`** This panel includes various widgets, such as sliders for light intensity, buttons for blinds control, and a temperature adjustment feature.

2. **Widget Configuration**: Each widget is assigned a unique ID for identification. For example, the light control slider is assigned the ID **`"light_control_slider."`**

3. **Macro Integration**: A macro is written and deployed on the device to listen for events triggered by the **`"Room Control Panel."`** The macro monitors user interactions, such as changes in the slider position or button presses, and translates these into commands for the respective room elements.

4. **Event-Driven Actions**: When a user adjusts the **`"light_control_slider,"`**

the macro sends a command to the room's lighting system to adjust the brightness accordingly. The temperature adjustment widget interacts with the room's climate control system to set the desired temperature.

Macros have limited functionality, and for advanced use cases, you can integrate the same way with third party Controllers (for example, Crestron, Lightware, etc). We will discuss controllers later in this chapter.

Now that we have explored the user-facing technologies let's shift our focus to the advanced audio-visual (AV) topics that operate behind the scenes.

Advanced AV Technologies

Now, let's explore some advanced topics in AV. These technologies play a crucial role in enhancing the overall collaboration experience, yet often remain unnoticed by the end users.

Let's start with third party sensors.

Sensors

Sensors in meeting rooms are integral to creating intelligent, responsive environments. These aren't limited to meeting rooms; we can find the same in smart home integrations as well, but we are discussing here in the context of meeting rooms.

Cisco Webex Room endpoints have inbuilt sensors that provide valuable data for optimizing meeting environments:

- **Presence and People Count**: These sensors facilitate real-estate optimization by tracking room occupancy and usage patterns
- **Air Quality and VOCs (Volatile Organic Compounds)**: These sensors detect pollutants in the air, contributing to healthier indoor environments
- **Noise Measurements:** Assessing ambient noise levels aids in designing more comfortable and conducive meeting spaces

Building upon the capabilities of the Cisco Webex Room endpoints, third-party motion, thermal, and temperature sensors (for example, from Lutron or Crestron) extend this functionality further.

Let's see, how automated environmental control systems use these sensors to make workspaces more efficient and comfortable.

- **Lighting Automation**: It integrates with sensors to activate lights based on room occupancy while also adapting to natural lighting conditions for energy efficiency.
    - Motion sensors trigger lights only in occupied spaces, reducing energy consumption

    - Automated lighting systems work with motorized shades to utilize natural light effectively
- **Window Shades Automation**: Motorized shades respond to lighting needs for video conferences or presentations, automatically adjusting to optimize screen visibility and room lighting.
- **HVAC Control via Sensors**: Sensors like Autani Wireless Room Controllers dynamically adjust the temperature, ensuring a comfortable and healthy environment based on real-time room usage.

Now that we've discussed sensors let's explore the role of in-room controllers in managing these technologies.

In-room Controllers

In-room controllers revolutionize complex audio-visual setups by centralizing control of various devices into a single, unified system. This integration ensures the seamless operation of essential components such as projectors, screens, sound systems, and video conferencing equipment. By transforming individual device management into a cohesive system, these controllers simplify AV setups, making them more efficient and user-friendly.

The scope of these controllers often extends beyond AV equipment, encompassing additional functionalities like lighting, window shades, and climate control within the room. This broader control spectrum allows for automated adjustments that significantly enhance the meeting experience. For instance, when a video conference is initiated, automated actions, such as dimming the lights, closing window shades, and optimizing audio levels, are triggered. This automation is convenient and ensures an uninterrupted flow during meetings or presentations.

In-room controllers integrated with video matrix switchers allow for sophisticated management of multi-source media distribution across multiple displays. For example, consider a large auditorium with multiple inputs like laptop connections, wireless presentation devices, cameras, and various output displays including main screens and repeater monitors. The video matrix switcher provides the ports for connecting and switching these sources and destinations. The in-room control system then provides the logic to route particular inputs to specific outputs as needed. This enables seamless distribution of multiple content sources across the appropriate screens.

Together, the matrix-switching capabilities and intelligent control logic facilitate dynamic and flexible presentations. Presenters can effortlessly transition between sharing different content with different display zones as required. This enhances the versatility of meetings and events, allowing speakers to share engaging, multi-source experiences tailored to this advanced AV environment.

Let's explore some popular products in the market, including Crestron and QSC. Similar solutions are also available from AMX, Lightware, and Extron. All Vendors have controllers and switchers that can be used interchangeably. Please ensure compatibility with Vendors.

- **Crestron Controllers**: Crestron's 4-Series (CP4, CP4N) is renowned for its advanced control capabilities over various devices. These controllers stand out for their extensive integration capabilities, robust programming options for custom automation, and reliability. They support multiple protocols and interfaces, catering to high-end conference rooms, corporate settings, and any space that demands detailed customization and integration. Crestron's strength lies in its customization and integration capabilities, making it the preferred choice for complex AV setups requiring high programmability and user-specific customization.
- **QSC Controllers**: The Q-SYS Core series, particularly Core 110f and Core Nano, highlight QSC's product range. These controllers are lauded for their exceptional audio integration, combining powerful audio, video, and control features into a single, scalable platform. Known for their audio DSP capabilities, QSC controllers are the go-to choice for environments where audio quality and processing are paramount, such as large conference spaces and auditoriums. QSC's focus on audio-centric setups makes it an ideal option for settings where sound quality is critical.

Each AV controller brand offers unique strengths tailored to specific use cases. The flexibility of these systems is critical; they can be customized or programmed to suit the unique requirements of any meeting space, ranging from compact huddle rooms to expansive conference halls.

Let's explore a use case demonstrating how these controllers can be integrated with Cisco video endpoints to create a seamless AV experience in meeting rooms.

Integrating lighting and AC automation with a Cisco touch panel involves a collaboration between third Party Vendor and Cisco. This integration offers solutions for common AV challenges without requiring custom programming or major changes. The key aspects include:

- **Plug-n-Play Solutions**: Utilizes built-in auto-switching on Crestron switchers for extending signals and expanding input numbers. This solution works out of the box with simple HDMI connections to the codec.
- **Configuration-Based Solutions**: These run on Crestron control systems, allowing various video switching and signal extension options. Installers use a web-based configuration page to set up the System, which can be easily replicated across multiple rooms.
- **Fully Custom Solutions**: Crestron Certified Drivers and Control Modules enable deep integration with the codec and customization through the

RoomOs API for bespoke conference rooms. This approach adds capabilities like lighting, climate, and shade control.

Crestron's DMPS Lite products employ the Cisco API for seamless integration, enabling direct communication with the WebEx room kit and Cisco Touch interface without complex programming or a control system. This makes it straightforward to deploy across multiple rooms.

The above explanation is based on Crestron's blog; you can find more details at https://www.crestron.com/News/Blog/October-2020/Crestron-and-Cisco-%E2%80%93-Better-Together.

Other vendors like Extron and Lightware have similar collaboration with Cisco.

Understanding Audio DSP (Digital Signal Processor)

An Audio DSP (Digital Signal Processor) is a specialized device used in sound processing and management, particularly in environments where high-quality audio is essential. It takes multiple audio inputs, such as microphones or line inputs, and processes these signals to produce a clear, balanced, and optimized audio output.

Let's explore some of the core functions of an audio DSP.

- **Multiple Audio Inputs**: Audio DSPs handle various input sources, from microphones to other audio line inputs, and mix, route, and switch between these inputs. This is especially important in settings like conference rooms or auditoriums, where multiple speakers or sound sources must be managed simultaneously.
- **Microphone Power and Management**: They provide microphones with the necessary (often phantom) power and manage their levels. This includes adjusting microphone gain (the microphone's sensitivity) and determining which microphones are active at any given time.
- **Expansion of Audio Capabilities**: Audio DSPs are crucial when the built-in audio processing of a device, like a video endpoint is insufficient. They allow for the expansion of audio capabilities, for instance, by integrating ceiling microphones in a large room to ensure even audio coverage or connecting to extended speaker systems to provide sufficient sound reinforcement for larger groups.
- **Sound Quality Enhancement**: DSPs enhance the overall sound quality by reducing noise (echo cancellation), managing feedback, and equalizing audio to adapt to different room acoustics. This results in clearer and more intelligible audio, vital for effective communication.
- **Customization of Audio Processing**: They allow for the customization of audio processing to suit specific needs. It can include setting up specific audio

profiles for different types of meetings or adjusting the audio processing to compensate for the acoustics of a room.

Consider a large conference room equipped with ceiling microphones. An audio DSP can be used to manage these mics effectively. It can power them, control which microphones are active at any moment (to avoid picking up unnecessary noise or feedback), and adjust their gain settings. Furthermore, the DSP can process the captured audio to enhance clarity, ensuring every participant receives a clear and balanced audio feed, whether in the room or joining remotely.

Some leading Audio DSP vendors are QSC, BSS Audio (by Harman), and Biamp.

QSC DSPs excel in integrated control processing and audio DSP; they have built-in controller processing and audio DSP, which reduces the need for additional control systems.

Advanced AV controllers and Audio DSPs complement Cisco's collaboration hardware, such as Webex Room Kits, by enhancing audio and video control capabilities in complex environments.

Now, let's shift our focus from the intricacies of hardware technology to the overall design and functionality of AV environments.

Environmental Considerations in AV Room Design

Environmental considerations are crucial in AV room design, impacting audio-visual systems' overall experience and effectiveness. Understanding how room acoustics, lighting, and layout influence AV setups is essential for creating optimal environments for communication and collaboration.

- **Room Acoustics**: Acoustics is a challenging yet fundamental aspect of AV room design. Understanding its impact on sound quality and the interplay of room dimensions, materials, and acoustic treatment is essential for creating an environment conducive to clear audio communication.
  - **Impact on Sound Quality**: The acoustic characteristics of a room significantly influence the quality of sound produced by AV systems. Poor acoustics can result in sound distortions, echoes, and unwanted reflections, which degrade audio clarity.
  - **Room Dimensions and Materials**: A room's size, shape, and construction materials affect its acoustics. Small rooms with hard, reflective surfaces tend to produce unnatural sounds, while larger rooms with absorbent materials sound more natural. Selecting appropriate materials for walls, ceilings, and floors is vital for achieving desired acoustic properties.

  - **Acoustic Treatment and Soundproofing**: Implement acoustic treatments like panels and diffusers to control reverberation and echoes, ensuring clear audio transmission. Soundproofing is critical to prevent external noise intrusion and maintain sound quality within the room.
  - **Microphone and Loudspeaker Directionality**: Position microphones and speakers strategically to maximize audio pickup and amplification, minimizing the impact of noise sources. It involves understanding the directional characteristics of these devices and aligning them to optimize sound quality and reduce unwanted noise interference.
- **Lighting**: Good lighting is imperative for videoconferencing and overall room aesthetics. It affects how participants are viewed and how comfortable they are in the space.
  - **Influence on Videoconferencing**: Lighting plays a pivotal role in videoconferencing environments. The ANSI/IES/AVIXA RP-38-17 standard provides guidelines for optimal lighting in videoconferencing rooms. Proper lighting enhances participant viewing, optimizes camera conditions, and improves overall communication and productivity of videoconferencing sessions.
  - **Glare Management**: Address the issue of glare, which can reduce screen visibility and cause eye strain. Utilize blackout shades and adjustable window treatments to control natural light.
  - **Layered Lighting Design**: Develop a layered lighting plan with separate controls for task, accent, and ambient lighting. Align lighting zones with seating arrangements and display locations to optimize visibility and reduce screen washouts.
  - **Strategic Lighting Placement**: Position lights to minimize glare on screens and ensure comfortable viewing for participants, enhancing the overall visual experience in the room.
- **Layout Considerations**: The physical layout of a room plays a significant role in the functionality and effectiveness of an AV setup.
  - **Speaker Placement**: Optimizing placement for the particular speaker and room dynamics provides the best acoustic results. Speaker placement depends on the room specifics, dispersion patterns, and manufacturer recommendations. General guidelines include angling stereo speakers inward, keeping speakers away from walls, positioning tweeters at ear level, and avoiding corners that can overemphasize bass.
  - **Room Layout**: The arrangement of furniture and other objects affects how sound waves travel and interact within a space. It's important to consider room layout in AV system placement to optimize sound distribution and minimize audio interference.

- **Room Shape and Furniture Placement**: Consider the impact of the room's shape, pillar placements, and furniture layout on lines of sight. An oblong shape or central table can obstruct views of the display.
- **Ergonomic and Functional Design**: Choose room layouts that facilitate easy viewing of displays and interaction among participants. Ensure the AV setup accommodates the natural flow of meetings and presentations.

Navigating the complexities of AV room design requires a structured approach. Let's outline a step-by-step methodology that addresses key environmental factors, ensuring that every aspect of the room's design contributes to an optimal AV experience.

This structured approach to AV room design encapsulates the essence of creating spaces that are functionally effective, aesthetically pleasing, and comfortable for users.

- **Understand Room Usage**: Describe typical meeting scenarios, occupancy, and functional requirements. It helps to determine the necessary AV components.
- **Evaluate Core Environment Constraints**: Conduct an acoustic analysis and identify potential noise sources. Assess lighting conditions to identify glare issues and mark areas with line-of-sight challenges.
- **Craft Design Strategies**: Implement acoustic treatment, layered lighting, and ergonomic room layouts. Design the space to support clear audio and visual communication while considering comfort and functionality.
- **Select AV Components Strategically**: Choose microphones, speakers, cameras, and display technologies that match the room's acoustic and visual characteristics. Ensure the equipment supports the intended use and enhances the user experience.

In short, integrating key environmental considerations like room acoustics, lighting, and layout forms the foundation of an effective AV environment. While we have highlighted some crucial aspects, it's important to recognize that this is not an exhaustive list. The field of AV design encompasses a wide range of expertise and adheres to comprehensive standards and guidelines.

Transitioning to a final aspect of AV technology, let's briefly explore hot desking and digital signage solutions. While these areas may seem peripheral, they are increasingly pivotal in modern collaborative environments.

Hot Desking and Digital Signage System

Hot desking is an office organization method where employees don't have permanent desks; instead, they choose various locations to work from throughout the day. This approach maximizes space efficiency and supports a flexible work environment. Hot desking gained traction due to shifts towards remote or hybrid work models, as it aligns with the need for adaptable workspaces.

Integration with room booking solutions is a key feature, allowing employees to reserve desks using familiar tools like mobile apps or online systems. These systems typically offer features like viewing floorplans and locating colleagues, facilitating smooth workspace management. Often, this is part of your Room scheduling system product/service.

Digital signage involves a network of digital displays for delivering tailored information and advertising. Managed centrally, digital signage uses a combination of hardware and software to execute its functionality. It's effective for increasing exposure, improving customer experience, and enhancing employee engagement.

Some of the key benefits of using Digital signage are:

- Reaching a broad audience with dynamic messaging
- Supporting real-time updates and consistent branding
- Cost-effective and environment-friendly compared to traditional print mediums.

Various solutions include large-format displays, interactive flat panels, mobile interaction displays, video walls, kiosk displays, outdoor displays, and speciality displays. These solutions serve different purposes, from interactive tasks to dynamic advertising in public spaces. Digital signage is also a virtual receptionist in lobbies, offering welcome messages, interactive wayfinding, real-time updates, visitor registration, and impressive video wall displays. This is often part of a broader workplace management suite, including additional capabilities like hotdesking, wayfinding, and digital signage. Some vendors offer end-to-end solutions encompassing both the software and hardware elements and some have partnerships/integrations with different vendors.

Cisco's Webex Room Navigator touch panels also allow extensive custom branding and digital signage functionalities suitable for corporate environments. It permits customized logos and backgrounds to match company branding in half-wake and awake states, enhancing corporate identity. When not used for meetings, the panel can display tailored content like announcements, calendars, or web pages. It allows organizations to utilize the panels as dynamic signage for internal communications and updates. However, the Webex Room Navigator has limited built-in digital signage capabilities and may require integration with third-party solutions like Appspace to unlock more advanced signage features.

Conclusion

This chapter covered several critical topics in unified communications - media resources, conferencing, and audio-visual solutions. We explored the different types of media resources and how they can be provisioned and assigned in CUCM to provide services like conferencing, transcoding, and media termination. The chapter also provided an overview of common voice and video codecs and how to configure codec preferences.

For audio-visual solutions, we explored the new tech that is changing how meeting rooms work. We looked at some examples from Cisco and other companies to give you an idea of what is currently available in the industry. This should help you understand what these systems can do and how they might fit into your setup.

In the next chapter, we will transition to collaboration cloud and hybrid solutions, including infrastructure deployed at the edge.

Multiple Choice Questions

1. What is the primary function of Media Resource Groups (MRGs) in CUCM?
    a. To manage voice mailboxes
    b. To segregate dialable address spaces
    c. To group media resources like transcoders, MTP
    d. To route calls between different devices
2. Which technology is essential for converting audio streams between different codecs in CUCM?
    a. Annunciator
    b. Music on Hold
    c. Transcoders
    d. Media Termination Point (MTP)
3. What is the role of an Annunciator in CUCM?
    a. To provide ringback tones
    b. To broadcast music on hold
    c. To deliver pre-recorded announcements
    d. To facilitate conference calls
4. What is the main advantage of wireless sharing in meeting rooms?
    a. Increased security
    b. Cable clutter reduction
    c. Faster data transfer
    d. Lower energy consumption

5. Which feature enables participants to join scheduled meetings with a single button press?
    a. Call Pickup
    b. OBTP
    c. Media Resource Groups
    d. Wireless Sharing

Answers

1. c
2. c
3. c
4. b
5. b

Further Reading

Same as in the last chapter, it is suggested to explore the following topics on your own to improve your understanding and broaden your perspective.. Remember to tailor your research based on your organization's specific needs and always discern between genuine insights and industry trends.

- **Voice and Video Codec Bandwidth Usage**: You can find lots of information on internet, or you can read this document from Cisco to see comparison of different voice codecs.
  https://www.cisco.com/c/en/us/support/docs/voice/voice-quality/7934-bwidth-consume.html
- **MTP Requirements**: Research when MTP is required or causes the call failure, specially over SIP trunk. You can find the information in Cisco's SRND document.
- **Research Different Meeting Room Booking Systems in the Market**: Explore what type of features different products have. How well do they integrate with your company's existing infrastructure or what value they will add if you deploy any of those in your environment.
- **Explore More About RoomOS:** You can find all the documentation about RoomOS here. I encourage you look at what's possible.
  https://roomos.cisco.com/doc/Welcome/Welcome

- **Explore Macros Available on GitHub**: There are many macros available for CE and RoomOs version. I encourage you to explore how they work and how they can help improve user experience in your environment: https://github.com/CiscoDevNet/roomdevices-macros-samples
- **Learn More About USB Passthrough with Cisco Endpoints**: This is a community-driven solution and not supported by Cisco TAC. It allows you to use the camera, microphone, and speakers of the Cisco device directly with your laptop, just by connecting them with a USB cable. We haven't covered this topic in this chapter as it is a very advanced topic. It's good to explore how it works. You can find the documentation here: https://roomos.cisco.com/macros/USB%20Mode%20Version%202

Chapter 7
Exploring Cisco Collaboration Cloud, Hybrid and Edge

Introduction

In this chapter, we begin exploring Collaboration services in the Cloud. We focus on the Webex suite, looking at its different services and then discuss hybrid scenarios, examining the various Webex hybrid services and how they benefit businesses. We go into detail on Cisco Expressway, briefly cover Cisco CUBE and wrap up the chapter by focusing on Edge servers in on-premises architectures.

Structure

We will discuss the following topics:

- Collaboration cloud
    - Webex Meetings, Messaging, Calling, Webinars and Vidcast
    - Webex Real-Time Media Models
- Webex Hybrid
    - Webex Hybrid Calendar and Directory Service
    - Webex Edge and Cloud-connected UC
- Edge Servers
    - Cisco Expressway
    - Cisco Unified Border Element

Collaboration Cloud

The shift towards Software as a Service (SaaS) for collaboration is a significant trend in the modern business landscape. SaaS offers cloud-based applications, simplifying access to collaboration tools like Video conferencing, Telephony, and Web conferencing without the need for on-site infrastructure.

Let's explore a few key points.

- **Scalability and Flexibility**: Traditional on-premises setups can be restrictive, particularly scaling. As businesses grow or their needs change, expanding an on-premises system often requires significant investment in hardware and software. SaaS platforms offer immense scalability. They allow businesses to easily adjust their service usage to match fluctuating demands, from scaling up for large meetings to scaling down in quieter periods without changing hardware.
- **Cost Considerations**: On-premises solutions typically involve substantial Capital Expenditures (CapEx) for hardware and Software. However, SaaS operates on an Operational Expenditure (OpEx) model with regular, predictable costs. SaaS offers a cost-effective solution for smaller businesses or those with variable needs. The subscription model negates the need for large upfront investments, making advanced collaboration tools accessible to a broader range of businesses.
- **Continuous Innovation:** SaaS providers can rapidly deploy new features and updates, keeping businesses at the forefront of collaboration technology. This agility contrasts with the slower innovation cycle of on-premises solutions, where updates often require lengthy testing and integration processes. SaaS platforms continuously improve with integrated updates without disrupting the user experience. This ensures businesses have access to the latest features and functionalities.
- **Reduced Operational Burdens on IT:** SaaS models significantly reduce the operational burden on IT staff. Maintenance tasks such as security updates, bug fixes, and system upgrades are managed by the SaaS provider. SaaS providers typically adhere to stringent security standards, ensuring data protection and compliance with regulatory requirements. This alleviates businesses from the complex task of managing these aspects in-house.

The shift from on-premises to cloud-based services in collaboration platforms fundamentally changes how integrations and system interactions are managed. Let's explore two key points:

- **Automation and Orchestration in Cloud Services**: Cloud-based services abstract the complexities of the underlying infrastructure, enabling more straightforward automation and orchestration processes. This contrasts with on-premises architectures, where automation often requires intricate knowledge of various components. Cloud services typically provide unified APIs across different features and offerings. This standardization simplifies integrating various services and tools, unlike the disparate interfaces often encountered in on-premises systems.

- **Partner Integration and Marketplace Evolution**: Third-party partners and service providers can integrate their solutions more easily in the cloud paradigm. The cloud offers a common platform with standardized APIs, making it simpler for partners to develop and integrate their applications.

  SaaS platforms often come with their own marketplaces, offering a variety of pre-built integration apps. These marketplaces are a hub for innovation, allowing businesses to extend their collaboration capabilities seamlessly. The availability of ready-made apps in these marketplaces democratizes access to advanced integrations. Companies can leverage integrations rather than custom development in on-premises solutions, even with limited budgets or technical expertise.

Now, let's explore Cisco's cloud-based collaboration services - the Webex suite.

Exploring the Cisco's Webex Suite

Cisco's Webex suite offers a comprehensive set of business communication and collaboration tools accessible through a unified application. This integration simplifies both the user experience and administrative management.

The unified user experience within the Webex suite eliminates the need to navigate between multiple apps for different tasks by offering:

- Seamless service integration, combining meetings, messaging, calling, and more in one interface
- Simplified feature activation, enabling new services directly within the app without additional downloads
- Consistent user interface across services, reducing the learning curve and enhancing adoption

Streamlined administrative management is achieved through the following:

- A Control Hub that provides administrators with a GUI for comprehensive service management
- API is available for Webex Control Hub, which allows administrators to manage various aspects of Webex services programmatically. The Webex Control Hub API provides several functionalities:
  - **Admin APIs**: For user management, licensing, and hybrid services
  - **Reports API:** For generating and managing reports on Webex service usage

  - **Device Management APIs**: To handle device peripherals and configurations, enhancing direct management capabilities from the Control Hub
- Webex also offers a variety of APIs that allow developers to integrate and enhance Cisco Webex services. These APIs have extensive capabilities for developers to create custom integrations, bots, and applications that leverage the robust features of the Cisco Webex platform.
  - Messaging API
  - Meetings API
  - Calling API
  - Devices API
  - Webex Assistant Skills API
  - FedRAMP API
  - Workspace Integrations API
  - Contact Center API
  - Embedded Apps API
  - Software Development Kits (SDKs) for various platforms, including iOS, Android, Browser, Node.js, and Java, to facilitate the development of Webex integrations and applications.

The Webex suite offers a range of key services designed to enhance collaboration and communication across teams and organizations:

- **Webex Meetings**: A video conferencing solution offering secure and inclusive collaboration experiences with features like recordings, transcriptions, immersive sharing, gesture recognition, and background noise removal
- **Webex Messaging**: Includes built-in messaging, file sharing, and whiteboarding to keep work moving between meetings
- **Webex Calling**: A modern business phone system with features like voice queues, HD voice, and Webex Go
- **Webex Events**: End-to-end event management software for industry trade shows, conferences, and summits, with features like event registration, check-in, and analytics
- **Webex Webinars**: An interactive webinar platform supporting up to 100,000 attendees, offering simple setup and delivery with audience engagement
- **Slido**: An integrated polling and Q&A tool for engaging audiences in meetings and events
- **Vidcast**: A solution for asynchronous video messaging that allows recording and sharing content without blocking calendar time

Built on a reliable platform, Webex integrates these services to support a variety of work environments and needs without complicating user experience.

We will not go through each service in detail but explore a few.

Webex Meetings

Webex Meetings redefines the video conferencing experience with features designed for clarity, convenience, and comprehensive collaboration. Let's explore some key features of Webex meetings:

1. **HD Video Conferencing**: Accommodates up to 1000 participants with high-definition video, adapting to various bandwidth environments for optimal quality.
2. **Advanced Screen Sharing**: Improved quality and frame rate, making detailed content easily viewable by all participants. Along with Whiteboard and annotation capabilities.
3. **Multi-Platform Meeting Access**: Join meetings from Webex apps for desktop and mobile, or web browser, PSTN dial-in, or SIP-enabled devices. Allows to join meetings hosted by third-party platforms like Microsoft Teams directly within the Webex app.
4. **Meeting Recording**: Record meetings with the option to manually add chapters. Automated transcription is also available.
5. **Dynamic Virtual Backgrounds**: Options for blurring, custom images, animated GIFs, or video files as backgrounds, offering personalization and enhanced visual engagement.
6. **Breakout Sessions**: Create smaller discussion groups within a larger meeting for focused collaboration.
7. **In-Meeting Chat and Polling**: Engage participants with text chat, live polls, and Q&A sessions enhanced by Slido integration.
8. **Enhanced Meeting Security**: Robust end-to-end encryption and other security protocols for highly secure meetings.
9. **Remote Desktop Control:** Allow hosts to take control of a participant's screen for hands-on troubleshooting.
10. **Meeting Roles and Delegation**: Assign host, cohost, and presenter roles for efficient meeting management.
11. **Audio Intelligence**: Enhances audio quality through features like background noise removal, music optimization, and tuning voice pickup based on room acoustics and multiple speakers.

12. **Language Intelligence**: Provides real-time closed captioning, post-meeting transcripts, and spoken language translation into over 100 languages to aid comprehension.
13. **Video Intelligence**: Uses AI to optimize video framing, tracking and focusing on active speakers, and adjusting camera settings to improve video quality.
14. **Collaboration Insights**: Analyzes collaboration patterns and provides visibility into insights like profiles of frequent collaborators and personal collaboration habits.
15. **Webex Assistant**: AI-powered voice-activated assistant for tasks, such as meeting organization, note-taking, decision tracking, and controlling devices. It also enables building custom skills tailored to specific needs.

Webex Messaging

Webex Messaging ensures that teamwork flows smoothly with features that support constant communication and resource sharing. Let's explore some key features of Webex Messaging:

1. **Continuous Team Collaboration**: Persistent, always-on chat rooms with enhanced file sharing and digital whiteboarding
2. **Customizable Workspaces**: Spaces for specific projects or teams with centralized resources
3. **Robust Secure Communication**: End-to-end encryption with stronger security protocols, ensuring the confidentiality and integrity of all conversations
4. **Seamless Meeting Integration**: Fluid transition from messaging to video meetings with improved interface and connectivity, enhancing user convenience
5. **Expanded Third-Party Integration**: Broader connectivity with productivity tools, offering a more integrated and unified workflow experience

Webex Calling

Webex Calling brings cloud innovation to business phone systems, transitioning from traditional on-premises PBX to a fully integrated cloud calling solution. This shift simplifies infrastructure and enriches communication capabilities with various advanced features. Let's examine the key features of Webex Calling that are transforming business communication:

- **Call Routing Features**: Intelligent call routing, call queues, auto attendants, and transcriptions.

- **Advanced Call Handling**: Call forwarding, simultaneous ring, call park, ad hoc conference calls.
- **Voicemail and Unified Messaging**: Visual voicemail, voicemail to email, secure voicemail.
- **Mobility Features**: Native mobile app, business phone number on mobile devices, WiFi calling.
- **Flexible Deployment Options**: Hybrid or fully cloud-based setup.
- **Interoperability**: Interoperable with existing telephony infrastructure.

Webex Calling provides various Public Switched Telephone Network (PSTN) options to cater to different business needs and preferences. These options include:

- **Cisco Calling Plan**: This is a simplified option where Cisco provides PSTN services as part of the Webex Calling package. It's an all-in-one solution that's easy to set up and manage, making it a convenient choice for businesses looking for a straightforward approach to integrating PSTN with their Webex Calling environment.
- **Cloud Connected PSTN (CCP)**: This option uses Cisco-certified partners for PSTN services. Cloud Connected PSTN offers flexibility to businesses, allowing them to choose a provider based on coverage, number availability, features, packaging, and pricing. It's managed through a single pane of glass, and once numbers are procured, administrators can assign and manage them across different providers in different countries directly through Control Hub. This option suits organizations that require more control over their PSTN services and prefer to work with specific providers.
- **Local Gateway**: For businesses that need to continue using their current carrier, have an existing long-term contract with their carrier, or require service in a remote branch office, the local gateway option allows them to pair Webex Calling with virtually any PSTN provider worldwide. This approach leverages existing provider relationships and on-premises hardware while delivering Webex Calling features to their users. The local gateway can be deployed as a standalone or integrated with the Cisco Unified Communications Manager. This option provides the most flexibility and is particularly useful for businesses with specific requirements or existing infrastructure they wish to utilize.

  The deployment of Local Gateways for Webex Calling can be configured in various ways, depending on the organization's specific requirements. Here are the key deployment models:

- **Standalone Local Gateway Deployments**: This model is suitable for organizations without any existing IP PBX. It applies to both single-location and multi-location deployments. In this setup, all calls that do not match

Webex Calling destinations are sent to the local gateway assigned to the location for processing. The local gateway routes calls from Webex Calling to the PSTN and vice versa.

- **Local Gateway Deployments with On-Premises CUCM**: This model is needed when Webex Calling-enabled locations are added to an existing Cisco UC deployment where Unified CM is deployed as the on-premises call control solution. It's also required for direct dialing between phones registered to Unified CM and phones in Webex Calling locations.

  In this deployment, Webex Calling sends calls that do not match the customer's Webex Calling destinations to the local gateway, including PSTN numbers and Unified CM internal extensions. The local gateway routes all calls from Webex Calling to Unified CM and vice versa. Unified CM then routes incoming calls to local destinations or the PSTN as per the existing dial plan.

Now, let's demystify the licensing structure for Webex Calling's PSTN connectivity options, we will understand how each choice impacts your overall licensing strategy. This explanation is for illustrative purposes, and licensing options may change. Consulting directly with Cisco's sales or account manager is best for the most current information and tailored advice.

For all three options, the underlying Webex Calling license is a prerequisite. Webex Calling offers different license types through the Cisco Collaboration Flex Plan, including:

- **Professional**: Full feature set for the entire organization, including UC, mobility, team collaboration, and meeting options
- **Basic**: Limited features without mobility or UC, suited for users who need a voice-only option
- **Workspaces/Common Area**: Limited calling features, ideal for areas, such as lobbies or break rooms

The PSTN option does not typically affect the type of Webex Calling license you choose; rather, it affects how your external calling capabilities are integrated and billed.

The licensing for the three Public Switched Telephone Network (PSTN) options in Webex Calling largely depends on the chosen PSTN connectivity method. Here's an overview of how licensing works for each PSTN option:

- **Cisco Calling Plans**: When you opt for Cisco Calling Plans, the PSTN service is bundled as part of the Webex Calling package. The licensing for Cisco Calling Plans is typically straightforward and unified. It's part of the Webex Calling license, meaning that you purchase a comprehensive package that includes both the calling capabilities of Webex and the PSTN services.

This option simplifies billing and administration since you're dealing with a single vendor (Cisco) for both Webex Calling features and PSTN connectivity.

- **Cloud Connected PSTN (CCP)**: In the case of Cloud Connected PSTN, you choose from Cisco-certified third-party PSTN providers. Licensing and billing for PSTN services are handled separately from the Webex Calling license. You will have a separate agreement with the chosen PSTN provider.

  This means that while you have a Webex Calling license for accessing the Webex suite of collaboration tools, the PSTN aspect is billed and managed through the third-party provider you select. However, integration allows for some level of management through Cisco's Control Hub.

- **Local Gateway**: When using a local gateway, you're essentially integrating Webex Calling with your existing PSTN services, which could be from any carrier you choose. The licensing for the local gateway option is more complex since it involves the Webex Calling license and any existing agreements you have with your PSTN provider. In addition, depending on your setup, there might be additional licensing requirements for the hardware or software that forms the local gateway (e.g., Cisco Unified Border Element (CUBE) licenses if you are using Cisco hardware for the gateway).

  This option provides the most flexibility regarding carrier choice but requires careful management to ensure compatibility and cost-effectiveness.

Before we explore the next service, let's take a moment to highlight two distinctive features that set Webex Calling apart.

Webex Go

Webex Go integrates Webex Calling into mobile devices using eSIM technology, allowing users to handle both personal and business communications on the same device. This feature enables access to Webex Calling's enterprise-grade functionalities, such as extension dialing, business voicemail, and call recording directly from the mobile's native dialer.

Webex Go enable users to add a business line to their personal mobile device or opt for a mobile operator option for a dedicated wireless business number. The service provides access to enterprise-grade features, such as extension dialing, call recording, and business voicemail, all delivered with superior call quality over the mobile network. Additionally, Webex Go simplifies call management by enabling users to transfer calls easily between Cisco devices and upgrade calls to full collaboration meetings with video and content sharing. Webex Go offers centralized device management through the Control Hub for IT administrators, allowing corporate policies and compliance measures to be applied.

To utilize Webex Go effectively, there are a few key prerequisites:

- **Licensing Requirements**: Users must obtain either paid or trial Webex Go licenses to access the service
- **Device Compatibility**: The service is compatible with unlocked mobile phones that support eSIM technology
- **Purchase Channels**: Webex Go services and licenses are available exclusively through Webex Calling certified partners

Currently, Webex Go is available in specific regions, including the U.S. and UK.

In summary, Webex Go merges personal and professional communication functionalities onto a single mobile device through eSIM technology, offering a practical solution for modern business needs. It simplifies mobile communication by integrating business calling features without needing additional applications, supported by Webex Calling's robust features.

For detailed information on Webex Go, please visit the official Webex help page:

https://help.webex.com/en-us/article/n2fha94/What-is-Webex-Go

Webex Calling for Microsoft Teams

The integration of Webex Calling with Microsoft Teams combines Webex's advanced calling features with the comprehensive messaging and collaboration environment of Microsoft Teams, allowing users to manage calls directly within the Teams interface. This integration simplifies workflows by enabling users to access Webex's enterprise-grade Telephony and audio intelligence directly from Teams without needing to toggle between different platforms.

The integration supports voice and video calls via the Webex interface within Teams, allowing for speed dial management, viewing recent calls, listening to voicemails, managing call settings, and forwarding options directly in Teams.

Setting up this integration requires a Webex Control Hub with a Webex Calling subscription and appropriate Office 365 licensing. Administrators can enable the Webex Call app in the Teams Admin Center, ensuring that it aligns with permission policies and is added to Teams setup policies. Users will need to authenticate with both Microsoft and Webex accounts to use Webex Calling features within Teams.

Notably, this integration does not incur extra licensing costs and applies to both CUCM on-premises environments and Webex Cloud Calling. It's designed to be client-side, making it relatively straightforward to implement. Features like multi-call window management and bidirectional presence synchronization can be configured in the Control Hub to ensure a seamless user experience across both platforms.

For more detailed instructions on configuring Microsoft Teams for Webex Calling, including permission policies, app installation, and presence sync permissions, visit the Cisco help page https://help.webex.com/en-us/article/ngmx08cb/Webex-Calling-for-Microsoft-Teams

Webex Webinars

Webex Webinars facilitates hosting large-scale virtual webinars, integrating various features to support interactivity and global accessibility. It can support events, allowing up to 100,000 attendees, providing scalability for different event sizes. The platform includes real-time translation capabilities for over 100 languages, broadening the potential audience reach. Features such as live polling, Q&A sessions, and emoji reactions are available to engage participants actively. Additionally, the platform offers customization options for branding, enabling organizations to align the webinar appearance with their branding guidelines. Pre-event rehearsal and practice tools are available for presenters to ensure smooth delivery. Webex Webinars also integrate with various external applications, enhancing workflow efficiency and accessibility features, including live interpreters' support and ensuring inclusivity for all participants.

The licensing model for Webex Webinars offers different tiers based on attendee capacity. Key aspects include:

- **Attendee Capacity Options**: Tiers for 1,000, 3,000, 5,000, 10,000, and 10,000+ attendees
- **Real-Time Translation Add-On**: Offers translation services in real-time from English to over 100 different closed-captioned languages, available at an additional cost

Vidcast (Video Messaging)

Vidcast, part of the Webex Suite, is Webex's solution for asynchronous video messaging. Vidcast addresses the need for asynchronous communication by allowing users to record and share video messages. This tool facilitates efficient information sharing without aligning schedules for live meetings. Users can create and distribute video content, enabling recipients to view and interact with the material at their convenience.

The service simplifies the sharing process, making it straightforward for users to distribute content across their organization or team.

Before we move to the next section, let's revisit the point about continuous innovation in SaaS services. One example is Webex's introduction of Real-Time Media Models (RMMs) and AI-related features. Cisco announced these advancements at WebexOne in October 2023, marking a significant leap towards enhancing hybrid work and contact center experiences through generative AI.

Webex Real-Time Media Models

RMMs employ generative AI to process and analyze audio and visual cues during meetings. This technology enhances the quality of media streams and generates contextual insights by understanding participants' tone of voice, gestures, and facial expressions. Features such as AI-driven audio codecs and super-resolution for video ensure that Webex services can deliver high-definition experiences even in challenging network conditions.

Let's understand its impact on Webex Services.

- **Audio and Video Quality Enhancement**: By dynamically processing media streams, RMMs maintain crystal-clear audio and video quality, regardless of bandwidth constraints. This results in a more consistent and reliable meeting experience.
    - The new AI Codec in Webex aims to deliver clear audio regardless of network conditions. It reduces audio choppiness and incorporates speech enhancement functions like noise removal and de-reverberation.
    - Super Resolution for Video uses generative AI to rebuild video packets in poor bandwidth conditions, ensuring high-definition meeting experiences even with limited bandwidth.
- **Contextual Insights and Summaries**: RMMs can track participants' actions, like gestures of approval or leaving the frame, incorporating these details into enriched meeting summaries. This contextual data adds a layer of understanding to digital interactions, making follow-ups more accurate and meaningful. RMMs analyze various audio and visual cues, including tone of voice, gestures, and facial expressions, to generate real-time insights. This data can be used for various purposes, such as improving communication and collaboration.
- **Accessibility and Efficiency**: The ability of RMMs to provide instant meeting summaries for participants who momentarily step away ensures continuous engagement.
- **Webex Contact Center Efficiency**: With the integration of RMMs in the Webex AI Assistant, contact center agents can receive context-rich suggested responses and summaries, improving customer interactions. Supervisors can use these insights to identify training opportunities and positive reinforcement without reviewing entire chat transcripts or call recordings.

The models are part of Cisco's broader generative AI strategy, aiming to add audio and video data into contextual formats aligned with generative AI workflows. You can find more details here: https://www.webex.ai/

This information on Webex Real-Time Media Models and AI enhancements is sourced from Cisco's WebexOne event and Cisco's official documentation. These features are subject to further development due to the rapid pace of technological advancements. For the most current application and functionality, directly testing these features is recommended to ensure they meet your specific requirements.

If you are looking to gain a more in-depth understanding of the architectural design and infrastructure of the Webex platform,, Cisco's live presentation titled "Webex Infrastructure & Platform - BRKCOL-2990" is a valuable resource. This presentation covers the nuances of Webex's design and architecture, providing insights into how Cisco has tailored its platform to meet the demands of modern collaboration.

Now, let's explore a hybrid scenario where organizations leverage both on-premises infrastructure and Webex cloud services. This approach allows for a seamless blend of on-premises control and cloud agility, offering a comprehensive solution for today's hybrid work environments.

Webex Hybrid

This shift towards a hybrid model underscores Cisco's commitment to innovation across both on-premises and cloud solutions, ensuring organizations can navigate their transition to the Cloud at their own pace while maximizing the benefits of Cisco's collaboration technologies.

Cisco offers solutions like Webex Media Node and Expressway Connectors, bridging on-premises systems with the Cloud. Webex Media Node optimizes media streams for Webex Meetings, reducing latency and bandwidth requirements, while Expressway Connectors facilitate secure connectivity between on-premises environments and Cisco cloud services. This hybrid approach not only maintains the robustness of on-premises systems but also leverages the scalability and innovation of cloud services, ensuring businesses have access to the best of both worlds.

Cisco Expressway facilitates seamless integration between on-premises infrastructure and Cisco's cloud services through a suite of connectors. Let's explore hybrid services which use these connectors:

- **Webex Hybrid Calendar Service**: This service integrates on-premises Microsoft Exchange with the Webex Cloud, utilizing the Expressway-based Calendar Connector. See the deployment guide for more details: https://www.cisco.com/go/hybrid-services-calendar
- **Webex Hybrid Message Service**: This service enables the exchange of messages and presence status between Cisco Webex messaging and Cisco Unified Communications Manager IM and Presence Service. See the deployment guide for more details: https://www.cisco.com/go/hybrid-services-message

- **Webex Serviceability Connector**: This connector facilitates the automation of diagnostic log collection and other serviceability tasks and is recommended to be hosted on Expressway for Cloud-Connect UC. See the deployment guide for more details: https://www.cisco.com/go/serviceability

To install these connectors, refer to their specific deployment guide. Additionally, ensure your Expressway-C connector host for hybrid services is up-to-date with the latest software release.

Installing Webex Hybrid Connectors on Cisco Expressway involves several steps and considerations. Here's a general overview of the process:

- **Preparation**: Before installing any connectors, ensure that your Cisco Expressway runs a supported version of the software and is properly configured for the deployment. Understanding your network setup and requirements for each connector you plan to install is important.
- **Installing the Connector Software**: Depending on the specific hybrid service (such as Hybrid Messaging, Hybrid calendar, etc.), you need to follow the respective deployment guide to install the connector software on your Expressway-C. This typically involves downloading and running the connector software from the Cisco website or the Expressway-C interface.
- **Connector Registration**: Register your Expressway-C connector host to the Webex Cloud. This is a crucial step in the installation process, enabling your on-premises environment to connect securely with Webex services.
- **Configuration**: After installation, configure the connector according to your organizational needs and the specific requirements of the service.

It's important to note that connectors are installed on Expressway-C rather than Expressway-E. This is due to the components' distinct roles within Cisco's architecture.

- Expressway-C and Expressway-E serve different functions in an architecture. Expressway-C (Core) is designed to operate within an organization's internal network. It typically handles tasks more aligned with internal management and integration with other Cisco Unified Communications solutions, making it suitable for hosting services and connectors requiring direct access to internal systems.
- Expressway-E (Edge) facilitates secure firewall traversal and provides connectivity between an organization's internal network and external networks, including the Internet. It acts as a border element, managing the traffic that enters or leaves the organization's network. Installing hybrid connectors on Expressway-E would expose them directly to the external network, which is not ideal from a security perspective.
- Hybrid services often require integration with internal systems such as Cisco Unified Communications Manager, Microsoft Exchange, or Active Directory.

Being within the internal network, Expressway-C can communicate more securely and efficiently with these systems than Expressway-E.

- Architectural best practices typically dictate that any application or service that requires direct access to internal network resources should be placed within the internal network for better control and security.

As you see in this *Figure 7.1*, we can deploy connector on dedicated Exp-C just for this purpose. It's deployed in internal network and communicates with Cloud on HTTPS. This figure shows hybrid calendar connector as example, communicating with On-prem exchange server.

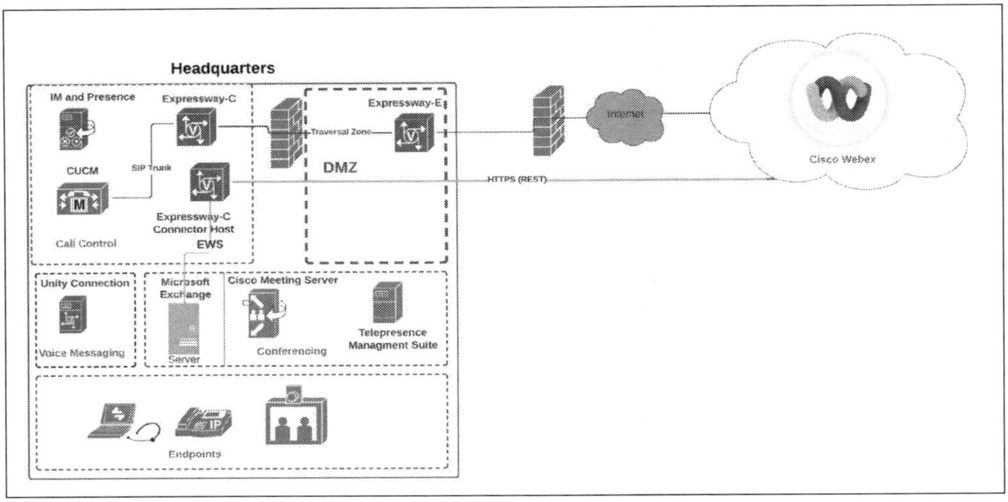

Figure 7.1: *Expressway Connector Host*

It's important to note that not all Webex Hybrid Services require deployment through Expressway. Below are examples of services with deployment requirements outside of Expressway.

- **Webex Hybrid Data Security**: Moves the Key Management Service (KMS) and other security-related functions to your enterprise data center for enhanced data security. See the deployment guide for more details: https://www.cisco.com/go/hybrid-data-security
- **Cisco Directory Connector**: Simplifies administrative experience by automatically synchronizing Microsoft Active Directory users with Webex user management. See the deployment guide for more details: https://www.cisco.com/go/hybrid-services-directory
- **Webex Hybrid Calling for Devices**: Provides hybrid call functionality for Room, Desk, and Cisco Webex Board devices, integrating them into your existing on-premises dial plan. See the deployment guide for more details: http://www.cisco.com/go/hybrid-call-webex-devices

Now that we've covered the basics of connector installation, it's time to look at the range of hybrid services available. We will only focus on a few key services.

Webex Hybrid Calendar Service

We discussed One Button to Push (OBTP) in *Chapter 6: Media Resources, Conferencing, and AV Solutions*, in the context of Webex Hybrid Calendar Service; it seamlessly integrates with your organization's existing calendar system to streamline meeting management.

Hybrid Calendar parses meeting details from the calendar system, including location, start and end times, and invitees. It populates the meetings list in the Webex App and provides a Join button (One Button to Push - OBTP). The Hybrid Calendar can also parse video addresses from calendar invitations, even for non-Webex meetings. When a supported address is detected, the meeting appears in the users' Webex App and is enabled for OBTP on Webex devices like scheduled rooms and desks that are enabled for the Hybrid Calendar.

The Expressway-based connector integrates Webex with Microsoft Exchange through an impersonation account. The Hybrid Calendar uses Exchange Web Services (EWS) to access calendar events and supports a range of mailbox operations but only uses a subset of commands for calendar use cases.

Webex Hybrid Directory Service

Cisco Webex Hybrid Directory Integration allows organizations to integrate their existing on-premises AD environment with the cloud-based Webex platform. This integration enables users to access Webex services using their existing corporate credentials, provides centralized management of user identities and permissions, and simplifies administration tasks such as user provisioning and de-provisioning.

Cisco Directory Connector automatically synchronizes Microsoft Active Directory users into Webex Control Hub. This ensures that user account information is always current in the Cloud, with the Active Directory remaining the single source of truth for all user account information mirrored in Control Hub.

When users attempt to log in to Webex, they are prompted to enter their email address. If the email address's domain portion matches an enabled hybrid AD integration domain, the user is redirected to the organization's identity provider (IdP), typically Microsoft Azure AD or Okta, to authenticate. The IdP verifies the user's credentials against the on-premises AD server and, if successful, grants them access to Webex.

Webex Hybrid Directory Service and Cisco Directory Connector refer to the same integration capabilities between on-premises Active Directory and the Webex Cloud. The names are synonymous and used interchangeably.

Webex Edge

Cisco Webex Edge is a suite of services consisting of three main components: Webex Edge Audio, Webex Edge Connect, and Webex Video Mesh.

Webex Edge is designed to enhance the quality and efficiency of Cisco Webex meetings and calls, especially for organizations using Cisco Unified Communications Manager. It also includes device management capabilities known as Webex Edge for Devices. Webex Edge for Devices allows on-premises endpoints to maintain on-prem registration while still accessing cloud-based monitoring and management through Control Hub.

Each component serves distinct purposes: enhancing audio and video call quality, optimizing network connections, and facilitating better control over on-premise devices.

Let's dive deeper into each part and understand their functionalities and technical operations:

1. **Webex Edge Audio**: Webex Edge Audio is a feature designed to optimize the integration between Cisco Webex meetings and an organization's telephony infrastructure. It achieves this optimization by rerouting audio calls that would traditionally traverse the Public Switched Telephone Network (PSTN) to an "on-net" path. It also provides cost savings for participants using callback from any phone by routing the callback via on-net Expressways and out through the organization's own PSTN gateways. This service connects to the Webex Cloud through Cisco Expressway without additional licenses, offering an end-to-end VoIP path for Unified Communications Manager-registered devices.

   In summary, Webex Edge Audio provides a dual benefit for organizations:

   a. **On-net call routing for Cisco endpoint users**: Allows meeting attendees using Cisco IP phones to join meetings via on-net call routing through Expressway/CUCM instead of the PSTN.

   b. **Cost optimization for callback PSTN**: For participants dialing into a Webex Meeting via callback, Edge Audio routes the return call through the enterprise's own PSTN gateways via Expressway instead of using the Webex Cloud telephony infrastructure. Leveraging existing on-prem PSTN connectivity enables organizations to reduce telephony/audio charges incurred in Webex Meetings.

   For step-by-step guidance on deploying and configuring Webex Edge Audio, refer to the official Cisco documentation available at:

   https://help.webex.com/en-us/article/4pldzd/Cisco-Webex-Edge-Audio-Deployment-Options

https://help.webex.com/en-us/article/xmsy7d/Cisco-Webex-Edge-Audio-Customer-Configuration-Guide

2. **Webex Edge Connect**: This service provides a dedicated, managed, Quality-of-Service (QoS) enabled IP link from a customer's premises to the Cisco Webex cloud through direct peering, such as via the Equinix Cloud Exchange. It offers enhanced meeting quality with consistent network performance and additional security compared to public internet-based connections. By leveraging a direct connection to the Webex backbone, Webex Edge Connect reduces congestion, packet loss, jitter, and delay, thus offering a more reliable and secure meeting experience.

3. **Webex Video Mesh**: Formerly known as Hybrid Media Service, this component is included within the Webex Edge service. Video Mesh allows local media processing for select Cisco Webex on-premises meeting attendees, improving video quality and reducing latency by not requiring media to traverse to the Cloud and back for call processing. It automatically cascades to the Cloud when on-premises resources are full or unavailable, ensuring all participants can join the meeting.

4. **Webex Edge for Devices**: Allows on-premises devices to stay registered while gaining access to cloud-only features and monitoring through the Control Hub. On-premises registration, device management, calling, and media services continue operating locally while benefiting from cloud services and device diagnostics. Current features include connection status monitoring, device diagnostics, historical analytics, cloud xAPI access, real-time media metrics, and log management.

Let's explore two popular Webex Edge services in detail - Webex Video Mesh and Webex Edge for Devices.

Webex Video Mesh

Webex Video Mesh, previously known as Hybrid Media Service, is a Cisco-designed solution to enhance video conferencing quality and efficiency by integrating Cloud and on-premises resources. This service aims to provide an optimal meeting experience by dynamically deciding whether to route video conferencing traffic through the local network (on-premises) or the Cloud based on various factors like location, resource availability, and network conditions. Here is a high-level view of how it works:

- When a user starts or joins a video conference, the System determines whether an on-premises Video Mesh Node can handle the call. This decision is based on factors, such as the availability of on-premises nodes, the current load, and the geographic location of the participants.

- If the criteria for on-premises handling are met, the call is routed to a local Video Mesh Node. If not, or if the on-premises node reaches capacity, additional participants are dynamically routed to the Cloud without interrupting the ongoing meeting.
- Video Mesh Nodes can optimize media streams in real-time. This includes adjusting video quality based on available bandwidth, performing transcoding when necessary, and minimizing latency by choosing the shortest path for media traffic.
- In case of a node failure, calls are automatically rerouted to either another on-premises node or the Cloud, ensuring high availability.

Keeping media traffic on-premises reduces the bandwidth needed from the enterprise network to the Internet and also reduces latency, increases video quality, and enhances the overall user experience.

Originating from Cisco's Meeting Server (CMS), the Webex Video Mesh Node has been specifically adapted to serve the Webex ecosystem, leveraging its foundational architecture. It can be deployed on a Cisco Meeting Server 1000 appliance or as a virtualized solution on VMware ESXi 6.0 or later. Post-deployment, these nodes need registration within the Webex ecosystem through the Webex Control Hub. This process involves assigning each node to a cluster by inputting the node's IP address into the Control Hub, thereby integrating the node with Webex. The architecture allows for the seamless addition of new nodes into the cluster, facilitating scalable expansion and enhanced redundancy.

Deploying Video Mesh Nodes within a cluster configuration is recommended to maximize capacity and ensure redundancy. Configured in an active/active setup, the clusters are designed to provide fault tolerance, allowing uninterrupted meeting continuity even if a node encounters an issue. This clustering capability ensures high availability and supports the dynamic allocation of endpoints to nodes based on current load and capacity, optimizing resource use. Moreover, it enables the System to cascade meetings across multiple nodes if needed, ensuring efficient handling of larger meetings without compromising the quality or performance.

Webex app and SIP endpoints registered on CUCM discover routes to Webex Video Mesh Node differently. Let's examine the differences.

- Webex app undergoes a discovery process to determine the most suitable Video Mesh Node or cluster for media termination. This process involves:
    - When a Webex app starts, it registers to Webex. Webex then returns the addresses of cloud media services and Video Mesh Node clusters provisioned for that Webex organization.
    - If a Video Mesh Node is unreachable (e.g., outside the corporate network without VPN access), the endpoint will default to using Webex cloud media services.

  - To calculate the round-trip delay time (RTD) between the endpoint and the media nodes. The endpoint aims to use a Video Mesh cluster with the shortest RTD, enhancing the overall meeting experience by reducing latency.
- SIP endpoints registered with Cisco Unified CM can leverage Video Mesh for Webex Meetings. This setup involves:
  - Configuring a SIP trunk on CUCM to point to a Video Mesh Cluster, which can be secured with TLS for encrypted media transmission.
  - Using a SIP route pattern in CUCM to direct calls to a specific domain (For example, sitename.webex.com) through the SIP trunk to the Video Mesh cluster.
  - The Video Mesh Node signals Webex to set up and host the meeting on a selected cluster node, directing SIP endpoint media accordingly.
  - If all nodes are at capacity, CUCM can reroute the call to Webex through the Cisco Expressway, demonstrating the flexibility and resilience of the Video Mesh solution in accommodating various meeting scenarios.

For the latest details and in-depth technical information, refer to Cisco's official documentation on Webex Video Mesh: https://www.cisco.com/c/en/us/td/docs/solutions/CVD/Collaboration/hybrid/12x/hybcvd/hms.html

Webex Edge for Devices

Webex Edge for Devices is a Cisco offering that combines on-premises device registration with cloud-based features and management. It allows organizations to leverage cloud-based monitoring, troubleshooting, analytics, and APIs while retaining on-premises device registration, management, calling, and media services.

To use Webex Edge for Devices, we need Control Hub Access and Webex Room Devices that support CE9.15.3 or higher. A key requirement is an HTTPS connection from the on-premises device to the Webex Cloud. This connection can also function through proxies. The onboarding process involves several key steps,

- The initial step requires downloading the Webex Device Connector desktop application from the Webex Control Hub. This application acts as a bridge, facilitating the onboarding of devices registered with Unified CM to the Webex Cloud. It utilizes the AXL API for Unified CM registered devices to fetch device names and MAC addresses.
- The Webex Device Connector establishes a secure HTTPS connection to Unified CM using TLS version 1.2. It validates the Unified CM (Tomcat) certificate before connecting, ensuring the received server certificate is trusted.

- Upon establishing a secure connection, the Device Connector retrieves device details and communicates with the Webex Identity Service to generate an activation code for each device. The devices then use this activation code to establish a TLS connection to the Webex Cloud and complete the onboarding process automatically.
- Devices linked to the Webex Cloud in this manner are then visible and manageable via the Webex Control Hub, allowing for centralized control and management of both cloud-registered and on-premises devices.
- Once Cisco endpoints are successfully onboarded to the Webex Cloud through Webex Edge for Devices, they communicate with the Webex Cloud securely and efficiently, leveraging multiple layers of security and communication protocols. Endpoints make multiple TLS (Transport Layer Security) and HTTPS connections to the Webex Cloud primarily for signaling purposes. These connections are outbound only from the on-premises devices to the Webex Cloud.
- Some HTTPS connections are upgraded to Secure WebSocket connections for dynamic, bidirectional communications. This allows for a continuous, open connection between the Cisco endpoint and the Webex Cloud, facilitating real-time interactions with minimal latency.

Cisco is trying to make the transition to these features easy and provides a pathway for easy migration to full cloud capabilities in the future.

Here's a comprehensive list of features available in Webex Edge for Devices:

1. Cloud-managed Software Upgrade:
    - Automatic Software upgrades when a new RoomOS software version is available
    - Stable builds are released roughly once a month, and Beta builds every other week
    - Ability to select software channels with a default stable channel
2. Webex Optimized Experience:
    - Two-way whiteboarding in Webex Meetings
    - Advanced mute options (mute on entry, unmute all, allow attendees to unmute)
    - Cohost capabilities (the device gets a cohost role when the paired device joins)
    - Transfer Host and Leave feature
    - Ability to lock meetings

   - Notifications of attendees in the lobby and the ability to admit attendees to a meeting from the device
   - Meeting recording capabilities
   - Sending reactions in a meeting via call controls or gestures
   - Webex Assistant for devices (enabling and disabling Webex Assistant in meetings)
   - Face Recognition feature
3. Control Hub Features for Admins:
   - Historical Device Usage Analytics
   - Online/Offline Connection Status
   - Device Diagnostics Messages
   - Cloud xAPI access

This is not an exhaustive list. Please check Cisco's documentation for more details. You can find Webex Edge documentation here: https://help.webex.com/en-us/article/cy2l2z/Webex-Edge-for-Devices

https://www.cisco.com/c/dam/en/us/td/docs/voice_ip_comm/cloudCollaboration/wbxt/whitepapers/webex-edge-devices-white-paper.pdf

One more hybrid service Cisco offers, which is similar but focused on On-Prem Infrastructure, is called CCUC (Cloud-connected UC).

While both (Webex Edge for devices and CCUC) services connect on-premises devices to cloud capabilities, their functionalities differ. Cloud-connected UC focuses more on management, analytics, and operational efficiency of the Unified Communications system (CUCM, IM&P, CUC, etc.). In contrast, Webex Edge for Devices enhances the meeting and collaboration experience by integrating on-premises devices (endpoints - Webex room series) with cloud-based features.

Cloud-Connected Unified Communications

The Webex Cloud-Connected Unified Communications (CCUC) is a part of Cisco's Webex suite, designed to enhance traditional on-premises Unified Communications (UC) systems with cloud-based functionalities. This integration aims to improve the Cisco Unified Communications Manager (CUCM) service by providing detailed analytics, streamlined operational processes, and troubleshooting tools through the Webex Cloud environment.

CCUC is accessible to organizations with an existing Webex setup through specific Cisco licensing agreements without additional licenses. Please check with your Cisco Account Manager for more details.

Let's take a look at some of the available features with CCUC:

- CCUC seamlessly connects with on-premises UC Manager clusters, bridging the gap between local systems and cloud technology to enable advanced features without the need for full cloud migration.
- One of the key aspects of CCUC is its telemetry and analytics capabilities. It collects data from on-premises infrastructure, which is then sent to the Cloud for analysis. This telemetry data is crucial for understanding performance and usage patterns. The analytics provided can help with capacity planning and resource optimization. Example:
    - Find out the distribution of calls by time
    - Find out calls made per device type
- CCUC offers tools for monitoring and managing the performance of UC systems. It gives administrators a global view of their on-premises UC and UCM cloud services, allowing for more effective and centralized management. Administrators can use CCUC to track and report various service quality and system performance KPIs. Example:
    - View call audio quality statistics
    - View statistics on audio and video calls
- CCUC also provides Web-based RTMT and integrates with Collaboration Solutions Analyzer to help administrators troubleshoot any issues.
- It also provides some additional features for end users, for example, Borderless CTI, Presence sync of CUCM registered phones with Webex, and auto-provisioning of Phones.

This is not an exhaustive list. Please check Cisco's documentation for more details. You can find CCUC documentation here:

https://help.webex.com/en-us/landing/ld-npxwpmz-WebexCloud-ConnectedUC/Webex-Cloud-Connected-UC#Get-Started

Now that we've explored Cisco's collaboration cloud service, the Webex suite, and its hybrid capabilities, let's discuss the role of edge servers in on-premises architecture, focusing on their function in connecting it to the Cloud or other external services.

Edge Servers

In a Cisco Collaboration deployment, an edge server like Cisco Expressway plays a crucial role in extending the reach of the network outside the organizational boundaries in a secure and controlled manner. It's used when the goal is to enable remote workers to access collaboration tools (like Cisco Jabber) from outside the corporate firewall without a VPN (and without compromising the security of the internal network) or to facilitate secure B2B communications.

Cisco Unified Border Element (CUBE) is also considered an edge gateway, but it serves a different purpose than Cisco Expressway. CUBE is focused on session control and connectivity (including SIP trunking) and used when the primary requirement is to interface with SIP service providers, manage voice and video sessions between different infrastructure (Interoperability scenarios between two different types of PBX), or when advanced voice/video session control and security is needed.

Expressway-E is always deployed in DMZ, but CUBE can be in DMZ or the internal network depending on your setup with ITSP.

As you see in *Figure* 7.2, Expressway-E is facing the internet and CUBE is connected to PSTN service. We have kept the figure simple, most often there is a static NAT done on the firewall facing the internet and CUBE may or may not be behind the firewall in DMZ.

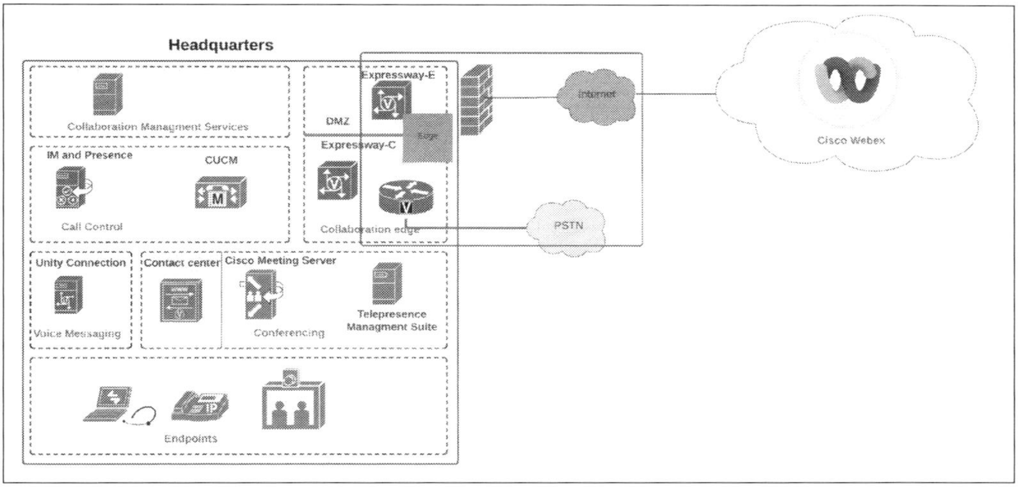

***Figure* 7.2**: *Edge Servers*

Let's explore Expressway and CUBE in detail.

Cisco Expressway

The Cisco Expressway Series originated from the Cisco Video Communication Server (VCS), which was primarily focused on enabling video conferencing capabilities across firewall barriers. The core functionality of VCS was to ensure that video conferencing traffic could securely traverse these network barriers without compromising the integrity or security of the enterprise's network. VCS was divided into two components: VCS Control (now Expressway-Core) and VCS Expressway (now Expressway-Edge).

Cisco later expanded VCS's capabilities into what is now the Expressway series. This evolution was marked by integrating voice, video, messaging, and mobile application communications, transforming it into a robust platform that supports a wider range of UC functionalities beyond just video.

The Expressway series is uniquely architected into two components: Expressway-Core (Exp-C) and Expressway-Edge (Exp-E), each serving distinct roles.

- Expressway-Core (Exp-C) is deployed within the enterprise LAN. Its primary function is to manage and control the registration, authentication, and routing of SIP (Session Initiation Protocol) devices and clients within the internal network. It acts as a gatekeeper for the organization's UC infrastructure, facilitating the seamless integration of Cisco's collaboration tools. It also hosts the connector required for hybrid services.
- Expressway-Edge (Exp-E) is positioned at the network perimeter, typically in the DMZ (demilitarized zone), acting as the public-facing gateway. Its primary role is to securely handle signaling and media traffic between the internal network and external entities over the Internet. This includes enabling B2B communications, remote access for mobile and teleworking users, and connectivity to cloud services.

By separating internal and external traffic handling, Cisco Expressway minimizes the internal network's exposure to potential internet threats. Exp-E, situated in the DMZ, is the only component directly exposed to external traffic, acting as a buffer zone that secures the internal UC environment managed by Exp-C.

The deployment options for Cisco Expressway can be categorized based on the scale of deployment and the platform choice, including virtual machine options and dedicated hardware appliances.

- **Small Deployment**: Ideal for Cisco Business Edition 6000 or supported VMware ESXi platforms, adhering to the required minimum hardware specification. This setup is for smaller environments with limited requirements.
- **Medium Deployment**: This represents the standard installation option, balancing performance and scalability for most organizations.
- **Large Deployment**: Designed for environments requiring extra performance and scalability capabilities, accommodating larger user bases and higher concurrent communication sessions.

Cisco Expressway is available as a CE Series appliance based on UCS hardware for organizations preferring dedicated hardware. The CE1200 appliance, for instance, is based on a UCS C220 M5L and can operate as either a medium or large capacity Expressway.

Installing Cisco Expressway as a virtual machine is a straightforward process, primarily involving the deployment of an OVA template through VMware's vSphere client. This method simplifies the initial setup and allows administrators to configure the System without dealing with complex manual installation.

After installation, the VM will boot and initiate the Install Wizard; it will allow admins to configure various settings, for example, network settings, root and admin credentials, and enable SSH and web UI. After the System has applied the configuration and rebooted, the Expressway is ready for use. Admins can now access the Expressway's web interface using a browser, allowing for further configuration and management.

Upon accessing the Cisco Expressway's web user interface, administrators are guided through the Service Setup Wizard to select the system type Expressway-C or Expressway-E. Based on the chosen series and type, you will select the services your Expressway system will provide. This could include but is not limited to, Cisco Webex Hybrid Services, Mobile and Remote Access, Jabber Guest Services, Microsoft gateway service, Registrar, CMR Cloud, and Business-to-Business calling. After selecting your services and restarting the System, it's customized to display only the menus and pages relevant to the services you've activated.

Some services are incompatible and cannot be selected simultaneously. For instance:

- Cisco Webex Hybrid Services can coexist with Business-to-Business calling but not with Mobile and Remote Access
- Due to technical limitations, Mobile and Remote Access can be paired with Registrar and Business-to-Business calling but not with Jabber Guest Services
- Microsoft gateway service requires a dedicated system and cannot coexist with other services

To summarize, depending on your needs, you can deploy the Expressway in different capacities. It can be scaled up in clusters and supports different services. Depending on service and system type, the underlying core component is the same for Expressway-C and Expressway-E; it serves a different role in architecture and needs to be configured accordingly.

Let's discuss a few important services/features in detail.

B2B Calling

B2B stands for "Business-to-Business" calling. It refers to making voice and video calls between organizations and businesses over the Internet using unified communications technology.

For example, employees at Company A need to communicate frequently with employees at Company B for meetings, sales calls, and collaboration or Company A wants to use a cloud service like Webex for video conferencing with partners and suppliers.

B2B calling enables this seamless inter-company communication using standards-based protocols like SIP over IP networks.

Cisco Expressway is a key component for enabling B2B communications between unified communications deployments and external entities.

It provides the following capabilities:

- **Firewall Traversal**: Expressway enables secure traversal of company firewalls for UC media and signaling. This allows internal users to make B2B calls securely via the Expressway solution. We will discuss firewall traversal later in the next section.
- **Intelligent Routing**: Dynamic DNS-based routing resolves and connects to external organizations and cloud services based on domain names.
- **Edge Deployment**: Expressway-E is deployed in the edge/DMZ to receive inbound B2B calls and route them internally.
- **Interoperability:** Standards-based SIP connectivity is used to interoperate with external UC infrastructure.

Here is how a typical B2B call works with Expressway:

1. Internal user, John calls external organization XYZ using URI
2. Call routes from CUCM to Expressway-C
3. Expressway-C sends the calls through the Expressway-E traversal zone (firewall traversal)
4. Expressway-E performs a DNS lookup on XYZ.com and finds the SIP proxy for XYZ
5. The call connects John and XYZ over the IP network

Expressway enables this B2B connectivity using standard IP and SIP while securing the internal UC environment. This improves workflows, avoids legacy circuits like ISDN, and reduces costs.

Before getting into the detailed scenario and configuration, let's understand how Cisco Expressway processes calls. It's crucial to understand different types of zones, dial plan options, including search rules and transforms, and the use of Call Processing Language (CPL). This is just a brief explanation.

Expressway utilizes zones to manage how calls are routed between different networks or servers. There are various types of zones/subzones, but we will stick to the most used ones.

Each zone serves a specific purpose:

- **Default Zone**: Used for calls to domains not explicitly handled by other zones. It acts as a catch-all for undefined traffic
- **Neighbor Zones**: Define SIP connections to adjacent systems like CUCM or another Expressway which are essential for direct, trusted communications. It's the same as the SIP trunk.

- **DNS Zones**: Used for routing calls based on DNS lookups, particularly useful for B2B communications when the destination is not statically defined.
- **Traversal Zones**: Specialized for linking Expressway-C and Expressway-E, facilitating firewall traversal for B2B calls.
- **Unified Communications Traversal Zones**: A traversal client or traversal server zone used for Unified Communications features such as mobile and remote access or Jabber Guest.

To route the calls, we need a dial plan. The dial plan in Expressway is a set of rules that govern how calls are routed. It includes:

- **Search Rules**: Determine the routing path for calls based on patterns in the dialed URI. They direct how Expressway queries zones to find the call destination. Search rules are similar to the Route pattern in CUCM.
- **Transforms**: Used to modify the SIP URI to match the expected format of the destination system or to conform to organizational policies.

Another important feature of Expressway is CPL. It allows the creation of advanced policy rules to manipulate how calls are processed as they flow through the System.

CPL scripts consist of a set of rule conditions and actions. It can check attributes like source IP, destination alias pattern, protocol, etc.

Some examples of what can be achieved using CPL in Expressway include:

- Allow or reject calls based on source, destination, or call attributes like time of day
- Modify/transform the source or destination aliases
- Forward/redirect calls to alternate numbers or endpoints
- Block specific codec types that are not permitted

CPL provides basic policy control using scripts directly on Expressway. It's one of the important features configured on Expressway-E to block all spam calls. Normally, local CPL on Expressway is enough; external policy services offer more advanced options deployed on external platforms if required.

Now that we have covered the basics, Let's understand how Expressway processes the calls:

- **Call Identification**: Expressway examines the source IP address and port number from where the call originated. The call is associated with a pre-configured zone based on the zone's IP and port configurations. If no specific zone matches, the call defaults to the Default Zone.
- **Pre-Search Transforms**: Any pre-search transforms configured are applied to the incoming alias to reformat or standardize it. This ensures the alias meets the consistent format required by search rules.

- **Policy Checking**: If integrated, external policy services are consulted to decide on call actions (allow, reject, redirect, or fork) based on administrator-configured rules. For local policy enforcement, configured Call Processing Language (CPL) scripts are checked against the call attributes, following a priority order.
- **Search Rule Application**: The transformed alias is matched against prioritized search rules in the configuration. These rules are based on patterns and dictate the routing zone for matching calls. Search rules are applied sequentially by configured priority. The call is routed according to the first matching rule, identifying the associated target zone.
- **Default Zone Routing**: If the transformed alias doesn't match any search rule, the call routes through the Default Zone.
- **Post-Search Transforms**: Post-search transformations configured for the identified target zone are applied, adjusting the alias to the format expected by the target zone.
- **Final Call Routing**: The call is routed via the selected target zone towards the destination endpoint or System. The handling of the call now depends on the configuration of the destination platform and how it processes incoming calls.

Now, let's understand the required configuration for the scenario by explaining high-level config.

Company ABC wants to enable:

- Outbound calls from CUCM endpoints to external B2B services over SIP
- Inbound calls from the Internet to CUCM endpoints

To achieve this, they will configure the SIP route pattern, SIP trunk, zones, search rules, and transforms.

- **CUCM Configuration:** CUCM serves as the call control system for ABC's IP phones, Jabber soft clients and TelePresence endpoints (Webex room endpoints)
    - A SIP trunk needs to be configured from CUCM to Expressway-C to route calls
    - A SIP route pattern like **.*@.*** matches any domain dialing and routes via the SIP trunk to Expressway-C. They use a wildcard pattern that captures all possible SIP URI calls not explicitly matched by other route patterns.
- **Expressway-C Configuration**: Expressway-C resides inside ABC's network and receives calls from CUCM over the SIP trunk.
    - A traversal zone named `To_ExpresswayE`, is set up with Expressway-E as the connection peer. This enables secure traversal connections between Expressway-C and Expressway-E

- Neighbor Zone is set up with CUCM
- As all calls from CUCM are sent to Expressway-C, we need a search rule to route calls for ABC's internal domain back to CUCM
- A search rule to route calls to external internet domains via the traversal zone
- We will need to set up transformations and local zone configuration.

- **Expressway-E Configuration:** Expressway-E resides in the DMZ and connects to Expressway-C.
  - A traversal server zone named `From_ExpresswayC`, is set up with Expressway-C as the connection peer
  - A DNS Zone to manage outbound B2B SIP calls to external domains
  - The default zone handles unsolicited incoming calls from external IP addresses. A SIP domain of abc.com is set to allow incoming calls to registered domains to be routed internally
  - Ensure there's a search rule that directs calls to the DNS Zone for any external SIP URIs

We also need to set up the DNS records. These DNS records facilitate the discovery and routing of SIP traffic between different entities over the Internet.

An overview of the SRV (Service) and A (Address) records required for this purpose, along with a brief explanation of how they function technically are as follows:

SRV Records

- `_sip._tcp.abc.com`: This SRV record is used for SIP (Session Initiation Protocol) traffic over TCP. It specifies the hostname and port number of the SIP server that should handle SIP traffic for the domain "abc.com."
- `_sip._tls.abc.com`: Similar to the `_sip._tcp` record but for SIP traffic secured with TLS (Transport Layer Security), offering encrypted SIP communications.

A Records

- `exp-e.abc.com`: An A record mapping the hostname of the Expressway-E server to its IP address. This is crucial for the SRV records to resolve to the correct server.
- `exp-c.abc.com`: Although not directly used by external entities for B2B communications, an A record for Expressway-C is necessary for internal resolutions and configurations.

Now, let's revisit the outgoing and incoming call flow for B2B in more detail.

Outgoing Calls from ABC Company to External Services:

1. **Initiating the Call**: A user at ABC Company initiates a call using SIP URI (e.g., user@example.com) from their Cisco Jabber client or video endpoint.
2. **SIP Route Pattern Matching**: The call request is directed to the Cisco Unified Communications Manager (CUCM), where a SIP route pattern matches the dialed SIP URI. This pattern is configured to route calls to the Expressway-C via a SIP trunk.
3. **Routing to Expressway-C**: Upon receiving the call, Exp-C performs initial processing. This includes verifying the call's destination and applying any relevant policies or transformations required for external communication.
4. **Expressway-C to Expressway-E**: Exp-C then forwards the call to Expressway-E. Exp-E acts as the border element interfacing with the external network.
5. **DNS Lookup and SIP INVITE**: Expressway-E does not have direct SIP trunks to all possible external services or businesses. Instead, it uses DNS zones to perform an SRV record lookup for the domain specified in the SIP URI, identifying the appropriate service endpoint for SIP communication. Based on the DNS query results, Exp-E sends a SIP INVITE to the external service (e.g., Zoom or Webex), establishing the call.

Incoming Calls to ABC Company from External Entities:

1. **Call Initiation**: When an external user attempts to establish a SIP call to a user at ABC Company using the SIP URI (e.g., **`user@abc.com`**), their SIP server initiates a DNS lookup to resolve the destination
2. **SRV Record Lookup**: The external entity's DNS query will first seek out SRV records associated with **`"abc.com"`** (e.g., **`_sip._tcp.abc.com`**). These records indicate which server (hostname) and port should handle the incoming SIP traffic for the domain
3. **A Record Resolution:** Once an SRV record points to a specific hostname (e.g., exp-e.abc.com), another DNS query resolves this hostname to the IP address of the Expressway-E server (using the A record)
4. **SIP INVITE Handling**: The Expressway-E server at ABC Company receives the SIP INVITE. If the call is allowed based on ABC Company's policies, Expressway-E forwards the call to Expressway-C
5. **Internal Routing**: Expressway-C, having a configuration for the organization's dial plan, routes the call to the appropriate internal endpoint (e.g., a Cisco Jabber user) via CUCM
6. **Call Establishment**: Once the internal endpoint is identified and available, the call is established, allowing the external and internal users to communicate

This DNS setup, utilizing both SRV and A records, is fundamental for enabling seamless B2B communication through Cisco Expressway, ensuring calls are accurately routed and connected across organizational boundaries.

Figure 7.3 illustrates the Cisco Expressway configuration enabling B2B communication between Company ABC and external entity example. The diagram shows user@abc.com registered to Cisco Unified Communications Manager (CUCM), which has a SIP trunk to Expressway-C. The SIP route pattern ".@." on CUCM matches any domain dialing and routes those calls via the SIP trunk to Expressway-C, which then processes the calls based on its configured rules and zones.

Expressway-C has a neighbor zone to CUCM for trusted communication, a traversal zone **`"To Exp-E"`** to securely connect with Expressway-E through the firewall, a search rule to route calls for the internal "abc.com" domain back to CUCM, and another search rule to forward external calls to Expressway-E. Residing in the DMZ, Expressway-E handles external communication with a traversal server zone "From Exp-C" connected to Expressway-C. It uses DNS zones for outbound B2B calls, performing SRV record lookups to route calls to the appropriate external domains. The default zone on Expressway-E allows incoming calls from outside and routes them to Expressway-C if destined for the **`"abc.com"`** domain.

The necessary DNS records, including SRV records for SIP traffic and corresponding A records for hostname resolution, are also shown for a better understanding. **`"_sips._tcp.abc.com"`** and **`"_sips._tcp.example.com"`** SRV records indicate the servers responsible for handling SIP calls over TLS, while **`"exp-e.abc.com"`** and **`"exp-e.example.com"`** A records map those hostnames to their respective IP addresses. The right side of the diagram shows a similar Expressway setup for the example.com domain, enabling seamless B2B communication between the two organizations. Incoming calls from abc.com to example.com would traverse the internet, reach example.com's Expressway-E, and then be routed to their Expressway-C, CUCM, and finally to the destination endpoint.

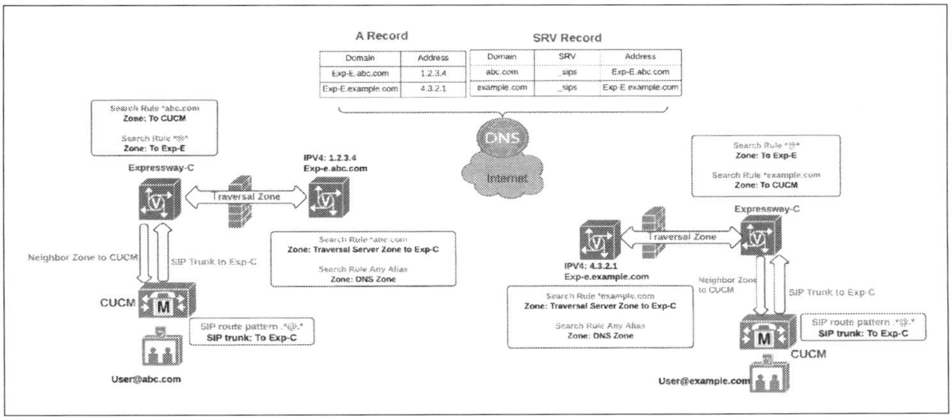

Figure 7.3: *Expressway Business-to-Business calling*

Now, let's move to another important topic: Firewall Traversal.

Firewall Traversal

A firewall protects the boundary between a private enterprise network and the public Internet. It controls traffic flow based on defined security rules. Typically, firewalls block unsolicited incoming requests while allowing some outbound requests.

This creates a challenge for enabling video communications between internal and external endpoints across the firewall. The firewall needs to permit the bidirectional signaling and media required for video calls without compromising security.

Cisco's Expressway firewall traversal architecture addresses this using a dedicated Expressway-E traversal server located in the enterprise DMZ or on the public Internet. It cooperates with an internal Expressway-C to enable secure firewall traversal for SIP-based communications.

The core components of the Expressway firewall traversal solution are:

- **Expressway-E**: Acts as the traversal server in the DMZ or on the public Internet
- **Expressway-C**: Located inside the enterprise network and acts as the traversal client
- **Firewall**: Protects the enterprise network perimeter and allows required Expressway traffic

The Expressway-E and Expressway-C work together using SIP-based application layer gateways (ALGs) to construct secure firewall-friendly signaling and media communication paths.

- The Expressway-C initiates outbound connections to the Expressway-E, so it can be established successfully through the firewall
- As we see in *Figure 7.4*, the Expressway-C maintains a persistent TLS connection to the Expressway-E by sending keep-alive packets, to keep the firewall paths open

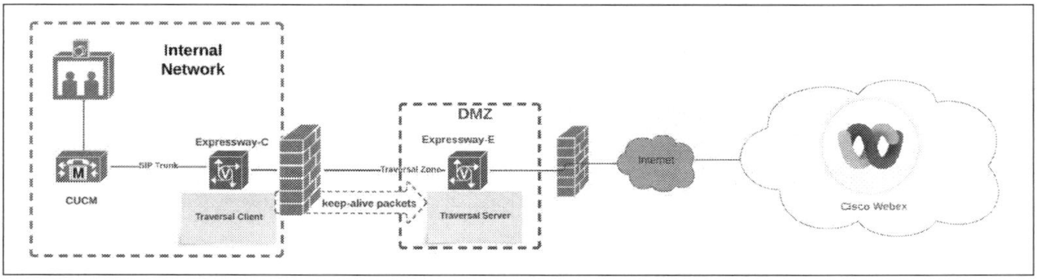

Figure 7.4: *Expressway Firewall Traversal*

- When an incoming call for Expressway-C arrives, Expressway-E uses the TLS connection to send the call signaling to Expressway-C
- Expressway-C then initiates any required media connections outbound to Expressway-E
- No inbound ports are open on Expressway-C, maintaining strong firewall security

This ensures that from the firewall's standpoint, all connections appear to originate from the trusted internal side.

An important aspect of Expressway firewall traversal is media demultiplexing:

- The firewall only allows outbound media connections from the internal network
- Thus, media for multiple calls must be multiplexed over the single TLS connection between Expressway-C and Expressway-E
- Expressway-E uses advanced demultiplexing techniques to forward each call's media over this firewall traversal tunnel

This minimizes required open ports and provides robustness against NAT changes.

Configuration for the traversal zone is very straightforward.

On Expressway-E:

1. Create a traversal server zone and specify the Expressway-C's authentication username in the Username field
2. Add the Expressway-C's authentication username and password credentials to the local authentication database
3. Configure the H.323 and SIP modes, ports and other additional settings

On Expressway-C:

1. Create a traversal client zone
2. Enter the same authentication Username and Password as configured on the Expressway-E
3. Configure the H.323 and SIP modes and ports to match the traversal server zone ports on the Expressway-E (and other additional settings)
4. Enter the Expressway-E's IP address or FQDN in the Peer 1 address field

The Expressway-E will authenticate the Expressway-C's credentials when it connects.

One of the important aspects is to ensure that required firewall ports are open through the firewall. To allow the Expressway solution to traverse the firewall, it must be configured to:

- Allow initial outbound connections from the Expressway-C client to the traversal ports on the Expressway-E server. SIP ports start at TCP/7001 and increment by 1 for every new traversal server zone
- Allow return traffic from the server ports back to the originating Expressway-C client system
- Not block or inspect SIP/H.323 protocols used for Expressway communications
- Media ports

You can find more details about ports here: https://www.cisco.com/c/en/us/td/docs/voice_ip_comm/expressway/config_guide/X14-0/ip_port_usage/exwy_b_ip-port-usage-configuration-guide-14.pdf

Let's move on to another important feature Expressway supports - MRA.

Mobile and Remote Access (MRA)

MRA facilitates endpoints such as Cisco Jabber to have their registration, call control, provisioning, messaging, and presence services provided by Cisco Unified Communications Manager (Unified CM) when the endpoint is not within the enterprise network. This technology is especially useful in today's global and mobile workforce, where employees increasingly work from remote locations and require reliable access to their organization's communication systems.

Users can access the same tools and services outside the office as they do within the office without needing to connect to a VPN. When a user attempts to connect to the corporate collaboration services (e.g., CUCM) from outside the network using a device or application (like Cisco Jabber), the MRA mechanism facilitates this by proxying the registration of the endpoint through Expressway-Edge and Expressway-Core to the CUCM.

Here's a high-level overview of the MRA flow:

1. **Initialization and Discovery**: When a user attempts to access services from a remote location, the device (for example, Cisco Jabber) uses DNS queries to discover the Expressway-Edge (Expressway-E) server. The device needs to be pre-configured with the external domain to perform this discovery.
2. **Secure Connection Establishment**: Once the Expressway-E is discovered, the device establishes a secure TLS (Transport Layer Security) connection to the Expressway-E. This connection is used for signaling and media encryption, ensuring secure communications.

3. **Authentication and Registration**: The Expressway-E forwards the authentication request to the internal Expressway-Core (Expressway-C), which communicates with the Cisco Unified Communications Manager (CUCM) or other unified communications services to authenticate the user. After successful authentication, the device is registered with the CUCM and can initiate or receive calls.
4. **Call Setup and Media Flow**: For a call, signaling information passes securely through Expressway-E and Expressway-C to the CUCM, which then sets up the call. The media path can be optimized based on the call's nature and the network's configuration, potentially flowing directly between endpoints or traversing the Expressway servers for media encryption and NAT traversal.
5. **Service Use**: Once registered, the device can use various services like voice and video calls, voicemail, presence information, and instant messaging, just as if it were connected directly to the corporate network.

The Expressway maintains a secure connection, allowing for ongoing communications without the need for VPNs, simplifying the user experience and enhancing security.

It's important to note that the specifics of the MRA flow can vary depending on the organization's network architecture, the Cisco Expressway version, and other configurations. For the most accurate and detailed information, refer to Cisco's MRA configuration guide https://www.cisco.com/c/en/us/td/docs/voice_ip_comm/expressway/config_guide/X14-2/mra/exwy_b_mra-deployment-guide-x142.html

Cisco Unified Border Element (CUBE)

Cisco Unified Border Element (CUBE) is an enterprise-focused Session Border Controller (SBC) integrated into Cisco's IOS and IOS XE software platforms. It facilitates simple and scalable session management across voice and video networks.

Key functionalities include:

- **Session Control and Security**: CUBE manages and secures voice and video traffic across the enterprise's border, handling signaling and media traversal between different VoIP protocols.
- **Interoperability:** It acts as a bridge for calls between various networks, ensuring compatibility across disparate VoIP protocols and codecs.
- **SIP Normalization**: CUBE can modify and normalize SIP messages, aiding in the integration of services and devices that use different SIP implementations.
- **Transcoding**: CUBE can transcode between audio codecs like G.711, G.729, and Opus to provide interoperability between endpoints. It also provides transrating between different packet rates.

- **Call Admission Control (CAC)**: CUBE can limit the number of active calls based on available bandwidth, preventing network congestion.
- **Security and Admission Control** - CUBE can apply security policies to allow or deny calls based on source/destination IP addresses, SIP domains, and other criteria. This enables protecting the core network from malicious attacks or excessive traffic.
- **NAT and Firewall Traversal** - CUBE supports NAT traversal and firewall traversal capabilities using STUN, TURN, ICE, and media latching to enable end-to-end VoIP calls across NAT/firewall boundaries.

Cisco Unified Border Element (CUBE) is supported on a range of Cisco router platforms running IOS-XE software:

- **Integrated Services Routers (ISR)** - Popular models include the 4000 Series ISRs, such as the 4451-X and 1000 Series ISRs, such as the 1100. These contain embedded voice processing capabilities.
- **Aggregation Services Routers (ASR)** - High-density router platforms like the ASR 1000 Series contain expansion slots for modular voice/DSP cards required for CUBE media functionality.
- **Cloud Services Router (CSR) 1000v** - Virtual router platform that runs CUBE as a virtual machine in Software but is no longer supported from Cisco IOS XE Bengaluru 17.4.1a onwards. If you use CSR 1000V, you must upgrade to Cisco Catalyst 8000V Edge Software (Catalyst 8000V).
- **Catalyst 8000v Edge Software** - A virtual router platform similar to CSR1000v, it can also run CUBE as a VM.

CUBE relies on internal DSP chips or installable DSP cards/modules for transcoding, transrating, and other media processing functions in physical routers. These are critical for interworking between different voice codecs and PSTN interfaces.

On virtual platforms like the CSR1000v and Catalyst 8000v, CUBE runs as a virtual machine without physical media resources. So, DSP-based functions like transcoding are not supported on these virtual CUBE variations.

Let's understand the high-level configuration of CUBE.

1. **Enable CUBE**: The process begins with enabling the CUBE functionality on a Cisco router. This usually involves entering specific commands in the global configuration mode of the router's CLI.
2. **Configure Trusted IP Address List for Toll-Fraud Prevention**: To secure the CUBE against unauthorized use, a list of trusted IP addresses is configured. Only traffic from these IPs will be allowed, preventing toll fraud.

3. **Determine Incoming Called Number Patterns**: Assess whether the incoming called number patterns are identical on both sides of the CUBE (for example, the patterns from the ITSP and the internal network).

   a. **If Yes**: Configure the number patterns to make them unique. This typically involves adding or removing prefixes or translating numbers so the CUBE can differentiate between inbound and outbound calls and route them correctly.

   b. **If No**: If the patterns are already unique, proceed to the next step.

4. **Configure Inbound and Outbound Dial Peers on Both Sides**: Dial peers for both inbound and outbound call legs on each side of the CUBE are configured. This sets up the CUBE to correctly process calls coming from and going to both the internal network (like a CUCM) and the external network (such as an ITSP).

5. **Configure Other Dial-Peer-Level Controls**: This involves setting up additional controls at the dial-peer level, which may include:

   a. **Voice Translation Rules:** To manipulate the calling and called numbers

   b. **DTMF Relays**: To ensure proper signaling of DTMF tones across different network segments

   c. **Payload Types**: To specify the type of codec payload used for the voice or video media

6. **Configure Interface Binding for Media and Control on Both Sides**: Interface binding associates the media (RTP) and signaling (SIP/H.323) to specific interfaces on the router. This ensures that media and control packets are sent and received on the correct network interfaces.

7. **Configure SIP Profiles**: SIP profiles are configured to define the attributes of SIP messages. This can include manipulating message headers, setting timers, and defining specific call setup and teardown behaviors.

8. **Configure Other Call Signaling Controls:** The final step involves setting up additional signaling controls such as - Registration and Authorization.

These are just high-level config steps. For detailed information on how to execute each of these steps and for more advanced configurations, refer to Cisco's official CUBE configuration guide: https://www.cisco.com/c/en/us/td/docs/ios-xml/ios/voice/cube/ios-xe/config/ios-xe-book.html

Conclusion

In this chapter, we explored the Webex Cloud and hybrid services. We started with the Webex suite, discussing various services such as Webex Meetings, Messaging, Calling, Webinars, and Vidcast. We discussed how these cloud-based offerings provide scalability, cost-effectiveness, and continuous innovation, empowering organizations to collaborate seamlessly across boundaries.

Next, we discussed the concept of Webex hybrid deployments, which bridge the gap between on-premises infrastructure and cloud services. We looked at key hybrid services like Webex Hybrid Calendar, Directory Service, and Webex Edge, understanding how they enable organizations to leverage the best of both worlds - the control and customization of on-premises systems and the flexibility and advanced features of the Cloud.

We then discussed edge servers, Cisco Expressway, and Cisco Unified Border Element (CUBE). Expressway facilitates secure firewall traversal and enables remote access and B2B communication. We also examined CUBE's role in session management, protocol interworking, and ensuring the security and quality of voice and video traffic at the network border.

In the next chapter, we will explore the role of protocols such as SIP, SDP, RTP, and RTCP in establishing and managing voice and video sessions.

Multiple Choice Questions

1. How does cloud collaboration primarily help organizations in financial terms?
    a. By increasing Operating Expenses (OpEx) due to higher subscription costs
    b. By eliminating the need for any IT expenditures
    c. By reducing Capital Expenditure (CapEx) through less need for on-premises infrastructure
    d. By shifting all financial responsibilities to cloud service providers
2. What is the key difference between Cisco Webex Meetings and Webex Webinars?
    a. Webex Meetings support larger audiences than Webex Webinars
    b. Webex Webinars allows for direct calling options, whereas Meetings does not

   c. Webex Meetings are ideal for small team collaborations, while Webinars are for large-scale events
   d. Webex Webinars are designed for interactive sessions, while Meetings are not

3. Where is the Webex Hybrid Calendar Connector typically deployed in a Cisco collaboration environment?
   a. EXP-C (Expressway-Core)
   b. EXP-E (Expressway-Edge)
   c. CUCM (Cisco Unified Communications Manager)
   d. CUBE (Cisco Unified Border Element)
4. How is the DNS Zone utilized in Expressway-E?
   a. For automatically registering devices with the Expressway-E
   b. To facilitate secure traversal of SIP traffic through firewalls
   c. To resolve domain names into IP addresses for call routing purposes
   d. As a security measure to prevent unauthorized call routing
5. What is the main benefit of firewall traversal using Cisco Expressway?
   a. It significantly increases the bandwidth available for video calls
   b. It allows for seamless communication between internal and external networks without compromising security
   c. It encrypts all video traffic passing through the firewall
   d. It provides a proprietary protocol for bypassing NAT and firewalls

Answers

1. c
2. c
3. a
4. c
5. b

Further Reading

Same as last chapter, it is recommended to explore the following topics on your own to improve your understanding and broaden your perspective.

- Compare Webex suite services and licensing with offerings from other vendors like Zoom and Microsoft. Understand the differences and their value propositions for businesses of various sizes.
- Examine the features of cloud-based collaboration tools for meetings, messaging, and webinars, and compare them with their on-premises counterparts.
- Investigate which other vendors offer hybrid solutions and understand how these solutions function.
- Research additional features of Cisco Expressway.
- Compare Cisco's CUBE with other Session Border Controllers (SBCs) on the market.

CHAPTER 8
Understanding Signaling and Media Protocols

Introduction

In this chapter, we will focus on the Signaling and Media Protocols used in Collaboration technology. We will start with the context on why these standards and protocols are important and who creates them, followed by briefly discussing how signaling and media flow work in Collaboration. We will then explore the SIP protocol in detail, discussing the call setup process, how different components work in SIP, various headers, and the Session Description Protocol. We will conclude this chapter by explaining the Media protocols RTP and RTCP.

Most of what we discuss in this chapter works behind the scenes and can be slightly different based on the scenario, vendor, and standard evolution, but the core concepts remain the same. Studying these basics will help you understand how these technologies and different products work.

Structure

In this chapter, we will discuss the following topics:

- The Significance of Standards and Protocols
- Signaling and Media in VoIP
- SIP Call Setup and Tear Down Processes
- SIP Components in Cisco's Collaboration Infrastructure
- SIP Headers and SDP
- Real-Time Media Protocols: RTP and RTCP

The Significance of Standards and Protocols

Since the rise of the Internet, technologies do not work in isolation anymore; they are often connected to the world. Different vendors/products in the market and their open-source alternatives exist for any technology. This has always created a challenge if other vendors are building a product for the same purpose. To have a unique selling point/feature, or, based on their expertise, they make it work in different ways and in such cases, it breaks the connected world. To mitigate this, the Industry has always come up with standards (a common ground) on how all these products will follow the same set of practices and use the protocols in the same way so they understand each other.

Take the Internet as an example. It is a network of networks with many networks connected to each other. The only reason it works is that there are a set of standards on how each network will share information with each other. Different networks may be deployed/configured in their own way, using different devices, but there are a set of standards on how they present and share the information. These standards often define Protocols.

While the terms "protocol" and "standard" are often used interchangeably, there is a subtle distinction between the two. Standards provide a framework or reference point for the development of protocols. They outline the requirements, best practices, and interoperability guidelines that protocols should adhere to. Standards are typically more abstract and high-level than protocols, serving as a blueprint for protocol development.

There are different protocols in different technologies. There are standard bodies that facilitate the discussions in industry; different people come together and propose the standard, which gets debated, modified, agreed upon, and published as RFC. These standards are usually converted into protocols or best practices. These are not enforced, instead recommended. Industry players/vendors follow these standards to maintain compatibility/interoperability. Still, there are always scenarios where vendors have an additional feature or an idea to optimize something using propriety methods, so they use some deviation/extensions in the protocol or consider the protocol/standard as a baseline and add their own methods to it.

Most vendors begin product development with a clear understanding of their market segment's relevant standards and protocols. This approach ensures that the product will be compatible with other products and systems in the ecosystem from the start. For VoIP products, this means integrating protocols such as Session Initiation Protocol (SIP) and Real-Time Protocol (RTP) and adhering to codec standards such as G.711 or G.729 for voice compression and decompression.

Let us understand this in the context of the Internet. The Internet Engineering Task Force (IETF) was formed to address the growing need for standardized protocols and practices to ensure the interoperability and smooth operation of the rapidly expanding Internet. Before the IETF's formation, the Internet was a collection of networks primarily used by academic and research institutions, and it operated on a variety of protocols that were not standardized. As the Internet began to grow and more organizations started to connect, the need for standardized protocols became evident to ensure that different networks could communicate with each other efficiently and reliably.

The Internet Engineering Task Force (IETF) is responsible for developing, testing, and implementing Internet standards. It is an open standards organization that uses open, well-documented processes to set Internet standards. The Internet Society's Internet Architecture Board (IAB) supervises the IETF. The IETF operates through drafting, discussing, and refining documents known as Requests for Comments (RFC), which, once approved, become standards.

The IETF is composed of volunteers from various sectors, including engineers, network administrators, researchers, and other interested individuals. There is no formal membership or selection process to participate in the IETF. Instead, anyone with an interest in Internet standards and protocols can contribute to the discussions, working groups, and document development. Leadership positions within the IETF, such as chairs of working groups or members of the Internet Engineering Steering Group (IESG), are selected through a nomination and consensus-building process among participants.

IFTF is not the only standard body. Several organizations define and maintain the technical standards for the Internet, IP, VoIP, network protocols, Ethernet, and other related technologies, each with its own focus area.

Below is a list of a few other key organizations and their primary areas of responsibility:

- **Internet Corporation for Assigned Names and Numbers (ICANN)**: ICANN is responsible for coordinating the maintenance and methodologies of several databases related to the namespaces and numerical spaces of the Internet.
    - **Internet Assigned Numbers Authority (IANA)**: IANA is responsible for the global coordination of the DNS Root, IP addressing, and other Internet protocol resources. It is managed by the ICANN.
- **World Wide Web Consortium (W3C)**: The W3C primarily focuses on standards for the World Wide Web. While it does not directly handle Internet protocols such as IP, it develops protocols and guidelines to ensure the long-term growth of the Web.
- **International Telecommunication Union (ITU)**: The ITU is a United Nations specialized agency that focuses on Information and communication

technologies. It includes standards related to VoIP and other telecommunications technologies.

- **Internet Society (ISOC)**: The Internet Society promotes the open development, evolution, and use of the Internet for the benefit of all people worldwide. It supports and promotes the work of the IETF and other standardizing bodies. To learn more about the relationship between ISOC and IETF, refer to RFC 8712.
- **3rd Generation Partnership Project (3GPP)**: 3GPP is a consortium of seven national or regional telecommunications standards organizations that develops technical specifications for cellular telecommunications network technologies, including radio access and the core transport network. 3GPP produces specifications for 2G, 3G, 4G, and 5G mobile communications systems and technologies to ensure global interoperability across vendors and operators.

Let us explore a few Protocols and Standards developed by IETF and ITU related to VoIP and Collaboration.

Protocols developed by the IETF are typically designed to be used across the global Internet and are open and freely available. For VoIP, the IETF concentrates on defining protocols that enable real-time communication over IP networks. The Internet Engineering Task Force (IETF) uses the Request for Comments (RFC) system for its documentation and standardization process.

Key IETF Protocols for VoIP:

- **Session Initiation Protocol (SIP)**: Protocol for initiating, maintaining, and terminating real-time sessions that include voice, video, and messaging applications. RFC 3261 explains the primary specification for SIP.
- **Real-Time Protocol (RTP)**: Defines a standardized packet format for delivering audio and video over the Internet. RFC 3550 defines RTP.
- **Session Description Protocol (SDP)**: Used with SIP to describe multimedia communication sessions for the purposes of session announcement, session invitation, and other forms of multimedia session initiation. RFC 8866 describes SDP.
- **Secure Real-Time Transport Protocol (SRTP)**: Provides encryption, message authentication, and integrity for RTP data. RFC 3711 specifies SRTP.

The ITU standards are often (not always) developed in the context of integrating with traditional telecommunication systems and may have a stronger focus on compatibility with legacy systems. If the standard is geared towards global telecommunication systems, involves integration with the public switched telephone networks (PSTN), or requires coordination among countries' telecommunication regulators, it likely falls under the ITU.

media transmission - the voice conversation. RTP provides ways to send real-time data such as audio and video over IP networks. Some key parts of RTP include:

- **RTP header**: contains information like timestamp, sequence number, and payload type
- **Payload**: the actual media data being carried
- **RTP Control Protocol (RTCP)**: allows monitoring of RTP session quality

Audio Codecs and Encoding Process

Endpoints use audio codecs to encode analog voice signals into a digital format that can be sent over IP. Common audio codecs used in VoIP include G.711, G.729, G.722, and Opus. The codec digitizes the audio, compresses it, and puts it into RTP packets that contain the encoded audio data in the payload part.

Example: G.711 is a codec that samples audio at 8 kHz and uses 64 kbps of bandwidth. It takes 8,000 samples per second, representing each sample by 8 bits, allowing for 256 different values.

The codec divides the digitized samples into frames, with each frame containing a certain number of samples. For instance, G.729 uses 10ms frames with 80 samples per frame. The frames are then passed through the codec algorithm to compress the data. Many VoIP codecs use linear predictive coding to remove redundancy between samples and frames. This compressed frame is then put into packets and sent over RTP.

The packetization interval determines how much audio data is put into each RTP packet. A common interval is 20ms, which means each RTP packet would contain two 10ms G.729 frames. The packetization rate directly affects bandwidth usage, delay, and error resilience. Smaller packets mean lower delay but more overhead, while larger packets are more efficient but can increase delay and jitter, which can hurt call quality.

RTP allows the packets to be carried over any transport protocol like UDP or TCP, with UDP being generally preferred since there is no retransmission of lost packets, which could delay real-time audio delivery.

These packets then follow the standard IP routing through network equipment such as routers and switches. At the receiving end, the RTP packets are received and passed through the jitter buffer to smooth out timing. The codec decompresses the audio data frames and converts the digital signal back into an analog audio waveform for the listener to hear through a speaker or phone.

Fitting the Pieces Together

The coordination between signaling protocols such as SIP to set up and manage the call, the RTP media transport to carry the voice packets, and the codec handling the encoding/decoding of audio allows two VoIP endpoints to communicate seamlessly.

Now that we have a solid understanding of how signaling, media, and codecs work together in VoIP, let us take a closer look at one of the most crucial aspects of VoIP communication: the SIP call setup and tear-down processes.

SIP Call Setup and Tear Down Processes

Session Initiation Protocol (SIP) is a signaling protocol for starting, managing, and ending real-time sessions involving video, voice, messaging, and other communication services between two or more participants over an IP network. It is an application-layer protocol that can work with different transport-layer protocols such as TCP or UDP. SIP is very flexible and can support many features such as call forwarding, call transfer, and conferencing.

The main functions of SIP are the following:

1. **Session Establishment**: Starting and setting up calls between two or more parties.
2. **Session Management**: Changing sessions that are already in progress, for instance, adding more people to a conference call.
3. **Session Termination**: Ending sessions either by the caller or the person being called.

SIP uses four main types of messages: requests, responses, provisions, and acknowledgments. The most common SIP messages are:

1. **`INVITE`**: Sent by the caller to start a session, with details about the media capabilities (audio, video, and so on.) using the Session Description Protocol (SDP).
2. **`Ringing`**: 180 (Ringing) response from the person being called, letting the caller know that the phone is ringing.
3. **`200 OK`**: This is sent by the person being called once they answer the call, indicating that the session can start.
4. **`ACK`**: The caller acknowledged that they received the 200 OK message.
5. **`BYE`**: Used by either party to end the session, followed by a final acknowledgment.

In a VoIP call, SIP first establishes the session between two endpoints, negotiating the parameters of the session, such as the codecs to be used and how RTP will transport the media. Once the session is established and the parameters agreed upon, RTP takes over the actual voice or video data transport. SIP may then be used again to modify or terminate the session.

Figure 8.1 shows the basic flow of a SIP call setup, media exchange, and call termination between a caller and callee with the help of a SIP server. Let us understand each step:

SIP Call Setup:

1. **INVITE from Caller to SIP Server**: The caller sends an **`INVITE`** request to the SIP server with information about their media capabilities and preferences.
2. **100 Trying from SIP Server to Caller**: The SIP server lets the caller know it received the **`INVITE`** and is trying to reach the callee.
3. **INVITE from SIP Server to Callee**: The SIP server forwards the **`INVITE`** to the callee.
4. **180 Ringing from Callee to SIP Server**: The callee's device sends a 180 Ringing response to the SIP server, indicating the phone is ringing but not yet answered.
5. **180 Ringing from SIP Server to Caller**: The SIP server relays the 180 Ringing to the caller.
6. **200 OK from Callee to SIP Server**: When the callee answers, they send a **`200 OK`** to the SIP server, confirming they have accepted the call.
7. **200 OK from SIP Server to Caller**: The SIP server forwards the **`200 OK`** to the caller.
8. **ACK from Caller to SIP Server, then to Callee:** The caller sends an **`ACK`** to the SIP server, which then forwards it to the callee, completing the call setup.

Media Session:

9. **Media Exchange (RTP)**: With the SIP session established, the actual voice or video data is exchanged directly between the caller and callee using RTP.

SIP Call Termination:

10. **BYE from Caller to SIP Server**: To end the call, the caller sends a **`BYE`** request to the SIP server.
11. **BYE from SIP Server to Callee**: The SIP server forwards the **`BYE`** to the callee.
12. **200 OK from Callee to SIP Server**: The callee responds with a **`200 OK`**, acknowledging the request to end the call.
13. **200 OK from SIP Server to Caller**: The SIP server sends a **`200 OK`** back to the caller, confirming the session has ended.

Session Ends

14. The session is now completely closed following the successful exchange of **BYE** and **200 OK** messages.

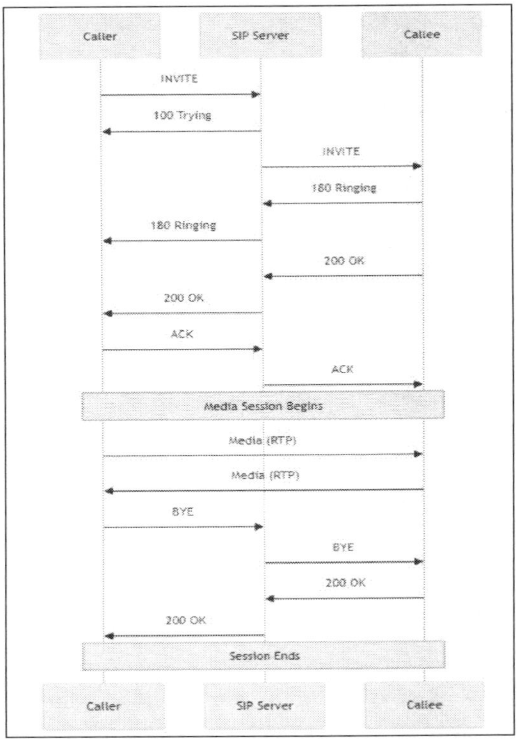

Figure 8.1: *SIP Call Setup*

Now that we understand how SIP manages call setup, media exchange, and call termination, let us look at the various SIP components that make up the infrastructure and explore how they work together to enable seamless VoIP communication, particularly within Cisco's Collaboration ecosystem.

SIP Components in Cisco's Collaboration Infrastructure

To grasp how Session Initiation Protocol (SIP) works within Voice over Internet Protocol (VoIP) systems, especially in Cisco's Collaboration environment, we need to understand the different SIP components and their functions. These components, including the Registrar, Proxy Server, and Back-to-Back User Agent (B2BUA), are crucial for setting up, routing, and managing SIP sessions. While there are several elements within the SIP ecosystem that facilitate various functionalities, we will focus on these three key components, as they form the core of SIP-based communication systems and are essential for understanding how SIP operates within Cisco's Collaboration environment.

Let us discuss each component, what it does, and how it relates to Cisco's Collaboration products.

SIP Registrar

The SIP Registrar plays a crucial role in SIP-based communication systems by handling registration requests from SIP devices, such as IP phones or softphones. When a SIP device is powered on, it sends a REGISTER message to the Registrar, informing the network of its current IP address and availability for receiving calls. This process allows the SIP system to maintain an up-to-date directory of all registered User Agents (UAs) and their contact information. In Cisco's Collaboration environment, the Cisco Unified Communications Manager (CUCM) serves as the SIP Registrar, among its other functions.

During the registration process, the SIP device provides an Address of Record (AOR), which acts as a unique identifier for the user. The AOR is typically in the form of a SIP URI, resembling an email address (example, **`sip:user@example.com`**). The AOR is essential in SIP as it serves as the user's public address, allowing SIP requests, such as incoming calls or messages, to be correctly routed to the user's current location.

The AOR usually contains the following information:

1. **User's SIP URI**: The unique identifier for the user (e.g., sip:user@example.com), used for routing calls and messages.

2. **Domain**: The domain of the SIP service provider, used for routing and registration purposes.

3. **User Display Name (optional)**: A human-readable name for the user.

4. **Parameters (optional)**: Additional parameters that can influence the routing of requests, such as transport protocol or user location.

5. **Authentication Details (optional)**: In some cases, the AOR may include credentials or tokens for user authentication.

Now, let us examine the registration process in more detail using the provided diagram *Figure* 8.2. The registration flow begins with the endpoint sending a **`REGISTER`** request, including the AOR, to the SIP Registrar. The Registrar processes the message, associates the AOR with the endpoint's IP address, and responds with a 200 OK message upon successful registration. The endpoint then sends periodic keep-alive **`REGISTER`** requests to maintain the registration, with the Registrar acknowledging each request with a **`200 OK`** response.

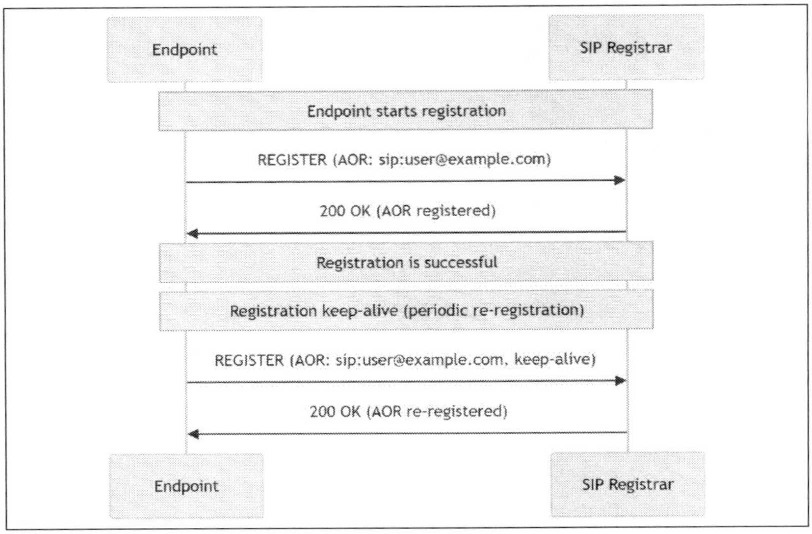

Figure 8.2: *SIP endpoint registration*

Registration Expiration and Refresh

To maintain the registration and ensure continuous reachability, the SIP device must periodically send **`REGISTER`** requests to the Registrar using the same Call-ID. This process, known as registration refresh or keep-alive, allows the Registrar to confirm that the device is still active and available at the registered contact address.

The **`REGISTER`** request may include an **`"Expires"`** header field specifying the duration of the validity of the registration. If absent, the Registrar assigns a default value, typically 3600 seconds (1 hour). To account for potential network issues, the endpoint must refresh the registration before expiration to maintain reachability, usually at a fraction of the expiration time. The Registrar may also include a **`"Min-Expires"`** header in its **`200 OK`** response, indicating the minimum allowed expiration time for future refreshes.

Authentication and Security

SIP Registrars often require authentication to ensure that only authorized endpoints can register and update their contact information. The most common authentication mechanism is the "Digest" scheme. When the Registrar receives a **`REGISTER`** request, it challenges the endpoint with a 401 Unauthorized response containing a nonce value. The endpoint then resends the **`REGISTER`** request with an "Authorization" header, including a hash of the username, password, nonce, and other parameters. The Registrar verifies this hash to authenticate the endpoint. To protect against eavesdropping and tampering, SIP messages can be encrypted using Transport Layer Security (TLS).

Multiple Contacts and Priorities

A single AOR can be associated with multiple contact addresses, representing different devices or locations where the user can be reached. The `"Contact"` header in the REGISTER request can include a `"q"` parameter, specifying the relative priority of each contact address, with higher values indicating higher priority.

Now that we understand the SIP Registrar's role in managing user registration, authentication, and maintaining up-to-date contact information, let us focus on another essential component: the SIP Proxy Server.

SIP Proxy Server

The SIP Proxy Server plays a crucial role in routing SIP requests to their intended destinations within a SIP-based communication system. As an intermediary, the SIP Proxy Server determines the next hop for each request based on the SIP message content and the server's internal routing rules. In addition to routing, SIP Proxy Servers can also perform authentication, authorization, and accounting functions.

One of the key responsibilities of a SIP Proxy Server is call routing. The proxy server uses the information contained in SIP headers, such as the Request-URI, To, and From headers, along with its internal routing tables to determine the most appropriate next hop for each request. The routing decision can be influenced by various factors, including the user's location, time of day, or other predefined policies. For example, a SIP Proxy Server can be configured to route calls to a user's office phone during business hours and to their mobile phone after hours. To ensure accurate call routing, the SIP Proxy Server may also consult external databases or directories to obtain a user's most up-to-date contact information.

Another powerful feature of SIP Proxy Servers is forking. Forking allows the proxy server to send an incoming request to multiple destinations simultaneously. This is particularly useful when users have multiple registered devices or when implementing call-hunting or call-forwarding features. For instance, if a user has a desk phone and a softphone registered, the SIP Proxy Server can fork an incoming call request, causing both devices to ring simultaneously. The call is then established with the device that answers first while the other device stops ringing. By leveraging forking, SIP Proxy Servers enhance user reachability and provide greater flexibility in handling incoming calls.

In Cisco's Collaboration environment, several components function as SIP Proxy Servers. The Cisco Unified Communications Manager (CUCM), being the core call control platform, acts as a SIP Proxy Server for devices registered to it. CUCM can route calls between internal endpoints and external entities via SIP trunks. The Cisco Expressway Series and Cisco Unified Border Element (CUBE) also serve as SIP Proxy Servers. These components play a vital role in routing calls between internal devices and external networks, such as SIP trunks connecting to Internet Telephony Service Providers (ITSPs) or between enterprise branches.

Now, let us examine the role of the SIP Proxy Server in a typical call flow, as illustrated in the provided diagram *Figure* 8.3.

UA1 initiates the call by sending an **`INVITE`** to the SIP Proxy. Upon receiving the INVITE, the proxy examines the request and determines the most appropriate route to reach UA2 based on its routing rules and the message content. The SIP Proxy then forwards the same **`INVITE`** to UA2, acting as a facilitator between the two User Agents without modifying the call state.

UA2 responds to the **`INVITE`** with a **`200 OK`**, which the proxy relays back to UA1. UA1 acknowledges the response with an **`ACK`**, establishing the session. Throughout this process, the SIP Proxy ensures the proper delivery of SIP messages between the User Agents.

Once the session is established, media flows directly between UA1 and UA2 using RTP, while the SIP Proxy remains uninvolved in the media exchange. To end the call, UA1 sends a **`BYE`** to the proxy, which forwards it to UA2. UA2 responds with a 200 OK, confirming the session termination. The proxy forwards this final response to UA1, marking the end of the call.

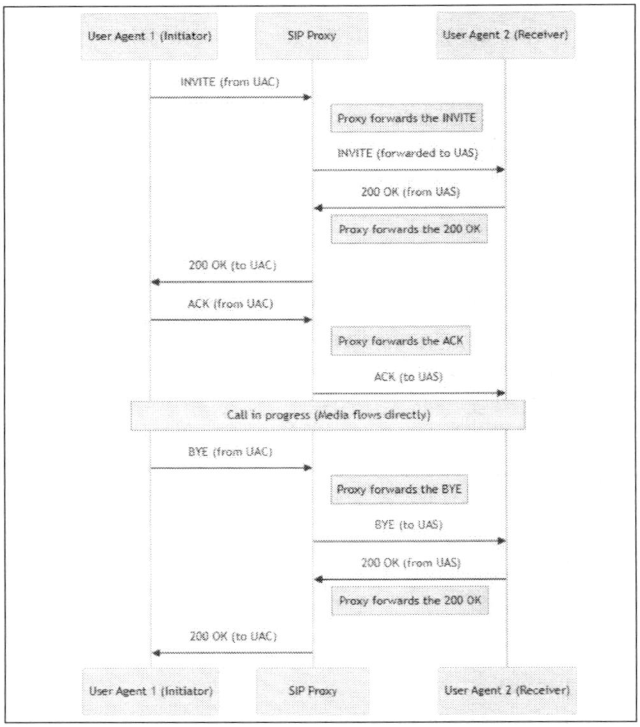

Figure 8.3: *Call flow through SIP Proxy*

Throughout this process, the SIP Proxy Server acts as a routing entity, ensuring that SIP messages are delivered to the appropriate destinations without modifying the session state or message content. This is a key difference between a SIP Proxy Server and a Back-to-Back User Agent (B2BUA), which actively participates in the call by terminating and re-originating SIP sessions. Let us now explore the concept of B2BUA and how it differs from a SIP Proxy Server.

Back-to-Back User Agent (B2BUA)

A Back-to-Back User Agent (B2BUA) is a SIP entity that sits between two User Agents (UAs) and actively participates in the SIP signaling and media flow. Unlike a SIP Proxy Server, which simply forwards messages between UAs, a B2BUA terminates the incoming SIP session, processes the request as a User Agent Server (UAS), and then initiates a new SIP session as a User Agent Client (UAC) to the destination UA. This unique position allows the B2BUA to control the SIP signaling and media completely.

In Cisco's Collaboration architecture, both the Cisco Unified Border Element (CUBE) and the Cisco Expressway function as B2BUAs. CUBE plays a crucial role in connecting different network zones, such as the internal network to the PSTN or between VoIP networks, while providing session control, security features, and transcoding services. Similarly, the Expressway serves as a border element, enabling secure communication between internal enterprise networks and external networks or the Internet.

B2BUAs offer several key features and benefits in Cisco's Collaboration environment:

1. **Topology Hiding**: CUBE and Expressway can hide the internal network topology from external entities by modifying SIP headers and masking IP addresses. This enhances security by preventing unauthorized parties from discovering the internal network's structure and components.

2. **Interoperability**: As B2BUAs, CUBE, and Expressway can facilitate communication between SIP endpoints that may not be fully compatible due to differences in SIP implementations, protocols, or features. They can translate and normalize SIP messages, ensuring seamless interoperability between diverse systems within the Cisco Collaboration ecosystem.

3. **Protocol Interworking**: CUBE and Expressway can enable communication between different protocols, such as SIP and H.323 or SIP and MGCP. This allows endpoints using different signaling protocols to communicate with each other, expanding the flexibility and reach of the Collaboration infrastructure.

4. **Security**: CUBE and Expressway provide security features such as SIP message validation, encryption, and authentication. They protect against SIP-based attacks by inspecting and filtering SIP traffic and can enforce security policies and access control rules to ensure that only authorized endpoints can establish SIP sessions.

Now, let us examine the role of the B2BUA in a typical call flow, as illustrated in the provided *Figure* 8.4

- UA1, acting as a UAC, sends an **`INVITE`** to the B2BUA to initiate a session with UA2. The B2BUA processes the request as a UAS, evaluates it based on its policies, and then generates a new INVITE as a UAC, sending it to UA2 on behalf of UA1.
- UA2, acting as a UAS, responds with a **`200 OK`**, indicating its willingness to establish the session. The B2BUA processes the response and forwards a new **`200 OK`** to UA1, completing the session establishment from UA1's perspective.
- UA1 sends an ACK to acknowledge the session establishment, which the B2BUA sends to UA2. With the session established, media flows between UA1 and UA2 through the B2BUA, which can perform functions like transcoding or recording.
- To end the call, UA1 sends a **`BYE`** to the B2BUA, which it sends to UA2. UA2 responds with a **`200 OK`**, confirming the termination. The B2BUA then sends a **`200 OK`** to UA1, completing the termination process.

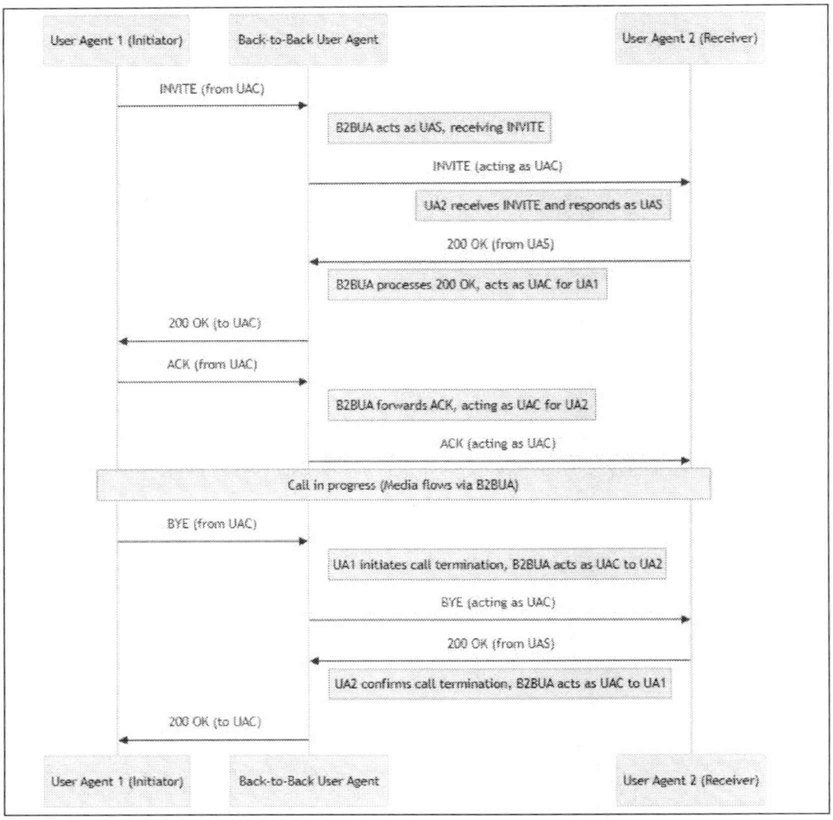

***Figure 8.4**: Call flow through SIP B2BUA*

Throughout this call flow, the B2BUA maintains two separate SIP sessions, one with each UA, allowing it to provide advanced features and apply policies to the communication. By acting as both UAS and UAC, the B2BUA can bridge different networks, enforce security measures, and enable seamless interoperability between various SIP endpoints and systems.

It is essential to know the core SIP components and their roles within Cisco's Collaboration infrastructure. However, to truly understand how SIP messages are constructed and exchanged, we need to explore SIP headers and the Session Description Protocol (SDP). These elements are crucial for establishing, modifying, and tearing down SIP sessions and negotiating media capabilities between endpoints.

Let us explore these building blocks.

SIP Headers and SDP

Session Initiation Protocol (SIP) messages are composed of a start-line, headers, and an optional message body. The headers contain essential information about the message, including the type of request or response, sender and recipient details, session specifics, and instructions for message handling. SIP headers follow a simple format: Header-Name: value.

Before discussing specific headers, it is important to understand two key concepts in SIP: transactions and dialogs.

A SIP transaction is a fundamental unit of interaction in SIP, consisting of a request and all responses to that request. They are identified by the combination of the CSeq header field (the sequence number) and the request method (example., **`INVITE`**, **`REGISTER`**). Transactions ensure that SIP requests are delivered reliably and responses are matched to their corresponding requests, even during network delays or failures. They also help in managing retransmissions and timeouts.

A SIP dialog represents a persistent peer-to-peer SIP relationship between two user agents. A dialog is established when a SIP request is sent from one user agent to another, and a response is received, creating a connection between the two endpoints. This connection persists for some time, allowing subsequent requests and responses related to the same call or session to be exchanged within the context of the dialog. Dialogs are identified by a combination of the Call-ID header, the local tag (from the From header), and the remote tag (from the To header in the response). Dialogs are essential for maintaining state information about a call, such as the call participants, the media being used, and any other session-related parameters negotiated between the endpoints.

Mandatory SIP Headers

Mandatory headers are crucial for the proper functioning of the SIP method. These headers provide the information required for a SIP message to be processed correctly. Let us explore each mandatory header in detail:

1. **`Via`**: The **`Via`** header is essential for tracking the path taken by the request through the SIP network. It is used for routing responses back to the requester and identifying the transport protocol and address to which the response should be sent. Each SIP entity that forwards the request adds its own **`Via`** header, forming a recorded route that the response can follow back to the originator.
   Example: **`Via: SIP/2.0/UDP 10.0.0.1:5060;branch=z9hG4bK776asdhds`**

2. **`From`**: The **`From`** header specifies the initiator of the request, including a display name (optional) and a SIP Uniform Resource Identifier (URI). The SIP URI represents the sender's address and is typically in the format **`"sip:user@domain".`** The **`From`** header also contains a tag parameter, which is a unique identifier for the dialog.
   Example: **`From: Alice sip:alice@example.com;tag=1928301774`**

3. **`To:`** The **`To`** header indicates the request's intended recipient. It is similar in format to the From header, containing a display name (optional) and a SIP URI. Initially, the **`To`** header does not include a tag parameter. However, when the recipient sends a response, a tag is added to uniquely identify the dialog.
   Example: **`To: Bob sip:bob@example.com`**

4. **`Call-ID:`** The **`Call-ID`** header serves as a unique identifier for a dialog or series of messages within a call. It ensures that all messages related to a specific call can be associated with each other. The **`Call-ID`** is generated by the caller and remains the same for all messages within a dialog.
   Example: **`Call-ID: a84b4c76e66710@pc33.example.com`**

5. **`CSeq:`** The Command Sequence (**`CSeq`**) header contains a sequence number and the method of the request. It is used to order transactions within a dialog and helps detect and prevent replay attacks. The sequence number increments for each new request within a dialog.
   Example: **`CSeq: 314159 INVITE`**

6. **`Max-Forwards`**: The **`Max-Forwards`** header limits the number of hops a request can make through the network. It is initialized by the sender and decremented by one each time the request is forwarded by a SIP entity. If the **`Max-Forwards`** value reaches zero, the request is discarded, preventing infinite loops in the network.
   Example: **`Max-Forwards: 70`**

These mandatory headers form the foundation of a well-structured SIP message. They provide essential information for message routing, dialog identification, and session management.

Optional SIP Headers

In addition to the mandatory headers, SIP messages can include optional headers that provide additional information and instructions to enhance the call setup, management, and termination processes. While not strictly required for basic SIP operation, these headers offer valuable functionality. There are many optional headers defined in the SIP specifications, but we'll focus on some of the most important ones:

1. **`Contact`**: The **`Contact`** header specifies the direct address at which the sender can be reached. It is particularly important in REGISTER requests, where it indicates the address to which future requests for the registered user should be sent. The Contact header is also crucial in responses to INVITE requests, providing the recipient with the direct address for subsequent requests within the dialog.
   Example: **`Contact: sip:alice@10.0.0.1`**

2. **`Content-Type`**: The **`Content-Type`** header informs the recipient about the type of message body, if any, that is attached to the SIP message. It is essential for the proper interpretation and handling of the message body. Common content types include **`"application/sdp"`** for Session Description Protocol (SDP) and **`"text/plain"`** for plain text.
   Example: **`Content-Type: application/sdp`**

3. **`Content-Length:`** The **`Content-Length`** header indicates the size of the message body in bytes. It is critical for the recipient to correctly parse the message body from the SIP headers. The Content-Length header must be present if the message contains a body.
   Example: **`Content-Length: 142`**

4. **`Record-Route and Route`**: The **`Record-Route`** header is inserted by SIP proxies to specify a route that subsequent requests in the dialog should follow. It allows the proxies to maintain a call state and stay involved in the signaling path. The **`Route`** header is used by the sender to specify a pre-determined path for the request to take through specific SIP proxies.
   Example: **`Record-Route: sip:proxy1.example.com;lr`**

   `Route: sip:proxy2.example.com;lr`
   The difference between **`Record-Route`** and **`Via`** is that Record-Route specifies a path for subsequent requests in a dialog, while **`Via`** tracks the path of a single request and its responses.

5. **`Allow:`** The **`Allow`** header lists the SIP methods supported by the user agent or server. It informs the recipient about the capabilities of the sender, helps in method negotiation, and prevents unnecessary requests.
   Example: **`Allow: INVITE, ACK, CANCEL, OPTIONS, BYE`**

6. **`Supported and Require`**: The **`Supported`** header lists the SIP extensions supported by the sender, while the Require header indicates which extensions must be supported by the recipient for the request to be processed successfully.
   Example: **`Supported: 100rel, precondition`**
   `Require: replaces`

These optional headers enhance the functionality and flexibility of SIP messages, allowing for advanced features, reliable message delivery, and interoperability between SIP entities.

Handling Unsupported Headers

SIP is designed to be extensible, allowing for the introduction of new headers and features. This extensibility enables vendors to add custom functionality to their SIP-based systems through the use of proprietary headers. Proprietary headers are typically prefixed with **`"X-"`** to distinguish them from standard headers. For example:

`X-Cisco-CallDuration: 120`

`X-Custom-Header: value`

However, not all SIP entities may support these extensions, which can lead to interoperability issues. To ensure that communication can still occur, even when proprietary or unsupported headers are present, SIP follows the "robustness principle," also known as Postel's Law. This principle states: "Be conservative in what you send; be liberal in what you accept."

In practice, this means that when a SIP entity receives a message with headers that it does not understand, it should ignore those headers and process the message as best as it can. This approach allows for backward compatibility and the gradual adoption of new features without breaking existing implementations.

For example, suppose a Cisco SIP phone sends a message with a proprietary header like **`"X-Cisco-CallDuration"`** to a non-Cisco SIP endpoint. In that case, the receiving endpoint should simply ignore the header and process the rest of the message normally. This ensures that the core communication can still occur, even if the proprietary functionality is not supported.

There are a few exceptions to this rule:

1. **Mandatory Headers**: All SIP entities must understand and process the mandatory headers (**`To, From, CSeq, Call-ID, Max-Forwards`**, and **`Via`**) for the message to be considered valid. The message should be rejected if a mandatory header is missing or malformed.

2. **Require and Proxy-Require Headers**: These headers indicate that a specific extension or feature must be supported by the receiving entity (**`Require`**) or

by proxies processing the request (**`Proxy-Require`**). If a SIP request contains a Require or Proxy-Require header with an option tag that the receiver or proxy does not understand, the request must be rejected with a 420 (**`Bad Extension`**) response. This prevents the use of features that are not supported by all parties involved in the communication.

By following these guidelines, SIP achieves a balance between extensibility and interoperability. It allows for the introduction of new features and proprietary extensions while ensuring that basic communication can still occur between SIP entities that may not support all the same capabilities.

In a Cisco Collaboration environment, this is particularly important as it enables interoperability between Cisco and non-Cisco SIP endpoints, as well as between different generations or models of Cisco devices that may support different sets of proprietary headers and features. By adhering to the robustness principle, Cisco devices can communicate effectively with a wide range of SIP entities while still leveraging Cisco-specific features when communicating with other Cisco devices.

Understanding SIP Headers with Example: INVITE and 200 OK

Now that we understand the various SIP headers and their roles in managing SIP-based communication, let us examine a sample SIP message exchange to see these headers in action.

One of the most common SIP message exchanges is the **`INVITE-200 OK`** transaction, which establishes a new SIP session. Let us examine a sample **`INVITE`** request and its corresponding **`200 OK`** response to understand how SIP headers are used in practice.

As shown in *Figure* 8.5, Alice initiates the communication by sending an **`INVITE`** request to Bob through the SIP server. This request includes crucial SIP headers such as **`Via, Max-Forwards, From, To`**, and **`Call-ID`**, which help in routing and managing the session setup. The SIP server forwards this **`INVITE`** to Bob, maintaining the integrity of the header information. Bob then sends a **`200 OK`** response, confirming the establishment of the session. This response follows the same path back to Alice, facilitated by the SIP server, indicating a successful connection.

Once the **`200 OK`** response is received by Alice, it confirms that both parties are ready, and the media session begins using RTP, allowing real-time audio or video data to be exchanged.

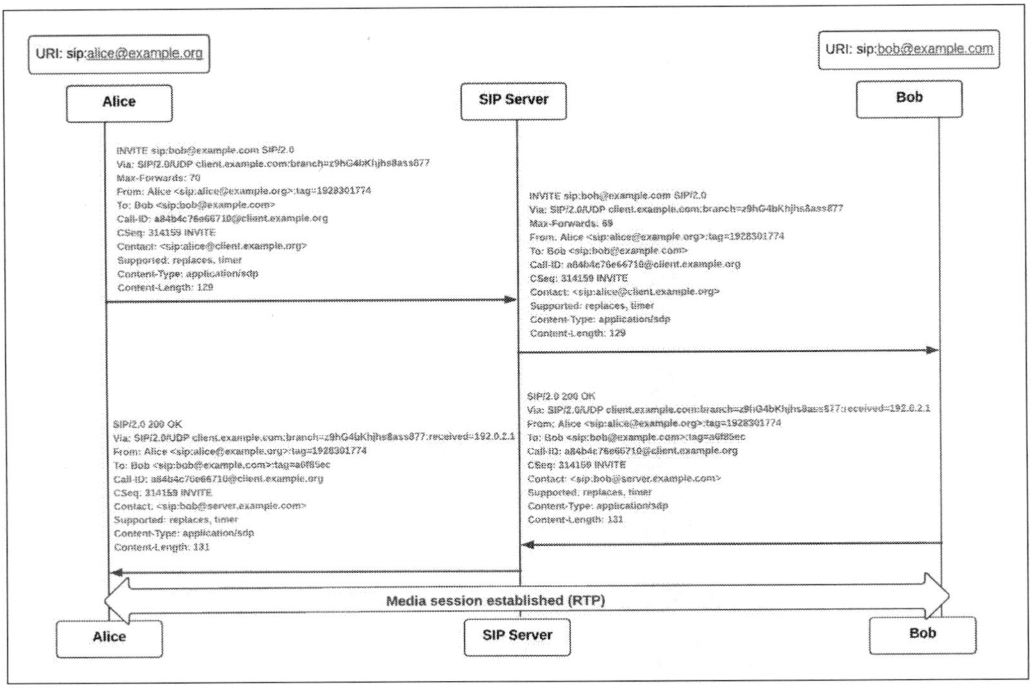

***Figure 8.5**: SIP INVITE and 200 OK Transaction Flow*

Now let us examine those headers in **`INVITE`** and **`2000K.`**

Sample **`SIP INVITE`** Request

In this **`INVITE`** request, the caller (Alice) is attempting to establish a new session with the callee (Bob). The request includes several important headers:

- **`Via`**: Indicates the transport protocol and the path the request has taken.
- **`Max-Forwards`**: Limits the number of hops the request can make to prevent loops.
- **`From`**: Specifies the caller's address and a unique tag for the dialog.
- **`To`**: Specifies the callee's address.
- **`Call-ID`**: Uniquely identifies this call.
- **`CSeq`**: Identifies the request within the dialog and includes the request method (INVITE).
- **Contact**: Provides the caller's direct address for subsequent requests in this dialog.
- **Supported**: Lists the SIP extensions supported by the caller.

- **Content-Type and Content-Length**: Describe the message body, which in this case is an SDP payload detailing the proposed media session parameters.

```
INVITE sip:bob@example.com SIP/2.0
Via: SIP/2.0/UDP client.example.com;branch=z9hG4bKhjhs8ass877
Max-Forwards: 70
From: Alice <sip:alice@example.org>;tag=1928301774
To: Bob <sip:bob@example.com>
Call-ID: a84b4c76e66710@client.example.org
CSeq: 314159 INVITE
Contact: <sip:alice@client.example.org>
Supported: replaces, timer
Content-Type: application/sdp
Content-Length: 129

v=0
o=Alice 2890844526 2890844526 IN IP4 client.example.org
s=Session SDP
c=IN IP4 client.example.org
t=0 0
m=audio 49170 RTP/AVP 0
a=rtpmap:0 PCMU/8000
```

Sample 200 OK Response

The **200 OK** response from the callee (Bob) indicates a successful session establishment. It includes many of the same headers as the INVITE request, with a few key differences:

- **Via**: Now includes the received parameter, indicating the source IP address of the request.
- **To**: Includes a unique tag generated by the callee for this dialog.
- **Contact**: Provides the callee's direct address for subsequent requests in this dialog.
- **Content-Type and Content-Length**: Describe the SDP payload, which now includes the callee's media session parameters.

```
SIP/2.0 200 OK
Via: SIP/2.0/UDP client.example.com;branch=z9hG4bKhjhs8ass877;re-
```

```
ceived=192.0.2.1
From: Alice <sip:alice@example.org>;tag=1928301774
To: Bob <sip:bob@example.com>;tag=a6f85ec
Call-ID: a84b4c76e66710@client.example.org
CSeq: 314159 INVITE
Contact: <sip:bob@server.example.com>
Supported: replaces, timer
Content-Type: application/sdp
Content-Length: 131

v=0
o=Bob 2890844527 2890844527 IN IP4 server.example.com
s=Session SDP
c=IN IP4 server.example.com
t=0 0
m=audio 49172 RTP/AVP 0
a=rtpmap:0 PCMU/8000
```

This sample exchange demonstrates how SIP headers work together to establish a new session. The mandatory headers ensure proper routing and identification of the dialog, while the optional headers provide additional information and functionality, such as the Supported header for extension negotiation and the SDP payload for media negotiation.

Understanding these headers and their roles is crucial for configuring, troubleshooting, and optimizing SIP-based communications in a Cisco Collaboration environment. Cisco devices, such as IP phones, video endpoints, and call control platforms (example, Cisco Unified Communications Manager), rely heavily on SIP headers to establish and manage sessions, negotiate capabilities, and ensure interoperability with other SIP-compliant systems.

Now that we have seen SIP headers in action let us move on to the Session Description Protocol (SDP) and explore its role in SIP-based media negotiation.

Session Description Protocol (SDP)

Session Description Protocol (SDP) is a protocol used in conjunction with the Session Initiation Protocol (SIP) and other signaling protocols to establish multimedia sessions in IP networks. SDP provides a standardized format for describing the parameters of a multimedia session, enabling endpoints to negotiate compatible media settings and participate in the session.

While SDP is not a part of SIP itself, it is commonly carried within SIP messages to convey information about the media capabilities and preferences of the endpoints involved in a session. This allows SIP to focus on session management tasks, such as establishing, modifying, and terminating sessions, while SDP handles the description of the media parameters.

SDP, defined in RFC 4566, provides a standard format for describing the metadata of a multimedia session, such as:

- Session name and purpose
- Time(s) the session is active
- The media types and formats offered
- Transport protocol and addresses (IP addresses and ports) for media streams
- Bandwidth requirements
- Contact information for the session originator

It is important to note that SDP itself does not deliver media or manage sessions; it is a format for describing the session parameters, allowing endpoints to negotiate compatible media settings and establish successful multimedia communication.

SDP Message Format

An SDP message consists of a series of lines, each beginning with a single-character field name followed by an equals sign (=) and the field value. The fields are grouped into sections, with each section starting with a specific field name.

Here is an example SDP message:

```
v=0
o=alice 2890844526 2890844526 IN IP4 host.example.com
s=Example SDP Session
c=IN IP4 192.0.2.1
t=0 0
m=audio 49170 RTP/AVP 0 8
a=rtpmap:0 PCMU/8000
a=rtpmap:8 PCMA/8000
m=video 49172 RTP/AVP 98
a=rtpmap:98 H263-1998/90000
a=fmtp:98 CIF=1;QCIF=1
```

Key SDP Fields are:

- **`v= (Protocol Version)`:** Specifies the version of the SDP protocol. The current version is 0.
- **`o= (Originator and Session Identifier)`:** This field contains the session's unique identifier, the originator's username, a session ID, a session version number, and the originator's IP address.
- **`s= (Session Name)`:** Provides a human-readable name for the session.
- **`c= (Connection Data)`:** Contains the IP address where the endpoint wants to receive the media stream. This field is crucial for troubleshooting, as it determines where the media packets are sent. The connection data can be specified at the session level or the media level.
- **`t= (Timing)`:** Specifies the start and stop times for the session. In the example above, **`"0 0"`** indicates that it's a permanent session.
- **`m= (Media Descriptions)`:** Defines the media type (example, audio, video), transport port (on which the endpoint expects to receive the media), protocol (example, RTP/AVP), and format (example, codec) for each media stream. In the example, there are two media lines: one for audio and one for video. The audio line specifies two payload types (0 and 8), while the video line specifies one payload type (98).
- **`a= (Attributes)`:** Provides additional information about the session or media, such as the RTP payload type mappings (**`a=rtpmap:`**) or format-specific parameters (**`a=fmtp:`**).

  It can also include information about the direction of the media stream. The **`"a=sendrecv"`** attribute indicates that the endpoint is willing to send and receive media, while **`"a=recvonly"`** means that the endpoint only wants to receive media and will not send any. Other possible values are **`"a=sendonly"`** (the endpoint will only send media) and **`"a=inactive"`** (the endpoint will neither send nor receive media).

  These attributes are important for negotiating the direction of the media flow and can be used to implement features like call recording or music on hold.

RTP payload types are used to identify the media format carried in RTP packets. They can be either static (predefined in RFC 3551) or dynamic (assigned dynamically in the SDP).

In the example above:

- "**`a=rtpmap:0 PCMU/8000`**" maps static payload type 0 to the PCMU (G.711 μ-law) codec with a clock rate of 8000 Hz.
- "**`a=rtpmap:8 PCMA/8000`**" maps static payload type 8 to the PCMA (G.711 A-law) codec with a clock rate of 8000 Hz.

- "**`a=rtpmap:98 H263-1998/90000`**" maps dynamic payload type 98 to the H.263-1998 video codec with a clock rate of 90000 Hz.

The **`"a=fmtp:"`** attribute is used to specify format-specific parameters. In the example, **`"a=fmtp:98 CIF=1;QCIF=1"`** indicates that the H.263 codec supports both CIF and QCIF resolutions.

SDP and the Offer/Answer Model

The Session Description Protocol (SDP) works within the Offer/Answer model framework, as defined in RFC 3264. The Offer/Answer model is a mechanism for two endpoints to agree on the media parameters for a session, and SDP is the protocol used to describe these media parameters.

In the Offer/Answer model, SDP is used as follows:

1. The offerer creates an SDP message (the offer) that describes its proposed media parameters, such as the codecs, transport protocols, IP addresses, and port numbers.
2. The offerer sends this SDP offer to the answerer using a signaling protocol such as SIP (example, in a SIP INVITE request).
3. The answerer receives the SDP offer and determines which media parameters it can support.
4. The answerer generates an SDP message (the answer) that includes its selected media parameters based on the received offer. The answer may also include additional information, such as the answerer's IP address and port numbers.
5. The answerer sends the SDP answer back to the offerer using the signaling protocol (example, in a **`SIP 200 OK`** response).
6. The offerer receives the SDP answer and learns which media parameters have been accepted by the answerer.
7. Both endpoints now share an understanding of the media parameters, and the session can be established using these negotiated parameters.

The Offer/Answer model allows endpoints to negotiate compatible media parameters before the session is fully established. The negotiated codec is influenced by various factors, such as the endpoint capabilities, codec preferences, bandwidth availability, and the configuration of intermediary devices like SIP proxies or media gateways.

In Cisco Collaboration environments, SDP is extensively used with SIP to establish voice and video sessions between endpoints. Cisco Unified Communications Manager (CUCM), Cisco Unified Border Element (CUBE), Cisco Expressway, and Cisco IP phones all use SDP to negotiate media capabilities and parameters during call setup.

For example, when a Cisco IP phone initiates a call through CUCM, it sends a SIP INVITE message containing an SDP offer. This offer includes the codecs, transport protocols, and other media capabilities supported by the phone. CUCM forwards this INVITE to the destination endpoint, which responds with a SIP 200 OK message containing an SDP answer, specifying the selected codec and media parameters for the call. CUCM then relays this answer back to the originating phone, allowing the endpoints to establish a compatible media session.

In the next chapter, we will explore various call flows involving SDP, such as early offer, delayed offer, and early media scenarios, to understand how media negotiation occurs in different situations.

It is important to note that SDP is not limited to audio codecs. It also negotiates video codecs, encryption parameters (example, SRTP), and other media-related settings. The Offer/Answer model and SDP provide a flexible and extensible framework for negotiating multimedia sessions in VoIP and video conferencing systems.

Once the media parameters have been negotiated using SDP, the media packets are transmitted using the Real-time Transport Protocol (RTP), and the Real-time Transport Control Protocol (RTCP) is used to monitor the quality of the media session and provide feedback to the endpoints. Let us move on to discuss RTP and RTCP in more detail.

Real-Time Media Protocols: RTP and RTCP

Real-time Transport Protocol (RTP) and Real-time Transport Control Protocol (RTCP) are essential protocols for real-time multimedia communication over IP networks. They are designed to handle the transmission of multimedia data with the sensitivity and efficiency required for real-time communication. RTP operates over User Datagram Protocol (UDP) to take advantage of its lower latency compared to Transmission Control Protocol (TCP), making it ideal for live audio and video streaming where timely delivery is crucial. RTCP provides feedback and control information about the RTP session, enabling monitoring and management of the multimedia transmission.

RTP (Real-time Transport Protocol)

RTP facilitates the real-time transmission of multimedia data by packetizing the media content. Each packet carries a portion of the content, such as a video frame or a snippet of audio, enabling the receiver to play the media as it arrives without waiting for the entire content to be delivered. This allows for low-latency streaming and interactive communication.

RTP incorporates several features to ensure the smooth and synchronized delivery of multimedia data. One of these features is timestamping. Each RTP packet includes a timestamp that indicates the sampling instant of the first byte in the payload. This timestamp helps the receiver reconstruct the original timing of the media and maintain proper synchronization during playback. Even if packets arrive out of order or experience varying network delays, the timestamps enable the receiver to reorder and playback the media correctly.

Another essential feature of RTP is sequence numbering. Each RTP packet is assigned a unique sequence number that increments with each subsequent packet. Sequence numbers allow the receiver to detect lost or out-of-order packets and take appropriate actions, such as applying error concealment techniques. By monitoring the sequence numbers, the receiver can ensure the integrity and continuity of the media stream.

RTP packets consist of a header and a payload. The RTP header contains critical information for processing and interpreting the media data. Let us explore some of the key header fields in detail:

- **Version (V):** This 2-bit field indicates the version of the RTP protocol being used. The current version is 2.
- **Padding (P)**: If set to 1, this 1-bit field indicates that the packet contains padding octets at the end, which are not part of the payload. The last octet of the padding contains a count of the padding octets.
- **Extension (X)**: If set to 1, this 1-bit field indicates the presence of an extension header between the standard header and the payload.
- **Marker (M)**: This 1-bit field is used at the application level and defined by the RTP profile. It can be used to mark significant events, such as the start of a talkspurt in audio or the end of a video frame.
- **Payload Type (PT)**: This 7-bit field identifies the format of the media payload carried in the RTP packet. It indicates the specific audio or video codec being used, such as G.711 for audio or H.264 for video. The mapping between payload types and codecs is defined in RTP profile specifications or through dynamic payload type assignment.
- **Sequence Number**: This 16-bit field is incremented by one for each RTP data packet sent. It allows the receiver to detect packet loss and restore the original packet sequence. The initial sequence number is randomly selected.
- **Timestamp**: This 32-bit field reflects the sampling instant of the first byte in the RTP payload. It is derived from a clock that increments monotonically and linearly in time, enabling synchronization and jitter calculations. The clock frequency is dependent on the media format and is specified in the RTP profile or payload format specification.
- **Synchronization Source (SSRC)**: This 32-bit field uniquely identifies the source

of the RTP stream within an RTP session. It is randomly generated. SSRC helps the receiver distinguish between multiple RTP streams coming from different sources and correctly associate them with their respective media content. If two sources were to have the same SSRC, it would lead to conflicts and confusion at the receiver, as it would not be able to associate the RTP packets with their respective sources correctly.

For example, in a video conference with multiple participants, each participant's audio and video streams would have different SSRCs, allowing the receiver to synchronize and playback the media from each participant correctly.

Now that we understand RTP, let us discuss RTCP.

RTCP

RTCP is a companion protocol to RTP that provides essential control and monitoring functionalities for real-time multimedia communication sessions. While RTP focuses on transporting media data, RTCP operates alongside RTP to ensure the smooth and efficient delivery of multimedia content.

RTCP packets are multiplexed with RTP packets on the same transport address using different port numbers. The RTCP port number is usually the next higher odd port number relative to the RTP port. For example, if RTP uses port 5004, RTCP would use port 5005.

RTCP packets are typically sent at a lower frequency compared to RTP packets to minimize the overhead. The RTCP transmission interval is dynamically calculated based on the session bandwidth and the number of participants. The interval is randomized to avoid synchronization issues and is adjusted to limit the RTCP bandwidth usage to a small fraction of the session bandwidth (typically 5% or less). RTCP also provides mechanisms for participants to report their reception statistics, enabling the sender to adapt its transmission rate based on the available bandwidth and the reported quality metrics.

RTCP packets follow a standard format that includes a header and one or more RTCP compound packets. The RTCP header contains the following fields:

- **Version (V)**: 2 bits indicating the version of the RTCP protocol. The current version is 2.
- **Padding (P)**: 1 bit indicating if there are padding octets at the end of the packet.
- **Reception Report Count (RC)**: 5 bits indicating the number of reception report blocks contained in the packet.
- **Packet Type (PT)**: 8 bits identifying the type of RTCP packet (example, SR, RR, SDES, BYE, APP).

- **Length**: 16 bits specifying the length of the RTCP packet in 32-bit words, excluding the header.

The main RTCP packet types are:

1. **Sender Report (SR)**: Sent periodically by active senders in an RTP session to report transmission and reception statistics. It includes information about the sender's packet count, octet count, timestamps, and reception reports from other participants.
2. **Receiver Report (RR)**: Sent by participants who are not active senders to report reception statistics. It includes information about the received packet count, octet count, packet loss, jitter, and timestamp information.
3. **Source Description (SDES)**: Carries source description items, such as the canonical name (CNAME) and other optional information about the participants in an RTP session.
4. **BYE**: Indicates the end of participation in an RTP session. It is sent when a participant leaves the session gracefully.
5. **Application-Specific (APP)**: Provides a mechanism for application-specific extensions to RTCP.

Each RTCP packet type serves a specific purpose in monitoring and managing the RTP session. Source Description (SDES) packets help in identifying and describing the participants in the session, and BYE packets indicate graceful termination of participation. Application-Specific (APP) packets offer flexibility for custom extensions and application-specific functionalities.

RTCP Sender Reports (SR) and Receiver Reports (RR) play an important role in providing feedback about the quality of the RTP transmission, including information about packet loss, jitter, and round-trip times. By analyzing the packet loss information in the reception report blocks, endpoints can figure out the quality of the network and identify any issues affecting the RTP transmission. If a high packet loss is reported, it indicates network congestion or problems with the media delivery, and the sender can adapt its transmission accordingly, such as by reducing the bitrate or applying error resilience techniques.

SR and RR packets include the following key fields:

- **SSRC**: 32 bits identifying the synchronization source of the originator of the report. SSRC stands for Synchronization Source, which is a unique identifier for the source of an RTP stream within a session.
- **Timestamp**: 64 bits representing the time when the report was sent, used for calculating round-trip times and jitter.

  Receivers can use the information in the SR packet to estimate the RTT by comparing the NTP timestamp in the SR packet with the local NTP timestamp when the packet is received. The difference between these timestamps represents the one-way delay from the sender to the receiver. By combining the one-way delay with the information in the corresponding RR packet, which includes the delay since the last SR packet, endpoints can estimate the RTT.

- **Sender's Packet Count**: 32 bits specifying the total number of RTP data packets transmitted by the sender since the start of the session.
- **Sender's Octet Count**: 32 bits specifying the total number of payload octets transmitted by the sender since the start of the session.
- **Reception Report Blocks**: Variable-length blocks containing statistics for each SSRC from which the sender has received RTP packets. Each block includes the SSRC, fraction lost, cumulative number of packets lost, extended highest sequence number received, interarrival jitter, and last SR timestamp.

  Interarrival jitter helps to measures the variation in the arrival times of RTP packets. Jitter is an important metric for assessing the stability and quality of the media delivery.

RTCP reports can be used with other QoE metrics, such as the Mean Opinion Score (MOS) or the Perceptual Evaluation of Speech Quality (PESQ), to provide a comprehensive assessment of the audio or video quality as perceived by the users.

RFC 3550 provides the core specification for RTP and RTCP. However, several related RFCs extend and enhance the functionality of RTCP. For example, RFC 3611 defines the RTP Control Protocol Extended Reports (RTCP XR), which provide additional metrics and diagnostic information. RFC 5506 introduces support for reduced-size RTCP packets to improve efficiency in low-bandwidth scenarios. Understanding these and other relevant RFCs can be helpful in troubleshooting complex issues.

Conclusion

In this chapter, we have explored the fundamentals of signaling and media protocols. We started by understanding the importance of standards and protocols in ensuring interoperability and seamless communication across different devices and networks. We also learned about the role of standard bodies such as IETF and ITU-T in developing and maintaining these protocols.

We explored how SIP enables the establishment, modification, and termination of multimedia sessions. We discussed the various components of SIP, including user agents, proxy servers, B2BUA, and registrars, and how they work together to facilitate communication. We also examined the SIP call setup process, including the different types of messages exchanged during a typical SIP session. Then, we learned about the structure of SDP messages and how they convey information, such as media types, codecs, and network addresses.

Then, we explored the media protocols, Real-time Transport Protocol (RTP) and its companion, the RTP Control Protocol (RTCP). We discovered how RTP enables the transport of real-time media data, such as audio and video, over IP networks. We also learned about the important role of RTCP in providing feedback and quality monitoring for RTP sessions.

By gaining a solid grasp of SIP, SDP, RTP and RTCP, you will be well-equipped to troubleshoot issues and design effective Collaboration solutions. In the next chapter, we will build upon this foundation and explore more advanced topics in Collaboration technology. We will discuss media negotiation concepts such as Early Offer, Delayed Offer, and Early Media. We will also examine how SIP flows vary in different scenarios, such as conferencing, call transfer and call forwarding. Additionally, we will touch upon the challenges of Network Address Translation (NAT) in Collaboration and the importance of Quality of Service (QoS).

Multiple Choice Questions

1. What is the primary purpose of signaling protocols in Collaboration technology?
   a. To transport media data between endpoints
   b. To establish, modify, and terminate multimedia sessions
   c. To provide quality of service feedback for media streams
   d. To encrypt media traffic for secure communication
2. In a SIP call setup process, which message is sent by the calling party to initiate a session?
   a. ACK
   b. BYE
   c. INVITE
   d. REGISTER
3. What is the purpose of the Session Description Protocol (SDP)?
   a. To authenticate users and authorize access to resources
   b. To describe the media capabilities and parameters of a session
   c. To provide end-to-end encryption for media streams
   d. To prioritize and manage network traffic for optimal performance

4. Which protocol is primarily used for transporting real-time media data, such as audio and video, in Collaboration technology?
    a. HTTP (Hypertext Transfer Protocol)
    b. RTP (Real-time Transport Protocol)
    c. SMTP (Simple Mail Transfer Protocol)
    d. FTP (File Transfer Protocol)
5. Which RTCP packet type is sent by active senders in an RTP session to report transmission and reception statistics?
    a. Sender Report (SR)
    b. Receiver Report (RR)
    c. Source Description (SDES)
    d. Bye (BYE)
6. What does the "m=" field in an SDP message represent?
    a. The media type and transport address for a session
    b. The encryption method used for media streams
    c. The maximum bandwidth allocated for the session
    d. The participant's display name and contact information

Answers

1. b
2. c
3. b
4. b
5. a
6. a

Further Reading

Same as the last chapter, to improve your understanding and broaden your perspective, it is suggested to explore the following topics on your own.

- Observe the protocols you come across while working on different tech products in your day-to-day tasks at work. Investigate which ones are standards or proprietary and try to find their corresponding RFCs or similar documentation (if applicable). Knowing where to find information when needed is a valuable skill.
- Familiarize yourself with the SIP core specification, RFC 3261. Read through it to understand its structure and how the information is presented. Familiarizing with the document's structure will save you time when you need to find key information for complex troubleshooting.
- Capture and analyze packet traces or logs of VoIP or video conference calls from various components of a Collaboration system, such as Cisco Unified Communications Manager (CUCM), Cisco Expressway, endpoints, or Cisco Unified Border Element (CUBE). Examine the headers and try to correlate them with the concepts you have learnt in this chapter.

CHAPTER 9
Deep Dive - Signaling and Media Protocols

Introduction

In the previous chapter, we explored the fundamentals of signaling and media protocols, focusing on SIP, SDP, RTP, and RTCP. Building upon this foundation, we will now explore the concept of media negotiation, exploring call flows such as Early Offer, Delayed Offer, and Early Media. We will also investigate how SIP flows vary in different scenarios, such as call transfer and forwarding.

We will then cover other essential protocols, such as DTMF relay and Fax over IP, which are crucial for integrating traditional telephony services with modern IP-based collaboration solutions. Then, we will address the challenges that Network Address Translation (NAT) poses in Collaboration environments and explore the techniques and protocols, such as STUN, TURN, and ICE, that help overcome these obstacles.

We will conclude the chapter by discussing the importance of Quality of Service (QoS) in ensuring a superior user experience in Collaboration solutions and the impact of network factors like latency, jitter, packet loss, and bandwidth limitations on voice and video quality.

Structure

We will discuss the following topics:

- SDP Offer/Answer: Delayed Offer, Early Offer, and Early Media
- Advanced SIP session Flows: Call Transfer, Forward
- Essential Protocols in IP Telephony: DTMF and Fax over IP
- NAT in Collaboration
- Network Performance Considerations and Quality of Service (QoS)

SDP Offer/Answer: Delayed Offer, Early Offer, and Early Media

In the previous chapter, we discussed the Session Description Protocol (SDP) and its crucial role in establishing multimedia sessions between endpoints. SDP is used to describe the media capabilities, parameters, and preferences of the participants in a VoIP call. The SDP offer/answer model, defined in RFC 3264, is the foundation for media negotiation in SIP-based VoIP systems.

To recap, the SDP offer/answer model involves one endpoint (the offeror) sending an SDP message describing the desired media characteristics for the session. The other endpoint (the answerer) receives this offer and responds with an SDP answer that includes the media characteristics it is willing and able to support. This process allows the endpoints to agree upon a common set of media parameters, ensuring compatibility and enabling successful media exchange.

In SIP call flows, timing when the SDP offer is sent can have significant implications for media negotiation. The SDP offer can be sent as part of the initial **`INVITE`** request by the Caller, or the **`INVITE`** can be sent without SDP. When the SDP offer is sent in the initial INVITE, it is known as an "Early Offer." Conversely, when the **`INVITE`** is sent without SDP, and the offer is instead sent in a subsequent message, it is called a "Delayed Offer." The choice between an Early Offer and a Delayed Offer affects how media negotiation is carried out and how the call is established. Before we discuss these flows, we must understand some essential concepts about SIP.

SIP uses request methods to initiate actions and response codes to indicate the outcome of those actions. The most common SIP request methods include:

- **`INVITE:`** Initiates a session or call
- **`ACK:`** Confirms the receipt of a final response to an **`INVITE`**
- **`BYE:`** Terminates a session or call
- **`CANCEL:`** Cancels a pending request
- **`REGISTER`**: Registers a user's contact information with a SIP registrar

SIP response codes are three-digit numbers grouped into classes:

- **`1xx (Provisional):`** The request is being processed, but the final outcome is not yet known (e.g., **`180 Ringing)`**
- **`2xx (Success)`**: The request was successfully received, understood, and accepted (e.g., **`200 OK`**)
- **3xx (Redirection)**: Further action is needed to complete the request (e.g., **`301 Moved Permanently`**)

- **`4xx (Client Error)`**: The request contains bad syntax or cannot be fulfilled by the server (e.g., **`400 Bad Request`**)
- **`5xx (Server Error)`**: The server failed to fulfill a valid request (e.g., **`500 Internal Server Error`**)

In SIP, responses can be either provisional (1xx) or final (2xx, 3xx, 4xx, 5xx). Provisional responses provide information about the progress of a request without terminating the transaction. Final responses conclude the transaction.

Provisional responses are unreliable by default, meaning they may be lost without affecting the transaction's outcome. However, some provisional responses, such as the 100 Trying and 180 Ringing, can be made reliable using the **PRACK** (Provisional Response **ACK**nowledgement) method described in RFC 3262. Reliable provisional responses ensure that the sender receives confirmation of their receipt.

The rules for sending SDP in SIP messages are as follows:

- SDP can be sent in an **`INVITE`** request, a reliable provisional response (using **PRACK**), a final **`200 OK`** response, or an **ACK** request.
- If the SDP offer is sent in the **`INVITE`**, the answer must be sent in the **`200 OK`** response.
- If the SDP offer is sent in a reliable provisional response, the answer must be sent in the **PRACK** request.
- If the SDP offer is sent in the **`200 OK`** response, the answer must be sent in the **ACK** request.

Media can only flow after the offer/answer exchange is completed, which occurs when the **ACK** is sent in response to the **`200 OK`**.

A non-failure response is a SIP response code that does not indicate an error or failure in processing the request. Non-failure responses include provisional responses (1xx) and successful final responses (2xx).

Building upon this foundation, we will now discuss various methods of media negotiation, including Early Offer, Delayed Offer, and Early Media. These concepts are essential for understanding how VoIP endpoints establish and modify media sessions, handle complex call scenarios, and provide enhanced user experiences. We will also explore the role of the **PRACK** (Provisional Response **ACK**nowledgement) method in providing reliable provisional responses and its significance in conjunction with Early Media.

Let's discuss Delayed Offer and their role in SIP call flows.

Delayed Offer

In a Delayed Offer scenario, the caller's initial **`INVITE`** request does not contain an SDP offer. Instead, the called party sends the SDP offer in the first reliable non-failure response to the **INVITE,** which is typically the final **200 OK** response. The Caller then provides the SDP answer in the **ACK** request, completing the offer/answer exchange. This approach allows the called party to have more control over the media negotiation process and enables interworking with legacy systems that may not support Early Offer.

One advantage of a Delayed Offer is that it allows the called party to generate an SDP offer based on its own capabilities and preferences rather than being constrained by the caller's offer. This is particularly useful in scenarios where the called party may need to allocate resources or gather information before generating the offer.

In a Cisco collaboration environment, the default behavior for endpoints and SIP trunks can vary. For endpoints, the default is typically an Early Offer, where the SDP offer is included in the initial **INVITE**. However, this behavior can be modified through the setting in the SIP profile associated with the endpoint. For SIP trunks, the default behavior depends on the type of trunk and the configuration of the attached devices. The "Early Offer support for voice and video calls" setting in the SIP profile associated with the trunk determines whether an Early Offer or Delayed Offer is used. It is important to ensure that the offer/answer exchange is compatible between the endpoints and the SIP trunk to avoid media negotiation failures.

In *Figure* 9.1, the Caller sends an **INVITE** without an SDP offer. The called party responds with a 180 Ringing, indicating the call is being processed. The called party then sends a **200 OK** response containing the SDP offer. The Caller responds with an **ACK** containing the SDP answer, completing the offer/answer exchange. At this point, media can flow in both directions between the Caller and the Called Party.

The figures and explanations provided in this chapter are simplified for easier understanding. In real-world scenarios, SIP messages often flow through additional components, such as SIP Registrars and SIP Proxies. However, the core concepts and message flows remain the same.

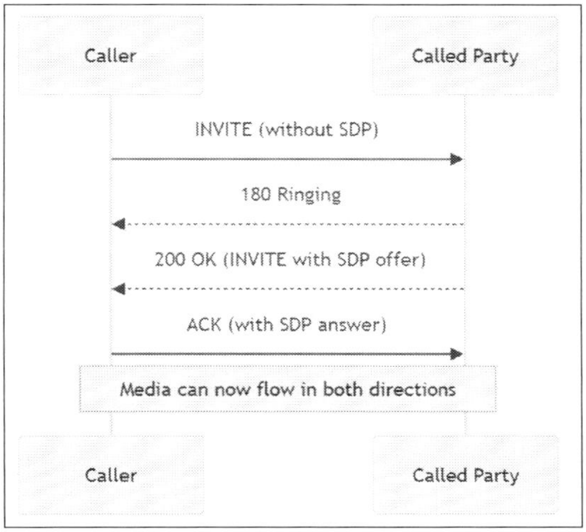

Figure 9.1: *Delayed Offer*

Early Offer

In contrast to a Delayed Offer, an Early Offer is a media negotiation approach where the Caller sends the SDP offer in the initial INVITE request. This allows the Caller to propose the desired media capabilities and parameters upfront, enabling faster call establishment and reducing the number of round trips required for media negotiation.

When using Early Offer, the Caller includes the SDP offer in the INVITE request, describing the media it wishes to use for the session. The Called Party then responds with a **`200 OK`** message containing the SDP answer, indicating which media parameters it accepts. The Caller acknowledges the **`200 OK`** with an **`ACK`** request, confirming the receipt of the answer and completing the offer/answer exchange.

One advantage of Early Offer is that it allows the Caller to specify its preferred media parameters from the outset, reducing the need for further negotiation. This can be particularly beneficial in scenarios where the Caller has specific media requirements or constraints, such as supported codecs or bandwidth limitations. However, Early Offer may not be suitable in all situations. For example, if the Called Party needs to allocate resources or gather information before generating the SDP answer, an Early Offer might not provide the necessary flexibility. In such cases, a Delayed Offer may be a more appropriate choice.

In *Figure* 9.2, the Caller sends an **`INVITE`** request containing the SDP offer. The Called Party responds with a 180 Ringing provisional response, indicating that the call is being processed. Next, the Called Party sends a **`200 OK`** response with the SDP answer, accepting or modifying the proposed media parameters. The Caller acknowledges the **`200 OK`** with an **`ACK`** request, completing the offer/answer exchange. At this point, media can flow in both directions between the Caller and the Called Party.

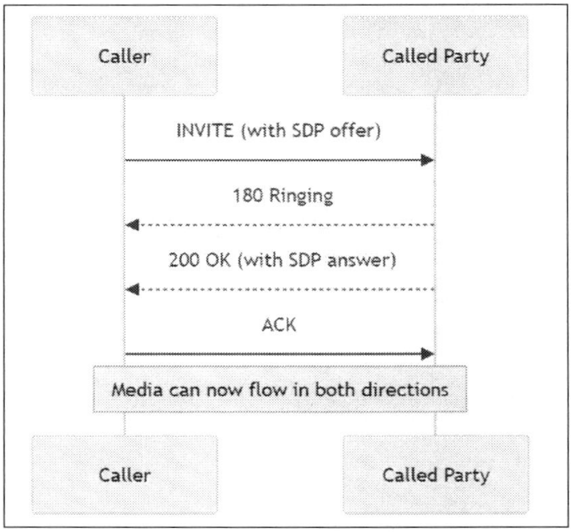

Figure 9.2: *Early Offer*

Early Media and PRACK

Early Media refers to the ability to exchange media (audio or video) between endpoints before a SIP session is fully established. This is useful in scenarios where the Caller needs to receive media from the Called Party before the call setup is completed, such as when the called party plays an announcement or provides a ringback tone.

In an Early Media scenario, the Called Party sends a reliable provisional response (1xx), such as 183 Session Progress, containing an SDP offer to the Caller. The Caller then sends a **`PRACK`** (Provisional Response **`ACK`**nowledgement) request with the SDP answer, confirming the receipt of the provisional response and establishing an early media session. The Called Party acknowledges the **`PRACK`** with a **`200 OK`** response.

The PRACK method, defined in RFC 3262, provides reliability for provisional responses. It ensures that the Caller receives the provisional response and allows for establishing early media sessions. Without **`PRACK`**, provisional responses are unreliable and may be lost, leading to issues with early media exchange.

In *Figure* 9.3, the Caller sends an **`INVITE`** request without an SDP offer. The Called Party responds with a 183 Session Progress provisional response containing an SDP offer. The Caller sends a **`PRACK`** request with the SDP answer, confirming the receipt of the 183 responses. The Called Party acknowledges the **`PRACK`** with a **`200 OK`** response. At this point, early media can flow from the Called Party to the Caller.

After the early media exchange, the Called Party sends a 180 Ringing provisional response, followed by a **`200 OK`** response to the **`INVITE`** request. The Caller acknowledges the **`200 OK`** with an **`ACK`** request, completing the call setup. Media can now flow in both directions between the Caller and the Called Party.

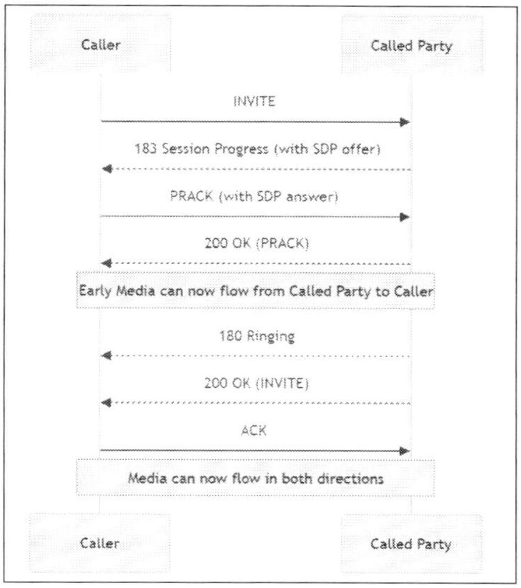

***Figure 9.3**: Early Media*

Let's discuss SIP call flows for advanced call scenarios, such as call transfer and forward, along with related SIP headers.

Advanced SIP Session Flows: Call Transfer and Forward

In this section, we will explore the SIP call flows and headers related to call transfer and call forwarding. These features enhance the flexibility and functionality of SIP-based communication systems, allowing users to manage and redirect calls efficiently.

Call Transfer

Call transfer allows a user to redirect an ongoing call to another party. There are two types of call transfer: blind transfer and attended transfer.

In SIP, the **REFER** method defined in RFC 3515, enables call transfer scenarios. The **REFER** method allows the transfer to be decoupled from the original call setup logic. It's a dedicated mechanism that doesn't require re-invoking all original call setup procedures.

It clearly indicates a transfer attempt and gives users or servers control over whether to accept the transfer.

- The **REFER** method in SIP is used to ask a recipient (an SIP user agent or an SIP server) to initiate an SIP request on behalf of the sender. It is commonly used to orchestrate call transfers.
- The **REFER** request contains a **"Refer-To"** header, specifying the transfer target's URI (Uniform Resource Identifier) – this is where the transfer should go. The URI can be a SIP URI or any other valid URI scheme. It's like saying, "Please start a call with this URI."
- The recipient of the **REFER** request responds with **202 Accepted** if it understands and accepts the **REFER** request.
- The **"Referred-By"** header is often included, indicating the entity requesting the transfer. This is for informational purposes and can help with authentication and authorization.

The **REFER** method provides a standardized way to initiate and manage call transfers in SIP, allowing interoperability between different SIP implementations.

Now that we understand the basics of **REFER,** let's discuss blind and attended transfer.

Blind Transfer

In a blind transfer, the transferring party does not wait for the transfer target to answer before completing the transfer. The transferring party sends a **REFER** request to the transfer target and then disconnects from the call, allowing the transferee and the transfer target to establish a direct call.

In *Figure* 9.4, we see the flow for a blind transfer. Initially, User A and User B are connected in a call with media flowing between them. User B (the transferor) then sends a **REFER** request to User C (the transfer target) with the **Refer-To** header containing User A's URI. User C accepts the transfer by sending a 202 Accepted response. User B then sends a **BYE** request to User A to terminate their call. Finally, User C sends an **INVITE** request to User A with the **Referred-By** header, indicating that the call was transferred by User B. The **200 OK** response from User A to User C completes the call establishment, and media starts flowing between User A and User C.

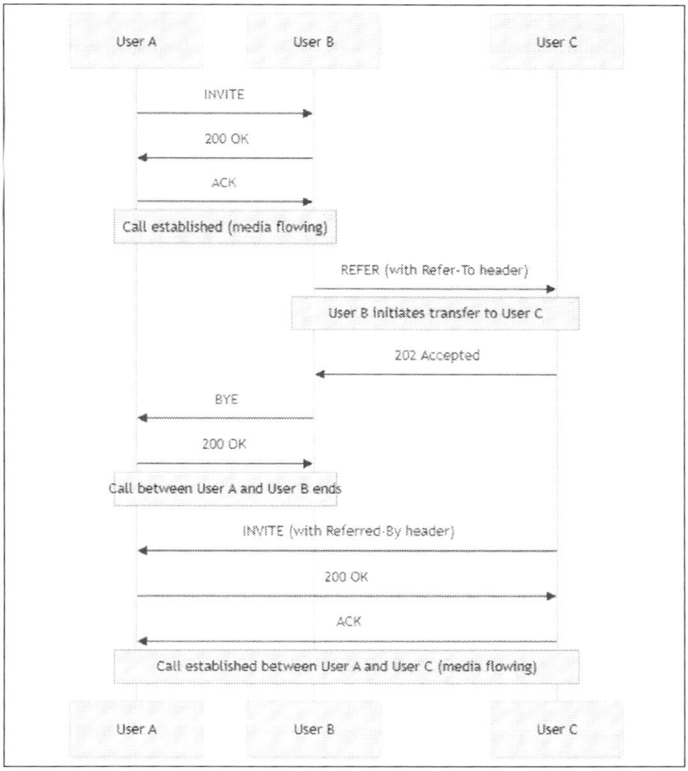

Figure 9.4: *Blind Transfer*

Attended Transfer

In an attended transfer, the transferring party establishes a call with the transfer target, consults with them, and then initiates the transfer. The transferring party waits for the transfer target to answer before completing the transfer.

In *Figure* 9.5, we see the flow for an attended transfer, where User A and User B are connected in a call with media flowing between them. User B then establishes a new call with User C and consults with them. After the consultation, User B sends a **REFER** request to User C, initiating the transfer. User C accepts the transfer and sends an

INVITE request to User A. Once User A answers the call, media flows between User A and User C, completing the attended transfer.

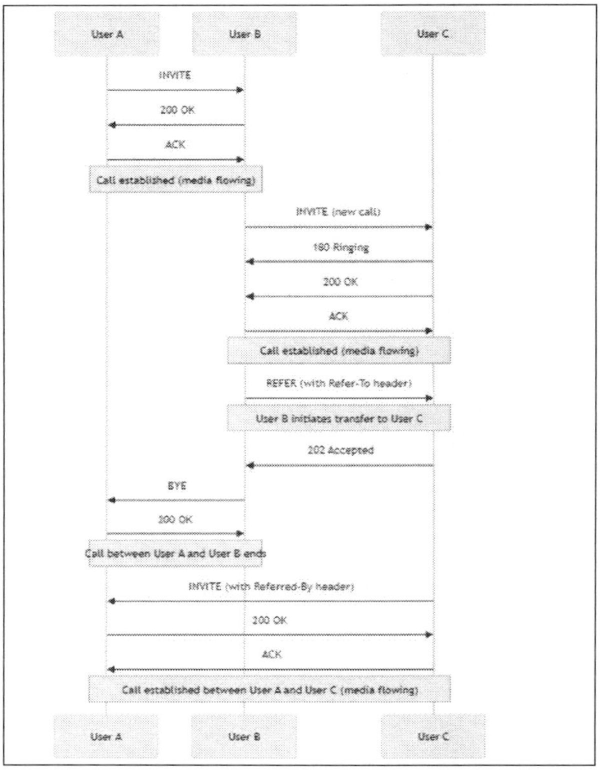

***Figure 9.5**: Attended Transfer*

Now that we've covered call transfer scenarios using the **REFER** method, let's discuss another important aspect of call management in SIP: call forwarding.

Call Forwarding

Call forwarding allows a user to redirect incoming calls to another destination based on certain conditions, such as when the user is busy, not answering, or unconditionally. SIP provides mechanisms to enable call forwarding through specific headers and response codes.

When a SIP user agent receives an incoming call that needs to be forwarded, it responds with a 3xx (redirection) response code. The most commonly used response codes for call forwarding are:

- **301 (Moved Permanently)**: This indicates that the user has permanently moved to a new URI, and all future requests should be directed to the new URI.

- **302 (Moved Temporarily)**: This indicates that the user has temporarily moved to a new URI, and the current request should be forwarded to the new URI.

In addition to the **`3xx`** response code, the SIP user agent includes a **`"Contact"`** header in the response. The **`"Contact"`** header contains the URI where the call should be forwarded. The receiving user agent then sends a new **`INVITE`** request to the URI specified in the **`"Contact"`** header to establish the forwarded call.

Call forwarding can be configured on the client side (the user's device) or the server side (the SIP server or proxy). Server-side call forwarding allows for centralized control and can be applied even if the user's device is offline or unreachable.

Let's look at a few common call-forwarding scenarios:

- **Call Forward Unconditional (CFU)**: In this scenario, all incoming calls to a user are immediately forwarded to another destination, regardless of the user's status.
- **Call Forward on Busy (CFB)**: In this scenario, incoming calls are forwarded to another destination only when the user is busy or already engaged in a call.
- **Call Forward on No Answer (CFNA)**: In this scenario, incoming calls are forwarded to another destination if the user does not answer within a specified time.

Figure 9.6 shows the flow for unconditional call forwarding in a Cisco deployment. Initially, the Caller sends an INVITE request to the Cisco Unified Communications Manager (CUCM), addressing it to the **`Original_Recipient's`** URI. The CUCM receives the INVITE request and checks the call forwarding settings for the **`Original_Recipient`**. Since unconditional call forwarding is enabled, the CUCM generates a 302 Moved Temporarily response, which includes the "Contact" header field specifying the URI of the **`Forwarded_Recipient.`**

The CUCM sends the 302 response back to the Caller. The Caller extracts the **`Forwarded_Recipient's`** URI from the **`"Contact"`** header and sends a new INVITE request to the CUCM, addressing it to the **`Forwarded_Recipient's`** URI. The CUCM receives the **`INVITE`** request and forwards it to the **`Forwarded_Recipient's`** endpoint.

The **`Forwarded_Recipient's`** endpoint responds with a **`200 OK`** response, indicating that the call is accepted. This response is sent back to the CUCM, which then forwards it to the Caller. The Caller sends an **`ACK`** request to the CUCM to acknowledge the successful establishment of the call, and the CUCM forwards the ACK to the **`Forwarded_Recipient's`** endpoint.

Finally, the media session is established between the Caller and the **`Forwarded_Recipient,`** with the CUCM acting as a signaling intermediary. Throughout this process, the CUCM adds the necessary **`"Diversion"`** or **`"History-Info"`** headers to the SIP messages to indicate that the call has been diverted and to maintain a history of the call's diversions.

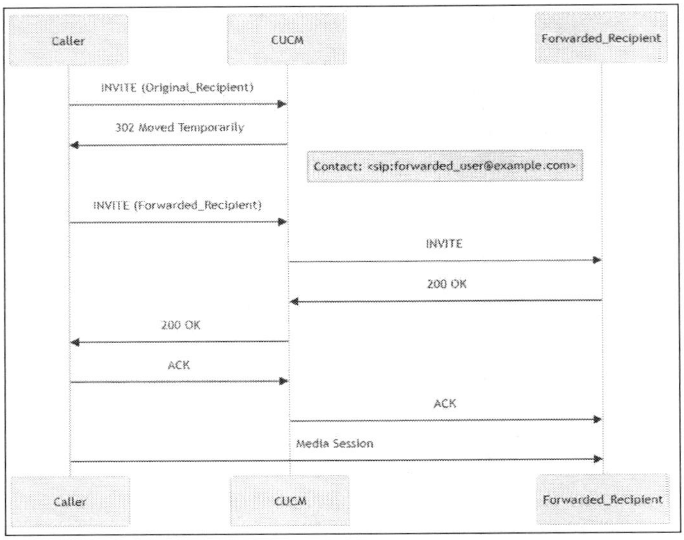

Figure 9.6: *Unconditional call forwarding*

When a SIP request is forwarded from its original destination to a new one, it's crucial to track and understand the request's journey. In SIP, two headers are commonly used for this purpose: the **"Diversion"** header and the **"History-Info"** header. While both headers provide information about call forwarding, they differ in functionality and standardization. Let's explore these headers in more detail.

The **"Diversion"** header is a non-standard header field that was introduced to indicate call forwarding information. It provides details about the original recipient, the new recipient, and the reason for the diversion. However, it's crucial to note that the **"Diversion"** header is not part of the official SIP specification and may not be widely supported by all SIP implementations.

The header contains the following parameters:

- **name-addr**: The URI of the original recipient.
- **reason**: The reason for the diversion, such as **"unconditional", "user-busy", "no-answer", "unavailable",** or **"time-of-day".**
- **counter**: An integer indicating the number of successive diversions that have occurred.

Here's an example of a **"Diversion"** header:

```
Diversion: <sip:user@example.com>;reason=unconditional;counter=1
```

In this example, the **"Diversion"** header indicates that the request was diverted from **"user@example.com"** to a new destination due to an unconditional call forwarding setting. The "counter" parameter shows that this is the first diversion that has occurred.

Now, let's move on to the **"History-Info"** header, which is the standard and more comprehensive solution for capturing request history information in SIP.

The **"History-Info"** header contains a list of entries, each representing a previous request destination. Each entry includes the URI of the recipient at that step, an index indicating the chronological order, and, optionally, the response code received from that recipient.

The header contains a list of entries, each representing a prior request destination. Each entry includes:

- **hi-entry**: The URI of the recipient at that step
- **index**: A string indicating the chronological order of the entries
- **rc**: The response code received from the recipient

Here's an example of a **"History-Info"** header:

```
History-Info: <sip:user1@example.com>;index=1,<sip:user2@example.
com>;index=1.1;rc=302
```

In this example, the **"History-Info"** header shows that the request was initially sent to **"user1@example.com"** and then forwarded to **"user2@example.com"**. The **"index"** parameter indicates the order of the entries, with **"1"** being the first destination and **"1.1"** being the second destination. The **"rc"** parameter represents the response code received from **"user2@example.com"**, which is **"302"** (Moved Temporarily), indicating that the request was temporarily redirected.

One advantage of the **"History-Info"** header is that it can convey more information than the **"Diversion"** header. It includes details such as the reason for each diversion (e.g., unconditional, user-busy, no-answer), privacy settings to control the visibility of history information, and the targeted Request-URI at each step.

For instance, the reason for each diversion can be included using the **"reason"** parameter, such as **"reason=unconditional"** or **"reason=user-busy"**. Privacy settings can be specified using the "privacy" parameter, like **"privacy=history"** to indicate that the history information should be hidden from subsequent entities. The targeted Request-URI at each step can be represented using the **"target-param"** parameter, providing the URI that was targeted for each forwarding step.

It's important to understand that both the **"Diversion"** and **"History-Info"** headers can be present in SIP responses, particularly in 3xx (redirection) responses. However, since the **"History-Info"** header is the standard solution and offers more comprehensive information, it is generally recommended over the non-standard **"Diversion"** header.

Now, let's discuss additional protocols, crucial in enabling various aspects of voice and multimedia communication over IP networks.

Essential Protocols in IP Telephony: DTMF and Fax over IP

In IP telephony, various protocols work together to enable seamless voice and multimedia communication. While SIP has been the focus of our discussion so far, it's essential to understand other key protocols that play crucial roles in managing and enhancing IP-based communication systems. In this section, we will explore Dual-Tone Multi-Frequency (DTMF) signaling and fax transmission over IP networks.

DTMF

Dual-Tone Multi-Frequency (DTMF) is a signaling method used in telephone systems to transmit the digits 0-9, the letters A-D, and the symbols # and *. DTMF is commonly used for interactive voice response (IVR) systems, voicemail navigation, and other applications requiring user input during a voice call.

In traditional analog telephone systems, DTMF tones are generated by the telephone keypad and transmitted in-band, meaning they are sent over the same audio channel as voice communication. However, in VoIP networks, the transmission of DTMF tones requires special handling to ensure reliable detection and prevent issues such as audio quality degradation.

When a user presses a key on their telephone keypad during a VoIP call, the endpoint (such as an IP phone or softphone) generates a DTMF tone. Each DTMF tone is a combination of two sine wave tones, one from a low-frequency group (697 Hz, 770 Hz, 852 Hz, 941 Hz) and one from a high-frequency group (1209 Hz, 1336 Hz, 1477 Hz, 1633 Hz). The specific combination of the two frequencies determines the digit or symbol being transmitted.

There are several methods for transmitting DTMF tones in VoIP networks:

1. **In-Band Audio**: This method sends the DTMF tones as regular audio samples within the RTP media stream. The tones are transmitted the same way as voice audio, using the same codec. However, this approach can lead to issues such as audio quality degradation, incorrect detection, and compatibility problems with certain codecs that use compression techniques.

2. **Out-of-Band Signaling (RFC 2833)**: RFC 2833 (updated by RFC 4733) defines a standardized method for transmitting DTMF tones out-of-band, separate from the audio stream. In this approach, the endpoint sends the DTMF tones as RTP events using a dedicated RTP payload type. The RTP event packets contain information about the DTMF digit, duration, and other attributes. This method allows for reliable DTMF transmission without affecting the audio quality.

3. **SIP INFO Method**: The SIP INFO method is another out-of-band signaling approach for transmitting DTMF tones. In this method, the endpoint sends a SIP INFO message containing the DTMF digit information to the remote party. The receiving endpoint then generates the corresponding DTMF tone locally. While this method is straightforward, it may not be supported by all endpoints and can introduce additional overhead in the signaling plane.

To ensure successful DTMF transmission in VoIP calls, the endpoints involved must negotiate and agree on the DTMF transmission method. The negotiation typically occurs during the session establishment phase using the Session Description Protocol (SDP).

In the SDP offer/answer exchange, the endpoints indicate their supported DTMF methods using the "telephone-event" media format. The most commonly used DTMF method is RFC 2833, which is supported by most modern VoIP endpoints and servers.

However, the endpoints may sometimes not support the same DTMF method, leading to interoperability issues. To address this, VoIP systems often implement DTMF relay mechanisms that convert between different DTMF transmission methods. For example, a DTMF relay can convert in-band DTMF tones to out-of-band RTP events (RFC 2833) or SIP INFO messages, ensuring compatibility between endpoints.

When a VoIP system receives a DTMF tone through in-band audio or out-of-band signaling, it must accurately detect and process the tone. The system's DTMF detector analyzes the incoming audio or signaling information to identify the specific DTMF digit or symbol.

DTMF detection algorithms typically involve techniques such as the Goertzel algorithm, Fourier analysis, or correlation-based methods to reliably identify the DTMF tones in the presence of background noise or audio distortions.

Once the DTMF digit is detected, the system can take appropriate actions based on the application or service logic. For example, in an IVR system, the detected DTMF digits are used to navigate menus, select options, or provide user input.

While DTMF signaling is widely used in VoIP systems, there are some challenges and considerations to keep in mind:

- **DTMF Tone Duration**: The duration of DTMF tones can vary depending on the sending endpoint and user behavior. VoIP endpoints and servers should be capable of accurately handling different DTMF tone durations.
- **DTMF Tone Level**: The amplitude of DTMF tones may differ based on the sending endpoint's configuration or the network conditions. Proper DTMF tone level detection and normalization are important to ensure reliable detection.

- **Echo and Double Detection**: In some cases, DTMF tones may be echoed back or detected multiple times due to network or endpoint issues. Proper echo cancellation and duplicate DTMF filtering mechanisms should be implemented to avoid false detections.
- **DTMF Compression**: DTMF tones may be distorted or lost during the compression process while using compressed audio codecs. Out-of-band DTMF transmission methods, such as RFC 2833, help mitigate this issue by sending DTMF information separately from the audio stream.
- **Security Considerations**: DTMF tones can control sensitive applications or services, such as the Bank IVR system. Proper security measures, such as authentication and encryption, should be implemented to prevent unauthorized access or manipulation of DTMF-based services.

By implementing reliable DTMF handling mechanisms, such as RFC 2833 or SIP INFO, and addressing challenges like tone duration, level detection, and interoperability, VoIP systems can provide seamless and accurate DTMF functionality to end-users.

When configuring SIP trunks in Cisco Unified Communications Manager (CUCM), administrators can define the DTMF signaling method to ensure compatibility with the connected endpoints or network elements.

CUCM provides several options for DTMF configuration on SIP trunks:

1. **RFC 2833**: This is the default and recommended DTMF signaling method in CUCM. It sends DTMF tones out-of-band using RTP events, as defined in RFC 2833 (and updated in RFC 4733). To configure RFC 2833 on a SIP trunk, navigate to the SIP Profile associated with the trunk and set the **`"DTMF Signaling Method"`** to **`"RFC 2833".`**
2. **No Preference**: When set to **`"No Preference",`** CUCM does not specify a preferred DTMF signaling method in the SDP offer. Instead, it relies on the negotiation between the endpoints to determine the DTMF method. This option provides flexibility but may lead to interoperability issues if the endpoints do not support the same DTMF methods.
3. **INFO**: CUCM can be configured to use the SIP INFO method for DTMF signaling. In this case, DTMF tones are sent as SIP INFO messages, separate from the audio stream. To enable the INFO method, set the “DTMF Signaling Method” to “INFO” in the SIP Profile.

It’s important to ensure that the DTMF signaling method configured on CUCM matches the capabilities and requirements of the connected endpoints or network elements.

Now that we’ve discussed the intricacies of DTMF signaling in VoIP environments, let’s focus on another important aspect of legacy communication adapted to work over IP networks: Fax over IP (FoIP).

Fax over IP (FoIP)

Fax over IP (FoIP) refers to the transmission of fax messages over IP networks, such as the Internet or private IP networks, instead of traditional analog telephone lines (PSTN). Traditional fax sends binary images of documents over the Public Switched Telephone Network (PSTN) using audio-frequency tones. FoIP, however, digitizes these images and transmits them as packets over IP networks.

FoIP technology is useful in scenarios where traditional PSTN lines are unavailable or integration with digital communication systems is desired. One of the most significant advantages of FoIP is its ability to support remote work and virtual offices. FoIP allows for faxing over the Internet, eliminating the need for physical fax machines and dedicated phone lines, which is ideal for remote workers and virtual offices. This enables employees to send and receive faxes from anywhere with an internet connection, enhancing flexibility and productivity.

Businesses and organizations that use Unified Communications (UC) systems can greatly benefit from FoIP by integrating fax services with their existing email, voicemail, and messaging services. This streamlines communication and reduces costs associated with maintaining separate fax infrastructure. FoIP also helps industries that heavily rely on faxing, such as the legal and healthcare sectors. These industries can leverage FoIP's improved efficiency and digital integration while complying with document transmission and privacy regulations.

Fax transmission was designed for analog telephone networks, which presented several challenges when adapting fax to IP networks:

1. **Real-time Requirements**: Fax communication relies on strict timing and real-time transmission of signals. IP networks can disrupt the timing-sensitive fax signals with their packet-based nature and potential for latency and jitter.

2. **Protocol Incompatibility**: Traditional fax machines use protocols like T.30 and T.4, which were not designed for IP networks. These protocols expect a continuous, uninterrupted communication channel, which is not inherent in packet-switched IP networks.

3. **Network Impairments**: IP networks can introduce impairments such as packet loss, delay, and jitter, which can degrade fax quality and cause transmission failures.

4. **Security**: Transmitting sensitive documents over IP networks introduces security concerns. Encryption and secure transmission protocols are necessary to protect fax data in transit.

Various FoIP protocols and techniques have been developed to address these challenges and enable reliable fax transmission over IP networks.

1. **T.38**: It is the most widely adopted FoIP protocol, standardized by the International Telecommunication Union (ITU). It defines a mechanism for transporting fax signals over IP networks using Real-time Transport Protocol (RTP) or UDP. It encapsulates the fax data and signaling information into IP packets and provides error correction and redundancy mechanisms to ensure reliable fax transmission.

   Key components of T.38 include the following:

   a. T.30 fax protocol for call control is carried over SIP

   b. Fax image data is encoded as T.38 packets

   c. Redundancy and retransmission procedures for reliability

   d. Support for various codecs like T.4, T.6, etc.

2. **T.37**: This ITU standard defines a method for sending and receiving faxes using email protocols, such as SMTP and POP3. With T.37, fax messages are converted into email attachments (typically in TIFF format) and transmitted over IP networks using email infrastructure. T.37 is commonly used in store-and-forward fax scenarios.

3. **G.711 Pass-through**: It is a simple method for transmitting fax over IP networks using the G.711 codec. In this approach, the analog fax signals are encoded using G.711 and transmitted as audio packets over the IP network. While G.711 pass-through is easy to implement, it is less reliable than T.38 and may not work well in networks with significant impairments.

4. **IP Brokering through Email**: This approach converts fax content into email attachments, delivering them using SMTP between fax servers. Key aspects are:

   a. Fax document rendered as TIFF/PDF attachment

   b. Email sent with meta info in headers

   c. SMTP transports email between fax servers

   d. Servers reconstitute fax from email

Implementing FoIP involves several key components and considerations. Organizations must ensure that their fax devices support IP interfaces and protocols to deploy FoIP successfully. This can be achieved through various means, such as using IP-enabled fax machines, fax adapters for analog fax machines, multifunction printers with fax server software, or fax gateways for PSTN interconnection.

The following components are typically involved in FoIP implementation:

- **Fax Endpoints**: Fax endpoints can be traditional fax machines with analog telephone adapters (ATAs) or IP-based fax servers supporting FoIP protocols. These endpoints send and receive fax documents over the IP network.

- **VoIP Gateways**: VoIP gateways, such as Cisco Integrated Services Routers (ISRs) or Cisco Voice Gateways (VGs), connect fax endpoints to the IP network. These gateways perform protocol conversion, signal processing, and interworking between fax and IP protocols.
- **Call Control and Signaling**: Call control and signaling protocols, such as SIP or H.323, are used to establish and manage FoIP calls. These protocols handle call setup, teardown, and negotiation of FoIP capabilities between the endpoints.
- **IP Network Infrastructure**: The IP network infrastructure, including routers, switches, and QoS mechanisms, ensures reliable FoIP transmission. Proper network design, bandwidth provisioning, and QoS configuration are essential to minimize network impairments and guarantee real-time performance for fax traffic.

To illustrate how FoIP works, let's consider a simple example of connecting fax machines to a Cisco Voice Gateway (VG) using MGCP (Media Gateway Control Protocol). The analog fax machines are connected to the FXS (Foreign Exchange Station) ports of the Cisco VG using RJ-11 cables. The VG is configured to support fax protocols like T.38 and set to use appropriate codecs such as G.711. MGCP controls and manages the VG, with a Call Agent (such as Cisco Unified Communications Manager) handling call setup and teardown. The Call Agent instructs the VG to establish connections and negotiate fax capabilities between the endpoints. With this setup, the Cisco VG handles the protocol conversion and transports the fax over the IP network, enabling seamless FoIP communication under the control of the MGCP Call Agent.

Now that we have discussed SIP and other essential VoIP protocols in detail, let's explore another critical aspect of collaboration networks: Network Address Translation (NAT) and its impact on voice and video communication.

NAT in Collaboration

Network Address Translation (NAT) is a technique used by routers and firewalls to modify packets' source and destination IP addresses as they pass through the device. NAT's primary purpose is to conserve public IPv4 addresses by allowing multiple devices on a private network to share a single public IP address. NAT also provides an additional layer of security by hiding the internal network topology from the outside world.

There are different types of NAT:

- **Static NAT**: One-to-one mapping between a private IP address and a public IP address is called Static NAT. It is useful when a device on a private network needs to be accessible from the Internet using a fixed IP address.

- **Dynamic NAT**: Many-to-one mapping where multiple private IP addresses are dynamically mapped to a single public IP address is called Dynamic NAT. It assigns a public IP address from a pool to a private IP address on an as-needed basis.
- **Port Address Translation (PAT) or NAT Overloading**: This extension of dynamic NAT allows multiple private IP addresses to share a single public IP address by using different port numbers. PAT enables thousands of private IP addresses to be translated to a single public IP address, conserving IPv4 address space.

In collaboration environments, NAT is commonly encountered in various scenarios where endpoints, services, and network segments are distributed across different locations and need to communicate with each other.

Collaboration solutions often need to connect to external services, such as cloud-based platforms, SIP trunks, or remote call control systems. These external services may be hosted by third-party providers or partners and typically reside outside the organization's network boundaries. When the collaboration system communicates with these external services, the traffic needs to traverse NAT devices at the edge of the organization's network. The NAT devices translate the collaboration system's internal private IP addresses to public IP addresses before forwarding the traffic to the external services. Similarly, incoming traffic from the external services undergoes NAT translation at the edge devices before being routed to the internal collaboration components. Proper configuration of NAT and firewall rules is essential to ensure secure and reliable communication between the collaboration system and external services.

Another common scenario is remote users. They connect to the corporate network using their home routers or mobile hotspots, which often have NAT enabled by default. When a remote user's device, such as a laptop or IP phone, connects to the corporate collaboration system (e.g., Cisco Unified Communications Manager), it obtains a private IP address from the home router's DHCP server. The home router performs NAT, translating the private IP address of the user's device to the public IP address assigned by the Internet Service Provider (ISP). As a result, the collaboration system sees the remote user's traffic originating from the home router's public IP address rather than the device's private IP address.

This NAT traversal scenario requires the collaboration system to have mechanisms to properly handle signaling and media traffic to and from remote users, ensuring successful communication.

Edge servers, such as Session Border Controllers (SBCs), Cisco Expressway, and Cisco Unified Border Element (CUBE), play a vital role in enabling seamless communication across NAT boundaries in these collaboration environments. These solutions employ techniques like STUN, TURN, and ICE to discover public IP addresses, establish direct media paths, and provide fallback mechanisms for media relay when needed.

Before we discuss these techniques, let's first understand the challenges in detail. NAT introduces several challenges for collaboration protocols, which rely on embedding IP addresses and port numbers within signaling messages and media streams.

Let's take a closer look at how these issues occur:

- **Signaling Protocol Issues:** Collaboration protocols like SIP, H.323, and MGCP include IP addresses and ports in their signaling messages to establish connections and negotiate media capabilities. For example, in SIP, the Via, Contact, and Record-Route headers contain the IP address and port of the endpoint or intermediate servers. When a signaling message traverses a NAT device, the NAT modifies the source IP address and port in the packet header to the public IP address and a translated port. However, the NAT does not modify the IP addresses and ports embedded within the signaling message payload, resulting in a mismatch between the packet header and the signaling information. This mismatch can cause issues with call setup, as the receiving endpoint may not be able to determine the correct IP address and port to send the response back to the originating endpoint. Additionally, the mismatch can lead to problems with call routing and media negotiation, as the signaling messages may contain incorrect or unreachable IP addresses and ports.
- **Media Connectivity Problems:** Media streams in collaboration protocols, such as RTP (Real-time Transport Protocol) and RTCP (RTP Control Protocol), carry the actual audio and video data between endpoints. When an endpoint behind a NAT sends a media packet, the NAT changes the source IP address and port of the packet to the public IP address and a translated port. However, the receiving endpoint may be unaware of this translation and will send the return media to the original IP address and port specified in the signaling messages (e.g., SDP - Session Description Protocol). As a result, the return media packets may not reach the originating endpoint, causing one-way audio or video, where one party can hear or see the other but not vice versa. In some cases, the media connectivity may fail entirely, with neither party able to receive the other's media.
- **Incompatibility with Certain NAT Types:** There are different types of NAT behaviors, such as full cone, restricted cone, port-restricted cone, and symmetric NAT. Symmetric NAT, in particular, poses significant challenges for collaboration protocols. In symmetric NAT, each outgoing connection from an internal IP address and port to a specific external IP address and port is mapped to a unique public IP address and port. This means that if an endpoint behind a symmetric NAT sends a packet to multiple destinations, each destination will see a different public IP address and port for the same internal endpoint. Collaboration protocols often expect consistent IP

addresses and port mappings for signaling and media, and the per-destination mapping of symmetric NAT can break this assumption. As a result, endpoints behind symmetric NATs may experience difficulties in establishing successful connections with other endpoints, leading to call failures or media connectivity issues.

Various NAT traversal techniques and solutions have been developed to overcome these challenges, such as STUN, TURN, and ICE. These solutions aim to discover the public IP addresses and ports of endpoints, establish direct media connections whenever possible, and provide fallback mechanisms for relaying media when direct connectivity fails.

Let's explore the key NAT traversal techniques in detail:

- **Session Traversal Utilities for NAT (STUN):** Session Traversal Utilities for NAT (STUN) is a protocol that enables endpoints to discover their public IP address and port as seen by the outside world. STUN is a client-server protocol where an endpoint (STUN client) sends a request to a STUN server, typically located on the public Internet. The STUN server responds to the client's request with the public IP address and port that it observes for the client. By obtaining this information, the endpoint can determine if it is behind a NAT and learn its public IP address and port mapping.

  STUN helps endpoints gather the necessary information to establish direct media connections with other endpoints. The STUN client sends a binding request to the STUN server, typically including the client's local IP address and port. The STUN server then responds with a binding response containing the public IP address and port the server sees for the client. The client can compare this information with its local IP address and port to determine the type of NAT it is behind and the mapping behavior. STUN is a lightweight protocol requiring no special configuration on the NAT devices. However, STUN has limitations and may not work with all types of NATs, particularly symmetric NATs, which create unique mappings for each destination IP address and port.

- **Traversal Using Relays Around NAT (TURN):** Traversal Using Relays around NAT (TURN) is a protocol that enables endpoints to relay media through a TURN server when direct connectivity between endpoints is not possible. TURN servers act as intermediaries, forwarding media packets between the endpoints. When an endpoint determines that it cannot establish a direct media connection with the other endpoint (e.g., due to restrictive NAT or firewall), it can request the TURN server to allocate a public IP address and port for media relay. The endpoint then sends its media packets to the TURN server, which forwards them to the other endpoint. Similarly, the other endpoint sends its media packets to the TURN server, which sends them back to the requesting endpoint.

TURN ensures that media can flow between endpoints, even in the presence of restrictive NATs or firewalls. However, TURN introduces additional latency and consumes more network resources than direct media connections. TURN is typically used as a fallback mechanism when other NAT traversal techniques, such as STUN or ICE, fail to establish direct connectivity. To use TURN, endpoints need to be configured with the address of a TURN server and authenticate with the server using credentials (username and password). The TURN server allocates a public IP address and port for each endpoint and relays media packets between them.

- **Interactive Connectivity Establishment (ICE):** Interactive Connectivity Establishment (ICE) is a comprehensive NAT traversal solution that combines STUN and TURN to establish the most efficient media path between endpoints. ICE is designed to work with various types of NATs and firewalls and provides a reliable mechanism for setting up direct media connections.

  The ICE process involves the following steps:

  1. **Gathering Candidates**: Each endpoint gathers a list of potential IP addresses and ports (candidates) it can use for media communication. These candidates include the endpoint's local IP address and port, the public IP address and port discovered through STUN, and the relayed IP address and port allocated by a TURN server.

  2. **Exchanging Candidates**: The endpoints exchange their candidate information through signaling messages, such as SDP (Session Description Protocol) in SIP. This allows each endpoint to know the available candidates of the other endpoint.

  3. **Connectivity Checks**: The endpoints perform connectivity checks by sending STUN binding requests from each of their candidates to the candidates of the other endpoint. These checks help determine the reachability and connectivity between the candidates.

  4. **Candidate Selection**: The endpoints select the best candidate pair for media communication based on the connectivity check results. ICE prioritizes direct connectivity (host candidates) over relayed connectivity (TURN candidates) to ensure the most efficient media path.

  5. **Media Flow**: Once the best candidate pair is selected, the endpoints establish the media connection and start exchanging media packets directly or through the TURN server, depending on the selected candidates. ICE provides a robust and flexible NAT traversal solution that adapts to different network conditions and NAT types. It maximizes the chances of establishing direct media connectivity and falls back to the TURN relay when necessary.

NAT traversal techniques are implemented and handled by the collaboration endpoints, such as IP phones, softphones, or video conferencing systems, and by the collaboration infrastructure components, such as call control servers and border elements. Proper configuration and support for these techniques are essential for seamless NAT traversal in collaboration environments.

In NAT environments, Expressway simplifies traversal between public and private networks by supporting dual network interfaces, separating LAN and WAN traffic. It also implements Interactive Connectivity Establishment (ICE), Traversal Using Relays around NAT (TURN), and Session Traversal Utilities for NAT (STUN) protocols to enhance media traversal across NAT. Expressway automatically detects the presence of NAT and adjusts its signaling and media traffic accordingly.

To configure Expressway for NAT traversal, we need to define NAT reflection rules. This ensures that Expressway-E, the external-facing component, can route traffic correctly by understanding its public-facing IP address as seen from the outside world. We should also properly configure the LAN and WAN interfaces on Expressway-E with IP addressing and default gateway settings to handle internal and external traffic separately. In the Expressway-E configuration settings, we can enable ICE, TURN, and STUN services. This allows us to specify the public IP address for STUN requests and configure TURN servers if needed for relay services. Additionally, we must configure firewall traversal settings to allow the necessary ports for SIP, H.323, and media traffic by opening UDP and TCP ports as required for communication and media traversal.

Cisco Unified Border Element (CUBE) is another essential component for managing NAT traversal in Cisco collaboration deployments. In NAT environments, CUBE plays a crucial role in normalizing SIP messages, handling media flows, and ensuring security across network boundaries. It offers key features such as SIP normalization, which allows it to modify SIP messages for compatibility across different VoIP systems and support NAT traversal. CUBE also provides flexibility in media handling, with configuration options for flow-through (where media passes through CUBE) and flow-around (where media is directed around CUBE) modes. This adaptability enables CUBE to accommodate different NAT scenarios effectively.

Now that we have explored the intricacies of NAT traversal and its impact on collaboration solutions, let's discuss critical factors that influence the overall user experience and network performance in collaboration environments: delay and Quality of Service (QoS).

Network Performance Considerations and Quality of Service (QoS)

Minimizing delay in voice and video communication is crucial for maintaining a high-quality user experience. The International Telecommunication Union (ITU) provides recommendations for acceptable one-way delay in voice applications through its G.114 standard. According to ITU-T G.114, the following one-way delay values are considered:

- `0-150 ms`: Acceptable for most user applications
- `150-400 ms`: Acceptable, but may impact the user experience
- `400+ ms`: Unacceptable for general network planning purposes

Several types of delay can contribute to the overall one-way delay in a collaboration system:

- **DSP Delay**: The time taken by the Digital Signal Processor (DSP) to process and encode/decode audio or video signals
- **Packetization Delay**: The time required to fill a packet with encoded audio or video data before it can be transmitted
- **Queuing Delay**: The time a packet spends waiting in a queue before being transmitted, often due to network congestion
- **Serialization Delay**: The time needed to place a packet onto the physical medium, depending on the link's bandwidth and the packet's size
- **Propagation Delay**: The time taken for a packet to travel from the source to the destination through the physical medium
- **De-jitter Buffer Delay**: The time introduced by the receiving endpoint's de-jitter buffer to smooth out the variations in packet arrival times (jitter)

To minimize the one-way delay, each component must be optimized through proper network design, configuration, and QoS mechanisms.

Quality of Service

Quality of Service (QoS) is a collection of tools and techniques that enable networks to provide differentiated treatment to specific types of traffic, ensuring that critical applications receive the necessary network resources and performance levels. In collaboration environments, QoS is crucial for maintaining the quality and reliability of voice, video, and data communications, especially during network congestion. It's important to note that QoS mechanisms are most effective when the network is experiencing congestion, as they help prioritize critical traffic and allocate limited resources efficiently. In the absence of congestion, QoS may not significantly impact traffic flow.

Several common network problems can impact collaboration traffic:

1. **Latency**: The time taken for a packet to travel from the source to the destination. High latency can lead to noticeable delays in audio and video communications.

2. **Jitter**: The variation in packet arrival times, causing packets to arrive out of order or with inconsistent delays. Jitter can result in choppy audio, video freezes, or distortions.

3. **Packet Loss**: The failure of packets to reach their destination due to network congestion, link errors, or other factors. Packet loss can cause audio dropouts, video artifacts, or complete call failures.

4. **Bandwidth Limitations**: Insufficient network bandwidth can lead to congestion, increased latency, and packet loss, impacting the overall quality of collaboration sessions.

Now that we understand the common network problems, let's discuss the specific QoS requirements for different types of traffic in collaboration environments.

Different types of traffic have specific QoS requirements to ensure optimal performance:

- **Voice**: Voice traffic is considered **`"benign"`** as it generates a steady and predictable stream of small packets. Voice traffic requires low latency (typically <150 ms one-way), minimal jitter, and minimal packet loss (usually <1%) to maintain good quality. To achieve this, voice traffic should be given the highest priority in the QoS hierarchy.
- **Video**: Video traffic is bandwidth-intensive and can be considered **`"greedy"`** as it consumes a significant portion of network resources. It is sensitive to latency, jitter, and packet loss, with specific requirements varying based on the video codec and resolution. Compared to voice, video traffic can tolerate slightly higher latency and jitter values.
- **Data**: Data traffic, such as file transfers, web browsing, or email, is often considered **`"bursty"`** because it generates intermittent bursts of packets. Compared to voice and video, data traffic is generally more tolerant of latency and jitter but may require reliable delivery and sufficient bandwidth. The QoS requirements for data traffic can vary depending on the specific application and user expectations.

Now, let's explore how to implement QoS in a collaboration network to ensure that each traffic type receives the appropriate treatment.

Implementing QoS

Several mechanisms and techniques can be employed to ensure that collaboration traffic receives the necessary QoS treatment. Let's explore these in more detail.

1. **Class Models**: QoS class models, such as the Differentiated Services (DiffServ) model, provide a framework for classifying and marking traffic based on its

QoS requirements. Traffic is assigned to different classes, each receiving a specific QoS treatment.

2. **Traffic Classification and Marking**: Collaboration traffic is classified based on various criteria (e.g., IP addresses, ports, protocols) and marked with the appropriate Class of Service (CoS) or Differentiated Services Code Point (DSCP) values to indicate its QoS requirements.
3. **Queuing and Scheduling**: QoS mechanisms, such as Low Latency Queuing (LLQ), prioritize collaboration traffic over less time-sensitive traffic. LLQ provides a dedicated queue for voice and video packets, ensuring they are serviced before other queues.
4. **Bandwidth Reservation**: Techniques like Call Admission Control (CAC) and Resource Reservation Protocol (RSVP) are used to reserve bandwidth for collaboration traffic, guaranteeing the necessary network resources are available.
5. **Congestion Management**: QoS mechanisms, such as Weighted Random Early Detection (WRED), can be employed to manage network congestion by selectively dropping lower-priority packets when congestion occurs, protecting high-priority collaboration traffic.

When implementing QoS in a collaboration environment, establishing trust boundaries and properly classifying and marking traffic at the LAN level are crucial.

QoS trust boundaries define the points in the network where QoS classification and marking are trusted and propagated. In collaboration environments, it is common to establish trust boundaries at the access layer switches, where endpoints are connected.

LAN-based classification and marking involve configuring access layer switches to trust the QoS markings (CoS or DSCP) set by collaboration endpoints or to reclassify and remark the traffic based on predefined policies. It is common for IP phones to mark the DSCP values of the voice and signaling traffic and then configure the access layer switches to trust these markings. This ensures that the voice traffic receives the appropriate QoS treatment as it traverses the network.

However, the process may be different for softphones running on computers. Softphones may not be able to mark the DSCP values of the voice traffic directly. In such cases, it is more common to either identify the softphone traffic at the access layer switch based on the IP address, port numbers, or other criteria and then mark the traffic accordingly. Alternatively, the softphone application can be configured to set specific DSCP values through registry settings in the Windows operating system, and then the access layer switch can be configured to trust these markings.

By effectively implementing QoS, organizations can ensure that their collaboration traffic receives the necessary prioritization and protection, even during network congestion. This results in a high-quality and reliable user experience.

Conclusion

In this chapter, we started by examining the concept of media negotiation, focusing on techniques such as Early Offer, Delayed Offer, and Early Media and their impact on SIP call flows and media stream establishment. We then investigated how SIP flows adapt to various scenarios, such as call transfer and call forwarding, providing insights into the specific headers and message exchanges that enable these advanced call features.

We then covered essential protocols and techniques, including DTMF relay and Fax over IP for integrating traditional telephony services with modern collaboration solutions. These technologies ensure seamless interoperability between diverse systems.

We also explored the challenges posed by Network Address Translation (NAT) in Collaboration environments, exploring the techniques and protocols, such as STUN, TURN, and ICE, that help overcomes the complications introduced by NAT in the flow of signaling and media traffic. Furthermore, we emphasized the importance of Quality of Service (QoS) in delivering a superior user experience, discussing the impact of network factors on voice and video quality.

In the next chapter, we will explore security in collaboration, data privacy considerations, and compliance with telecom regulations in different geographies. Additionally, we will discuss the importance of emergency calling functionality and explore disaster recovery planning and recovery strategies for Collaboration solutions.

Multiple Choice Questions

1. What is the primary difference between a Delayed Offer and an Early Offer in SIP call flows?
    a. Delayed Offer sends the SDP Offer in the initial INVITE, while Early Offer sends it in the 200 OK response.
    b. Delayed Offer sends the SDP Offer in the 200 OK response, while Early Offer sends it in the initial INVITE.
    c. Delayed Offer and Early Offer are synonyms for the same concept.
    d. Delayed Offer is used for video calls, while Early Offer is used for audio calls.

2. What is the purpose of the PRACK (Provisional Response ACKnowledgement) method in SIP?
    a. To acknowledge the receipt of a final response
    b. To cancel a pending request
    c. To provide reliable delivery of provisional responses
    d. To register a user's contact information with a SIP registrar
3. Which SIP method is used to initiate a call transfer?
    a. **`INVITE`**
    b. **`BYE`**
    c. **`REFER`**
    d. **`CANCEL`**
4. What is the purpose of the Session Traversal Utilities for NAT (STUN) protocol?
    a. To relay media through a server when direct connectivity is not possible
    b. To enable endpoints to discover their public IP address and port
    c. To establish the most efficient media path between endpoints
    d. To provide encryption for signaling and media traffic
5. According to ITU-T G.114, what is the acceptable one-way delay for most user applications?
    a. 0-50 ms
    b. 0-150 ms
    c. 150-400 ms
    d. 400+ ms

Answers

1. b
2. c
3. c
4. b
5. b

Further Reading

Same as the last chapter, explore the following topics on your own to improve your understanding and broaden your perspective.

- Investigate the various settings in collaboration infrastructure components, such as Cisco Unified Communications Manager (CUCM) or Cisco Expressway, that influence SDP negotiation. Understand how these settings determine whether an endpoint or SIP trunk will use an Early Offer, Delayed Offer, or Early Media.
- Explore the SIP session flows for advanced telephony features, such as conference calling and call hold/resume. Analyze the SIP messages exchanged during these call scenarios, focusing on the specific headers and message sequences.
- Obtain packet captures of calls that use DTMF signaling, such as interactive voice response (IVR) systems or voicemail navigation. Analyze the packet captures using tools like Wireshark to identify and interpret DTMF tones.
- Observe how DTMF tones are represented in the captured packets, whether they are sent in-band or out-of-band, and how they are encoded (e.g., RFC 2833, SIP INFO).
- Dive deeper into QoS mechanisms and how they are implemented in your collaboration environment. Understand the QoS configuration on network devices, such as routers and switches, and how they prioritize and manage collaboration traffic.

CHAPTER 10
Security, Compliance and Recovery

Introduction

In today's digital landscape, organizations face increasing security threats that can exploit vulnerabilities in UC systems, such as protocol weaknesses, Voice over IP (VoIP) attacks, and endpoint or infrastructure vulnerabilities. These threats constantly evolve, making it crucial for organizations to stay vigilant and proactive in their security measures. Successful attacks can lead to devastating consequences, such as data breaches, unauthorized access, service disruptions, and financial losses. Additionally, as businesses expand globally, compliance with various regulations and industry standards, such as data privacy regulations like GDPR and HIPAA and country-specific telephony regulations, becomes increasingly complex and essential to prevent severe penalties, legal repercussions, and reputational damage. In addition to security and compliance, organizations must also prioritize recovery strategies to minimize the impact of inevitable disruptions. Whether caused by data loss, system failures, or cyberattacks, downtime can have significant consequences for businesses that rely on UC services for critical communications. To mitigate these risks, organizations must develop and regularly test robust disaster recovery plans (DRP) that enable quick restoration of services in the event of a disruption.

In this chapter, we will explore specific security measures, compliance considerations, and recovery strategies that are essential for safeguarding and maintaining the integrity of UC solutions. By prioritizing these critical aspects, organizations can mitigate risks, protect their assets, and deliver reliable and secure communication services to their users.

Structure

In this chapter, we will discuss the following topics:

- Security
  - Transport Layer Security and Certificates
  - Secure Communication Protocols in Cisco UC
  - Security Measures and System Hardening in Cisco UC
  - Preventing Toll Fraud in Cisco UC
- Recovery Strategy
  - Disaster Recovery Planning (DRP) for Cisco UC
  - Backup and Restore
- Compliance
  - Data Privacy and Cisco UC
  - Regulations Affecting Cisco UC Services
  - Emergency Calling in Cisco UC

Security

Security is a vast topic. With the rise in cyber-attacks, security has become important.. In most organizations, specific teams manage security, but security is everyone's job. It is important for UC admins to be aware and do their best to maintain the security aspect of the UC infrastructure.

In this section, we will start with Transport Layer Security, Certificates, and Public Key Infrastructure. We will then explore the protocols used in Unified Communications to make communication secure. Then, we will discuss the security measures in Cisco UC Infrastructure components. Before moving to the next section, we will discuss toll fraud and its prevention in Cisco UC.

Transport Layer Security and Certificates

Imagine a global organization with employees distributed across multiple locations. The organization relies on a UC solution to enable seamless voice, video, and messaging communication among its employees. The UC infrastructure includes various components, such as IP phones, video endpoints, and softphone clients, which communicate over the organization's network and the Internet.

Now, let us consider the risks associated with unsecured communication in this scenario:

- **Eavesdropping**: If the communication channels are not encrypted, an attacker could intercept and listen to the conversations, potentially gaining access to sensitive business information or personal discussions.

- **Data Tampering**: An attacker could modify the transmitted data without proper integrity checks, leading to miscommunication or fraudulent activities.
- **Impersonation**: If the identities of the communicating parties are not verified, an attacker could impersonate a legitimate user or device and gain unauthorized access to the UC system.

The organization must enable a robust security protocol like Transport Layer Security (TLS) to mitigate these risks and ensure secure communication. TLS provides encryption, integrity, and authentication, addressing the security concerns.

TLS is a cryptographic protocol that provides secure communication over a network. It is widely used in UC environments to protect SIP signaling and media traffic. TLS uses a combination of symmetric and asymmetric encryption, along with certificates, to establish a secure connection.

Certificates and Public Key Infrastructure (PKI) play a crucial role in securing communications within a network, including Unified Communications (UC) environments.

To understand their significance, let us first discuss the fundamental security concepts they address: authentication, integrity, and encryption.

- **Authentication** is verifying the identity of a user, device, or entity in a communication. It ensures that the entities involved are who they claim to be.
- **Integrity** assures that data has not been altered or tampered with during transmission. It ensures the data received is exactly as sent by the originator, without any modification.
- **Encryption** converts plaintext data into a coded form (ciphertext) to prevent unauthorized access. Only those who have the key can decrypt and access the original data.

There are two main types of encryption: symmetric and asymmetric.

- **Symmetric encryption** uses a single secret key for both encryption and decryption. The same key is used to encrypt the plaintext and decrypt the ciphertext. Symmetric encryption is fast and efficient but requires a secure method to exchange the secret key between the communicating parties.
- **Asymmetric encryption** uses a pair of keys: a public key and a private key. The public key is widely distributed and can be used by anyone to encrypt data, while the private key is kept secret and is used to decrypt data encrypted with the corresponding public key. Asymmetric encryption is slower than symmetric encryption but eliminates the need for secure key exchange.

Now that we understand the role of certificates and encryption in securing communication, let us look at how TLS establishes a secure connection between a client and a server. The TLS handshake process is a critical step in setting up an encrypted communication channel, and it involves the exchange of certificates and the negotiation of encryption parameters.

The TLS handshake process involves the following steps:

1. The client sends a **"ClientHello"** message to the server, indicating its supported TLS versions and cipher suites.
2. The server responds with a **"ServerHello"** message, selecting the TLS version and cipher suite to be used. The server also sends its certificate, which contains its public key.
3. The client verifies the server's certificate by checking its digital signature and ensuring it is issued by a trusted CA.
4. The client generates a random session key, encrypts it with the server's public key (obtained from the certificate), and sends it to the server.
5. The server decrypts the session key using its private key.
6. The client and server use the shared session key for symmetric encryption of the subsequent communication.

You can find an excellent interactive illustration of TLS 1.2 and 1.3 here or on other sites on the Internet: https://tls12.xargs.org/

One of the most important things to note is that TLS uses asymmetric encryption to exchange keys securely between the client and the server. Once a secure channel is established, TLS switches to symmetric encryption for the remainder of the session for efficiency, using the securely exchanged keys.

This process involves certificates, which are digital documents that bind a public key with an entity's identity (such as a server or a domain). The certificate is issued by a trusted authority known as a Certificate Authority (CA). Before issuing a certificate, the CA verifies the identity of the entity requesting it. Once issued, the certificate can be used to establish secure communications.

Certificates and Public Key Infrastructure (PKI) in Cisco UC

A certificate contains critical information that aids in authentication, integrity, and encryption:

- **Subject**: The entity's identity (example, a website, server).
- **Issuer**: The identity of the CA that issued the certificate.
- **Valid From/To**: The certificate's validity period.

- **Public Key**: The public key corresponds to the private key owned by the subject.
- **Digital Signature**: A cryptographic signature by the issuing CA verifying the certificate's integrity.

Each of these elements plays a part in establishing secure communications.

Certificates help verify that the server you are connecting to is correct and not an imposter. The server's public key, embedded in the certificate, encrypts data sent from the client to the server, ensuring that only the server can decrypt it with its private key. Certificates also ensure the data exchanged has not been altered or tampered with during transit.

Certificates can be Self-signed or CA-signed. Self-signed Certificates are generated and signed by the entity itself, not by a CA. While they can provide encryption, their authenticity cannot be independently verified, limiting their trustworthiness outside internal networks. Self-signed certificates are often used for testing or internal purposes but are not recommended for production environments.

CA-issued Certificates are signed by a trusted Certificate Authority (CA). Because CAs are trusted entities, their certificates are widely accepted as valid and authentic, making CA-issued certificates essential for secure communications over the Internet. Devices or servers generate a key pair (public and private key) and create a Certificate Signing Request (CSR). The CSR contains the device's public key and identifying information. The CSR is then sent to a CA, which verifies the requester's identity and signs the certificate with its own private key. The signed certificate, containing the device's public key and the CA's digital signature, is returned to the device. The device now has a valid certificate that can be used for authentication, integrity, and encryption.

Public Key Infrastructure (PKI) is used to establish trust on a larger scale. PKI is a framework that defines the roles, policies, and procedures needed to create, manage, distribute, use, store, and revoke digital certificates. It includes components such as CAs, registration authorities (RAs), and certificate repositories. In a PKI hierarchy, there is a root CA at the top, which is the ultimate trusted authority. Below the root CA, there can be intermediate CAs that issue certificates on behalf of the root CA. This structure forms a chain of trust, where each certificate is signed by the CA above it in the hierarchy.

This hierarchical structure allows for scalability and flexibility in certificate management. The Root CA can delegate the issuance of certificates to multiple intermediate CAs, which can then issue certificates to servers or other entities as needed.

It is crucial to protect the private key of the Root CA, as it is the foundation of trust for the entire PKI. If the Root CA's private key is compromised, the entire chain of trust is broken, and all certificates issued by the Root CA and its intermediate CAs can no longer be trusted.

In practice, the Root CA is often kept offline and used only for signing intermediate CA certificates. This helps to minimize the risk of the Root CA's private key being compromised. The intermediate CAs are then responsible for issuing and managing server certificates, providing an additional layer of security and flexibility.

As you see in *Figure* 10.1, the Root CA sits at the top of the hierarchy and self-signs its own certificate, establishing itself as the ultimate trusted authority. The Root CA then signs the certificates of Intermediate CA 1 and Intermediate CA 2, delegating the authority to issue server certificates to these intermediate CAs. Intermediate CA 1 signs Server Certificate 1 and Server Certificate 2, while Intermediate CA 2 signs Server Certificate 3 and Server Certificate 4. This hierarchical structure allows for scalability and flexibility in certificate management, enabling the Root CA to delegate the issuance of certificates to multiple intermediate CAs, which can then issue certificates to servers or other entities as needed.

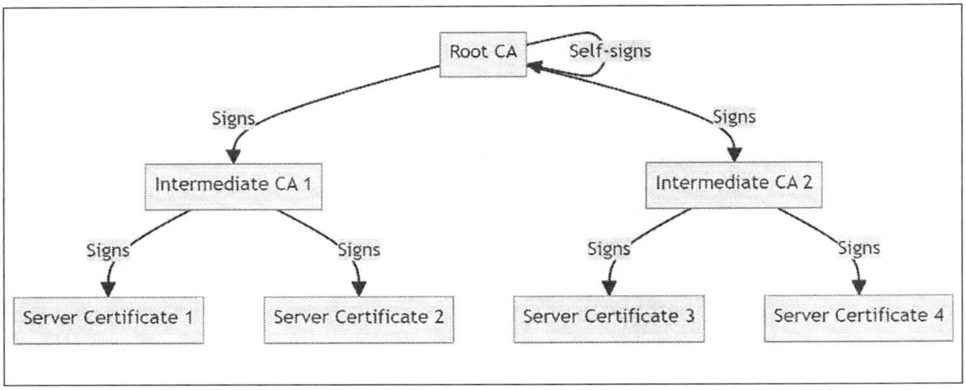

Figure 10.1: *PKI Hierarchy and Chain of Trust*

When a certificate is presented, the recipient can trace the chain of trust back to the root CA to verify its validity. Each intermediate CA's certificate is signed by the CA above it, and the root CA's certificate is self-signed. By verifying the chain of trust, the recipient can determine whether a certificate is trustworthy. The fundamental principle here is that your device must inherently trust the Certificate Authority (CA) that signed the server's certificate you're communicating with. This trust is established through a hierarchy of certificates, leading back to a root CA that your device already trusts.

As you see in *Figure* 10.2, the device inherently trusts the Root CA, as its certificate is pre-installed in the device's trust store. When the device receives Server Certificate 1 or Server Certificate 2 during a TLS handshake, it verifies the certificate by tracing the chain of trust back to the Root CA. For Server Certificate 1, the device verifies that it was signed by Intermediate CA 1 and then verifies that Intermediate CA 1's certificate was signed by the trusted Root CA. Similarly, for Server Certificate 2, the device verifies that it was signed by Intermediate CA 2 and then verifies that Intermediate CA 2's certificate was signed by the trusted Root CA. By successfully verifying the chain of trust up to the trusted Root CA, the device establishes trust in the server's certificate.

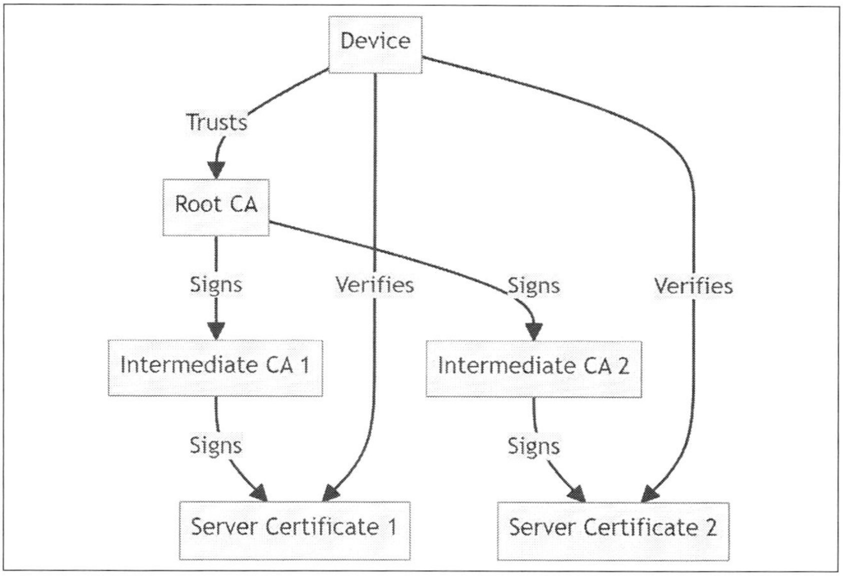

***Figure 10.2**: Device Verifying Server Certificate Trust*

This chain of trust is crucial in PKI as it allows devices to verify the authenticity of certificates issued by CAs that they may not directly trust. As long as the device trusts the Root CA, it can extend that trust to certificates issued by intermediate CAs signed by the Root CA. By utilizing the chain of trust, PKI provides a scalable and efficient method for establishing trust in certificates, enabling secure communication between devices and servers in UC environments and beyond.

It is important to note that for the chain of trust to be established, the device must have the Root CA's certificate pre-installed or manually added to its trust store. This is typically done by the device's manufacturer or the IT admin in the case of a private PKI.

PKI can be implemented using public CAs or private CAs.

- **Public CAs** are external authorities recognized and trusted by operating systems and browsers globally. They issue certificates for use on the Internet, where entities need to establish trust with the general public. For public CAs, your device likely already trusts the root CA since its certificate is pre-installed in your device's trust store. The chain of trust is verified up to this pre-installed root certificate. Public CAs, such as DigiCert or Symantec, are trusted third parties that issue certificates to the public. They follow strict guidelines and are audited regularly to maintain trust.

- **Private CAs** operate within an organization and are not automatically trusted outside of it. They issue certificates for internal use, where trust is established through internal mechanisms. Private CAs offer control over the certificate lifecycle tailored to organizational security policies. For private CAs, for your device to establish trust, the root certificate of the private CA needs to be manually installed in your device's trust store. Once installed, the device can verify the chain of trust up to the trusted private root CA. Private CAs are operated by organizations for internal use. Private CAs issue certificates specifically for the organization's own devices, users, and services.

When implementing and managing a PKI for a Cisco UC environment, it is essential to consider that most organizations already have an internal PKI infrastructure, often based on Microsoft Active Directory Certificate Services (AD CS). This internal PKI is usually managed by a separate team. Cisco UC administrators should collaborate with the PKI team to ensure that the certificates issued for UC components meet the specific requirements outlined in Cisco's documentation.

The typical process for obtaining certificates for UC servers involves the following steps:

1. Generate a Certificate Signing Request (CSR) on the UC server. The CSR contains the server's public key and the requested certificate attributes.
2. Submit the CSR to the internal CA for signing. The PKI team will verify the request, ensure the necessary attributes are present, and sign the certificate using the CA's private key.
3. Retrieve the signed certificate from the CA and upload it to the UC server.
4. Restart the relevant services on the UC server to ensure that the new certificate is properly loaded and used.

It is important to note that the certificate requirements may differ depending on the server's role and its interaction with external entities. Servers within the internal network, such as Cisco Unified Communications Manager (CUCM), Cisco Unity Connection (CUC), Cisco Contact Center Express (UCCX), and Cisco Expressway-C, typically obtain certificates signed by the internal CA. These servers primarily communicate with other internal components and endpoints, which trust the internal root CA.

However, edge servers such as Cisco Expressway-E, which interact with external entities (example, remote endpoints or other organizations), may require certificates signed by a public CA. External entities may not trust the organization's internal root CA but will likely trust a well-known public root CA. In such cases, the UC administrators should request certificates from a trusted public CA, ensuring that the certificates meet both Cisco's requirements and the industry standards for publicly trusted certificates.

Certificate Types in CUCM and Their Usage

Cisco Unified Communications Manager (CUCM) uses several types of certificates for different services and purposes. Here are the main certificate types in CUCM and their usage:

- **CallManager Certificate**: This certificate secures SIP and SCCP communication between CUCM and endpoints and between CUCM and other UC components. It is used for the CallManager service, which is CUCM's core call-processing service.
- **Tomcat Certificate**: The Tomcat certificate secures the CUCM web-based administrative interface. It ensures that communication between the administrator's web browser and the CUCM administrative interface is encrypted using HTTPS.
- **CAPF (Certificate Authority Proxy Function) Certificate**: The CAPF certificate is used to issue and manage certificates for endpoints in a secure manner. CAPF is a service that runs on CUCM and acts as a proxy between the endpoints and the CA. It authenticates endpoints and issues certificates to endpoints on behalf of the CA.
- **Trust Verification Service (TVS) Certificate**: The TVS certificate is used by the Trust Verification Service, which is responsible for verifying the identity of endpoints and determining their trust status.

You will see these on the **`Cisco Unified Operating System Administration`** page under **`Security > Certificate Management`**. From here, you can generate a CSR and upload the signed certificate as well.

CUCM uses multiple certificates for different services to provide a granular security level and compartmentalize the impact of a potential certificate compromise. If a single certificate were used for all services and that certificate was compromised, it would affect the entire CUCM system. By using separate certificates for each service, the impact of a certificate compromise is limited to that specific service, making the system more resilient.

While we have covered the main certificate types used in CUCM, it is important to note that different Cisco UC servers may have different certificate requirements based on their specific roles and functionalities.

Now that we have a solid understanding of PKI and certificates and their usage in Cisco UC, let us discuss the secure communication protocols commonly used in UC environments: TLS, SRTP, and SIPS.

Secure Communication Protocols in Cisco UC

In this section, we will discuss briefly three main protocols in Cisco UC for securing communication- TLS, SIPS, and SRTP.

TLS and SIPS are protocols used to establish secure communication channels, but they operate at different layers and serve different purposes.

TLS is a cryptographic protocol that provides secure communication over a network. It operates at the OSI model's transport layer (Layer 4) and is used to secure various application layer protocols, such as HTTP (HTTPS), SMTP, and SIP.

TLS ensures the confidentiality, integrity, and authenticity of the data exchanged between the communicating parties. TLS is widely used in Cisco UC environments to secure SIP signaling traffic between UC components, such as CUCM, Cisco Unity Connection, and endpoints. It ensures that the SIP messages exchanged between these components are encrypted and protected from eavesdropping and tampering. It is important to note that TLS is applied on a hop-by-hop basis, meaning that each segment of the communication path is secured independently.

SIPS is a signaling-level protocol used to establish secure end-to-end SIP communication between endpoints. It is a Uniform Resource Identifier (URI) scheme used in Session Initiation Protocol (SIP) to indicate that the entire communication path between the endpoints should be secured using TLS. When a SIP URI is prefixed with "sips:" instead of "sip:", it indicates that TLS should be used for all hops in the communication path, from the sender to the recipient. This differentiates SIPS from TLS, which is applied on a per-hop basis. When a SIP call is initiated using a SIPS URI, the endpoints establish a TLS connection for SIP signaling, and the media is typically secured using Secure Real-time Transport Protocol (SRTP).

SRTP is a security protocol used to encrypt and authenticate real-time media traffic, such as voice and video, in IP-based communication systems. It provides confidentiality, integrity, and authentication for Real-time Transport Protocol (RTP) packets, which carry the media data. SRTP uses symmetric key encryption to encrypt the media payload and adds an authentication tag to each RTP packet to ensure its integrity and authenticity. The symmetric keys used for SRTP encryption and authentication are typically derived from a master key, which is securely exchanged between the endpoints using a key management protocol, such as Session Description Protocol Security Descriptions (SDES) or Datagram Transport Layer Security for Secure RTP (DTLS SRTP).

In Cisco UC environments, SRTP is commonly used with TLS to provide a complete security solution. TLS secures the SIP signaling traffic, while SRTP secures the media traffic. This combination ensures that both the signaling and media communication channels are protected from eavesdropping and tampering.

It is important to note that while SRTP can be used independently of TLS, it is generally recommended that they be used together for enhanced security. TLS provides secure key exchange and authentication for the signaling channel, while SRTP encrypts and authenticates the media channel. Using SRTP without TLS may leave the signaling channel vulnerable to attacks, which could compromise the security of the media communication.

In some scenarios, TLS can be used without SRTP, providing security for the signaling channel only. However, this approach leaves the media traffic unencrypted and vulnerable to interception. It is generally considered a best practice to use both TLS and SRTP to ensure end-to-end security for both signaling and media communication in Cisco UC environments.

Several settings and parameters need to be configured to enable TLS and SRTP in a Cisco UC environment. Here are some key configuration elements:

1. **On SIP trunks**: In CUCM, create a SIP Trunk Security Profile with the **`"Device Security Mode"`** set to **`"Encrypted."`** This profile determines the security settings for SIP trunks for signaling. Apply this SIP Trunk Security Profile to the SIP trunk. Then, in SIP Trunk Configuration, set the **`"SRTP Allowed"`** checkbox to enable SRTP for media encryption on the SIP trunk. This allows the CUCM to enable secure and nonsecure media calls over the trunk.
2. **On endpoints**: Create a Phone Security Profile with the **`"Device Security Mode"`** set to **`"Encrypted"`** and the **`"Transport Type"`** set to **`"TLS."`** This profile is assigned to Endpoints to enable secure signaling and media. Configure the endpoints (IP phones, softphones, etc.) to use the appropriate Phone security profiles and ensure they have the necessary certificates installed.

By configuring these settings and parameters, you can enable TLS and SRTP in your Cisco UC environment to secure both signaling and media communication.

Now, let us look at other security measures to make UC infrastructure more secure.

Security Measures and System Hardening in Cisco UC

In this section, we will discuss the concepts of Mixed Mode and tokenless operations in Cisco UC environments. We will also cover some security settings and best practices for system hardening.

Mixed Mode and CTL/ITL in CUCM

Cisco Unified CM supports two security modes: Nonsecure Mode and Mixed Mode.

When you install Cisco Unified CM for the first time, the default security mode is

Nonsecure Mode. In this mode, security features are not enforced, and the system operates without signaling or media encryption.

Mixed mode enables security features and provides support for authenticated or encrypted devices. It requires using the Certificate Trust List (CTL) file for authentication and encryption.

These are high-level steps to configure Mixed Mode:

1. Enable the Cisco Certificate Authority Proxy Function (CAPF) service on the publisher.
2. Enable the Cisco CTL Provider service on the publisher.
3. Run the CLI command utils ctl set-cluster mixed-mode on the publisher.
4. Restart the Cisco CallManager and Cisco TFTP services on all nodes in the cluster.
5. Reset all devices to register with Cisco Unified CM using the new CTL file.

You can also verify the Cluster security mode from the GUI of CUCM. Navigate to **`CUCM Admin Page > System > Enterprise Parameters`** and look for Cluster security mode under Security parameters. If it is set to 1, it means it's in mixed mode, and 0 means it's in non-secure mode.

In the past, Cisco UC environments relied on physical USB eTokens to store and manage cryptographic keys and certificates. These eTokens were used to authenticate devices and establish secure connections. However, managing and distributing USB eTokens across a large number of devices was complex and costly.

With the introduction of the tokenless solution in Cisco Unified CM 10.0 and later, the need for physical USB eTokens was eliminated. The tokenless approach simplifies the management of secure communications by using certificates without requiring physical tokens.

In a tokenless environment, endpoints use a Locally Significant Certificate (LSC) issued by the CAPF to establish secure connections. The LSC is a device-specific certificate that uniquely identifies the endpoint. Additionally, endpoints have a Manufacturer-Installed Certificate (MIC) pre-installed by the manufacturer, which is used for initial authentication with Cisco Unified CM during registration.

The following are the steps to secure Cisco UC endpoints in a tokenless environment:

1. Configure the CAPF service and enable the generation of LSCs.
2. Configure phone security profiles with the **`"Device Security Mode"`** set to **`"Encrypted"`** and the "Transport Type" set to "TLS".

3. Apply the security profiles to the endpoints.
4. Ensure that Cisco Unified CM is in Mixed Mode and has the necessary certificates (example, CAPF certificate) installed.

With the combination of LSCs and MICs, secure authentication and communication between endpoints and Cisco UC components can be achieved without the need for physical USB eTokens.

It is important to note that the specific steps and configurations may vary depending on the Cisco UC platform and version being used. Always refer to the official Cisco documentation for the most up-to-date and detailed instructions on configuring security features for your specific environment.

Transitioning from the general security features, let's explore the specific security hardening measures implemented in Cisco Unified Communications Manager (CUCM) and Cisco Unity Connection (CUC).

System Hardening in Cisco UC

Cisco UC platforms, such as Cisco Unified Communications Manager (CUCM), Cisco Unity Connection, and Cisco Expressway, come with a set of default security settings that provide a baseline level of protection.

Some examples include:

- **Default password policies**: Cisco UC platforms enforce default password policies, such as minimum password length, complexity requirements, and password expiration, to ensure that strong passwords are used.
- **Role-based access control (RBAC)**: Cisco UC platforms implement RBAC, which limits user access to specific resources and functions based on their assigned roles and permissions.

To further enhance the security of Cisco UC systems, consider implementing the following best practices:

- Regularly apply security patches and updates to keep the system up to date and protected against known vulnerabilities.
- Use strong, complex passwords for all UC components and user accounts, and enforce regular password changes.
- Limit administrative access to UC systems and use secure protocols, such as SSH and HTTPS, for remote management.
- Implement network segmentation to isolate UC traffic from other network traffic and apply appropriate access control lists (ACLs) to restrict unauthorized access.

- Enable logging and monitoring to detect and respond to security events and anomalies in a timely manner.

It is important to note that these are just some examples of default security settings and best practices.

In addition to the default security settings and best practices mentioned earlier, Cisco has taken extra steps to harden the CUCM and CUC platforms to provide a robust and secure foundation for enterprise communications.

Here are some of the key security hardening features built into CUCM and CUC:

- **Customized and Hardened OS**: CUCM and CUC don't use a standard, off-the-shelf operating system. Instead, they utilize a customized and hardened version of the OS specifically tailored for the platform. This includes removing unnecessary modules, disabling unused services, and applying proprietary security enhancements to critical components like OpenSSL. By minimizing the OS footprint and attack surface, Cisco reduces the risk of potential vulnerabilities.
- **Restricted Access and Controlled Interfaces**: To prevent unauthorized access, native interfaces to the guest OS, database, runtime, and other internal components are not exposed. Administrators can only interact with the system through Cisco-provided secure interfaces, such as the web-based GUI, CLI (accessed via SSH), or API. This approach ensures that all access points are properly authenticated, encrypted, and auditable.
- **Closed-System Software Stack**: CUCM and CUC operate as closed systems, meaning that all software components are provided, tested, and digitally signed by Cisco. This includes the OS, database, applications, and any additional modules. Administrators cannot install third-party software or make changes to the underlying components, ensuring the integrity and stability of the platform.
- **Granular Access Control**: Even with restricted access, Cisco implements granular control over administrative privileges. Root access to the guest OS is disabled by default, and administrators must use their designated credentials to access the system through the provided interfaces. In exceptional cases, temporary remote access can be granted to Cisco support personnel, but this is closely controlled and monitored by the customer.
- **Multi-layered Intrusion Prevention**: CUCM and CUC employ a multi-layered approach to intrusion prevention. This includes enabling SELinux in enforcing mode, which provides mandatory access controls to limit the privileges of applications and services. Additionally, a host-based firewall (IPTables) is configured to restrict network traffic and apply rate limiting based on the specific services running on the server.

- **Comprehensive Audit Logging:** To maintain accountability and facilitate incident response, CUCM and CUC generate detailed audit logs for various components, including the OS, database, and application layers. These logs capture critical events, user actions, and system changes, enabling administrators to monitor and investigate any suspicious activities.
- **Rigorous Compliance and Certification**: CUCM, CUC, and other Cisco UC products undergo regular testing and validation to ensure compliance with stringent security standards. This includes certifications such as FIPS 140-2, Common Criteria, and Department of Defense STIGs. By adhering to these standards, Cisco is committed to providing a trustworthy and secure communications platform.

Cisco provides detailed security guides and recommendations for each UC component, which should be consulted to understand the available security features and configurations comprehensively.

Now, let us move to another important topic: Toll fraud prevention.

Preventing Toll Fraud in Cisco UC

Toll fraud, also known as telephony fraud or voice fraud, is a significant concern in Cisco UC environments. It occurs when unauthorized individuals gain access to an organization's telephony system and make expensive long-distance or international calls, resulting in substantial financial losses. Attackers can exploit vulnerabilities in UC systems, such as weak passwords, misconfigured dial plans, or exposed gateways, to make unauthorized calls. These calls can quickly accumulate, leading to significant costs for the organization.

Toll fraud can lead to financial losses and reputational damage, as the organization's phone numbers may be used for illegal activities, such as scams or fraud schemes. In this section, we will discuss some of the techniques and best practices to prevent toll fraud in Cisco UC components.

- **On Cisco Expressway:**
    - Implement Call Processing Language (CPL) rules in the default zone to block unauthorized call patterns. CPL rules allow you to define specific criteria for allowing or blocking calls based on the called number or pattern.
    - Configure strict search rules and transforms to control which calls are allowed through Expressway and to manipulate the called numbers if necessary.
    - Use the **`"Reject calls to unknown domains"`** setting to prevent calls to unrecognized domains, which could potentially lead to toll fraud.

  - Utilize **`"Call Policy"`** rules to control which calls are allowed based on the source and destination of the call.
- **On Cisco Unified Communications Manager (CUCM):**
  - Restrict access of the PSTN partition only to the necessary trunks and devices. For example, if calls from Expressway-C to the CUCM SIP trunk are not expected to reach the PSTN, ensure that the PSTN partition is not associated with the Calling Search Space (CSS) assigned to that trunk.
  - Implement **`"Forced Authorization Codes" (FAC)`** for PSTN calls to require users to enter a valid code before making outbound calls, adding an extra layer of authentication.
  - Configure Call Admission Control (CAC) to limit the number of simultaneous calls and prevent excessive call traffic that could indicate toll fraud activity.
  - Enable **`"Call Detail Record" (CDR)`** and **`"Call Management Record" (CMR)`** logging to capture detailed call information for auditing and fraud detection purposes.
- **On Voice Gateways:**
  - Implement specific and restrictive dial plans to control which numbers can be dialed out. Avoid using vague or overly permissive dial peers that could be exploited for toll fraud.
  - Use **`"Translation Rules"`** to manipulate dialed digits and restrict access to unauthorized numbers or patterns.
  - Consider blocking calls to premium-rate numbers or international destinations that are not required for business purposes.
- **On Cisco Unity Connection:**
  - Configure **`"Restriction Tables"`** to control outbound calling capabilities from voicemail ports. Restrict access to unnecessary destinations and limit the number of digits that can be dialed out.

These are just a few recommendations. There may be more UC infrastructure components where you should ensure that toll fraud is not possible due to misconfiguration.

Additionally, here are some general recommendations:

- Regularly review and update call routing configurations, dial plans, and CSS/partitions to ensure they align with the organization's calling policies and prevent unauthorized access to sensitive destinations.
- Monitor call detail records (CDRs) and call management records (CMRs) for suspicious activity, such as high call volumes to unusual destinations or long call durations.

- Implement real-time alerts and notifications for potential toll fraud incidents, such as calls to known high-risk numbers or excessive call charges.
- Collaborate with your telecom service provider to implement additional fraud prevention measures, such as call blocking or rate limiting for high-risk destinations.
- Educate users about toll fraud risks and best practices, such as not sharing voicemail passwords and reporting suspicious call activities.

By implementing these techniques and best practices across your Cisco UC environment, you can significantly reduce the risk of toll fraud and protect your organization from financial losses and reputational damage.

For a detailed understanding, it is recommended to read the Security chapter of "Preferred Architecture for Cisco Collaboration 12.x Enterprise On-Premises Deployments" (https://www.cisco.com/c/en/us/td/docs/solutions/CVD/Collaboration/enterprise/12x/120/collbcvd/security.html).

Now, let us move to the next section: Recovery.

Recovery Strategy

Recovery is a critical aspect of any Unified Communications (UC) deployment, as it ensures the continuity of services in the event of a disaster or system failure. In today's fast-paced business environment, downtime can lead to significant financial losses, productivity disruption, and reputational damage. A comprehensive recovery strategy, including Disaster Recovery Planning (DRP) and data backup, is essential for minimizing the impact of disruptions and ensuring the timely restoration of UC services.

It is crucial to understand the importance of recovery planning and to have a deep knowledge of the available tools, techniques, and best practices for implementing effective recovery strategies in Cisco UC environments. By proactively preparing for potential disruptions and having well-defined recovery processes in place, organizations can minimize downtime, protect critical data, and maintain the availability and reliability of their UC services.

In this section, we will explore the key aspects of Disaster Recovery Planning (DRP) for Cisco UC, including its importance, key components, and implementation considerations.

Disaster Recovery Planning (DRP) for Cisco UC

Disaster Recovery Planning (DRP) is the process of creating a structured approach to prepare for, respond to, and recover from a disaster or unexpected event that disrupts UC services. A well-designed DRP helps organizations minimize the impact of disruptions, ensure the timely restoration of critical UC functions, and maintain the continuity of communication services.

In UC environments, DRP is essential for several reasons. First, it minimizes downtime by enabling organizations to quickly respond to and recover from disruptions, reducing the duration of UC service unavailability. Second, DRP strategies, such as regular backups and data replication, help safeguard critical UC data, including configuration settings and user information. Third, many industries have specific regulations and standards requiring organizations to have documented recovery plans and procedures. Finally, by ensuring the timely restoration of UC services, DRP helps organizations maintain business continuity and minimize the impact of disruptions on productivity and customer service.

DRP plans should be designed to address various aspects of disaster recovery, from identifying potential risks to implementing recovery procedures.

Key components of a well-rounded DRP include:

- **Risk assessment**: Identify potential risks and vulnerabilities that could impact UC services, such as hardware failures, network outages, or natural disasters.
- **Business impact analysis**: Assess the potential impact of disruptions on critical UC functions and prioritize recovery efforts based on business requirements.
- **Recovery objectives**: Define Recovery Time Objectives (RTO) and Recovery Point Objectives (RPO) for UC services, specifying the maximum acceptable downtime and data loss.
- **Backup and replication strategies**: Implement regular backup and replication mechanisms to protect critical UC data and configuration settings.
- **Failover and redundancy**: Deploy redundant UC components and establish failover mechanisms to ensure high availability and minimize single points of failure.
- **Disaster recovery procedures**: Develop detailed step-by-step procedures for responding to and recovering from different disaster scenarios, including roles and responsibilities.
- **Testing and maintenance**: Regularly test (at least once a year) and update the DRP strategy to validate its effectiveness, identify gaps, and ensure that recovery procedures remain up to date with changes in the UC environment.

When implementing DRP in Cisco UC environments, organizations can follow these best practices to ensure effective disaster recovery:

- **Leverage Cisco's high availability (HA) features**: Implement HA features, such as redundant servers, clustering, and load balancing, for critical UC components like Cisco Unified Communications Manager (CUCM), Cisco Unity Connection, and Cisco Expressway.

- **Implement backup and restore capabilities**: Use Cisco's built-in backup and restore tools, such as the Disaster Recovery System (DRS) for CUCM and Unity Connection and the Backup and Restore feature for Cisco Expressway, to regularly back up system configurations and data.

  In addition to Cisco's built-in tools, organizations can leverage third-party backup solutions compatible with Cisco UC systems. These solutions often provide additional features like centralized management, advanced scheduling options, and integration with enterprise backup infrastructures.

- **Establish geographically dispersed redundancy**: Deploy UC components across multiple geographically dispersed data centers or cloud regions to ensure service continuity in case of a localized disaster.

One critical component of a comprehensive DRP is a robust backup and replication strategy. Let us explore that briefly.

Backup and Restore

Regular backups ensure that organizations have access to recent copies of their critical UC data and configurations, enabling them to restore services quickly during a disaster.

Several factors should be considered when designing backup schedules and retention policies for Cisco UC environments. Consider the following recommendations:

- Schedule full backups regularly, such as weekly or monthly, depending on the data change rate and the acceptable level of data loss.
- Implement a retention policy that aligns with business requirements and regulatory obligations. Retain backups for a sufficient period to meet data recovery and compliance needs.
- Store backups on separate or off-site storage systems to protect against local disasters.
- Regularly test the integrity and recoverability of backups to ensure they can be used for successful restoration.

These are just a few recommendations to help organizations develop a robust backup strategy for their Cisco UC environments. It's crucial to have an organization-wide discussion around these topics to ensure alignment and consistency with the overall disaster recovery plan. It is essential to document the plan in detail and ensure that all relevant stakeholders understand their roles and responsibilities. By having a well-thought-out and clearly communicated plan in place, organizations can respond quickly and effectively when faced with urgent situations that require service restoration. This proactive approach minimizes confusion and enables a coordinated effort to restore critical UC services, ultimately reducing the impact of disruptions on business operations.

Compliance

Compliance is a critical aspect of deploying and managing Cisco Unified Communications (UC) solutions. As UC systems handle a significant amount of sensitive data, including personal information and confidential business communications, it is essential for UC administrators to understand and adhere to various data privacy regulations and industry-specific requirements. Non-compliance can lead to legal consequences, financial penalties, and reputational damage.

In this section, we will explore the key aspects of compliance in Cisco UC environments, focusing on data privacy, regulations affecting UC services, and best practices for ensuring compliance. We will also examine the significance of emergency calling in Cisco UC and discuss the technical considerations and best practices for implementing and maintaining emergency calling functionality.

Data Privacy and Cisco UC

Data privacy is a critical concern in today's digital world. As more personal information is shared and stored across various systems, it is essential to ensure that sensitive data is handled securely and complies with relevant regulations. When it comes to Cisco Unified Communications (UC) solutions, data privacy presents unique challenges and responsibilities for UC administrators.

Cisco UC services, such as voice, video, and messaging, handle a wide range of personal data, including user identities, contact information, call records, and voicemail messages. This data is highly sensitive and must be protected according to data privacy regulations and industry standards. The sensitive nature of the data processed by UC systems highlights the importance of implementing strong data protection measures and following privacy best practices.

From a general data privacy perspective, regulations like the General Data Protection Regulation (GDPR) have raised the bar for how personal data should be collected, processed, and protected. GDPR defines personal data as any information identifying a person, such as their name, email address, phone number, or IP address. Under GDPR, organizations must have a valid reason for processing personal data, such as getting consent from the individual or having a legitimate business need.

UC administrators face several challenges when it comes to ensuring data privacy compliance. One major challenge is the difficulty in separating business and personal data. In many cases, UC systems are used for both work and personal communication, making it hard to distinguish between them. This complicates the process of identifying and protecting personal data, as it may be mixed with business-related information.

Additionally, UC administrators have a greater responsibility regarding data privacy, as they often have access to a wide range of sensitive data across multiple systems and applications. With this access comes the duty to handle personal data in a way that respects individual privacy rights and ensures compliance with relevant regulations.

To address these challenges, UC administrators must adopt a privacy-focused approach in designing, deploying, and managing Cisco UC solutions. This involves implementing data privacy principles, such as:

- **Data Minimization**: Collecting and processing only the minimum amount of personal data needed for a specific purpose. UC administrators should review data collection practices and disable unnecessary data gathering to reduce the risk of privacy breaches.
- **Purpose Limitation**: Clearly state the reason for collecting personal data and ensure it is used only for that purpose. UC administrators should inform users about the purpose of data collection and obtain their consent when required.
- **Data Security**: Putting in place appropriate technical and organizational measures to protect personal data from unauthorized access, accidental loss, or destruction. This includes encrypting UC data both in transit and at rest, enforcing strong access controls, and regularly monitoring for security threats.
- **Data Retention**: Defining and enforcing data retention policies that specify how long UC data should be kept and when it should be securely deleted. UC administrators should ensure that personal data is not kept longer than necessary and is securely disposed of when no longer needed.
- **Privacy by Design**: Incorporating privacy considerations into the design and configuration of UC systems from the start. This involves assessing privacy impact, implementing privacy-enhancing technologies, and regularly reviewing and updating privacy practices.

By following these principles and staying up-to-date with the latest data privacy regulations, UC administrators can help ensure that Cisco UC deployments respect individual privacy rights and maintain compliance with applicable laws and standards.

In addition to understanding data privacy principles, UC administrators must also be aware of the specific regulations that apply to Cisco UC services.

Regulations Affecting Cisco UC Services

Numerous regulations impact Cisco UC services at a general level and specific to the telecommunications industry.

- **General Data Protection Regulation (GDPR)** is a data privacy regulation applicable to organizations that process the personal data of European Union (EU) citizens. UC administrators must make sure that personal data handled by UC systems is properly protected through encryption, access controls, and secure data storage. They must also have ways to fulfill data subject rights, like the ability to access, correct, or delete personal data when requested. GDPR also requires organizations to keep detailed records of data processing activities, including why the data is processed and what types of personal data are involved. UC administrators should work closely with legal and compliance teams to ensure that UC systems and processes meet GDPR requirements.

- **Health Insurance Portability and Accountability Act (HIPAA)** is a U.S. federal law that establishes data privacy and security provisions for safeguarding medical information. It applies to healthcare providers, health plans, and healthcare clearinghouses that handle protected health information (PHI). UC systems that handle protected health information (PHI) must follow HIPAA's Security Rule, which requires appropriate administrative, physical, and technical safeguards to ensure PHI's confidentiality, integrity, and availability. This includes encrypting PHI both at rest and in transit, implementing strict access controls, and regularly monitoring and auditing UC systems for potential security breaches. UC administrators in healthcare organizations must work with compliance officers to ensure that UC deployments meet HIPAA requirements and protect patient privacy.

These are just two examples of general data privacy regulations. Many other regulations, such as the California Consumer Privacy Act (CCPA) and the Personal Information Protection and Electronic Documents Act (PIPEDA) in Canada, may apply to Cisco UC deployments depending on the industry and geographic location.

In addition to general data privacy regulations, there are also country-specific telecommunications regulations that impact Cisco UC deployments.

The Telecom Regulatory Authority of India (TRAI) has specific regulations for Voice over Internet Protocol (VoIP) services in India. One important requirement is the Tail-End Hop-Off (TEHO) restriction, which means companies cannot mix VoIP and PSTN calls across different locations to avoid national and international call charges. For example, a call from an IP Phone in the Pune office to a cell phone in Delhi must be routed through the Pune local PSTN gateway and not over the WAN to use Delhi's local PSTN gateway. Another example is if the IP Phone in the Pune office is in VoIP call with an IP Phone in the Mumbai office, they cannot add the PSTN participant in the same call.

To comply with this regulation, UC deployments in India often use PBX's Location-Based Routing (LBR) features, such as the Geolocation feature in Cisco Unified Communications Manager (CUCM). LBR is a generic term for this feature and is commonly available in different IP PBX. Local PSTN breakout can be usually controlled by CSS and Partition in CUCM but the challenge is to control supplementary features such as transfer, conference, and so on. LBR features such as Geolocation in CUCM ensure that calls are routed through the local voice gateway, preventing toll bypass.

Organizations in India that provide services like tele-banking, tele-medicine, e-commerce, call centers, and other IT-enabled services using telecom resources (and IP PBX or On-Prem Contact centers) are called Other Service Providers (OSPs). These OSPs need to get a special license from the Department of Telecommunications (DoT). Non-OSP entities do not provide these services, so they don't need an OSP license. OSPs must follow TRAI regulations, which may include keeping detailed call records, saving logs for a specific time, and being subject to audits. Breaking these regulations can lead to fines and penalties. UC administrators in India must know these requirements and put in place the necessary technical measures to ensure compliance.

Other countries in Asia have similar regulations related to toll bypass. UC administrators should research and follow the specific regulations for their deployments in those countries.

In China, there are strict regulations about data retention and processing of citizen data outside the country. Also, a China Direct Inward Dialing (DID) number cannot be assigned to a user outside China. UC administrators deploying systems in China must ensure that data storage and processing follow these regulations and have the necessary approvals (if required) from relevant authorities.

These examples show how important it is to understand and follow country-specific telecommunications regulations when deploying Cisco UC solutions. UC administrators must work closely with legal and compliance teams to ensure their deployments meet all applicable requirements and avoid potential penalties or legal consequences.

Emergency Calling in Cisco UC

Emergency calling is a critical feature in Cisco UC systems, as it enables users to quickly and reliably connect with emergency services in case of life-threatening situations. Ensuring the proper implementation and functionality of emergency calling is not only a regulatory requirement in many countries but also a moral responsibility for organizations deploying UC solutions.

Implementing emergency calling in Cisco UC systems involves several technical considerations:

- **Location information**: Accurate location information is crucial for emergency services to respond quickly to calls. In Cisco UC systems, location information can be provided through various means, such as:
    - **Static locations**: Assigning fixed locations to IP phones based on their physical location.
    - **Dynamic locations**: Network-based location discovery mechanisms, such as Cisco Emergency Responder (CER), are used to determine the location of IP phones dynamically. CER tracks devices by their connection to LAN

switch ports and IP subnets, enabling it to determine the device's location dynamically.

  - **Softphone locations**: Prompting softphone users to manually update their location information or use GPS-based location services on mobile devices.

- **Emergency call routing**: Emergency calls must be routed to the appropriate Public Safety Answering Point (PSAP) based on the caller's location. UC systems use Emergency Location Identification Numbers (ELINs) or Emergency Response Locations (ERLs) to associate caller locations with the correct PSAP.
- **Emergency notification:** In addition to routing emergency calls to the PSAP, UC systems can also notify designated personnel, such as security or facilities staff, when an emergency call is placed. This can be achieved through email, SMS, or phone notifications.
- **Call admission control**: During emergency situations, it is essential to prioritize emergency calls over regular call traffic. Cisco UC systems can use call admission control (CAC) mechanisms to ensure that emergency calls are given priority and can be completed even during network congestion.
- **Redundancy and failover**: Emergency calling functionality must be resilient and available even during system failures or outages. Implementing redundancy and failover mechanisms, such as backup PSTN connections or geographically dispersed UC clusters, can help ensure the continuity of emergency calling services.

Now, let us explore the requirements in different countries.

Emergency Calling in Different Countries

Emergency calling requirements and numbers vary from country to country. While some countries have a single emergency number, others have separate numbers for different emergency services, such as police, fire, and ambulance.

Here are a few examples:

- **United States and Canada**: 911 (single number for all emergency services)
- **United Kingdom**: 999 (single number for all emergency services)
- **European Union**: 112 (single number for all emergency services, alongside country-specific numbers)
- **Australia**: 000 (single number for all emergency services)
- **India**: 112 (single number for all emergency services, introduced in 2019)
  - Police: 100
  - Fire: 101
  - Ambulance: 102

Each country has its own regulations and technical requirements for emergency calls, which can include location information transmission, emergency call routing, and prioritization of emergency calls over regular call traffic.

In addition to connecting with public emergency services, many organizations have their own in-house security or emergency response teams. These teams handle emergencies within the enterprise premises and coordinate with public emergency services when necessary.

Organizations may configure their UC systems to notify the in-house emergency response team when an emergency call is placed. This notification can take the form of phone calls, SMS messages, or email alerts, including details such as the caller's location and callback number.

The configuration of emergency calling in UC systems can range from simple call routing configurations and user education to integrating with specific products and services to meet regulatory requirements.

For example, in countries without strict location information transmission requirements, UC administrators may configure the system to route emergency calls to the appropriate emergency numbers and educate users on how to place emergency calls using the UC system. However, in countries with more stringent requirements, such as the United States, which has E911 regulations, UC administrators need to integrate their systems with solutions like Cisco Emergency Responder (CER) and work with emergency calling service providers to ensure that accurate location information is transmitted to the Public Safety Answering Point (PSAP).

Let us examine the E911 requirements and technical implementation in the United States. Please note that regulatory requirements for E911 can vary by jurisdiction within the United States. This variability can affect the specifics of how emergency calling solutions are implemented and managed, so we will keep the explanation generic and high-level.

The technical implementation of E911 involves the following components and processes:

- **Location Information**: The caller's location information is typically provided in the form of an Emergency Response Location (ERL) or a dispatchable location, which includes the street address, building, floor, and room number. This information is stored in a database and associated with the caller's phone number or endpoint. Cisco's Emergency Responder (CER) is an emergency call management solution that dynamically tracks the location of IP phones and associates them with ERLs. CER uses network discovery protocols (CDP, LLDP) and SNMP queries to determine the location of IP phones and update the ALI database. ERLs in CER represent specific geographic areas, such as buildings, floors, or rooms. Each ERL is associated with a unique Emergency Location

Identification Number (ELIN), which is a phone number used to identify the caller's location to the PSAP.

- **Emergency Call Routing**: When an emergency call is placed, the call is routed to the appropriate PSAP based on the caller's location. The telephony service provider or the enterprise's emergency call routing solution, such as CER integrated with CUCM, typically handles the routing.
- **Location Information Transmission**: The caller's location information is transmitted to the PSAP using the Automatic Location Identification (ALI) database. The ALI database is a centralized repository that contains the location information associated with each phone number or endpoint. When an emergency call is placed, the phone number or endpoint identifier is used to query the ALI database, and the corresponding location information is retrieved and sent to the PSAP.

  For example, CER integrates with the ALI database maintained by the emergency calling service provider. CER updates the ALI database with the ERL and ELIN information associated with each IP phone. When an emergency call is placed, the service provider queries the ALI database and retrieves the location information to be sent to the PSAP.
- **Presence Information Data Format - Location Object (PIDF-LO)**: PIDF-LO is a standardized XML format used to convey location information in IP-based emergency calling systems. It includes details such as the location type (example, civic or geodetic), location data (example, street address, latitude/longitude), and location uncertainty. Modern implementations can use next-generation 911 (NG911) systems that directly accept data formats like PIDF-LO over IP-based networks, bypassing traditional PSTN-based ALI lookups.

  CER supports the generation and transmission of location information using the PIDF-LO format. When an emergency call is placed, CER includes the PIDF-LO location information in the SIP signaling messages sent to the service provider, which then forwards the information to the PSAP.
- **Service Providers**: Emergency calling service providers play a crucial role in handling the mapping and transmission of location information. They work with enterprises to ensure that the location information associated with each endpoint is accurate and up to date. When an emergency call is placed, the service provider is responsible for querying the ALI database, retrieving the location information, and sending it to the PSAP in the appropriate format (example, PIDF-LO) using protocols such as Session Initiation Protocol (SIP) or HTTP-Enabled Location Delivery (HELD).

It is important to note that the specific implementation details may vary depending on the service provider and the local E911 regulations. Implementing E911 solutions, especially in complex environments, requires thorough testing and validation to ensure that location information is accurate and emergency calls are routed correctly.

Cisco UC administrators should work closely with their emergency calling service providers and refer to Cisco's documentation, such as the Cisco Emergency Responder Administration Guide, for detailed configuration and integration instructions.

The collection and transmission of real-time location information for E911 purposes raise important privacy concerns. While this information is crucial for emergency responders to locate and assist callers in need quickly, it is essential to implement measures that protect the privacy of individuals and prevent unauthorized access or misuse of the data. Enterprises must ensure that the location information collected and stored for E911 purposes is protected against unauthorized access, use, or disclosure. This includes implementing appropriate security controls, such as encryption, access controls, and data retention policies, to safeguard sensitive location data.

Conclusion

In this chapter, we explored the essential aspects of security, compliance, and recovery in Cisco UC environments.

We started by discussing the importance of TLS and certificates in securing communications and the role of PKI in establishing trust. Next, we looked at secure communication protocols such as TLS, SRTP, and SIPS, which protect sensitive information in UC systems. We also covered security measures, system hardening techniques, and best practices for preventing toll fraud.

We then highlighted the importance of a comprehensive disaster recovery strategy, including regular backups, failover mechanisms, and thorough testing. By implementing robust recovery measures, organizations can minimize downtime and ensure the availability of vital communication channels.

We then discussed the importance of complying with data privacy regulations and industry standards, such as GDPR and HIPAA, when managing Cisco UC solutions. Additionally, we emphasized the critical role of emergency calling in Cisco UC, discussing technical considerations and best practices for accurate location information and proper call routing for emergency services. We also examined E911 regulatory requirements and implementation details in the United States.

In the next chapter, we will explore troubleshooting techniques and tools to effectively manage day-to-day UC operations and ensure optimal performance of the collaboration infrastructure.

Multiple Choice Question

1. What is the purpose of Transport Layer Security (TLS) in Cisco UC environments?
    a. To encrypt media traffic between endpoints
    b. To secure SIP signaling traffic between UC components
    c. To authenticate users and grant access to UC services
    d. To prioritize emergency calls over regular call traffic
2. Which of the following is NOT a key component of a comprehensive Disaster Recovery Plan (DRP) for Cisco UC?
    a. Risk assessment
    b. Business impact analysis
    c. Employee training and awareness
    d. Backup and replication strategies
3. What does the acronym SRTP stand for in the context of secure communication protocols?
    a. Secure Real-time Transport Protocol
    b. Session Initiation Protocol over TLS
    c. Signaling and RTP Transmission Protocol
    d. Secure Reliable Transport Protocol
4. Which data privacy regulation applies to organizations that process the personal data of European Union (EU) citizens?
    a. HIPAA
    b. GDPR
    c. CCPA
    d. PIPEDA
5. What is the purpose of the "SRTP Allowed" checkbox in the SIP trunk configuration on Cisco Unified Communications Manager (CUCM)?
    a. To enable SRTP for media encryption on the SIP trunk
    b. To allow the SIP trunk to fall back to RTP if the endpoints do not support SRTP

   c. To prioritize SRTP traffic over non-SRTP traffic on the SIP trunk

   d. Both a and b

6. What is the purpose of conducting regular testing and maintenance of a Disaster Recovery Plan (DRP)?

   a. To validate the effectiveness of the DRP and identify gaps

   b. To update the DRP to reflect changes in the UC environment

   c. To ensure that recovery procedures remain up to date

   d. All of the above

Answers

1. b
2. c
3. a
4. b
5. d
6. d

Further Reading

Same as the last chapter, explore the following topics on your own to improve your understanding and broaden your perspective.

- PKI, Certificates, and Certificate Attributes:
  - Dive deeper into Public Key Infrastructure (PKI) and its role in securing communications. Study the different attributes in certificates and their significance in authentication and encryption.
  - Investigate the specific certificate requirements for various UC components, such as Cisco Unified Communications Manager (CUCM), Cisco Expressway, and Cisco Meeting Server (CMS). Refer to the Cisco's doc for detailed information:
    - Maintain and Operate guides for CUCM 12.5
      https://www.cisco.com/c/en/us/td/docs/voice_ip_comm/cucm/security/12_5_1/cucm_b_security-guide-1251/cucm_b_security-guide-1251_chapter_011101.html

    - Expressway Configuration guide for 12.5 or 14.0

      https://www.cisco.com/c/en/us/td/docs/voice_ip_comm/expressway/config_guide/X12-5/exwy_b_certificate-creation-use-deployment-guide.html

      https://www.cisco.com/c/en/us/td/docs/voice_ip_comm/expressway/config_guide/X14-0/cert_creation_use/exwy_b_cisco-expressway-certificate-creation-and-use-deployment-guide-x14-0.html

    - CMS certificate guidelines

      https://www.cisco.com/c/dam/en/us/td/docs/conferencing/ciscoMeetingServer/Deployment_Guide/Version-3-5/Certificate-Guidelines-for-all-Deployments-3-5.pdf

      https://www.cisco.com/c/en/us/support/docs/conferencing/meeting-server/214618-generate-csr-and-apply-certificates-to-c.html

- Security Measures in UC Components:
    - Explore the various security features and configurations available in different UC components.
    - Consult the Cisco documentation for each product to gain insights into the specific security measures and best practices.
- Toll Fraud Prevention:
    - Analyze the spam call hits on your Expressway-E and understand how spam calls attempt to exploit dial plans for toll fraud.
    - Review your baseline PSTN usage and engage with your PSTN/SIP provider to discuss the mechanisms they have in place for anomaly detection and alerting, such as unexpected call volumes through your PSTN connection.
- Disaster Recovery Planning (DRP):
    - Assess your organization's current DRP strategy and documentation.
    - If no documented DRP exists, create a sample plan to understand the process and considerations involved.
    - Investigate the scheduled backups, their storage locations, and the documentation of the backup process.
    - Conduct a scenario analysis to determine the potential data loss in the event of an infrastructure failure or ransomware attack, and evaluate if the Recovery Point Objective (RPO) aligns with your organization's tolerance for data loss.

- Regulatory Compliance:
    - Research the specific regulatory requirements applicable to your organization based on its global presence and industry.
    - Examine the different policies and controls in place to ensure compliance with relevant regulations.
    - Consider the impact of regulations on UC deployments and the necessary steps to maintain compliance.
- Emergency Calling:
    - Investigate the emergency calling requirements for your UC deployment across different geographical locations.
    - Compare and contrast emergency calling functionality in enterprise environments with consumer applications such as Uber, Android, and iOS.
    - Study how location sharing and emergency calls are implemented in these consumer apps to gain insights into user experience and functionality. You can research on your own or refer to the following for Uber, Android, and Apple.

      https://www.uber.com/en-IN/blog/ubers-emergency-button-and-the-technologies-behind-it/

      https://support.google.com/android/answer/3467281#turn-location-on-off

      https://www.apple.com/legal/privacy/data/en/location-services/

CHAPTER 11
Troubleshooting Techniques and Tools

Introduction

Effective troubleshooting is a critical skill for anyone working with technology, whether you are an operations engineer responsible for maintaining and supporting production systems or an architect deploying new solutions. Troubleshooting is not just about resolving issues; it is about doing so efficiently, minimizing downtime, and preventing future occurrences.

In this chapter, we will explore Cisco's recommended troubleshooting framework, which provides a systematic approach to problem-solving. We will use real-world examples to illustrate how this framework can be applied to diagnose and resolve issues efficiently in Cisco Collaboration environments. Beyond the standard framework, we will also discuss practical tips and techniques to enhance your troubleshooting skills and help you navigate complex scenarios.

Finally, we will introduce you to various powerful tools designed specifically for troubleshooting Cisco Collaboration technologies.

Structure

In this chapter, we will discuss the following topics:

- Troubleshooting Approach
  - Cisco's Troubleshooting Framework
  - Real-World Insights (Beyond the Framework)
- Cisco Collaboration Troubleshooting Tools

Troubleshooting Approach

Developing strong troubleshooting skills is not about memorizing a list of common issues and their solutions. Instead, it is about cultivating a systematic approach to problem-solving. This approach involves breaking down complex problems into smaller, more manageable components, gathering relevant information, and applying a logical process of elimination to identify the root cause.

Fundamental technical knowledge is the foundation of effective troubleshooting. You must first understand how the technology works to diagnose and resolve issues. This understanding allows you to ask the right questions, identify potential points of failure, and determine the most appropriate course of action. Without a solid grasp of the underlying principles, you will be working in the dark, relying on guesswork and trial and error.

In addition to a systematic approach and technical knowledge, specialized tools can significantly expedite the troubleshooting process. These tools, such as log analyzers, network monitoring software, and diagnostic utilities, provide valuable insights into system behavior and performance. Although these tools may vary slightly for different technologies, we will focus on Cisco Collaboration-related tools in this chapter. They can help you quickly identify anomalies, pinpoint the source of problems, and gather the evidence needed to support your conclusions.

Cisco's Troubleshooting Framework

To help you approach troubleshooting systematically, Cisco has developed a framework that can be applied to any technical issue, including those related to Cisco Unified Communications (UC). This framework consists of eight steps:

1. **Define the Problem**: Start by clearly stating the issue. Identify the specific symptoms you are observing and list the potential causes that could be contributing to the problem. This step helps you focus your efforts and ensures that everyone involved is on the same page.

2. **Gather Facts**: Next, collect as much relevant information as possible. This may involve talking to affected users, consulting with other administrators, or using diagnostic tools to gather data. The more facts you have, the easier it will be to narrow down the list of potential causes.

3. **Consider Possibilities**: With the facts, start eliminating potential causes that do not fit the evidence. This process of elimination helps you focus on the most likely culprits, saving time and effort in the troubleshooting process.

4. **Create an Action Plan**: Once you have identified the most probable cause, develop a plan to address it. The key here is to change only one variable at a time. This approach makes it easier to determine whether a particular change has resolved the issue or if you need to try something else.

5. **Implement the Action Plan**: Put your plan into action, carefully following each step and testing along the way to see if the symptoms disappear. Be sure

to document any changes you make so you can refer back to them later if needed.

6. **Observe Results**: As you implement your action plan, monitor the results using the same fact-gathering methods you used in Step 2. This will help you determine whether your changes are having the desired effect or if you need to adjust your approach.

7. **Verify Problem Resolution**: Analyze the results of your actions to determine if the problem has been resolved. If the symptoms have disappeared and the system functions normally, you can consider the issue resolved.

8. **Record Findings**: If the problem persists, document your findings, including the steps you have taken, the results you have observed, and any new information you have gathered. Then, loop back to step 4 and create a new action plan based on the next most likely cause. If the problem is resolved, document the root cause and the steps taken to resolve it for future reference.

By following this systematic approach, you can confidently tackle even the most complex Cisco UC issues, knowing you are working through the problem logically and efficiently.

Real-World Insights (Beyond the Framework)

While Cisco's troubleshooting framework provides a solid foundation for approaching technical issues, it is important to recognize that its application may vary depending on the context and situation. The core principles remain the same, but how you navigate the steps can differ based on factors such as your role, the environment you are working in, and the information available to you.

For example, suppose you are part of an internal IT team responsible for managing the infrastructure for a specific service. In that case, you would likely have access to extensive documentation and insider knowledge about the setup and configuration. You may also be aware of recent changes or have access to internal change management tools and historical data on similar issues. This additional context can help you move through the troubleshooting steps more quickly, as you have a better starting point for identifying potential causes.

However, even in this scenario, it is crucial not to let familiarity lead to overconfidence. Just because an issue seems similar to one you have encountered before does not mean the root cause is the same. Skipping the fact-gathering and diagnostic steps can lead to incorrect assumptions and waste of time. Always approach each problem systematically, even if you think you know the answer.

If you work for a consulting company or provide shared technical support to multiple customers, you may have limited context and less access to internal information. In these situations, strictly adhering to the troubleshooting framework is even more important. Gathering as much relevant information as possible becomes critical to understanding the unique environment and identifying the root cause of the issue.

Regardless of the context, one of the most important aspects of troubleshooting is working with a comprehensive data set. While asking questions and gathering information from users is valuable, collecting facts from the systems is equally important. This approach allows you to cross-reference user-provided information with objective data, ensuring a more complete picture of the problem. Relying solely on user input can have its drawbacks. Users may not remember all the details, especially if the issue was intermittent or occurred in the past. They may also be busy or unresponsive, leading to delays in the troubleshooting process. By proactively gathering system data, you can continue progressing even if user input is limited or slow to arrive.

Once the issue has been identified and understood, it is important to provide a temporary workaround to minimize downtime and user impact if the fix requires significant time. After thorough analysis, the focus should shift to implementing a permanent fix and determining how to prevent the same issue from occurring in the future. If the same problem has arisen recently, it should be analyzed as a problem ticket to identify the root cause and necessary actions.

One of the worst approaches to fixing an ongoing issue is changing various settings without identifying the root cause, hoping the problem will resolve itself. This can lead to unexpected consequences and create new issues down the line. When working on different issues, the best practice is to collect logs from various components, analyze them, and understand what is happening within the system. This analysis should point to the potential source of the issue unless it indicates that a recent change to the system or architecture is causing the problem. In such cases, the decision to revert or modify the change should be based on facts and evidence. Every action has consequences, and it is crucial to understand how each action will impact the service.

Let us discuss an example to help you understand Cisco's troubleshooting framework and other practical tips.

Example: A user reports via the helpdesk that they cannot make any calls from their phone.

1. **Define the Problem**
    a. **Symptom**: The user is unable to make calls from their phone.
    b. **Potential causes**: Phone configuration issues, network connectivity problems, call control system failures, or user error.
2. **Gather Facts**
    a. Was the phone working before? If yes, when was it last known to be working?

   b. Are other users in the same location or department experiencing similar issues?
   c. Have there been any recent changes to the user's phone configuration or the network?
   d. Is the phone registered and showing the correct status on the call control system (CUCM)?
   e. Collect logs from the phone, network devices, and call control system for analysis.
3. **Consider Possibilities**
   a. Based on the gathered facts, narrow down the potential causes.
   b. If the issue started after a recent configuration change, that might be the culprit.
   c. If other users are experiencing similar issues, it could be a network or call control system problem.
   d. If the phone is not registering correctly, focus on network connectivity and call control system settings. You can also look at the CUCM logs and check each step of the Phone registration flow.
4. **Create an Action Plan**
   a. Prioritize the most likely causes based on the facts and possibilities.
   b. Develop a step-by-step plan to test and address each potential cause.
   c. Ensure the plan changes only one variable at a time to isolate the root cause effectively.
5. **Implement the Action Plan**
   a. Execute the action plan, testing after each change to determine if the issue is resolved.
   b. If a temporary workaround is needed, implement it to minimize downtime while working on a permanent fix.
   c. Keep detailed notes of the actions taken and their results.
6. **Observe Results**
   a. After each change, test the phone to see if the user can make calls successfully.
   b. Monitor the phone and call control system logs to verify that the issue has been resolved.
   c. Confirm with the user that they are able to make calls without any problems.

7. **Verify Problem Resolution**
    a. If the user can make calls and the logs show no further issues, consider the problem resolved.
    b. If the issue persists, revisit the gathered facts and consider other possibilities.
8. **Document Findings**
    a. Record the root cause of the problem and the steps taken to resolve it.
    b. Update any relevant knowledge bases or troubleshooting guides to help other team members resolve similar issues more efficiently in the future.
    c. If the same issue has occurred recently, analyze it as a problem ticket to identify the underlying cause and prevent future occurrences.

By following Cisco's structured troubleshooting framework and applying practical tips, you can effectively resolve issues like the one in this example. This systematic approach helps minimize downtime, improve problem-solving efficiency, and prevent the recurrence of similar issues in the future.

While having a solid troubleshooting methodology is essential, access to the right tools can significantly streamline the process and provide valuable insights. In the next section, we will explore some of the key tools available for troubleshooting the Cisco Collaboration environment.

Cisco Collaboration Troubleshooting Tools

Maintaining a high level of uptime and meeting business SLAs in a Cisco Collaboration environment requires a proactive approach and a well-designed monitoring strategy. Even with redundancy built into the system, failures can still occur due to various factors. To stay ahead of potential issues, it is crucial to have observability at both the system and service levels.

Monitoring tools come in different forms, each with its benefits and limitations. SNMP-based tools like SolarWinds provide basic monitoring capabilities for Cisco Collaboration components, such as up/down status and a few other metrics. However, their scope is limited. Syslog or log aggregation tools can offer more detailed insights, while custom scripts using APIs can be used to check specific aspects of the system.

In an on-premises environment, a Collaboration service is typically composed of multiple components working together. It is important to note that rarely a single tool can monitor the service end-to-end from a user experience perspective. For example, monitoring CUCM, its services, phone status, and gateway status does not necessarily guarantee that a call from a user to the PSTN will work seamlessly. In this context, third-party tools are available in the market to simulate PSTN call testing end-to-end, providing a more comprehensive view of the service.

Implementing these monitoring tools can help IT proactively identify issues before users or the business reports them. In reactive scenarios, these tools can also help minimize troubleshooting efforts and reduce downtime by providing valuable data and insights.

While we would not cover every available tool in detail, let us explore some popular Cisco tools that can help troubleshoot Collaboration issues.

1. **Dialed Number Analyzer (DNA)** is a powerful tool in CUCM that helps troubleshoot call routing issues by simulating call flows. For example, suppose a user reports that calls to a specific extension are not reaching the intended destination. In that case, DNA can be used to trace the call flow and identify any misconfigurations in the dial plan or route patterns. This tool is handy when dealing with complex dial plans or onboarding new users or departments.

   As you can see in *Figure 11.1*, DNA is accessible from the Cisco Unified Serviceability page of CUCM. It is located under the Tools menu, making it easily accessible for troubleshooting purposes.

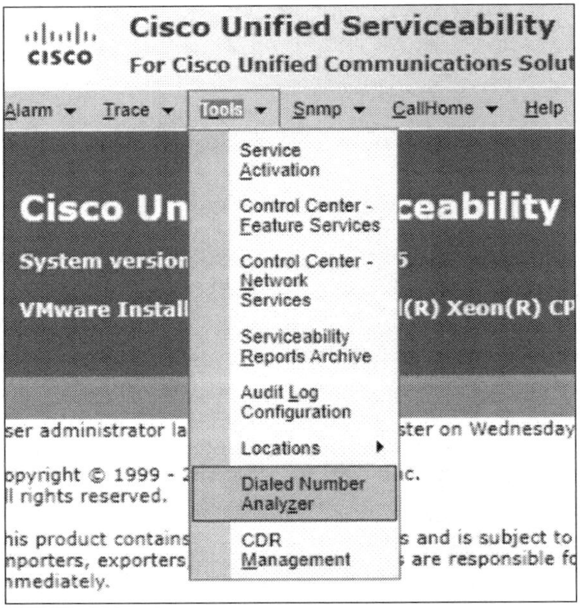

Figure 11.1: *Tools- Dialed Number Analyzer*

When you click on the Dialed Number Analyzer (DNA) option from the Cisco Unified Serviceability page, it opens a new page with various analysis options.

As shown in *Figure* 11.2, the Analysis dropdown menu provides several choices, each designed to help troubleshoot specific aspects of call routing. The **"Phones"** option allows you to analyze call flows originating from a particular phone, while the **"Gateways"** option focuses on call flows through specific gateways. The **"Trunks"** option helps examine call routing via trunks, and the **"Dump DA Information"** provides detailed diagnostic information about the digit analysis process. Lastly, the **"Multiple Analyzer"** option enables you to run multiple call flow simulations simultaneously. Let us take a closer look at the **"Analyzer"** option, which is the most commonly used tool for troubleshooting call routing issues.

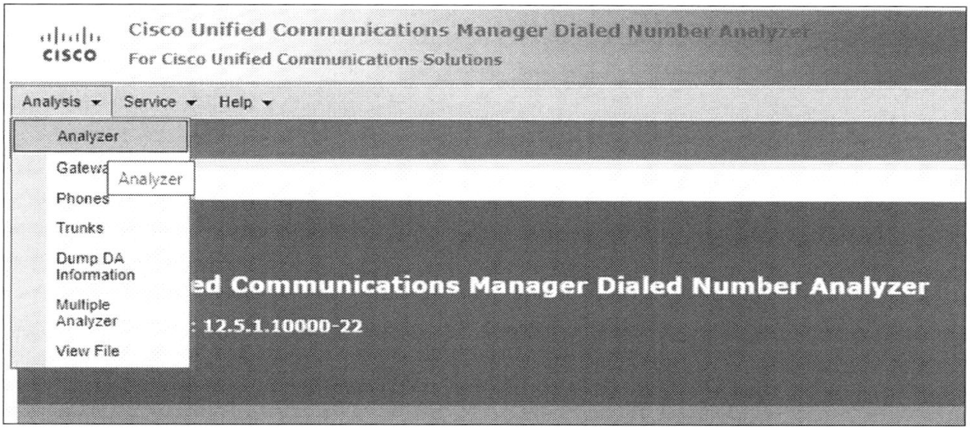

Figure 11.2: *DNA - Analysis - Analyzer tool*

In *Figure* 11.3, we can see a more detailed view of the DNA results after running the Analyzer. The red box highlights some key information that helps in interpreting the results and troubleshooting call routing issues. The **"Calling Party"** field shows the number or extension of the party initiating the call. In this example, it is set to **"1000"**. The **"Dialed Digits"** field displays the digits dialed by the calling party. Here, we can see **"911234567890",** which represents a destination number or a specific sequence of digits to test the call flow. The **"Calling Search Space"** dropdown allows you to select the appropriate calling search space for the simulated call. This determines the partitions and route patterns that will be considered during the digit analysis process. The **"Device Time Zone"** setting lets you specify the time zone for the simulated call, which can be relevant when dealing with time-based call routing rules or restrictions. Finally, the **"Time"** field allows you to set a specific time for the simulated call, which can be useful for testing time-of-day routing rules. By providing these input parameters, DNA can simulate a call flow based on the specific conditions you want to test. The results will show you the step-by-step process of how the dialed digits are analyzed, transformed, and routed based on the configured dial plan, partitions, and route patterns. This information helps pinpoint any misconfigurations or issues in the call routing logic, making it easier to troubleshoot and resolve problems.

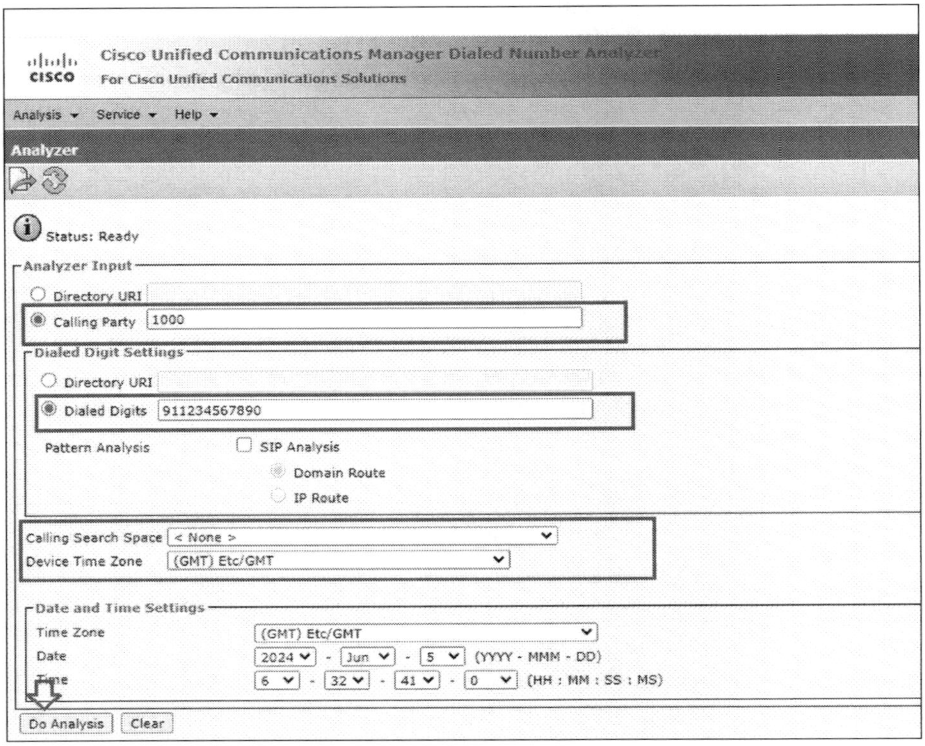

Figure 11.3: *DNA - Using Analyzer tool*

2. **Route Plan Report** in CUCM provides a comprehensive overview of the system's dial plan, including route patterns, route lists, and route groups. This is useful when optimizing the dial plan or identifying unused or misconfigured route patterns. For instance, the Route Plan Report can help identify overlapping or redundant patterns.
   The route plan report is available from the Cisco Unified CM Administration page in CUCM.

3. **CLI Commands** are available on CUCM, CUC, UCCX, and Expressway and are used to gather system information, monitor performance, and troubleshoot issues. For example, on CUCM, the **`"utils dbreplication runtimestate"`** command can be used to check the database replication status between cluster nodes, helping identify any replication issues. CLI commands are handy for advanced troubleshooting when GUI access is limited or unavailable.
   You will find the CUCM cli reference guide here. Similarly, you can also look for different product cli reference guides.

https://www.cisco.com/c/en/us/support/unified-communications/unified-communications-manager-callmanager/products-command-reference-list.html

4. **Logs** are available on all products. They provide information about system events, errors, and warnings, which is essential for understanding system behavior and identifying potential issues. RTMT is commonly used to download the logs from CUCM, CUC, and UCCX, but it can also be done using **`cli`** commands.

   By default, logs may not be detailed and only contain errors. As shown in *Figure 11.4*, You can change the trace level for CUCM from the Cisco unified serviceability page in CUCM under Trace Configuration for each node/service. If these are set to Detailed, they contain most information but can consume lots of disk space and impact system performance.

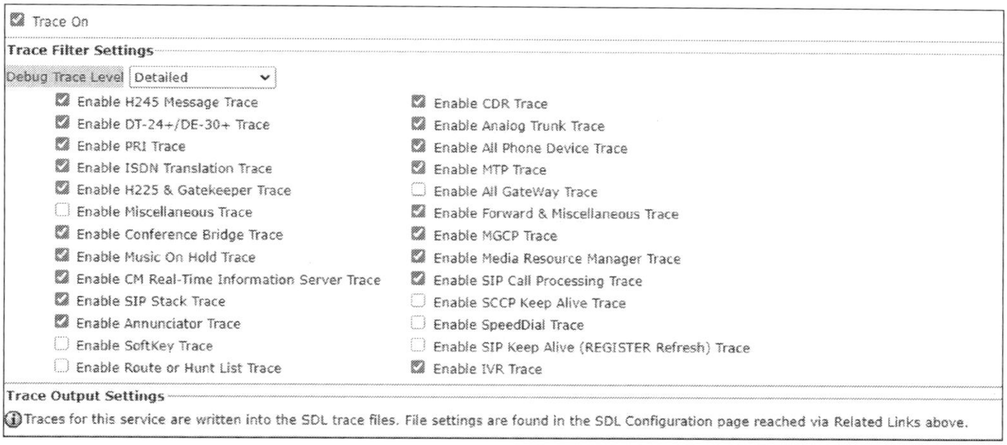

Figure 11.4: *CUCM detailed traces*

   For Expressway, you can download and see the logs from **`Status > Logs`** in GUI. Debugs and packet capture can be enabled from **`Expressway GUI maintenance> Diagnostics > Diagnostic logging.`**

5. **Real-Time Monitoring Tool (RTMT)** is a versatile Java-based application designed to help administrators monitor and manage Cisco Unified Communications Manager (CUCM) and Cisco Unity Connection (CUC) environments. RTMT provides a user-friendly interface that offers real-time insights into the health and performance of your Cisco UC system.

   To use RTMT, you first need to download it from the Cisco Unified Communications Manager administration interface and install it on your PC. When you launch RTMT, you will be prompted to enter the IP address or hostname of the CUCM or CUC server you want to monitor and your authentication credentials. Upon connecting to the server, RTMT establishes a link and collects real-time data, performance metrics, and logs.

Some of the key features and benefits of RTMT include:

- Real-time system health monitoring, including CPU usage, memory consumption, and disk space utilization.
- Performance monitoring of call volume, call quality, and network statistics.
- Customizable alerts and notifications for proactive issue detection and response.
- Comprehensive reporting and diagnostic tools include the Call Quality Summary, Alert Summary, Trace and Log Central, and Syslog Viewer.

Now let us connect to RTMT and explore its interface and capabilities.

As you see in *Figure* 11.5, the RTMT main page provides a user-friendly navigation menu on the left side, allowing you to access various monitoring and management features.

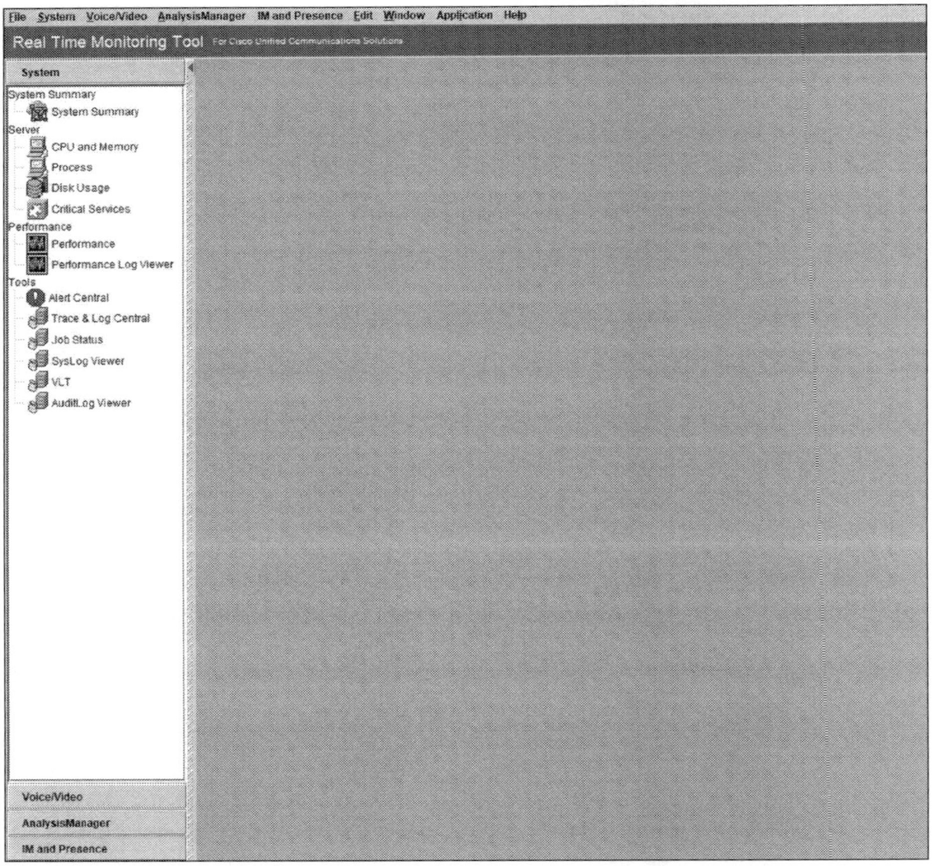

Figure 11.5: *Cisco RTMT Main page*

Under the **"Voice/Video"** section, you can access a range of tools specifically designed for monitoring voice and video services in your Cisco UC environment, as shown in the following *Figure 11.6*.

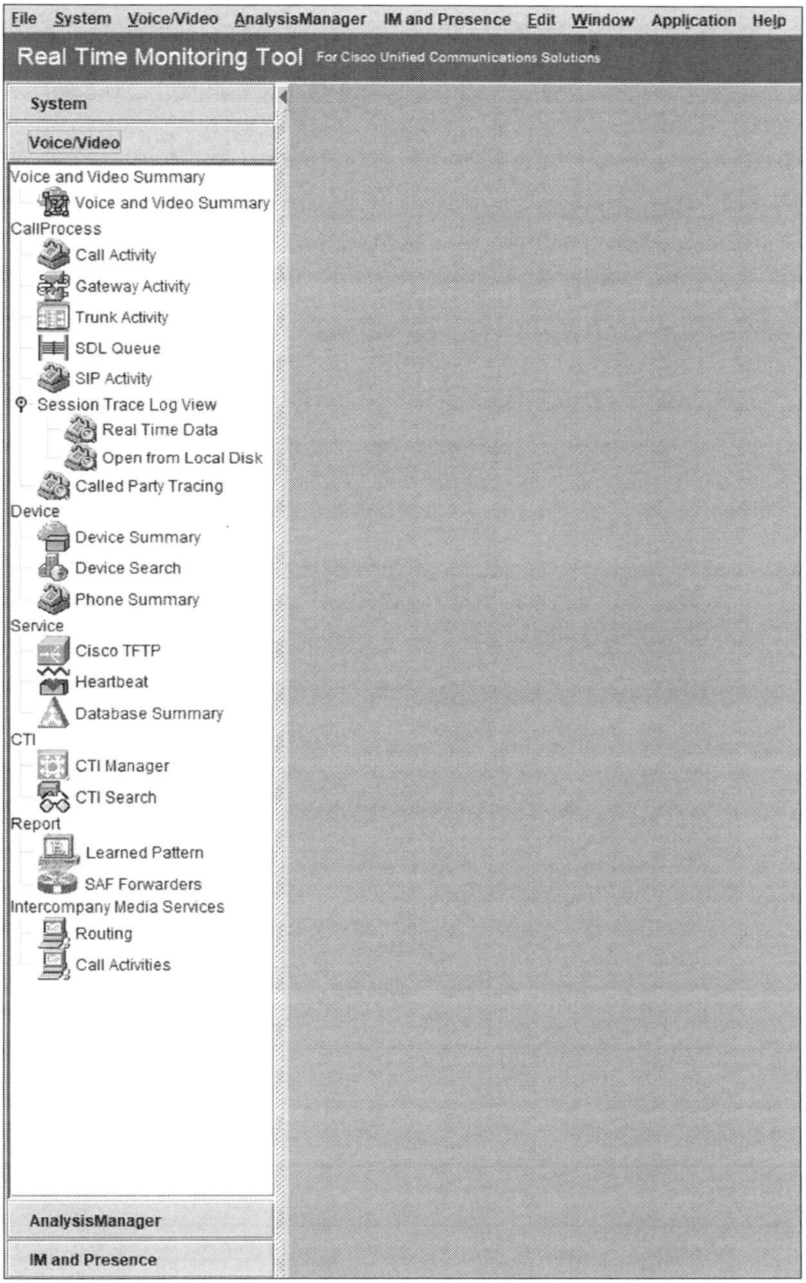

Figure 11.6: *Cisco RTMT Voice Video page*

In the "**Voice/Video**" section, you can monitor call activity, gateway activity, trunk activity, and more. This allows you to gain real-time insights into the performance and health of your voice and video services.

Lastly, let us take a closer look at the process of collecting Cisco Unified Communications Manager (CUCM) logs using RTMT. As shown in the *Figure* 11.7, RTMT allows you to collect various types of logs from your CUCM servers, including trace files, crash dumps, and install logs.

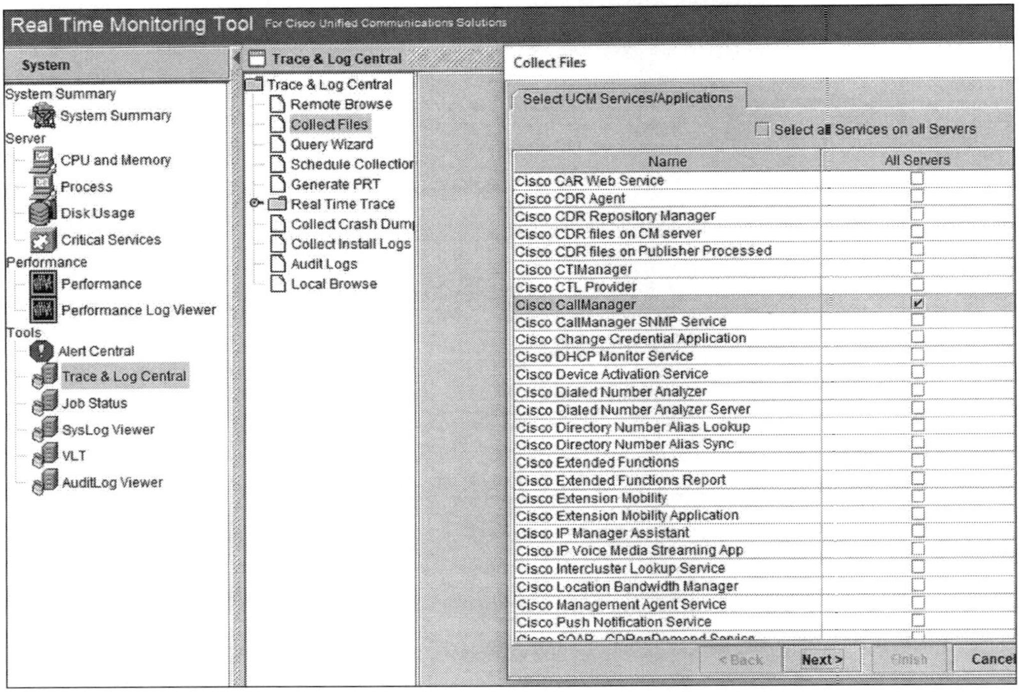

***Figure* 11.7**: *Cisco RTMT Collecting logs*

6. **Cisco Bug Search** tool allows you to search for known bugs and issues across Cisco's product portfolio, including Cisco Collaboration products. To use the Bug Search Tool, simply navigate to the Cisco Bug Search page (https://bst.cloudapps.cisco.com/bugsearch/) and enter relevant keywords, product names, or bug IDs to search for specific issues. The tool provides detailed information about each bug, including its status, severity, and available workarounds or fixes. If the URL to the tool has been changed, search for the Cisco bug search tool online using a search engine to find the most up-to-date link.

   By leveraging the Bug Search Tool, administrators can:

   - Check if an encountered problem is a known issue with a documented workaround or resolution.

- Stay informed about the latest software updates, patches, and bug fixes for their Cisco Collaboration products.
- Proactively address potential issues by identifying and resolving known bugs before they impact their environment.

7. **Collaboration Solutions Analyzer (CSA)** is a powerful web-based tool provided by Cisco that offers a suite of diagnostic and troubleshooting utilities for Cisco Collaboration products. CSA is designed to help administrators and support engineers quickly identify and resolve issues in their Cisco UC environment. To access CSA, you need to log in with your Cisco account. As the URL for CSA may change over time, it is recommended that you look for "Collaboration Solutions Analyzer" using a search engine to find the most up-to-date link.

   CSA consists of five main tools, each serving a specific purpose in the troubleshooting process:

   - **Log Analyzer:** This tool allows you to upload logs from your collaboration devices and automatically detect and help troubleshoot issues. The Log Analyzer can pinpoint problems related to call setup, registration, and media processing by analyzing log files. It provides a streamlined and efficient way to diagnose issues without manual log analysis.
   - **CollabEdge Validator**: The CollabEdge Validator is designed to speed up your Mobile and Remote Access (MRA) feature deployment or troubleshooting process. It offers a step-by-step validation wizard that guides you through the configuration and helps identify potential issues. This tool is handy when setting up MRA for the first time or experiencing problems with MRA connectivity.
   - **SRV Checker**: The SRV Checker tool helps you validate your public domain's DNS service records and connectivity for various collaboration services, such as Cisco Webex, Cisco Unified Communications Manager, and Cisco Expressway. By ensuring that your DNS records are correctly configured, you can avoid issues related to service discovery and connectivity.
   - **B2B Call Tester**: This tool enables you to test inbound and outbound calls to and from your collaboration deployment. It is particularly useful for verifying the proper functioning of your Cisco UC system's external communication capabilities. The B2B Call Tester helps identify potential call routing, signaling, and media handling issues by simulating real-world call scenarios.
   - **UC Crashdump Analyzer**: The UC Crashdump Analyzer provides root cause analysis (RCA) for application crashes on various Cisco Collaboration products, including CUCM, IM&P, CUC, and UCCX (running on the UCOS platform). By analyzing crash dump files, this tool helps pinpoint the

specific cause of application failures, enabling administrators to take appropriate corrective actions.

Using these tools, administrators can speed up troubleshooting, find and fix problems faster, and keep their Cisco Collaboration systems healthy and performing well. Combined with a step-by-step troubleshooting approach, these tools help administrators tackle different issues and keep the user experience running smoothly.

Conclusion

In this chapter, we explored the essential aspects of troubleshooting Cisco Collaboration environments. We began by exploring Cisco's recommended troubleshooting framework, which consists of eight key steps: defining the problem, gathering facts, considering possibilities, creating an action plan, implementing the plan, observing results, verifying problem resolution, and documenting findings. By following this structured approach and applying it to real-world examples, you can effectively diagnose and resolve issues in your collaboration infrastructure.

In addition to the standard framework, we discussed practical tips and techniques to enhance your troubleshooting skills. These included the importance of understanding the fundamentals of collaboration technology, leveraging past experiences, and adapting the framework to different contexts. We also emphasized the value of providing temporary workarounds to minimize downtime while working on permanent solutions.

We introduced a range of tools specifically designed for Cisco Collaboration technologies to support your troubleshooting efforts.

In the next chapter, we will explore the available APIs and automation in Cisco Collaboration and discover how these technologies can streamline operations and reduce manual efforts.

Further Reading

Same as the last chapter, explore the following topics on your own to improve your understanding and broaden your perspective.

- Pick a few past or ongoing issues in your Collab environment and run them through the Troubleshooting framework discussed in this chapter. If you do not manage the operations, you can skip this point.
- Use the Dialed number analyzer and Route plan report in CUCM and check them against your existing dial plan. You can also investigate similar functionality in the Expressway.
- Find cli commands for CUCM for the following:

    - How do you check the database replication status in the CUCM cluster?
    - How do you check which services are up and running and which services are stopped?
    - How do you restart a particular service from the CLI?
    - How do you check the version in active and inactive partitions?
- Do the following using RTMT:
    - Check active alarms, disk space, CPU, and memory information for CUCM and CUC.
    - Collect logs from CUCM for the Call manager service for all nodes in the cluster. Only collect logs for the last two hours.
- Capture debugs from Expressway.
- Use CSA to analyze the logs you collected from CUCM and the Expressway.
- Search for open bugs in your current CUCM version or on CUCM 12.5.1.
    - You can also search by product name.

CHAPTER 12
Automation and APIs in Cisco Collaboration

Introduction

In this chapter, we will explore the role of automation and APIs in Cisco Collaboration products. We will start by discussing the benefits of automation and the importance of APIs in enabling it. Then, we will dive into the specific APIs available for various Cisco Collaboration products, including Webex Devices, SBCs, Voice Gateways, Cisco Meeting Server, Unified Communications Manager, Expressway, and Webex. We will also cover how developers can access resources and learn more about these APIs through Cisco DevNet.

Structure

In this chapter, we will discuss the following topics:

- Introduction to Automation and APIs
- APIs in Cisco Collaboration Products
    - Webex Devices
    - SBC and Voice Gateway
    - Cisco Meeting Server
    - Cisco Unified Communications Manager (CUCM)
    - Cisco Expressway
    - Webex

Introduction to Automation and APIs

Automation streamlines processes reduces manual effort, and enhances overall efficiency. By leveraging automation, IT teams can simplify complex tasks, minimize human error, and free up valuable time to focus on more strategic initiatives.

There are various benefits of automating repetitive tasks; a few key benefits are the following:

- **Efficiency**: Automation handles tasks more swiftly than human counterparts, especially repetitive or bulk operations.
- **Accuracy**: With precise programming, automation reduces the chances of errors that are common in manual processes, especially in repetitive and tedious tasks.
- **Scheduling**: Automation allows for the scheduling of tasks during off-peak hours, which minimizes operational disruptions.

Application Programming Interfaces (APIs) are crucial for enabling automation in Cisco Collaboration. An API is a set of rules and protocols that allows different software applications to communicate and exchange data with each other. In simpler terms, APIs provide a structured way for developers to interact with a system, much like a menu in a restaurant, which provides a structured way for customers to order their food. This structured interaction enables developers to retrieve information, perform actions, and integrate functionality into their own applications.

Traditionally, administrators and users interacted with collaboration systems through graphical user interfaces (GUIs). While GUIs provide a user-friendly way to configure and manage the system, they have limitations when it comes to automation and integration. APIs allow programmatic access to the system, enabling developers to automate tasks, build custom integrations, and extend the functionality of the collaboration platform.

Cisco Collaboration products support various API types; a single product often offers multiple APIs. This allows developers flexibility in how they interface with these systems. However, having an API available does not guarantee that all functions can be performed through it. The specific actions that can be conducted via an API depends on what the vendor chooses to expose through their software and document accordingly. To support different API types and features in products, collaboration vendors like Cisco need to do the following:

- Vendors need to create clear and well-documented API endpoints and schemas. This documentation is crucial for developers to understand available functions, access methods, and response formats.
- Implement secure authentication and authorization mechanisms.
- Provide Software Development Kits(SDKs) and libraries in popular programming languages. These kits may contain libraries that abstract some of the complexities involved in direct API calls, making development more straightforward.
- Offer comprehensive documentation, code samples, and developer resources.
- Continuous support and maintenance for APIs to ensure they function

correctly, remain secure, and are updated with new features or necessary fixes.

There are various types of APIs available, each with its own characteristics and use cases. Let us take a closer look at some of the most popular API types in the industry.

- **Representational State Transfer (REST) APIs**: REST is a widely adopted architectural style for designing networked applications. It uses HTTP methods (GET, POST, PUT, DELETE) to interact with resources and exchange data in lightweight formats such as JSON or XML. Authentication in REST APIs is commonly done using API keys, which are like passwords that allow access to the API, or OAuth, which is a secure way to grant access to your data without sharing your password, or JSON Web Tokens (JWT), which are a type of token that is used to authenticate requests.
- **Simple Object Access Protocol (SOAP) APIs**: SOAP is a protocol that uses XML for exchanging structured data between systems. SOAP APIs define a set of rules for communication, including message format, encoding, and processing. Authentication in SOAP APIs often uses WS-Security, which supports various authentication mechanisms, such as username/password, X.509 certificates, and security tokens.
    - **Administrative XML (AXML) APIs**: AXL is a SOAP-based API provided by Cisco for managing and configuring Cisco Unified Communications Manager (CUCM).

Let us explore the specific APIs available for different Cisco Collaboration products and how they enable automation and integration capabilities.

APIs in Cisco Collaboration Products

The Cisco Developer portal at developer.cisco.com is a practical starting point. This resource is handy for those looking to automate operations or develop custom applications within the Cisco ecosystem.

On Cisco DevNet (developer.cisco.com), developers can find API documentation, SDK documentation, and data models to understand how to interact with Cisco's collaboration products programmatically. Cisco also offers interactive tutorials, hands-on exercises, example code implementations, and solutions in the Code Exchange, demonstrating how to use Cisco's APIs in real-world scenarios. Additionally, developers can access a testing environment with pre-built Cisco platforms, APIs, SDKs, and solutions for experimentation and development.

While access to all the resources is free, some activities, like labbing, may require a login. You can log in using your Cisco credentials or a Google, GitHub, or Webex account.

Now, let us look at some of the specific APIs available for Cisco's collaboration products.

Webex Devices

In *Chapter 6, Media Resources, Conferencing, and AV Solutions*, we briefly introduced the APIs available for Cisco Webex Devices. In this section, we will focus more on the xAPI and its role in automating operational tasks. xAPI supports both command-line and HTTP-based commands, enabling developers to integrate these devices into automated workflows.

xAPI provides four primary interaction mechanisms with Cisco video devices:

- `Command`: Execute actions on the device, such as dialing a number, adjusting the volume, or muting the microphone. These are direct commands that affect how the device operates in real time.
- `Status`: Access read-only state values that indicate the system's current condition or settings. This includes information like whether the system is in a call, the current volume level, or the connection status.
- `Config`: Modify permanent system settings such as the device's name, default system volume, and other preferences that persist after the device is restarted or turned off.
- `Event`: Receive notifications about specific incidents that occur at particular moments, such as when a meeting is starting or when a user interacts with a custom button. These are singular events that provide timely information.

xAPI enables various use cases, such as automating device settings across multiple devices, monitoring and alerting based on device statuses in real-time, adjusting configurations dynamically in response to specific situations or feedback, and implementing event-driven responses to automate actions based on specific events detected by the system.

You can find more details about xAPI here https://roomos.cisco.com/xapi

Alongside xAPI, the CE Deploy tool offers a no-code solution for performing bulk operations on Cisco Webex Devices. CE Deploy is a web-based application that simplifies the management and deployment of Cisco collaboration endpoints, whether they are registered to the Webex Cloud or Cisco Unified Communications Manager (CUCM).

You can find the CE-deploy here: https://github.com/voipnorm/CE-Deploy

As you see in *Figure 12.1*, its interface is divided into several sections, including Deployment, History, Documentation, Settings, Design, Support, and About. The Deployment section, which is currently selected, provides options to configure the deployment settings.

Under the Deployment section, administrators can specify the login credentials, such as the username and password, for accessing the devices. They can choose to perform operations on a single device, multiple devices using sites, or multiple devices using CSV files. On the right side of the interface, CE Deploy offers a range of tools and features. The Macro Factory tool allows administrators to add, delete, activate, and deactivate macros for the entire deployment. The Button Factory enables the creation and management of custom button panels on the endpoints.

Other tools include Touch Screenshot for capturing screenshots of the touch screen on the endpoint and Inventory for downloading the latest inventory data and collecting serial numbers for all endpoints and peripherals. It also allows you to simultaneously send xAPI commands to multiple Cisco devices and provides options to take backups and gather logs in bulk. This makes managing device settings and troubleshooting issues across a large network easier.

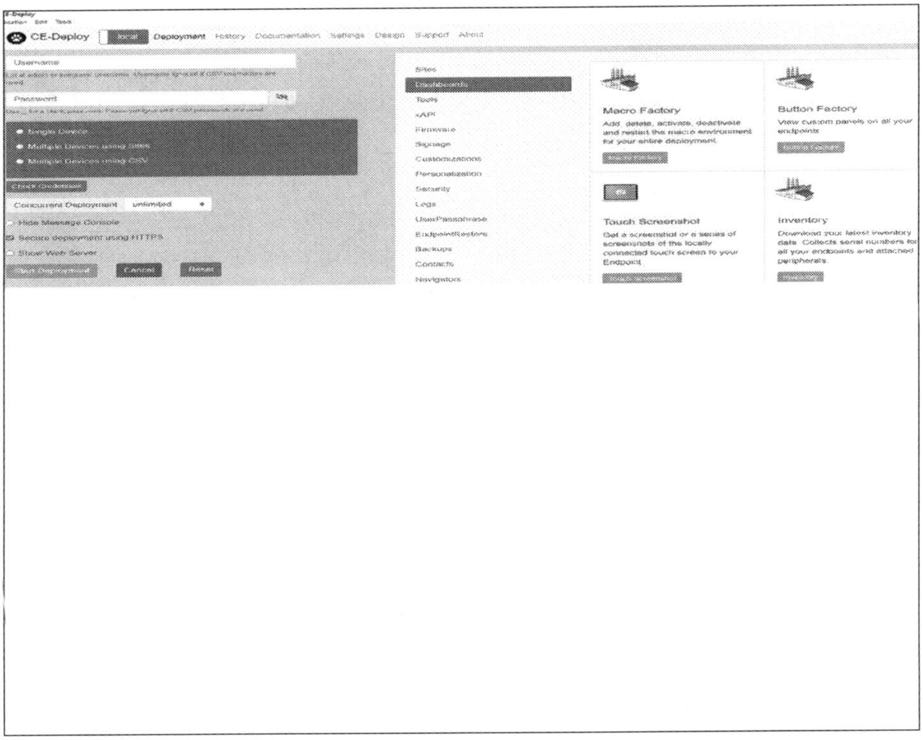

Figure 12.1: *CE Deploy tool interface*

SBC and Voice gateway

Cisco provides several automation options for Voice Gateways and SBCs based on IOS-XE, including model-driven programmability with NETCONF and RESTCONF and tool integrations like Ansible.

- **NETCONF and RESTCONF**: These protocols use YANG Data Models for structured configuration and management of network devices, ensuring transactional integrity where configurations are fully applied or rolled back in case of errors.
    - NETCONF is a standard protocol for managing network devices defined by the IETF. It uses XML-based data encoding and provides a structured way to retrieve, configure, and modify device settings.
    - RESTCONF is a REST-like protocol that provides a more modern and web-friendly approach to network device configuration and management. It uses HTTP methods (GET, POST, PUT, DELETE) to interact with the device's configuration and operational data, making integrating with existing tools and workflows easier. RESTCONF supports both XML and JSON data formats, providing flexibility in data representation and making it compatible with a wide range of programming languages and frameworks.
- **Ansible**: Unlike NETCONF and RESTCONF, which interact directly via APIs, Ansible automates IOS-XE devices using SSH and CLI commands. It is widely used for its simplicity and does not require direct API interactions, making it suitable for various automation scenarios without the complexity of dealing with APIs directly. Ansible's playbooks use a simple syntax written in YAML, which makes them easily understandable and writable even for those who might not have extensive programming expertise. This lowers the barrier to entry for automating network configurations and operations. Ansible does not require any agents to be installed on the network devices it manages. It communicates using standard protocols like SSH and uses existing CLI commands.

  Ansible's functionality is extended through modules that encapsulate specific network commands or operations. For Cisco IOS-XE, there are specific modules that allow for detailed and tailored management of devices. You can find more details here: https://developer.cisco.com/learning/modules/intro-ansible-iosxe/

Cisco Meeting Server

The CMS REST API offers a flexible and powerful way to interact with the Cisco Meeting Server. It enables developers to programmatically manage meetings, users, and call controls, enhancing custom integrations and automation capabilities. The REST API uses standard HTTP methods (`GET`, `POST`, `PUT`, `DELETE`) to perform operations, making it accessible and easy to integrate with existing systems and workflows.

Cisco provides a Postman collection specifically designed for the CMS REST API to simplify API testing and development. Postman is a popular API development tool that allows developers to explore, test, and document APIs efficiently.

The CMS Postman collection can be found on GitHub: https://github.com/ciscocms/cms-postman-collection

This collection includes a set of pre-defined API requests covering various CMS REST API functionalities. It is a valuable resource for developers, providing ready-to-use examples and templates for interacting with the API.

Cisco Unified Communications Manager (CUCM)

CUCM offers two primary APIs: the Administrative XML (AXL) API and the Serviceability XML (SXML) API. These APIs enable developers and administrators to automate various tasks, retrieve system information, and extend CUCM's functionality.

Administrative XML (AXL) API:

- The AXL API is a SOAP-based API that allows developers to perform administrative tasks and retrieve configuration data from CUCM.
- It provides a wide range of operations, including managing users, devices, lines, call routing, and more.
- With AXL, developers can automate provisioning tasks, synchronize CUCM data with external systems, and build custom applications that interact with CUCM.
- The AXL API uses XML payloads for request and response data and supports HTTPS for secure communication.
- Cisco provides the AXL API's detailed documentation and WSDL files, enabling developers to generate client code and integrate CUCM functionalities into their applications.

Serviceability XML (SXML) API:

- The SXML API is another SOAP-based API that focuses on serviceability and monitoring aspects of CUCM.
- It allows developers to retrieve real-time data and statistics related to system performance, call quality, device status, and so on.
- With SXML, developers can build monitoring and reporting tools, integrate CUCM data with network management systems, and gain insights into the health and usage of the Unified Communications system.
- Similar to AXL, the SXML API uses XML payloads and supports HTTPS for secure communication.

You can find more details about it here :

https://developer.cisco.com/site/axl/

https://developer.cisco.com/site/sxml/discover/overview/

Cisco Expressway

Cisco Expressway offers a robust REST API for integration and automation. The API allows developers to programmatically interact with the system to perform configuration, monitoring, and management tasks.

The Expressway REST API is self-documented using the RESTful API Modeling Language (RAML) version 0.8. RAML provides a structured and human-readable format for describing the API endpoints, request/response schemas, and authentication requirements.

Developers can access the RAML definitions for their Expressway system at **`https://<Expressway FQDN or IP address>/api/raml`**

The self-documentation makes it easier for developers to understand and integrate with the API, reducing the learning curve and development time.

For example, one thing you can do by API is fetch the active alarms from the expressway, which can help with monitoring. Any issues with the configuration or status usually lead to alarms in the expressway.

The base URL to access the Expressway REST API is **`http://<Expressway FQDN or IP address>/api.`** For example, to access the system information, use **`https://<Expressway FQDN or IP address>/api/provisioning/sysinfo.`**

Webex

Webex offers a comprehensive set of APIs that enable developers to integrate various aspects of the Webex platform into their applications, websites, and services. The unified and consistent nature of these APIs makes it easier for developers to access and utilize Webex functionality compared to on-premises deployments, where each component may have its own distinct API.

To use the Webex APIs, developers need a Webex account by Cisco Webex Common Identity (CI). Authentication is required to access the Webex APIs. When making API requests, an Authorization HTTP header must be included to identify the requesting user. The header must also include an access token, which can be a personal access token, a Bot token, or an OAuth token from an Integration or Guest Issuer application.

Personal access tokens are short-lived tokens for testing and development. They can be obtained from the Webex for Developers portal and expire 12 hours after login. For production applications, it is recommended to use an Integration and obtain an access token using the OAuth 2.0 authorization framework.

The base URL for the Webex REST API is https://webexapis.com/v1/. API requests and responses use JSON format, and the APIs support HTTP methods such as GET, POST, PUT, and DELETE.

The Webex APIs cover a wide range of functionalities; here are a few of them.

- **Admin APIs**: The Admin APIs allow administrators to programmatically manage Webex users, licenses, and hybrid services. Some key functionalities include creating and updating user accounts, viewing license usage and available roles, managing hybrid services licenses and users, and retrieving information about hybrid clusters and connectors.
- **Messaging APIs**: The Messaging APIs enable developers to integrate Webex messaging functionality into their applications. Some key functionalities include managing spaces (create, read, update, delete), interacting with bots, and handling file attachments.
- **Meetings APIs**: The Meetings APIs provide access to Webex Meetings features, allowing developers to create, manage, and control meetings programmatically. Some key capabilities include scheduling meetings, inviting participants, managing meeting preferences and options, handling recordings, and retrieving meeting details and reports.
- **Calling APIs**: The Calling APIs enable developers to integrate Webex Calling functionality into their applications. They provide access to various calling-related features, such as managing users and devices, configuring call settings and preferences, handling call history and recordings, and controlling call flows and routing.
- **Webex Status API**: The Webex Status API provides programmatic access to real-time status information about Webex services. It allows developers to retrieve status summaries, component statuses, incident details, and scheduled maintenance information.

Conclusion

In this chapter, we explored automation and APIs within Cisco Collaboration products. We discussed the benefits of automation and the importance of APIs in enabling it. We covered the specific APIs available for Webex Devices, SBCs, Voice Gateways, Cisco Meeting Server, Unified Communications Manager, Expressway, and Webex. By leveraging these APIs, organizations can streamline their workflows and enhance the efficiency of their collaboration infrastructure. In the next chapter, we will explore how to find documentation and discuss emerging trends in collaboration.

Further Reading

Explore the following topics on your own to improve your understanding and broaden your perspective:

- Explore all the available learning labs https://developer.cisco.com/learning/search/?categories=Collaboration&contentType=track,module,lab&page=1
- If you are a beginner to Automation and API, maybe start with these two learning modules: https://developer.cisco.com/learning/modules/dne-intro-rest-api/ https://developer.cisco.com/learning/modules/dne-intro-coding-and-apis/
- Explore the Collaboration Repos in Code Exchange, you will find some scripts made by others, which can be a good starting point: https://developer.cisco.com/codeexchange/search/?categories=Collaboration
- Explore and use the sandbox to do hands-on practice: https://developer.cisco.com/site/sandbox/
- Explore the community where you can ask questions: https://community.cisco.com/t5/devnet-collaboration/ct-p/j-developer-collab

CHAPTER 13

Additional Resources and Emerging Trends

Introduction

In this final chapter, we will explore the various resources available to help you stay informed and grow as a collaboration professional. We will also discuss the emerging trends shaping the future of Cisco Collaboration.

Additional Resources

Knowing how to find the correct information is crucial for success as a collaboration administrator or architect. Even in the CCIE exam, Cisco provides a documentation CD for candidates to refer to when needed. It is impossible to memorize everything, and while experience teaches us a lot, technology evolves quickly, making it essential to verify information from official documentation.

Cisco offers various types of documentation and resources that come in handy during different phases of designing, deploying, and managing Collaboration solutions. These resources help ensure that you have access to the most up-to-date and accurate information. In this section, we will primarily refer to Cisco Unified Communications Manager (CUCM) 12.5.x documentation as an example, but you can find similar resources for other Collaboration products.

Design and Planning

- **Cisco Collaboration Solutions Design Guidance**: This page has lots of resources that provide guidance on designing, sizing, and planning Collaboration solutions. https://www.cisco.com/c/en/us/td/docs/voice_ip_comm/uc_system/design/guides/UCgoList.html
- **Cisco Collaboration product support documentation**: This page has many resources for a specific product and release, including compatibility information, release notes, design guides, configuration examples, and

technical references. https://www.cisco.com/c/en/us/support/unified-communications/collaboration-systems-release-12-5/model.html

- **Cisco Collaboration Virtualization**: This page is helpful when designing and planning virtualized Collaboration deployments. It provides guidance on supported platforms, sizing considerations, and best practices. https://www.cisco.com/c/dam/en/us/td/docs/voice_ip_comm/uc_system/virtualization/cisco-collaboration-virtualization.html

Operations and Maintenance:

- **CUCM product support documentation**: This page provides a comprehensive list of documents for CUCM, including configuration guides, data sheets, end-of-life notices, install and upgrade guides, maintain and operate guides, command references, release and compatibility information, security advisories, and troubleshooting guides. https://www.cisco.com/c/en/us/support/unified-communications/unified-communications-manager-callmanager/series.html#~tab-documents
- **Cisco Community**: The Cisco Community is a valuable resource where you can connect with other professionals, ask questions, and find solutions to common issues. https://community.cisco.com/t5/collaboration/ct-p/4691-collaboration-voice-video
  https://community.cisco.com/t5/webex-community/ct-p/webex-user
- **Cisco Support Tools**: Cisco offers a variety of support tools to help manage your devices, licenses, and notifications. Some examples include:
  - **My Notifications**: Create custom alerts for critical product support subjects, including Security Advisories, Field Notices, End of Sale/Support Announcements, Software Updates, and Known Bugs.
  - **My Devices**: Manage lists of your devices and view contract details.
  - **Device Coverage Checker**: Check service contract coverage for your devices.
  - **Product License Registration**: Register and manage your product licenses.

  https://www.cisco.com/c/en/us/support/web/tools-catalog.html

In addition to the documentation and support resources mentioned, the Cisco Live On-Demand Library is also very valuable. It' is a free collection of sessions from global Cisco Live events. These sessions cover a wide range of topics related to Collaboration, including:

- Product updates and roadmaps
- Best practices and case studies
- Technical deep dives and demonstrations
- Troubleshooting and maintenance techniques

By accessing these on-demand sessions, you can learn from Cisco experts and industry professionals at your own pace. The library is continuously updated with new content from recent events.

Emerging Trends

In this section, we will explore some of the emerging trends in Cisco Collaboration and how they are shaping the future of work.

- Web conferencing has largely replaced audio-only conferences, becoming the preferred method for remote meetings and Collaboration. Even when all participants join as audio-only, fewer people use PSTN dial-in options due to improved internet penetration. Web conferencing allows for the seamless integration of additional modalities, such as screen sharing, within the same meeting. As a result, dedicated audio-only bridge products are becoming a thing of the past.
- Shift Towards Persistent and Topic-Focused Chat Instant Messaging (IM) has evolved from one-on-one conversations. As global organizations increasingly rely on asynchronous communication, tools like Cisco Webex Teams, Slack, and Microsoft Teams provide a platform for ongoing discussions and Collaboration. Additionally, the popularity of tools like Vidcast and Loom demonstrates the growing demand for asynchronous video communication.
- Generative AI (GenAI) is a hot topic across various industries, and Collaboration is no exception. In the context of conferences and chats, GenAI can be used to generate meeting summaries, identify action points, and provide real-time translation. However, the most significant impact of GenAI is expected to be in contact centers, where conversational AI and intelligent bots can revolutionize customer service and support.
- The future of Collaboration lies in hybrid architectures, and there will always be a place for On-prem infrastructure. While many collaboration solutions are shifting to Software as a Service (SaaS) models, not all customers are ready for a complete cloud transition. SaaS offers benefits such as faster innovation, an OpEx model, easy scalability, and reduced skill requirements. However, it also has drawbacks, including limited data sovereignty (for example, EU vs. US regulations), higher long-term costs due to per-user subscription-based licensing, and potential security risks in the event of a breach.
- As a result, many customers may prefer to maintain on-premises solutions while integrating with cloud services and adopting a hybrid model. This approach allows organizations to balance the benefits of cloud collaboration with their specific requirements for data control, costs, and security.
- Some vendors will shift towards commodity hardware for endpoints, focusing on software optimization. However, hardware will still offer unique advantages

and features, such as on-device AI processing, which will drive innovation in endpoint design and functionality.

- As competition watchdogs focus on promoting fairness and innovation, there will be a push for greater interoperability between collaboration solutions from different vendors. This trend will reduce vendor lock-in and encourage the development of open standards and APIs.
- Large organizations are increasingly adopting a multi-vendor approach to Collaboration, utilizing products from different providers to meet their diverse needs. This trend is driven by factors such as department-specific requirements, mergers and acquisitions, and the desire to leverage best-of-breed solutions. As a result, interoperability and seamless integration between collaboration platforms will become even more critical.

While the collaboration landscape continues to evolve with new technologies, vendors, and deployment models, it is essential to focus on the fundamentals. Understanding the core concepts, protocols, and architectures that underpin collaboration solutions will provide a solid foundation for navigating the ever-changing market.

Different vendors and deployment options, whether on-premises or cloud-based, may offer unique features and benefits, but they also share many similarities. By concentrating on the foundational elements of collaboration technologies, the knowledge and skills you acquire will remain relevant and valuable even as new ideas and trends emerge.

Rule 11 of RFC 1925 states, "*Every old idea will be proposed again with a different name and a different presentation, regardless of whether it works.*" This highlights the cyclical nature of technology trends and the importance of discerning the core concepts behind new propositions.

Conclusion

In this final chapter, we explored the various resources available to help you stay informed and grow as a Cisco Collaboration professional. From official documentation and support tools to community forums, these resources are essential for staying up-to-date with the latest updates and best practices and effectively managing your collaboration environment.

We also discussed the emerging trends shaping the future of Cisco Collaboration, such as the rise of web conferencing, the shift towards persistent chat, the impact of AI, the move towards hybrid architectures, and the increasing adoption of multi-vendor environments.

Keep learning, stay curious, and leverage the resources available as you continue your journey in the field of Cisco Collaboration. Remember, the knowledge and skills you have gained throughout this book will serve as a solid foundation, enabling you to adapt and thrive in an ever-evolving industry.

Index

A

B

D

I

M

N

P

Q

R

S

Made in United States
Orlando, FL
04 November 2026

90200519R00223